ARCANE AMERICA

MYNDERSE LIBRARY

SENECA FALLS, NY 13148

Presented by

Ann and Don Cramer

in memory of

Elaine Woodmancy

ARCANE AMERICA

101 of the Best Places You Never Heard of

Jack Edward Shay
and
Betty Casey

Copyright © 1999 by Jack Edward Shay and Betty Casey.

Library of Congress Number: 98-87854
ISBN#:   Hardcover   0-7388-0127-5
           Softcover   0-7388-0128-3

All rights reserved. No part of this book may be reproduced or transmitted in any form or by any means, electronic or mechanical, including photocopying, recording, or by any information storage and retrieval system, without permission in writing from the copyright owner.

This book was printed in the United States of America.

To order additional copies of this book, contact:
Xlibris Corporation
1-888-7-XLIBRIS
www.Xlibris.com

MYNDERSE LIBRARY
31 FALL STREET
SENECA FALLS, NEW YORK 13148

CONTENTS

INTRODUCTION 15

ALABAMA
THE SMALL WORLD OF A
   HUNCHBACK MONK 21
THE GREATEST MASSACRE IN
   WHITE AMERICAN HISTORY 24
THE BATTLE THAT MADE A PRESIDENT 28

ALASKA
A BIG BLUE GLACIER YOU CAN
   WALK ON AND EAT 33
AMERICA'S SCENIC HIGHWAY 1 -
   BUT NOT THE ONE YOU THINK 36

ARIZONA
A DRIVE YOU'LL NEVER FORGET 43
THE LODGE BY THE HIDDEN BRIDGE
   IN THE VALLEY 47

ARKANSAS
THE NATIONAL PARK THAT
   DOESN'T LOOK LIKE ONE 55

CALIFORNIA
THE PASS WHERE MOTHER NATURE
   MADE ANIMALS OF MEN 63
"THE PLACE GOD FORGOT" 69

THE ASHES OF AN ADVENTURER,
    THE LEGACY OF A LAUREATE 73
AMERICA'S OTHER "OLD FAITHFUL" 78
A KNIGHT TO REMEMBER...
    WHEN TIME STOOD STILL 81
THE GLASS CHURCH WITH THE OCEAN VIEW 84

COLORADO
THE MILE-HIGH GRAVE IN THE
    MILE-HIGH STATE 91

CONNECTICUT
SHERLOCK'S HOME 97
A SUBTERRANEAN PRISON 101

DELAWARE
AMERICA'S FIRST CRY OF CONSCIENCE 109

FLORIDA
A DESERTED ISLAND WITH
    TOURS AND A FESTIVAL 115
"DARLING" GATORS UP CLOSE 121

GEORGIA
AMERICA'S CONCENTRATION CAMP 127
THE SHRINE TO A DEATH THAT
    STOPPED THE WORLD 132

HAWAII
HAWAII'S ST. VALENTINE'S DAY MASSACRE 141
A JOURNEY TO HEAVEN...AND INTO HELL 147
A WALK ALONG THE CLIFFS
    WHERE MOVIES ARE MADE 155

IDAHO
WHERE THE SUN STILL RISES
   OVER BLOWN-OUT BRAINS 161
THE DAY THE SUN WENT OUT
   ON THE SUNSHINE 167

ILLINOIS
THE BEATIFIC BAHA'I BEHEMOTH BY THE LAKE 175
THE CAVE WITH SKELETONS IN ITS CLOSET 179
THE GODS' ROCK GARDEN 183

INDIANA
THE TOMBSTONE WITH LIPSTICK PRINTS 187
CRIME TIME IN NASHVILLE 192

IOWA
BRIDGES ON THE WAYNE 199

KANSAS
AN UNHOLY GARDEN OF EDEN 205
THE GHOST TOWN OF THE UNBURIED 211

KENTUCKY
A MUSEUM TO A CHICKENMAN 217
THE COKE CAPITAL OF KENTUCKY 221

LOUISIANA
THE WORLD'S LONGEST BRIDGE OVER WATER 227
THE VALHALLA OF PIRATES AND WITCHES 229

MAINE
THE DESERT THAT ATE A FARM 237

MARYLAND
THE HOUSE WHERE A BABE WAS BORN 243
A RAVEN'S GRAVE, A PLOTTER'S PLOT 247

MASSACHUSETTS
THE REAL ADAMS FAMILY 253
FLOWERPOTS AND POTHOLES 257

MICHIGAN
MICHIGAN'S MOTORIZED MUSIC MECCA 261
THE WOODWORKER WHO USED
    WOOD OTHERS WOULDN'T 265

MINNESOTA
AMERICA'S GREAT MISSISSIPPI RIVER HERO 273
JOURNEY TO THE CENTER OF THE TURF 278

MISSISSIPPI
A HUMBLE PALACE FOR THE LITTLE KING 283
AMERICA'S FIRST INTERSTATE HIGHWAY 286

MISSOURI
THE ROOT OF JESSE 293
THE BOTANICAL GARDEN THAT
    PLANTED ITS FOUNDER 298

MONTANA
THE MOUNTAIN PASS WHERE HEROES PASSED 303

NEBRASKA
THE ROCK OF THE AGES 309

NEVADA
SILVER...WITH A SLIVER OF SPIELBERG 315

NEW HAMPSHIRE
WHERE AMERICANS LIVED...
    2,000 YEARS BEFORE CHRIST 321
THE FINAL MISSION OF SANDY SLOANE 324

NEW JERSEY
 THE MINIATURE KINGDOM
    THAT KILLED ITS KING 331
THE BURNING SANDS OF SOUTHERN NEW JERSEY 337

NEW MEXICO
BULLETS, BLOOD, AND A BOY NAMED BILLY 343

NEW YORK
THE BUCKING BRONCOS OF BROOME COUNTY 351
THE TREASON THAT SHOCKED THE NATION 357
BENEATH THE PEEL OF THE BIG APPLE 361
THE RESORT WHERE PEOPLE CAME TO DIE 371
THE SUNNY SIDE OF THE SEA 376

NORTH CAROLINA
THE WOMAN WITH A THOUSAND CHILDREN 383
WALKING IN THE FOOTSTEPS OF THE
    LAST OF THE MOHICANS 387

NORTH DAKOTA
THE FORT WHERE SOLDIERS
    VANISHED INTO THE MIST 393
 THE MUSEUM IN A MALL
    FOR A FORGOTTEN MAN 398

OHIO
RIDING OUT WEST...AND WRITING OUT WEST 409
TOMB WITH A VIEW 414
THE WONDERFUL WIZARD OF WOOD 417

OKLAHOMA
THE GREATEST INDIAN WHO MAY NEVER
    HAVE LIVED 423
THE UNBUILT HOME OF THE MOST BELOVED
    AMERICAN 427

OREGON
WHERE AMERICA'S RICHEST MAN GOT RICH 435

PENNSYLVANIA
A KOZIAR CHRISTMAS 441
THE BIRTH OF THE BRETZEL 444
A LITTLE MAN, A LITTLE TOWN,
    A LARGE LEGACY 448
THE ISLAND OF NO RETURN...ALMOST 452

RHODE ISLAND
AMERICA'S MOST FAMOUS $1 PAINTING 459

SOUTH CAROLINA
AMERICA'S FIRST GREAT CIVIL WAR BATTLE 465

SOUTH DAKOTA
REESE'S PEEWEES 473
THE SACRED SOIL OF THE SIOUX 475

TENNESSEE
TENNESSEE'S TRIBUTES TO A LEGEND 483
THE SEA THAT NEVER SEES THE LIGHT OF DAY 490

TEXAS
THE ALAMO YOU REMEMBER 495
A DOUBLE DOSE OF DALLAS DELINQUENTS 499
A TEXAS-SIZED TRENCH IN THE
    PANHANDLE PLAINS 503

UTAH
THE MOUNTAINS OF THE MORMONS...AND THE
   ROADS TO THEM 509

VERMONT
A DOUBLE DIP OF CHIPS AND QUIPS 515
THE LIBRARY OF POOR LONELY VERSES 518

VIRGINIA
A TRIP TO TOBACCO ROAD 525
THE GREATEST MAN YOU NEVER HEARD OF 529

WASHINGTON
WASHINGTON'S FAVORITE FAIRY FOOD 537
THE LONELY KNOLL OF NESPELEM 541
THE WOMAN WHO WED TO GO WEST 545

WASHINGTON, D.C.
BLOOD, SEX, AND LINCOLN'S SKULL 551

WEST VIRGINIA
GOD'S GOLD 561

WISCONSIN
LIONS AND TIGERS AND BARABOOS 571
A SECLUDED SLICE OF SCANDINAVIA 575

WYOMING
HOW TO GO TO HELL IN WYOMING 581

BIBLIOGRAPHY 585

TO OUR PARENTS, JACK EDWARD SHAY, SR. AND MARIE BEATRICE SHAY, AND JOSEPH AND HELEN BEUHNER...WHO TRAVELED WITH US TO ALL THE SITES IN THIS BOOK...EITHER DIRECTLY ALONGSIDE OR AS ETERNAL INSPIRATIONS WITHIN THE MOST CHERISHED RECESSES OF OUR MEMORIES.

INTRODUCTION

You hold in your hands a compilation of 101 of the least-known, most interesting sites within the United States. It results from more than a decade of touring the country under a variety of circumstances. As we made our way across America, often bound for big-ticket destinations - the Grand Canyon, Mount Rushmore, San Francisco, Cape Cod - we encountered, sometimes purely by chance, equally intriguing places tucked away in isolated recesses of the countryside. Eventually, we decided to ferret out as many of them as practical.

Of the hundreds of such sites visited, 101 were culled for thematic variety, general interest, geographical balance, and emotional poignancy. They include battlefields, historic sites, museums, cemeteries, miniature worlds, natural wonders, national and state parks, wildlife refuges, scenic drives, little-known trails, houses, religious centers, deserted islands, gardens, inexplicable mysteries, hidden sites buried in the middle of nowhere, Indian reservations, underground worlds, manufacturing centers, and corners of forgotten importance within America's largest city. Some are breathtakingly beautiful, others are frighteningly bizarre. All are memorably unique.

Some sites have never before been written of, except in regional publications of limited scope and circulation. Almost all are virtually unknown outside their immediate vicinities or states. You will find no Statues of Liberty, no Yellowstones, no Disneylands among them. You may find yourself recognizing a particular name, cultural relationship, or historical fact here or there. But you'll probably not know that a certain site in a certain part of a certain state actually commemorates that little bit of trivia you once learned years ago in school.

For the most part, the sites are easily reachable. We specifically tried to include places within proximity to major tourist destinations so they might easily be tacked onto pre-arranged trips. Most sites can also be toured within an hour or two.

The book was also created with a nod to armchair travelers, people who might never be able to venture beyond the horizons of their imaginations. Considerable narrative background has been provided to bestow the proper significance to each site and paint a more vivid picture for those who must rely on our words for their impressions.

At first, we endeavored to represent all 50 states equally with two locations (and one for Washington, D.C.). We soon discovered an inescapable reality: not all states are created equal. Some overflow with glamorous tourist stops but run a little short of the special brand of rather anonymous Americana we attempted to collect. Some states, even after days of travel and hundreds of miles, barely supplied one or two places that fit our needs; others showered us with a dozen or more. We decided simply to use sites we deemed best, as long as each state was represented at least once.

Most travel books become rapidly outdated. Sites open and close unpredictably. Hours of operation and admission fees change, often annually. What costs $3 one year might cost $4 the next. Phone numbers change. To try to avoid this trap, we used generic terms. For example, admission fees may be "modest" or "nominal" (usually $1-3 by late-1990s benchmarks), "moderate" ($4-6), "average" ($7-10), and so forth. A "modest" $2 admission in 1999 may balloon to $7 by 2005, but, even allowing for inflation, it will most likely still be considered "modest" by price standards of its day. Likewise, "normal" or "customary" daytime hours, a recurrent phrase throughout the book, refers to a place that opens around 9 or 10 a.m. and closes around 4 or 5 p.m. On rare occasions, when we felt it essential, we provided current specifics.

Also, some sites may close to visitation, either temporarily (for renovation and so forth) or permanently (for relocation, business considerations, and such). All these sites were open at the writing of this book; to the best of our knowledge, they remain open at publication date.

Finally, directions can be misleading, too. Road designations change. New highways come into existence; old ones are relegated to secondary status. You need only an atlas to find the sites featured in this book. We started you out by providing the state and the appropriate county or city of each site. Then we supplied further relevant directions.

The sites are often their own reward. They are not designed to be the backbone of a two-week-long trek across America (although they can be). But they help flesh out some of the dry time between big cities and beaches, malls and theme parks. They are often thought-provoking and haunting, even sad, and sometimes elicit unexpected emotional jolts. And for the traveler, whether real or imaginary, with the kindred soul, they may be the very substance of America, an unobtrusive, soft-spoken, arcane America, an America of subtle imagination and wispy memory...perhaps, even, an America at its best...an America of remembrance.

ALABAMA

THE SMALL WORLD OF A HUNCHBACK MONK

A world in miniature exists just east of Cullman, Alabama on four acres of the St. Bernard Abbey. Incredibly, it is the work of a single man, a deformed, diminutive native of Bavaria who became a Benedictine monk in America. A back injury suffered while working on one of St. Bernard Abbey's buildings rendered him a hunchback which, in turn, gave the otherwise ascetic-looking man a near-dwarflike appearance.

Undaunted by the physical deformity that ruined his looks while still a youth, he set about monastic life with humility and dedication. While tending the furnaces and the various steam gauges in the abbey's power plant around 1912, he began whiling away the time by fashioning small buildings from any scrap material at hand. He placed his finished products in the abbey gardens, and the college's gift shop sold others as souvenirs.

As his collection and artistry - he relied on either his memory or photographs - grew, people from outside the abbey began touring the gardens to see the little village he had wrought. The tramp of increasing visitors necessitated moving the buildings to a more accessible site. And in 1934, a landscaped hillside that had formerly been a rock quarry became the Ave Maria Grotto.

Brother Joseph Zoettl continued crafting his tiny world until 1958 when, at 80, he completed one of his largest structures, the Lourdes Basilica Church, destined to be his last major work.

A modest man, he continued toiling in the mundane power house throughout the years he created the grotto. When visitors saw him, clad in work overalls, laboring among the sculptures, they often mistook him for a groundsman and asked if the sculptor was yet alive. "Oh, yes, he lives in the monastery," he answered simply and then went about his routine work, deflecting the accolades that surely would have come his way.

He died on October 15, 1961 and is buried with fellow monks in the abbey cemetery. The white cross marking his grave, indistinguishable from the scores of other such identical monuments dotting the consecrated ground in perfect symmetry, says simply: "1878 FR. CONV. JOSEPHUS ZOETTL O.S.B. R.I.P. 1961."

Though the miniature world is on the grounds of a Benedictine abbey, sharing space with a chapel, dining hall, gift shop, and interdenominational retreat center, it is also a microcosm that presents some 150 precise reproductions of some of the world's most historic and famed edifices. Most of the miniatures represent actual buildings or municipal districts that either possessed religious origins or somehow acquired spiritual status.

Yet many reproductions evoke more of ancient times, militarism, and cultural and mythological symbolism than of Christianity. Consider seeing the Statue of Liberty and the Leaning Tower of Pisa alongside the shrines at Lourdes and Fatima. The Hanging Gardens of Babylon (complete with water), Noah's Ark, and the Tower of Babel share space with California's famed chain of Franciscan missions: Carmel, Dolores, San Juan Capistrano. The Alamo, where renowned frontiersmen David Crockett and James Bowie died fighting the Mexican army for Texan independence, adjoins the Chapel of St. Therese.

Monte Cassino, the fifth-century Italian mountaintop Benedictine abbey pounded by Allied bombers in World War II, rises again from a hill in the grotto. Ancient Rome comes to life with startlingly real facsimiles of the Pantheon and Colosseum. The Holy Land springs anew with tableaus depicting virtually every facet of Christ's life from the Bethlehem cave to the Garden of Gethsemane and Calvary's hill.

And along the way, you encounter fantasy scenes such as the

Temple of the Fairies, Hansel and Gretel, and a dragon.

As amazingly lifelike as the reproductions are, the materials used to construct them are even more remarkable. Scrap material of all types - rocks, bricks, glass shards, tiles, pipes, seashells, beads, chandelier pendants - formed the basis for the grotto; cement became the unifying glue. Oddball items jut from the unlikeliest places, defying discovery by all save those in the know. Green fishing net floats adorn the Tower of Thanks. Cold cream jars help form the Temple of the Fairies. Mobile's Cathedral of the Immaculate Conception sports a pair of toilet ball floats for its twin domes. Blue ink bottles compose the blue cross within the Cave of the Guardian Angel. Colored marbles, cement, and glass make up an American flag.

The Ave Maria Grotto is open daily from 7 a.m. to sunset and offers snacks and picnic facilities. Visitors can easily tour it in an hour, although photographers and aficionados of miniature creations may want to allow more time. A paved sloping path affords easy access to the hillsides on which the buildings have been fashioned.

The grotto is fewer than five miles east of Interstate Highway 65, about halfway between Birmingham and Huntsville. From the interstate, take U.S. Highway 278 east past Cullman and look for signs for St. Bernard Abbey and the grotto.

For those searching for something else to do in the area, the 270-foot-long Clarkson Covered Bridge, an imposing structure built on stone piers, rises 45 feet above Crooked Creek (the site of the 1863 Civil War Battle of Hog Mountain) east of Cullman. Also just east is Lewis Smith Lake, one of Alabama's premier recreational meccas with over 500 miles of shoreline. Cullman hosts a number of festivals including: the Hank Williams, Jr. Look-Alike Contest in April; the July Classic Street Machines gathering; go-cart races Labor Day weekend; and Oktoberfest during two weeks in October.

THE GREATEST MASSACRE IN WHITE AMERICAN HISTORY

At noon on the oppressively torrid day of Monday, August 30, 1813, a thousand Creek warriors, naked except for dabs, stripes, and swirls of garish red and black paint smeared across their bodies and decorative cow tails hanging from their waists, assaulted a crudely constructed one-acre stockade in the southwestern part of what is now Alabama.

The Creeks were embroiled in a civil war resulting from a greater war enveloping it, the highly unpopular War of 1812 between Great Britain and the United States. Oddly enough, the Creeks were fighting one another over a white issue - white American western expansion onto Indian lands. Some Creeks, generally considered pacifists, had aligned themselves with the American settlers because they thought it foolhardy to try to halt the inevitable white conquest of the continent. Other Creeks, the more bellicose, supported the British and Spanish, who opposed the United States in the War of 1812, as a means of resisting expansion they considered unjust. Making matters worse, many Creeks had intermarried with white Americans, creating a race of half-breeds, some of whom were more white than Creek in language, dress, and acculturation.

In many cases, the Creek warriors who charged the stockade that humid August day were more biologically white than the supposed "white" settlers who defended the settlement against them. It was a confusing war.

The commander of the stockade, a lawyer and militia officer

named Daniel Beasley, was known to hit the bottle. He mistakenly believed his fort impregnable and refused even to bolt the gate, jeopardizing the lives of the hundreds of militiamen, civilians, and slaves - male and female...white, black, and red alike - who had banded together the previous month to hastily build the fort as protection against the uncertain tenor of the times.

The defense of the fort lasted till late afternoon when the attackers won the day and allowed the battle to degenerate into a massacre. The warriors grabbed babies and infants by their feet, slamming them against stockade walls. They stripped, scalped, and mutilated all the men and hacked women apart at the middle. They cut female abdomens open and yanked fetuses out from pregnant wombs, then squashed the unborn babies with their feet.

When the slaughter ended about 5:00 that afternoon, no one remained to eat the noontime meal that the women had prepared just before the attack had started.

In all, anywhere from 247 to more than 500 men, women, and children of the stockade perished in the assault. A few managed to escape. The massacre became the largest slaughter of white civilians - or a group predominantly comprising white civilians - by Native Americans in the history of the United States, before or since.

Few people have heard of the massacre at Fort Mims. The location is as remote in geography as the event is obscure in history. The site is in diminutive Tensaw in rural Baldwin County, west of State Highway 59. To reach it, motorists must drive 2.9-miles west on County Road 80, then a quarter-mile north at an intersection, and finally a tenth of a mile west at an elbow turn. The fort's site lies due north through the trees.

Only a marker and a flagpole stand vigil over the lonely site. And the place is usually deserted - except for one weekend each year.

But that weekend, the last one in August, commemorates the anniversary of the massacre in spirited style. The re-enactors, an amalgam of living history professionals, local historians, and civic groups, are spearheaded by Donnie Barrett and the 21st Alabama Infantry and 1812 Militia. The group ranges throughout the South, giving historically authentic performances. The Fort Mims orchestration is one of the most dramatic you'll ever see - made all the more poignant by its being staged on the very ground where the real bloodbath took place.

Between re-enactments, visitors listen to period music and folk groups, engage in raffles and tomahawk-throwing contests, watch Native American ceremonial dances, demonstrations of early pioneer life, and military drills, and talk with the re-enactors about the painstaking lengths to which they go to ensure historical fidelity in costume, weaponry, speech, and manner. Food can be obtained from vendors on the premises.

On Saturday evening, following a traditional catfish dinner for event participants and sponsors, the public is invited to attend a campfire tour of the tents and bonfires (when performing, re-enactors eschew modern conveniences, sleeping within period tents in the great outdoors, as if transplanted back to 1813). America has many re-enactment groups specializing in various of our nation's wars; the Fort Mims cadre is one of the best.

The ambitious Fort Mims Restoration Association, created in 1986, runs the yearly events. The group hopes to eventually reconstruct the fort and surround it with parking and picnic facilities and a museum. Regardless when plans materialize, the stalwart organization intends to continue the annual re-enactments.

The last weekend in August at the riverine site is usually very sticky, so a minimum of exertion is recommended. Let the re-enactors do the tussling and grappling and rolling around the battlefield.

Less than a mile from the site, Boat Yard Lake can provide some recreational water and fishing opportunities. And the grave of William Weatherford ("Red Eagle"), the half-blood Creek who led the charge against the fort, is nearby, just northwest of the equally small hamlet of Little River. Directional markers point the way, and re-enactment organizers can help with directions.

For those who may want to spend a day at the re-enactment and then see something else, the colorful city of Mobile - with the Battleship Alabama, Bellingrath Gardens, Fort Conde, and architectural gems of the Deep South - lies fewer than 50 miles southwest, and the popular sand stretches and beachfront stores of Gulf Shores are about 65 miles due south.

Fort Mims is so obscure that few people outside that portion of Alabama even know about the re-enactments, making them a hidden treasure ripe for discovery. The sponsors are friendly and will ensure your day is pleasant, especially if you tell them you're from out of state and are not descended from Fort Mims survivors.

There is a slight admission charge, a dollar or so.

If you elect to visit Fort Mims any other time of the year, you'll probably find it a very lonely place inhabited only by droves of summer mosquitoes.

THE BATTLE THAT MADE A PRESIDENT

On March 27, 1814, a soldier destined to be president led an army against a Creek Indian village in what is now east-central Alabama. Outnumbering the Creeks three to one, the army bottled them up at Tohopeka, a town of 300 log huts inside a peninsula formed by the horseshoe-like bend of the Tallapoosa River. The militia and infantry assaulted a barricade, some five to eight feet high, that protected the village.

The battle quickly became a rout. Nearly everyone in the town - close to 1,000 Creeks - went down. Women and children died; an aged Indian man, who sat pounding cornmeal, keeled over from the bullet of a soldier whose only concern lay in boasting of having killed anyone in the battle. The future president called the engagement a "slaughter" stopped only by "the darkness of the night."

The soldiers flushed out hiding Indians the following day and gunned them down. The victors also skinned the dead bodies, a lamentable practice of the day that yielded bizarre souvenirs: bridle reins fashioned from the limbs and torsos of human beings.

The fatalities indicate the one-sidedness of the battle: nearly 1,000 Creeks...49 attackers.

The battle became known as Horseshoe Bend and occurred in the midst of what is truly America's "forgotten war," a war that needs a date in its title to place it in time for modern Americans. Yet ironically, the War of 1812 produced both the poem whose words have become the "Star-Spangled Banner" and the only time the nation's capital has been burned. It also created the national legend of an obscure Tennessee militia officer who suddenly became the toast of the nation, the superstar hero of his day, and eventually the president of the country. His presidency resulted nearly directly from two smashing victories in the War of 1812: the Battle of New Orleans (the subject of a hit 20th-century rock and roll song) and the earlier Battle of Horseshoe Bend.

Hidden within the War of 1812 was an even more unknown contest called the Creek War. It needed only eight months to run its course and concluded with the fight at the Horseshoe. But in that short span, it became a devastating war of annihilation. Nearly every battle degenerated into total massacre. And when it ended, the Creeks were a broken nation, stripped of their last real chance of retaining their land, culture, and destiny.

The Creek War also helped make the careers of David Crockett, the famed frontiersman, and Sam Houston, who participated in the vanguard of the frontal assault of the barricade at Horseshoe Bend and whose bravery caught his commander's eye, assisting the young political protege in becoming a legislator, governor, and pre-eminent hero of the Texas War for Independence. And most dramatically, the war gave Andrew Jackson a hero's halo and led him down the road to the White House.

Horseshoe Bend is now a 2,040-acre national military park - the only battleground of the sanguine Creek War to be so designated. A visitor center provides an orientation on Creek society, the white spirit of westward expansion, and the war that ensued when different cultures met.

But the battlefield is the park's highlight, appearing very much as it did in 1814. Though the "horseshoe" loop of the Tallapoosa can only be seen from the air, visitors drive along a roughly parallel three-mile road as it winds around the important points. Nothing of the original buildings and breastworks survives, and the site is given to meadows and forests.

Horseshoe Bend is remarkably compact and carries nothing of the cluttered look and glut of historical markers of more popular battlefields. The drive is relaxing, and a 2.8-mile nature walk meanders alongside, connecting the principal sites. Fewer than 20 wayside markers tell the story in simple terms: no minute-by-minute movements of corps and brigades, just the tragic playing out of two cultures in clash.

An hour or two in the visitor center and on the grounds will acquaint you with this hidden fold of America's fabric. You will likely see few other visitors during your stay.

Horseshoe Bend is off State Highway 49 in rural Alabama, about five miles south of New Site and 12 miles north of Dadeville. Alexander City, 18 miles west, is the nearest sizable city. Restaurants, lodging, and amenities provide comfort along the way.

A National Park Service brochure, warning of "hazards such as poisonous snakes, poison ivy, and biting fire ants," advises visitors to exert "caution while boating and while walking along the riverbank." But generally, Horseshoe Bend is a safe place to wander, and adherence to the roadways ensures a harmless visit. The battlefield, museum and bookstore are free and open during customary daytime hours.

Martin Lake, one of Alabama's largest water recreation sites, lies just west and south. And Birmingham and Montgomery, two of the state's three largest cities, are fewer than 100 miles away.

ALASKA

The enormity of Exit Glacier...dwarfing the person near its base.

A BIG BLUE GLACIER YOU CAN WALK ON AND EAT

Everyone knows Alaska is chock-full of Eskimoes, polar bears, and lots of snow - whether in the form of flakes, ice, or glaciers. Snowflakes and ice are quite common wherever snow falls in the continental United States (or "down south," as the Alaskans refer to the Lower 48). Glaciers are another matter. And Alaska has glaciers like Maine has lobsters.

Simply put, glaciers are huge packs of icy snow that gradually move down mountains. They start at high elevations with snow that accumulates on and around mountains to a depth of usually at least a hundred feet (and frequently much more) without melting. The passage of time and the pressure of even more snow atop previous layers convert the original packed snow into ice. The inclination of the mountains on which the snow has become deeply embedded, the normal pull of gravity, and the continual addition of more fallen snow induce the icy tentacles of the snow mass to move downward, usually at an imperceptible pace to human eyes, rearranging the underlying landscape in the process, often creating craters, lakes, and other topographical features. Eventually, the moving snowfield reaches the open sea where it breaks apart into icebergs or moves into a lowland area where warmer temperatures accelerate the melting of the ice.

Most Alaskan visitors see the more accessible areas - the big cities and the "inside passage" tours that cruise alongside glaciers - and skip one of the most impressive sights of them all...because it is hidden and remote.

Currently only a shadow of its former self at three miles in length and with a descent of "only" 2,500 feet, Exit Glacier lies just northeast of Seward in the northern angle of Kenai Fjords National Park. Not only can you see it clearly from the road, you can also walk right up to it and atop it.

Exit is one of many glaciers within the expansive Harding Icefield, which numbers in its reach more than 30 glaciers and at times packs ice a mile deep, blanketing underlying flatlands and the Kenai Mountains on the south-central portion of the Kenai Peninsula that juts into the Gulf of Alaska. Nearly a baby compared to other glaciers many times its size, Exit's ice is what remains of a much larger glacier that stretched to what is now Seward on Resurrection Bay in another era. Essentially an icicle dripping off the Harding Icefield, Exit is still active and in a state of "retreat," uncovering new layers of bedrock to modern eyes.

Like all glaciers, Exit is deceptive. From a distance, it appears much smaller and less colorful than it is. A closer investigation reveals a sizable chunk of ice. As an Alaska Natural History Association brochure attests, "The height and width are difficult to judge. When viewed with people at its base, however, the true size and power can clearly be felt."

Not only will Exit grow to mammoth proportions as you walk closer, its color will also change from a dirty white to a bluish-white with brighter shades of blue bursting forth from the furrows of the crevasses. The brilliant blue tint springs from compact crystals within the ice receiving and absorbing the red part of sunlight and bouncing back the blue part, though the eyes can see only the final resultant color, not the entire process. If you are so inclined, you can sample the glacier as well. It will taste very much like what it ultimately is destined to be: water.

A ranger station is not far from the base of the glacier. It offers literature and information on the glacier and schedules nature walks and icefield hikes on weekends from Memorial Day to Labor Day.

A range of snow activities like camping, hiking, skiing, and mountaineering are permitted on Exit, which presents panoramic views of the gigantic icefield, but the footing is tricky...and slippery when wet. Only veteran climbers should consider a hiking conquest of the glacier.

Kenai Fjords National Park covers more than 670,000 acres, and the Harding Icefield sees anywhere from 400-800 inches of snow every year. Exit is the only part of the park that can be reached by car. Intrepid souls can see the rest of the park in or on kayaks, boats, airplances, and cross country skis. Waters of the fjords can be very treacherous, and backpackers should always be alert for crevasses and loose sheets of ice.

The park operates a visitor center in Seward (daily from Memorial Day to Labor Day and weekdays the rest of the year) with programs and information on the various activities.

Exit is roughly 125 road miles south of Anchorage. It can be reached by driving south on the Seward Highway. At milepost 3.7 (or 3.7 miles north of Seward), look for a gravel road to the west. Go nine miles on this bumpy road to the ranger station and parking and camping facilities. Then a half-mile trail leads up to the base of the glacier. That's the easy part.

But even if you go no farther, you can see the immensity and magical color of the glacier up close. It will take a whole day to make the drive from Anchorage to Exit and back, allowing time to explore the glacier. If you decide to tackle the glacier head-on at greater length, first know what you're doing, then check with the rangers, and finally allow much more time. The park has no lodging or eating facilities, but nearby Seward does.

AMERICA'S SCENIC HIGHWAY 1 - BUT NOT THE ONE YOU THINK

Many travelers nominate California Highway 1 - the coastal drive along the Pacific - as America's most scenic road. Others swear by U.S. Highway 1 connecting the Florida Keys.

But one overlooked road, offering views every bit as spectacular, lies much farther north.

Most visitors to our largest state go to Anchorage, Fairbanks, or Juneau...and maybe Denali National Park. Yet the 126 miles of Alaska's Seward Highway, separating Anchorage from Seward (on the northern end of Resurrection Bay), pass along some of America's most majestic mountains and glaciers galore.

The 250-mile round trip can be done either as a single day's jaunt or a multi-day trek with pauses along the way to savor the tempting diversions.

You pick up the Seward Highway - or State Highway 1, as it is known there - near downtown Anchorage, Alaska's largest city and the point of arrival for most tourists. The view becomes superb in short order as the road works its way through the city, into massive Chugach State Park, and along the north shore of Turnagain Arm, an inlet discovered and named by British explorer James Cook in 1778 while searching for a suspected northwest passage.

If the day is fair, you can feast upon the waters of the estuary glistening in the reflection of the sun's rays beneath a panoply of some of the highest snow-packed peaks you've ever seen - the Kenai Mountains of the Kenai Peninsula. The road parallels the tracks of the Alaska Railroad, the continent's northernmost railway, and offers glimpses of the distinctive blue and gold engines as they roll by. Each bend of the highway unveils either new peaks or at least different views; the promontories never have a chance to grow stale. Salmon and beluga whales occasionally romp in the sometimes-limpid, sometimes-turbulent waters, while Dall sheep and mountain goats heedlessly munch the meadows atop the roadside cliffs.

At Bird Point, you may see a tidal bore - a rippling wave that can swell as high as six feet and roll in at 15 miles an hour.

At length, you approach Girdwood, a small town fostered by a gold strike across Turnagain Arm in the late 1800s that now serves as headquarters for the Alyeska Winter Sports Arena.

Continuing, you enter the expansive Chugach National Forest and reach the easternmost extent of the water, take a marked side road, and come face to face with Explorer, Middle, Byron, and Portage Glaciers and the huge white and blue icebergs floating in 660-foot-deep Portage Lake (and calved from the glacial mass). Full activities, including a boat tour through the bergs, are available. During the summer, the Begich-Boggs Visitor Center (named for Congressmen Nick Begich and Hale Boggs - the latter the father of newscaster Cokie Roberts - who died in a 1972 plane crash in the area) serves as the start of professionally conducted nature walks. On rare occasions, 50-plus-mile-per-hour winds roar through the Portage Valley.

If you explore on your own at this point, you may come across a bear (though the odds are against it). Refrain from feeding or challenging him. If he sees you, stand your ground, neither retreating nor advancing, and wave your arms and talk in a normal voice. If the bear does not leave and moves closer, become more assertive; talk louder and make noises. If the bear still does not leave and actually touches you, keep your wits and discern his color. If he is brown, fall face downward or curl up in the fetal position with your hands covering the back of your neck, pretend you're dead, and wait for him to leave; if the bear is black, he won't fall for the ruse and, if you survive the ensuing scuffle, you'll have a marvelous story to tell for the rest of your life. To minimize sighting a bear in the first place, announce yourself in advance by traveling in a group and by making noise (singing, talking) as you walk.

Meanwhile, back on the drive, the Seward Highway traverses the Kenai Peninsula generally south by southwest through a succession of lakes, creeks, ski areas, and mountains.

At Tern Lake Junction, Highway 1 turns abruptly west, and the Seward Highway resumes its southerly course as Highway 9, running by Moose Pass (where sometimes you may indeed pass by moose) and skirting the Kenai Lake just west of Mother Goose Glacier on its inexorably mountainous journey to the deep water port of Seward, the end of the road.

It may seem like a lengthy trip, especially if you stop along the way. But actually, you'll only travel an insignificant fraction of the total distance through the southern heart of Alaska (the state is one-fifth the size of the continental United States, twice the size of Texas).

Most visitors don't head all the way down to Seward from Anchorage, instead turning back at Portage Glacier or boarding the train for Whittier to the east. But if you continue all the way, you'll be positioned to explore glacier-laden Kenai Fjords National Park and the waters of Resurrection Bay, which enter the Gulf of Alaska where killer whales frolic.

Seward has numerous eating and lodging facilities and claims to be the birthplace of the state flag and the start of the Iditarod Trail ("blazed by Alaska natives and...used extensively during the Gold Rush era to move mail and supplies from the ice free port of Seward to the gold fields of Nome," according to an historic marker on 4th Street at Railway Avenue). In addition to fishing tournaments and derbies, mountain-flanked Seward also sponsors the annual Fourth of July Mount Marathon Race where participants scamper up and down all 3,022 feet of the peak (a midget compared to the other points ringing the town of 2,000).

The return trip to Anchorage provides the same grandeur of

blue skies and waters swirling around snow-encrusted mountains - only in reverse.

A leisurely drive along Alaska's first designated National Forest Scenic Byway will give you a taste of everything the frozen giant is famous for - from clear lakes to snowy spires that pierce the clouds, from bee-size mosquitoes to "bear claws" (apple fritters nearly equivalent to loaves of bread). You may leave the state marveling at the many ways, shapes, and forms in which Alaska manages to showcase the white stuff that falls from the sky.

ARIZONA

A DRIVE YOU'LL NEVER FORGET

It's been called the scariest drive in the continental United States and, mile for mile, one of the most beautiful drives in the world. President Theodore Roosevelt simply called it a cross between the Grand Canyon and the Alps and "the most sublimely beautiful panorama Nature has ever created."

It's Arizona's Apache Trail - 40-plus miles of two- and sometimes one-lane travel through and around dust, blinding sun, herds of cows, desert cacti and scrub, U-curves that cling precariously to precipitate mountainsides, aqua lakes, the world's largest masonry dam, huge drops in elevation, and some of the most awe-inspiring scenery in the world.

Arizona has become a big tourist attraction in recent decades because of its hot, dry climate and stunning mountains and canyons. Most visitors head for the highly publicized sites - the Grand Canyon, Tucson, Sedona - and bypass the opportunity to drive the decidedly different Apache Trail.

It can be a mistake. The Apache Trail provides a microcosm of everything Arizona is famous for - desert flora, craggy mountains, declivitous canyons - and it also presents something Arizona is not so renowned for - water, in the form of three lakes, prime for fishing, boating, and photographic activities. Those who fear heights and snaking trails that constantly weave left and right through and around mountainsides are best advised to forgo the trail and remain safely at poolside back at the hotel. But for those who thrive on such thrills, no finer recommendation can be made.

To reach the Apache Trail, head east from Phoenix on U.S.

Highways 60/89 (Apache Boulevard) through Tempe and Mesa and into Apache Junction and look for signs for State Highway 88 (the Apache Trail) and follow them. You will instantly lose the traffic as you drive northeast through the southernmost extremities of the Tonto National Forest, a tract about the size of Connecticut.

The Apache Trail meanders around the west and north faces of the Superstition Mountains, a ruggedly beautiful range clearly visible to your right (east). Immediately off the road will be a complex of restaurants and shops designed to look like an old Western town and offering a spectacular view of the Superstitions.

Once back on the trail, you will encounter scenery that provided a daily backdrop for life among the Anasazi, Hohokam, and Salado tribes centuries before white men ever saw such sights. The trail itself, constructed and paved for modern man in the early years of the 20th century in order to transport laborers and equipment to the site where Roosevelt Dam was to rise, follows an old path employed by the Apaches in winding around the Superstitions. According to the story, they chose to skirt the mountains rather than directly penetrate them so as not to challenge their mightiest divinity, the Thunder God, whom they believed resided on the pinnacles of the Superstitions, occasionally humbling them with awesome electrical storms.

The scenery becomes breathtaking, and pull-offs invite you to take in the natural beauty of Weavers Needle and the 7,000-foot-high Four Peaks Mountain.

About 12 miles into the drive, you suddenly catch your first glimpse of Canyon Lake, one of the trail's three picturesque manmade lakes created from damming the Salt River. The other lakes (Apache and Roosevelt) come farther along the trail and lend a clear blue tint to the spectrum of colors shining from the mountains and canyon crevices. The lakes offer fishing, boating, camping, and eating opportunities. Canyon Lake has a 100-passenger steamboat at the ready, and Apache and Roosevelt Lakes have motels and restaurants. Roosevelt is the biggest and most popular, but

Apache, with depths over 200 feet, might be the most scenic and enchanting.

At about 17 miles, you enter Tortilla Flat (population six), a tourist stop because of its food, lodging, gifts, and post office.

About a mile after passing Horse Mesa Road on the left, at roughly 22 miles into the trek, the pavement ceases, giving way to a graded dirt road not suited for large RVs or station wagons or vehicles that fishtail. While generally pothole-free, the dirt road is extremely rough in places and makes you feel you're driving over a washboard; your teeth involuntarily clack against one another as you talk.

Still, this is the premier part of the trail, fetching the best scenery of all. A mile and a half on the dirt road brings you to Fish Creek Hill for a majestic view of Fish Creek Canyon and a sinuous drive that simulates the effect of motoring into the Grand Canyon and drops 800 feet in elevation in about a mile of actual driving distance.

Twenty miles later, after descending nearly to water level for a unique canyon bottom experience, you reach Roosevelt Dam, the heart of the Salt River Project which pumps water into Phoenix, transforming it from a 19th-century desert into today's sprawling population center. The ponderous structure rises to your left, emphatically concluding the Apache Trail with a dramatic exclamation point.

At this point, you have three choices: turn around and go back (be aware of the sun; you might not want to face it, as it sets in the west, particularly since you will be driving back on the side of the road immediately adjacent to the plummeting cliffs...and there are no guard rails); turn north onto State Highway 188, take it to the intersection with State 87, and return south to Phoenix on 87; or travel east on State 88 to the intersection with U.S. 60 and return west to Phoenix on 60, a circuitous route that yields more gorgeous scenery (including the Tonto National Monument - mountainous cliff dwellings of the Salado Indians that you can actually walk onto), but tacks on scores of additional miles.

If you decide to tackle the Apache Trail in a day, start early; it easily consumes the bulk of an entire day. Better yet, consider a combination driving/lodging or camping/boating trip and give it a few days. Boats are rather cheaply obtained at any of the marinas.

If you do nothing else in Arizona other than the trail, you can truly say you've experienced the wide diversity of the state. But remember to drive cautiously; the trail is its own reward, but only if you return to Phoenix under your own power. And be careful if you hike into the Superstitions; they're enticing, wildly beautiful, and sometimes deadly.

THE LODGE BY THE HIDDEN BRIDGE IN THE VALLEY

In 1877, a peripatetic Scottish seaman named David Douglas Gowan wandered central Arizona in search of gold. He found instead a band of Apaches intent on adding him to their trophy case. He outdistanced them within the mountains, but his situation turned desperate when they trapped him in a valley made fertile and green by a stream. In unfamiliar terrain, he seized the only possible escape route before him - a natural arch, with a cavernous, dark hole beneath, which suddenly appeared in front of him. Staring death in the face, he raced into the recess, climbed its slippery wall, and wedged himself into a tight crevice on a ledge beyond sight.

He waited. For three days, he remained secluded, fearful of his fate should he dare surface. At length, he dared to emerge and found his pursuers gone. He developed a fondness for the valley in which his miraculous cave nestled and homesteaded it.

What David Douglas Gowan had stumbled upon was the world's largest known travertine bridge reposing in a bowl-like valley in the midst of the mountainous hills of Arizona's Tonto Natural Forest, south of the Mogollon Rim. A 183-foot-high arch spans a 400-foot-long tunnel over a 150-foot width. Spring water had created the bridge by dropping off travertine sediment over a period of more years than anyone who ever lived could remember. Five acres of level valley land conceals the hidden rim of the opening under the bridge.

Travertine is a calcite - or limestone - that builds up from ground or surface mineral water. Most natural bridges build "down" when wind or water erodes rock, sculpting a bridge through millions of years. Travertine, by contrast, forms when water brings limestone, deposits it, and adds to it, essentially creating a natural outcropping that grows upward and outward.

Eventually, David Douglas Gowan invited his nephew, David Gowan Goodfellow, also of Scotland, to join him in the valley in near-dead center Arizona. Young David and his wife Lillias reached Arizona a few years later, in the 1890s, and entered the valley - Pine Creek Canyon - 500 feet beneath Buckhorn Mesa. They found Uncle David and his roughhewn cabin at the bottom, after a descent that nearly took Lillias' breath away. "I fervently wished that I had never come to Arizona," she later admitted. "I honestly believed that I could never reach the cabin alive if I ever started down over the precipice; and I was sure if I ever did get there, I would never be able to climb out again."

She and her husband eventually inherited the valley from their uncle when the sailor-Civil War veteran-sea captain-sheepherder-miner-gadabout died at 83.

The valley consisted of 160 acres which allowed the Goodfellows land enough for a more durable house, gardens, orchards, pastures, vineyards, and, of course, the secluded natural bridge beneath the plain. Word of the bridge gradually spread, and the Goodfellows sensed a ready-made cottage industry - and began literally building cottages. Aided by sons David and Harry, David Gowan Goodfellow carved a steep road from the side of Buckhorn Mesa to allow gentler access to the valley of the giant arch.

A good thing became even better. A steady stream of visitors necessitated larger and more permanent lodging. David Goodfellow, Jr., the engineering grandson of David Douglas Gowan, constructed a hotel that rose to completion in 1927. The cozy lodge accommodated a book-lined lobby- sitting room and a dining room on the first floor, individual bedrooms on the second, and a rooftop rumpus room on the third. A sheltered porch flanked the south and west sides of the bottom story; a screened-in outdoor porch, complete with beds, adjoined some of the rooms on the second story; and the eagle's nest on top provided airy looks at the sun's rising and setting.

The lodge did well for years afterward, introducing civility and comfort to the middle of a new state still considered scarcely more than a desolate desert. The Goodfellows kept the place running till 1948 when it entered periods of different ownership, neglect, and legal actions.

In the mid-1980s, owner Clifford Wolfswinkel and architects Kevin Van Der Molen and Jim Garrison rescued the building from decay. Securing the lodging ranch a spot on the National Register of Historic Places, they renovated it as close to the original structure as possible. The resultant 10 rooms radiated antiquity, from the names emblazoned on the doors of the suites ("General George Crook," for example, honored the cavalry commander who had once watered his troopers' horses in Pine Creek) to the interior furnishings which included original walnut dressers, metal and brass beds, wicker rockers and dinette sets, brass lamps, French window doors, and patterned wallpaper. Old-time pictures, portraits, and paintings hung everywhere. Bathrooms were often shared and came with clawfoot tubs. Suites purposely avoided televisions and telephones to better promote serenity. Nearly everyone who stayed at the Tonto Natural Bridge Historical Lodge trekked down to see the bridge, but the real attraction became the building whose unobtrusive placards gently reminded parents to curb their children's rambunctiousness and whose welcome flyers announced, "Most of our guests come here for peace and quiet...music and loud noises, especially on the porches and in the Observation Lounge, travel easily...."

After dinner, guests repaired to the observation lounge to watch "classic movies" of bygone eras on "a big screen television" (the only concession to entertainment modernity on the premises). Other visitors strolled the grounds to watch the day's sun become history behind the towering mountains. Guests retiring to the veranda at night or turning out the lights in their suites to gaze at the stars through screened porches often noticed skunks, deer, even javelinas out for their evening constitutionals.

Antiques rested everywhere: a plow and remnants of wheeled rigs outdoors; Lillias' pedal organ in the lobby; hanging flowerpots on the veranda; potbellied stoves and butter churns. The lodge's limited capacity ensured a greater degree of tranquility amidst the natural beauty of the valley.

Then in October 1990, Arizona bought the 160-acre site for $3 million and transformed the hidden paradise into a state park - the bridge, the cavern, the grottoes scalloped into the walls, the spindly threads of a waterfall, the hiking trails, the rushing stream, the flower gardens and picnic area, the grassy plain, the lodge. The state announced plans to improve the slippery descent into the cave and add more information about the geologic history of the natural wonder, refurbish the swimming pool and strengthen the scary, declivitous entrance road - a hair-raising, dust-kicking dirt trail - into the valley.

Upon acquiring the historic property, park management immediately closed portions of the site in need of being "upgraded" to conform with laws governing state parks. Direct access to the bridge stopped; the often primitive trail to Gowan's natural treasure was closed, and visitors no longer could clamber across the rocks and pools underneath the arch so "re-growth" could begin. Regretfully, the lodge closed its doors to overnight guests, although a recent brochure dangled a carrot: "The lodge is not yet available for overnight use, but plans are under way."

The house's gift shop and lobby remain open, and the brochure advertises a phone number for lodge tours. The main surface trail affords four views of the bridge, and the half-mile Gowan Loop Trail descends into the creek bed with an observation deck, peering into the great maw, at the bottom. Two other trails cut across the terrain, one near a small waterfall, the other near the creek bottom, but well clear of the bridge.

Tonto Natural Bridge State Park, as it is now known, lies hidden to all but the initiated in its placental valley, about 90 miles north of Phoenix and 10 miles north of Payson on State Highway 87, and then three miles west on a dirt road. Signs point the way.

Even if improved somewhat, the entrance road may still be a bit daunting, but it's worth it. Just close your eyes (unless you're driving) and wait till the car stops in the parking lot at the bottom. Trailers and motorhomes exceeding 16 feet are currently prohibited.

See the bridge. If the lodge has reopened, indulge your other senses there (phone 602-476-4202 for current information). Immerse yourself in quietude. Watch the sun set. Feel the breeze. Hear the rustling noises at night. Allow romance to once again enter your life. Leave the alarm clock back home.

Many better-known sites are nearby: Sedona, the high-profile New Age capital of the Southwest with its elegant craft shops and restaurants and massive doses of red rock monoliths; Jerome, a very commercial "ghost town;" and natural formations and cultural landmarks like Montezuma Castle and Tuzigoot National Monuments and Meteor Crater.

ARKANSAS

THE NATIONAL PARK THAT DOESN'T LOOK LIKE ONE

Of the more than four dozen national parks, one holds the twin distinction of being the smallest and most different. Imagine a national park whose main features don't include a canyon or a waterfall or a glacier or a volcano or a snow-encrusted crag or a sea of sawgrass. Imagine instead a mule-powered trolley ride past old buildings or a rubber-tired amphibious vehicle colloquially called a "duck." Fathom further the caprice of checking into a national park in the center of a busy town, being greeted by a uniformed ranger, and then slipping out of your clothes and into a whirlpool bath and you have an accurate picture of the 18th and most unique national park.

Hot Springs National Park's whirlpool baths and massages, duck tours, and mule trolleys, while not sponsored by the park, are operated by private concessionaires in accordance with rules established by the Department of the Interior, the Park Service's mother.

The Arkansas park arose around natural hot springs, 47 pools of mineral water that has been rippling out of the earth's fissures at 143 degrees Fahrenheit for thousands of years and that even today issues forth at nearly a million gallons a day. Hot Springs' water starts as rain falling through porous slits in the earth's surface before traveling downward in obedience to gravity until it enters nether regions of much warmer rock which heats it, cleansing it of any impurity. Along the journey, the water erodes various minerals from the rock, pulverizing them into liquid form and absorbing them. Finally, 4,000 years later, the hot, pure, enriched water gushes in springs to the surface, aided by faults that draw it upward.

Scientists conjecture that prehistoric Indians came across the bubbling springs as many as 10,000 years ago, observed the phenomenon, bathed in the cooler pools, and drank the water from nearby cold springs. Historians theorize the first white visitors to the "Valley of the Vapors" may have been Hernando de Soto and his Spanish conquistadores in 1541. French, Spanish, and American travelers knew of the springs in succeeding centuries, and President Thomas Jefferson commissioned an exploration of the area in 1804. Americans journeyed to it for its therapeutic waters, and the federal government acquired much of it in 1832 to protect it, indirectly making it the first "national park" (although that phrase was still nearly a century in the future).

The springs grew in popularity when wooden houses replaced the first primitive tents on the site and later still when opulent palatial buildings replaced the wooden houses as treatment centers. In 1921, the newly created National Park Service officially drew Hot Springs into its fold.

The advent of leisure time, family vacations, and high-speed freeways following World War II curtailed use of "The National Spa" and "The Nation's Health Sanitarium," as it was called, and the ornate bathhouses along Central Avenue - the heart of both the park and town of Hot Springs - went belly up, one by one. Most still stand in various stages of faded elegance, and only the Buckstaff Bathhouse still operates.

Of the nine buildings composing the park along Central Avenue between Reserve Avenue and Fountain Street, only one - the Fordyce Bathhouse - is open free to the public as a visitor center and historic relic. Tours usually start in the basement, the location of the Fordyce Spring; the modern buildings, following the example of the tents and makeshift wooden structures of the 19th century, enclosed the springs to allow guests a privacy and luxury unavailable to earlier people who merely drank the water or plunked themselves in it as it exited the bowels of the earth.

The first floor presents an information desk, gift shop, and theater where the mens' cooling and pack rooms used to be. The ladies' versions of those treatment rooms provide glimpses of the past: the steam cabinet room swathed rheumatic, syphilitic, jaundiced, and obese bodies with 30 minutes of 115-140-degree steam to make them sweat, quicken, and grow hot; attendants in the pack room swabbed sweaty bodies with moist packs and wrapped them in sheets; the cooling room allowed guests to relax in bathrobes or sheets, lounge on cots, read, chat, or nap as their temperatures returned to normal.

Though people of all stations and means could avail themselves of the treatment, in reality only the wealthy could afford to journey to the springs. The central men's bathhall, occupying the center of the first floor, showcases the affluence: a domed skylight holds 8,000 pieces of stained glass picturing an erotic tableau of Neptune's daughter holding court amongst mermaids, dolphins, and fish swimming untrammeled in swirls of water - elegant extravagance for patrons able to surmount the economic throes of the Depression.

A video entitled "The Process of Bathing Today" continuously plays in an exhibit room of the second floor alongside period artifacts relating to the hot water therapy, photos of famous visitors, and text plaques (like the one that recounts Majestic Bathhouse bathing attendant Jim Lemons' recollection of Prohibition bootlegger and mob kingpin Al Capone being "a good tipper....All those gangsters, they were just people.").

An adjacent exhibit room focuses on the history of the Hot Springs community, the spa society, and how the water reaches its unique temperature.

The remainder of the floor peaks into the bygone majesty of the massage rooms, the mechanotherapy room (a veritable gym with a rowing machine, electric horse, and stationary bicycle), and the dressing rooms.

The third floor nearly shimmers with its gilded glance at yesterdays gone by. A full-size gymnasium provides the most up-to-date equipment favored by earlier generations - the Nautiluses of their day. A beauty parlor and Hubbard tub room, utilized for underwater treatment, complement the staterooms rented out for rest and dressing purposes following the baths. And the rectangular assembly room presents an aristocratic ambience seldom seen today - a large space where guests congregated in their finery to discuss the day's topics under a vaulted stained glass ceiling overlooking sunburst glass doors, tile floors, sconce lights, wicker furniture, and ferns. Concerts often entranced guests, and the sheet music for "Avalon" and other melodies of a quainter era still grace the piano. The ladies' and men's parlors, where the sexes could retreat in blissful segregation, occupy either end, a delicate Knabe grand piano in the former, a billiard table, Victrola, game implements, and a spittoon in the latter.

A garden roof atop the building, where guests formerly sunbathed under the open sky or listened to concerts staged in the bandstand behind the bathhouse, is no longer open.

The Fordyce premiered in 1915 when Colonel Samuel Fordyce opened his Renaissance Revival mansion with its copper-framed marquee.

Adjoining the Fordyce on either side and currently closed (excepting the Buckstaff) are: the Superior Bathhouse which shut down in 1983 after enjoying the longest continuous run of all area bathhouses; the Hale, a brick and stucco edifice dating to 1892 but altered twice in the 20th century; the Maurice, a Mediterranean house that replaced a Victorian building in 1911 and which featured interior halls with imaginary water creatures on stained glass ceilings; the ceramic tile-domed Quapaw which, when opened in 1922, replaced two earlier bathhouses of wooden construction; the Ozark, built on the order of a mission with two ornamental towers and decorative scrolls and shields mimicking the ancient Roman baths; the neoclassical Buckstaff of 1911 vintage which has outlasted all its competing cousins from the golden age (1892-

1936); and the Lamar, built in 1923, with its California look, spacious muraled lobby, sun porch, and art deco details. Some of the historic houses are slated to be renovated and opened by private businessmen for purposes other than those responsible for their original construction...but under Park Service guidelines.

A thermal water cascade emptying into a pool just north of Bathhouse Row entices the more adventurous to wade in at mid-calf level (be careful; it's hot). And the Maurice Historic Spring, the park's initial display spring, is visible between the Hale and the Maurice. A casual quarter-mile walk along Central Avenue takes in the facades of Bathhouse Row, and a stroll along the Grand Promenade behind the houses affords views of America's greatest collection of historic bathhouses as well as two open, gurgling hot springs and several thermal fountains.

The park includes neighboring mountains that hug the valley enveloping the city of Hot Springs. Though not as popular as the bathhouses, they feature several driving roads, a dozen and a half relatively short and easy (most are well under a mile) hiking trails, a couple picnic sites, and a campground.

The 216-foot Hot Springs Mountain Tower, charging a moderate rate for its elevator ride, just atop the crest east of Bathhouse Row, delivers a nice view of the Ouachita Mountains and the Hot Springs valley they encase but a poor view of the bathhouses themselves (thanks to a tree-lined incline behind them).

The town's current operating bathhouses - Arlington Hotel, Buckstaff (the only one within the park), Downtowner Motor Inn, Hot Springs Health Spa, Hot Springs Park Hilton, Libbey Memorial Physical Medical Center, and Majestic Hotel - offer total packages (100-degree thermal water baths, steam cabinet hot packs, needle showers, and massages) for prices ranging from $20-30 (mid-1990s rates). Niceties like whirlpools and sitz baths (where the limbs rest outside the tub and the water concentrates on the lower back) sometimes cost extra. Hours and days of operation vary wildly; call 800-SPA-CITY or 501-321-2277 (the Convention & Visitor's Bureau) for information.

The Fordyce visitor center/museum opens daily during daytime hours.

Everything - park tour, bath, "duck" ride, tower view, etc. - will take a day. The city and its environs provide riverboat cruises, wax museums, alligator farms, aquariums and zoos, country music shows, riding stables, theme parks, Biblical pageants, miniature worlds, and lakes. If you go in the foreseeable future, expect to see signs and banners proclaiming Hot Springs the home of Bill Clinton.

You can get unlimited free samples of the famed mineral water from drinking fountains at the Fordyce or you can pay for the water in bottles sold at stores throughout the area. Either way, it will taste the same.

Hot Springs National Park is just southwest of the center of Arkansas, 55 miles from Little Rock on U.S. Interstate Highway 30 and U.S. Highway 70.

CALIFORNIA

THE PASS WHERE MOTHER NATURE MADE ANIMALS OF MEN

In the spring of 1846, hundreds of eastern and midwestern men, women, and children began a great westward walk across the continent to the new Pacific Coast territories.

They were neither the first nor the last to make the 2,000-mile epic journey west in search of new lands, lives, and fortunes. But that year's group was destined to go down in history.

They set out on different trails and on different dates throughout the spring, converging generally on one trail in Nebraska and pushing on into Wyoming. There, in July, near the South Pass through the Rocky Mountains, the various groups made a decision either to follow the established northern route through Wyoming, Idaho, and down into Nevada or to take a chance on a newly discovered southern "cutoff" route through Utah and Nevada that reputedly saved 200 miles...this in a time when cumbersome covered wagons routinely groaned under their weight, broke down, and often moved only a dozen miles a day. Most of the emigrants chose the sure northern trail, but about 90 people, relying on the purported shortcut, veered south.

The latter group arduously cut a road through the Wasatch Mountains, abandoning their possessions to lighten the load, and lost some of their livestock while enduring fourscore miles of the Great Salt Lake Desert; the cutoff, to their discomfiture, became no shortcut at all. When the two divergent trails joined in Nevada, the southern party found itself left behind in the dust of the northern party. Summer surrendered to fall, and the treacherous snow-capped Sierra Nevada Mountains still remained in the way.

Internal bickering, threats of Indian interference, scarce provisions, and violent death marred their progress. Finally, in early November, the strung-out party reached the vicinity of Truckee Lake where a negotiable pass cut through the mountains near the Nevada-California border. But snow had already fallen, an ominous sign for travelers still 100 miles shy of their destination, low on provisions, and facing dead ahead a mountain range notorious for sudden blizzards.

The party stopped to regroup, gain strength, and begin anew. But the snows continued to fall, and the journeyers splintered into groups and dug in for the winter.

On November 20, Patrick Breen wrote in his diary: "came to this place on the 31st of last month that it snowed we went on to the pass the snow so deep we were unable to find the road, when within 3 miles of the summit then turned back to this shanty....it continueing to snow all the time we were here we now have killed most party of our cattle having to stay here untill next spring & live on poor beef without bread or salt"

Conditions worsened. On November 29, he added: "still snowing now about 3 feet deep....killed my last oxen today....hard to get wood."

What followed was America's most tragic case of intense starvation and desperate cannibalism - the final horrible throes of the ill-starred Donner Party. Only half the expedition survived the unrelenting winter snows and managed to reach the end of the trail.

Three separate sites around the modern town of Truckee, California today tell the pathetic tale.

The smallest site lies along the south side of Donner Pass Road (Old Highway 40), just west of the Truckee school on the outskirts of town. A large white wooden cross rises behind a plaque in a boulder marking the site of the Graves cabin, one of three principal locations where various doomed travelers sequestered themselves for the winter.

Donner Memorial State Park, the most extensive of the three sites, lies a fraction of a mile west. The park commemorates the locations of the Breen and Murphy cabins and features the Pioneer Monument, a bronze cluster of emigrants peering west, in the direction of their illusory promised land, atop a 22-foot-high pedestal of stone and cement - the exact height of the 1846-47 snows at their deepest.

The Emigrant Trail Museum is open during normal daytime hours and charges a nominal fee. It displays textboards, photographs, and artifacts relevant to the Sierra Nevada Mountains, the pioneers, the California Gold Rush, the railroad, and western logging operations. It also explains the Donner Party story in pictures, words, and personal items belonging to various members - mementoes of that excruciatingly bitter winter. Dioramas show key scenes in the Donner Party's fight for survival. One exhibit, featuring a tree trunk, explains that 12-foot-high stumps shot up from the ground around the Donner camps in the spring, a somber indication of the depth the snow had reached when the doomed pioneers had cut off the tops of the trees for shelter and firewood the previous fall and winter. An emotional 25-minute narrative film, with riveting text and photography by Barbara Sutherland, runs every hour in a theater whose walls sprout evocative paintings of the heroism and suffering of the Donner Party.

The third site is several miles away, just east of U.S. Highway 89, three miles north of its junction with Interstate Highway 80 northeast of Truckee. A marker identifies the side road as "Donner Camp Picnic Ground Historical Site Tahoe National Forest." At the end of the cul-de-sac, a parking lot leads to a circular boardwalk and dirt trail looping around the site of the Alder Creek Valley where party leader George Donner, his family, and his brother's family pitched tents against trees to ward off the cold. "On October 28, 1846 the six covered wagons brought west by George and Jacob Donner and their families halted here for repairs," says a plaque emplaced within a boulder. "By March of 1847 one half of the party of 22 adults and children had died of starvation and cold. They came west seeking a new life and found misery and death."

A wooden marker with a lengthy text and roster of the fates of the individual Donners stands nearby. Straight ahead, via the loop trail, a meadow, formerly a forest, holds the remains of a double-pronged pine tree where the Donners erected one of their tents. The site is quiet, tranquil, nonthreatening; its occasional visitors shake their heads when contemplating how the peaceful clearing once held human lives as pawns.

Touring all three sites, a rarity for most visitors, will consume at least a couple hours, allowing for driving, hiking, and viewing time. Donner Memorial State Park also includes a portion of three-mile-long Donner Lake (formerly Truckee Lake) with boating, fishing, waterskiing, swimming, camping, picnicking, and hiking opportunities. The recreational portion of the park is open from Memorial Day to mid-September; a separate fee is charged.

A sobering stop because of the nature of the event it commemorates, the museum also contains a book and video store and receives the lion's share of visitors (the other two sites are primarily unknown and unvisited).

Though small, Truckee possesses a sizable shopping district.

The Donner Party sites are 10-15 miles north of numerous spots on the north shore of Lake Tahoe, a prime vacation destination and one of America's most scenic lakes. And Reno, the self-styled "Biggest Little City in the World," with its gambling glitz and glitter, lies just 30 miles northeast along Interstate 80, just across the Nevada border; it affords a more hedonistic slice of life than that dished out by Mother Nature 150 years earlier in a time when a blizzard meant not merely a day off from school but a date with destiny.

An altar of invocation, a tank of devastation...
silenced forever now in the place that God forgot.

"THE PLACE GOD FORGOT"

It's a strange place, smack-dab in the middle of nowhere in California's great southern desert - 30 miles east of Indio, 60 miles west of Blythe. Occupying a slight rise just north of Interstate Highway 10 and south of the southernmost reaches of Joshua Tree National Park, it grows scrub brush and sand as it squats and stares at the Little San Bernardino, Orocopia, and Chuckwalla Mountains all around it.

It includes a gas station, a combination 24-hour restaurant-convenience store-curio shop, an antique store, two double-room cottages, an automotive fix-it store, trailers to house the few people who man the businesses, and a cluster of disengaged jeeps and disarmed tanks, their gun nozzles pointing skyward. In one corner of the desert, holding its own against the clumps of greenery within which lizards scamper, an alfresco stone chapel with appendant altar and rows of wooden plank benches peers up at the stars at night as if to see if they hold answers to the prayers of long-gone years.

Welcome to Chiriaco Summit...which is, aside from those few people who tend the businesses, a ghost town usually not listed on state maps.

A couple generations ago, when the businesses had yet to spring up, when the tanks and jeeps rolled for real over the brush weeds, scattering lizards left and right with their thunder, people who passed by called it "The place God forgot." The crustiest fighting general who ever wore an American uniform described it as "desolate and remote" and opined "If you can work successfully here, in this country, it will be no difficulty at all to kill the assorted sons of bitches you will meet in any other country."

The general was George S. Patton, Jr., the controversial tank conqueror of North Africa and Europe in World War II. He came to Chiriaco Summit in early 1942, with America freshly plunged into war on two global fronts, charged with establishing a desert training center that would turn men into machines capable of surviving combat in Africa's Sahara Desert against the German Army. Patton chose 18,000 square miles of desert from Pomona, California east to Phoenix, Arizona and from Yuma, Arizona north to Boulder City, Nevada and set up 11 different training camps where men trained under the intense conditions of a living desert. Chiriaco Summit became Camp Young, his administrative center. As an historical plaque at the site says:

> Between 1942 and 1944 over one million men trained on the surrounding desert and participated in the most realistic war games under the harshest conditions imaginable. In a very important sense, many battles of World War II were won on these desert lands during those maneuvers.

The desert training center bears the distinction of being the largest military staging and maneuvering area anywhere in the history of the world.

Patton drove his men hard, insisting they run a 10-minute mile in the desert under scorching heat and burdened with uniforms, backpacks, and rifles. He nixed the suggestion that his men take time off to construct water tanks: "They have no time to do anything except learn to fight." He shared desert accommodations with them until July when he was sent to Europe for the real thing. But his policies endured for the next two years.

The empty tanks and jeeps and cannon at Chiriaco Summit guard the General Patton Memorial Museum constructed at the entrance to old Camp Young.

The eclectic museum exhibits artifacts from many of America's armed conflicts but focuses most of its space on Patton, his army, and the desert training. The customary military paraphernalia (photographs, paintings, decommissioned rifles, German flags and weaponry, uniforms, field radio kits, mess kits) are in abundance and complement displays germane to the subject: a photograph of a soldier in training shaving with canteen water that has reached a temperature of 100 degrees; dogtags, a tube of IPANA toothpaste, combs, lighters, and typewriters left behind at the training center; a sabre and fencing foil owned by Patton; and a lifesize wax figure of the general surrounded by flags.

A 25-minute film on Patton's life with reminiscences by soldiers who served under him plays in an adjoining theater.

Among the most memorable displays are a huge topographical bas relief map depicting the locations of the various desert training camps, a silk map of France carried by an 82nd Airborne soldier who parachuted into Normandy on D-Day, and a collection of sacramentals removed from a bombed-out Catholic church in Cassino, Italy on November 8, 1943.

And outside, trails weave to and around the tanks, jeeps, artillery, and stone altar where, slightly more than a half-century ago, tens of thousands of men played war games in earnest. The skeleton for a planned bronze statue of Patton rises from its temporary pedestal by the tanks; when finished, it will assume a place of honor at the museum's entrance.

Picnic tables hold the ground in front of the museum. A book store and gift shop wait inside the entrance.

A moderate admission is charged; touring the inside and outside and viewing the film should take an hour or so. The museum opens daily, except Thanksgiving and Christmas, during customary daytime hours.

The museum is only a few years old, and comparatively few people stop by because Chiriaco Summit is primarily a pit stop for motorists and truckers on the 90-mile stretch between Indio and Blythe. But if you're ever traveling that desolate stretch of I-10 and turn off at the spectral Chiriaco Summit for gas, food, or rest, as we did, and suddenly, inexplicably come across tanks, military vehicles, and a larger-than-life bronze of a general in the unlikeliest of places, at least you'll understand the story behind the glory.

THE ASHES OF AN ADVENTURER, THE LEGACY OF A LAUREATE

His personal motto included words among the most poignant ever penned:

> I would rather be ashes than dust! I would rather that my spark should burn out in a brilliant blaze than it should be stifled by dry rot. I would rather be a superb meteor, every atom of me in magnificent glow, than a sleepy and permanent planet. The proper function of man is to live, not to exist. I shall not waste my days in trying to prolong them. I shall use my time.

A life scarred by a troubled, delinquent adolescence fostered those words. The life ultimately proved to be short - 40 years - and checkered. Periods of benighted profligacy alternated with bouts of lavish success and intense idealism and one devastating emotional and financial setback.

It began on the West Coast on January 12, 1876 when John Griffith Chaney was born out of wedlock to a roustabout father who had wanted the fetus aborted and a mother who had twice turned to suicide in desperation. The father skipped town, and the mother later married John London who adopted the infant.

The boy grew up troubled, perhaps owing to a rather distant

relationship with a mother whose quirks included ritualistic seances and longshot financial plans that usually backfired. "I guess Jack was a pretty good boy when you come to figure it all out," she once assessed, "but he fell in with bad company. He used to have terrible fights with the boys of the neighborhood. He got to going down to the waterfront. He became awfully bossy in the house. We couldn't stand him sometimes."

The troubled teen gave short shrift to school and took up the life of a vagabond. He quarreled, drank, and went to sea where witnessing the braining of seals for their pelts profoundly affected him. Arrested for vagrancy in Niagara Falls, he spent a month in a Buffalo slammer and observed the brutality of the law and the effects of forced homosexual sex on hapless inmates. For awhile, he embraced the life of a hobo and rode the nation's rails.

As an adult, he entered into a marriage more of convenience than love and encouraged a side romance with another woman. The day after his marriage ended in divorce, he wed a woman who matched his flair for adventure.

He joined the Socialist Party and vocally criticized abject conditions of life for oppressed, penurious victims. He also espoused certain views that would be most charitably called racist. A world traveler, especially in the Far East and the South Seas, he picked up a number of diseases common to voyagers. In addition to problems encountered from his alcoholic and gluttonous tendencies, he also suffered from a variety of skin, gum, and sexual diseases. A stringent medication taken to counteract yaws adversely affected his kidneys. He turned to dangerous drugs like heroin, morphine, and opium to alleviate chronic intestinal pain.

He also had a brilliantly luminescent side as well. His mind soared with high ideals, compassion, and revolutionary concepts that would improve the lot of any man who had, like him, extracted meaning from misery in a life of poverty.

He enjoyed enormous success as a writer, selling articles and short stories and publishing his first book in 1900, when he was only 24. For about a decade during his prime, he became America's most popular novelist and one of its best paid. A daily regimen of writing a thousand words yielded more than four dozen books and hundreds of shorter works in both fiction and nonfiction. He sailed the South Pacific for two years and went to Asia as a war correspondent. He opened his house to friends who came calling.

When he died on November 22, 1916, at 40, of either gastrointestinal uremic poisoning or an overdose of morphine that recent speculation has termed potentially suicidal, Jack London had secured a reputation as one of the world's most revered writers. "Call of the Wild," "The Sea Wolf," "White Fang," and others had seen to that.

California's Jack London State Historic Park holds the remains of the famed author-adventurer, as well as his home for the final five years of his life and the ruins of his elaborate $80,000 Wolf House mansion that he ordered built yet never lived in because a fire of controversial origin consumed most of it on August 22, 1913. The 800-acre park, with remnants of his farm operations, a small lake, and biking and hiking trails, provides the greatest sense of London's persona and legacy anywhere in the world.

A museum and visitor center now occupy the House of Happy Walls, the home London's widow built after his death and lived in until her own passing in 1955. Two floors of artifacts, paintings, and photographs introduce London to a contemporary world that may only know him from his likeness on a postage stamp of recent vintage: a second-floor study bearing furnishings from his actual study, including the roll-top desk at which he wrote; a 1915 bust rendered by Finn Frolich; some of his books, seafaring equipment, and war memorabilia; a display case claiming London received over 600 rejection slips before achieving success and including a letter identified as his first rejection slip, a note from The Saturday Evening Post that says, "We have found the 'Sunlanders' a story of exceptional interest, and we should wish to give it a place in our columns were it not for our policy to exclude the tragic from the magazine. We thank you cordially for giving us an opportunity to examine this manuscript, and hope that you have in hand some tales of a more cheerful nature."; his bed, formerly in the nearby cottage, where he spent more time reading than sleeping; and several films that show his toothy smile and divulge his disinterest in mechanical instruments, including the typewriter which he eschewed in his writings in favor of a quick, sloppy scrawl that his wife deciphered and typed. A short film, set to a period ragtime melody, shows a robust London with his wife, driving a manure spreader, feeding pigs, brushing his favorite saddle horse, and happily waving farewell only six days before his death, seeming to undercut the theory that he may have committed suicide.

A half-mile southeast of the museum, through a forested trail that warns of poison oak and rattlesnakes, are short paths leading to both the stone remains of the tragically uninhabited Wolf House and the gravesite. The massive house, rustic yet comfortable, included an outdoor pool, library, secluded study, fireproof basement repository for valuables, two-tiered living room, guest rooms, a dining room for 50, fireproof walls, and an earthquake-proof concrete foundation. Its extant towers and intact walls appear eerie and bear mute testimony to a magnificent dream suddenly gone askew.

The grave is among the humblest in the country. A sign on a four-sided picket fence announces simply "JACK LONDON'S GRAVE." And inside the square enclosure, another sign recounts:

> Jack London once remarked to his wife Charmian and his sister Eliza that, "I wouldn't mind if you laid my ashes on the knoll where the Greenlaw children are buried. And roll over me a red boulder from the ruins of the Big House." On November, 26, 1916, in a silent ceremony, Charmian London placed her husband's ashes on the chosen knoll under this stone. After she passed away in 1955, Charmian's ashes were also laid to rest here.

A mossy boulder, porous with age, stands its solitary vigil near the marker. Weeds and grass grow high all around and commingle at its base. The graves of David and Lillie Greenlaw, the pioneer children he had referred to, are nearby, within their own picket-fenced enclosure. Except when busloads of schoolchildren visit, the site is still, its silence broken only by occasional chirps of birds.

The cottage in which Jack and Charmian London lived for five years is now undergoing restoration and will eventually house its rightful furnishings currently on display in the museum. It is a quarter-mile walk from the west parking lot. Though not open as of this writing, its front steps lead to two window-enclosed porches; the smaller one on the left is London's study where he wrote during his last years; the larger one on the right is where he died.

The California Department of Parks & Recreation operates the site at 2400 London Ranch Road in Glen Ellen, and the museum is open daily during normal daytime hours except on the major holidays of Thanksgiving, Christmas, and New Year's Day. The park itself stays open a couple hours longer. An average per-vehicle fee is charged.

State rangers who run the location say as many as 300 schoolchildren a week can visit when school is in session and as many as a million visitors a year stop by or use the park facilities, but our visit yielded considerably fewer people - one busload of kids and a dozen other visitors.

Even breezing through the museum, gravesite, ruins, and cottage will take a minimum of an hour because of the hiking involved. If you are particularly fond of Jack London or open to being touched by the legacy of a captivating spirit who managed to squeeze memorable stories out of a lifelong affinity for independent thinking and an unshackled wanderlust, you will want to stay several hours.

The park is easily marked on London Ranch Road, just off State Highway 12 in Glen Ellen, about 60 miles north of San Francisco and equally close to Point Reyes National Seashore and the Pacific Ocean.

AMERICA'S OTHER "OLD FAITHFUL"

It has the same panache, the same timing, the same name, and even works up a full head of steam like its more famous Big Daddy in Wyoming. It's tucked into northern California's Mount St. Helena and Palisades foothills.

The discovery of this Old Faithful dates back to before the 1906 San Francisco earthquake. Like its famous forebear, it behaves predictably, sending a jet of 360-degree water 60-150 feet into the air (although the former figure is what you're more likely to see). Major eruptions average every 40 minutes, around the clock, and last two to four minutes. Minor eruptions go off much more frequently, but tend to have shorter life spans. Our visit saw four eruptions in an hour, lasting about a minute and 20 seconds each time.

The people who operate the site at California's Old Faithful in Calistoga in the famous grape-growing, winemaking Napa Valley maintain there are only three regularly erupting geysers in the world: the one in Yellowstone National Park; one in New Zealand's Geyser Fields; and theirs (other geysers, including some in Nevada and Wyoming, erupt either continuously or with less predictability). If true, then Americans have a choice of only two "Old Faithfuls," and the one in California is more accessible and provides more intimacy because of its sparser crowds.

California's geyser also boasts an attractive setting, hemmed in by palm trees and a small bamboo jungle set against 4,500-foot Mount St. Helena and the Palisades peaks - former active volcanoes now gone dormant. Taped informative messages, lasting two or three minutes each, emanate from loudspeakers between eruptions and provide scientific facts on the nature of geysers and this one in particular.

Changes in barometric pressure, tectonic stresses, and the moon and tides affect the eruption frequency and height of Old Faithful's column. All geysers spring from locations where underground water, heat, and fissures and cavities lie in conjunction. Calistoga receives its water from an underground river, and its heat comes from hot magma or lava within the earth.

Noticeable changes in the eruption performance of Calistoga's geyser have signaled the onslaught of several major California earthquakes, including the Loma Prieta temblor that struck San Francisco in 1989.

Roughly 20 picnic tables and benches, all positioned for a good view, nearly surround the geyser. A snack bar and gift shop are nearby, and the snaking paths in the bamboo forest provide a good hide-and-seek place for kids to blow off their own steam while waiting for the next big one. An average admission is charged - a bit steep if you're only staying for one eruption, but worth its cost if you plan on hanging around for more than one and are a camera buff intent on capturing the geyser performing against the backdrop of the palm trees and the mountains.

Naturally, as with all geysers, certain rules should be adhered to. The water cools considerably upon reaching the air but is still hot and should be admired from a distance.

Though the setting is intimate, with only a handful of people watching an average eruption, that privacy is one of Old Faithful's greatest plusses. And seeing Yellowstone's Old Faithful requires a trip to the park and then a lengthy interior drive to reach it; Calistoga's geyser can be handily approached and seen.

Operating daily during normal daytime hours, Old Faithful is in Calistoga in Napa County at the junction of State Highways 29 and 128, 25 miles northwest of the city of Napa. Dozens of California wineries offering tours and tastings are just south, both on the road to Napa and along State Highway 12 to Schellville, as well as interspersed throughout the region. Hot water and sparkling wine can mix to make an enjoyable day. And the Petrified Forest, created by the volcanic eruption of Mount St. Helena three million years ago, is just a few miles west of Calistoga on Petrified Forest Road.

A KNIGHT TO REMEMBER...WHEN TIME STOOD STILL

It commanded a gorgeous view of the most scenic inlet on perhaps the most scenic lake in America. And it treated guests to a slice of life in the lap of luxury that most people could only dream of.

If you came to this mock Scandinavian castle during the 1930s and wartime '40s, you arrived at the $500,000 mansion and outbuildings with your cares solidly back home.

Copied after Scandinavian wooden domiciles and stone castles, the mansion arose in 1928-29, bedecked with original furnishings imported from Europe and exact handcrafted duplicates, leaded stained glass windows and Oriental rugs, an enclosed courtyard with a wildflower-studded sod roof, and an intriguing blend of authentic antiques and modern conveniences.

You came there for the summer, from late June to mid-September, and your stay ranged from a day to an entire season.

You received lavish treatment with no expense spared, as though the country had never heard the word "Depression." A maid knocked on the door of your private bedroom at 7 a.m. to awaken you. She laid out your day's attire, even flicked on the heater in the bathroom if the lakeside temperatures had dipped too low during the night. You ate with your hostess and other invited guests in the dining room an hour later.

Then you mingled with others in either the morning room or the living room and marveled at the beauty of the lake. You went swimming, sunbathing, fishing, hiking, riding (horses were always at your disposal).

Mail - real mail, letters, valued correspondence, not catalogs, flyers, and solicitations - came by boat around 11:30 or so. Lunch arrived an hour later, followed by a nap or quiet reading or letterwriting.

Tea was served at 4 p.m., either inside by the fireplace on cool days or under an umbrella out on the terrace overlooking the lake on warm ones. Sometimes you would be ferried to nearby Fannette Island, a private outcropping owned by your hostess, to have your tea in a 16-foot-square stone teahouse built atop the highest crag.

Then you read some more, played cards, strolled the paths, and watched squirrels gambol about before taking your dinner seat at 6:30. You dined on the finest foods served on exquisite servicewear including fingerbowls with wildflowers skimming the water. Next you partook of an after-dinner walk, followed by more social conversation, card games, and perhaps a private concert.

At 9:30 p.m., you either followed the lead of your elderly hostess and went to sleep or indulged in dancing or bowling or watched a movie elsewhere on the lake. If you used your own vehicle to get there, staffmembers washed and gassed it for you upon your return.

Your day might also have included a picnic or a moonlight cruise on the lake, all expenses paid.

If your hostess needed to go to her nearby winter home, you would be invited to accompany her for a day of shopping and dining while she tended business.

It was a world of leisure and luxury that no longer exists, a world where time seemed to stand still, where nothing was rushed, where everything had its place, a world made possible by Lora Josephine Knight, a wealthy society matron, philanthropist, and hostess who opened her mansion - Vikingsholm, on Emerald Bay on the southern shore of the California side of mountain-ringed Lake Tahoe - as a summer home in 1930. She built in the Scandinavian style because the bay and its surrounding mountainous terrain reminded her of Norwegian fjords. Widowed in her first marriage to an affluent businessman, divorced from her second husband, and having seen her only child die at a young age, she plunged wholeheartedly into the construction of Vikingsholm and turned it into a guest house for her friends. She summered there until 1945 when she died at 82.

The state now owns Vikingsholm, and you can no longer go there and do any of the things you could have when it was privately owned. But you can visit and take a half-hour guided tour and let your imagination carry you back to a more relaxed and orderly time.

Tours of Vikingsholm approximate the summer season, usually weekends from Memorial Day until mid-June and daily thereafter until Labor Day, during customary daytime hours. Tours depart every half-hour and include a maximum of about four dozen; a nominal fee is charged.

The Fannette Island teahouse, since victimized by vandalism and aging, can be reached by private boat. It is Lake Tahoe's only isle.

Vikingsholm is off State Highway 89 at Emerald Bay in the southwestern corner of Lake Tahoe. A roadside parking lot accommodates dozens of cars but is frequently full because the drive along Emerald Bay renders spectacular views. From the parking lot, a moderately steep mile-long trail descends to Vikingsholm.

Though the tour lasts less than a half-hour, your stay will total a couple hours when factoring in the time necessary to walk down and back, stroll the grounds, and visit the gift shop.

Most people coming to Lake Tahoe stumble upon Vikingsholm, and a good many just pass it by when they discover the mandatory two-mile round trip hike.

But it remains a nostalgic look at the past and can easily fit into a vacation on Tahoe's south shore which includes D. L. Bliss and Emerald Bay State Parks, beaches, historic sites, water recreation, and, on the Nevada side, casinos and glass-bottom paddlewheeler cruises. It can also be a refreshing antidote to the fast-paced, thrill-a-minute, self-absorbed society we have become in the years since Lora Knight died.

THE GLASS CHURCH WITH THE OCEAN VIEW

It all began in 1688 in Stockholm, Sweden when a Lutheran bishop fathered a child destined to grow up to become a Renaissance man who would speak nine languages, pen more than a hundred essays and books in various scientific disciplines, play music, serve in the Swedish Diet's House of Nobles, invent an ear trumpet for the deaf, and record and interpret dreams.

In a life that spanned more than eight full decades, he became a mining official who engineered Sweden's first algebra and calculus texts, a physiologist who blazed new trails in understanding the functions of the brain, ductless glands, and the nervous system, a physicist who prefigured Albert Einstein, an eminent scientist, cosmologist, and mathematician, and an astronomer who promoted the nebular theory of planetary formation.

In his 50s, he received a series of what he considered divine visions and then spent nearly the last 30 years of his life in exclusive pursuit of theology, writing 30 volumes either interpreting or augmenting Christian tenets. He became clairvoyant, assumed mystical powers, and claimed to converse with spirits.

Later generations called him the "Northern Plato." Nineteenth-century philosopher-essayist Ralph Waldo Emerson said he was "A colossal soul" who "lies vast abroad on his times, uncomprehended by them, and requires a long focal distance to be seen" and "One of the missouriums and mastodons of literature" who "is not to be measured by whole colleges of ordinary scholars." Twentieth-century humanitarian-author-lecturer Helen Keller labeled him a "Titan Genius" and "one of the noblest champions true Christianity has ever known." Novelist-critic Henry James, who spanned both centuries, lauded his "incomparable depth and splendor" and said "that he alone of men has...dared to bring creation within the bounds of consciousness....He grasped with clear and intellectual vision the seminal principles of things."

Revered and persecuted in his lifetime, he underwent a heresy trial in his native land in his 80s and died in London, England in 1772 at 84, hoping Christianity would assimilate his writings and transform them into "The New Church." He died believing that "the church is within man, and not without him."

After his death, Emanuel Swedenborg's writings gained greater currency and came to America in 1784. Three years later, the world's first Swedenborgian church - the Church of the New Jerusalem - arose in London, promulgating what today might be called a holistic approach to Christianity. By 1792, Baltimore, Maryland had its own Swedenborgian church. Third President Thomas Jefferson invited a Swedenborgian minister from Baltimore to deliver a sermon to Congress. Missionaries spread the faith westward across the continent; among them was John Chapman, who gained greater celebrity for concurrently sowing the seeds for another type of sustenance during his peripatetic journeys under the pseudonym "Johnny Appleseed."

The American branch of the church preached spiritual freedom and advocated responsibility in the liberating social movements of the 19th century. A Swedenborgian university in Ohio became the nation's second coed college.

In the early 20th century, a California Swedenborgian named Elizabeth Schellenberg conceived a plan for a wayfarers' chapel that would jut out above the Pacific Ocean and offer prayerful reflection and tranquility to travelers. A fellow Swedenborgian, Narcissa Cox Vanderlip, donated land on the Palos Verdes Peninsula, south of Los Angeles. The project remained dormant through the Depression and World War II but gained new life when Lloyd Wright, son of America's distinguished architect Frank Lloyd Wright, agreed to design the building.

Dedicated and opened for services and private meditation in 1951, the Wayfarers Chapel is one of only two and a half dozen Swedenborgian churches in America and, in all likelihood, the most attractive.

Though modest-sized, the chapel comprises glass panels on its sides and roof, all rising above a floor hewn of local stone and laced with California redwood beams to provide a striking edifice seeking "to correlate the environment, the natural setting that existed, with the architectural constructs," in Wright's words. It commands an eminence overlooking the Pacific near Abalone Cove and Portuguese Point. Clear days provide a misty glimpse of Santa Catalina Island, 25 miles off in the distance.

Joining the chapel is a 50-foot stone tower surmounted by a golden cross and cradling 16 bells. Illuminated at night, the cross acts as a beacon for ships coming to port; the bells chime on the quarter-hour and unleash cascades of music during special services and weddings.

A flowered colonnade connects the tower with a visitor center and provides shaded benches and panoramic vistas of the land as it steeply tapers off to yield to the ocean. Gardens flank the inner side of the colonnade and sprout profusions of seasonal flowers and plants of Biblical origins. Walkways thread the gardens and surround a compact gift shop. A small hillside stream, trickling between carefully planted greenery, and a triangular reflecting pool with spouting fountain jets complete the air of calm that reposes over the acres of sloping lawns and brilliantly colored flowers.

The "glass church," as it is often called, rises amidst coastal redwood trees, with ferns and plants ringing its inner walls, appearing to be a chapel growing out of a lush jungle.

Because of its serene beauty, the chapel hosts more than 600 annual marriages, so chances of running into a wedding party are better than average. Sunday worship occurs at 11 a.m., and special services take place throughout the year. An outdoor amphitheater of grass with natural terraces presents concerts, dramas, and a special Easter sunrise service. A visitor center continuously shows related videos.

More than 100 lights illuminate the walkways, gardens, and reflecting pool at dusk, when the sun sets over the Pacific.

Visitors are welcome to attend any non-private service and utilize a self-guiding brochure to experience the harmony between God, the Swedenborgian beliefs, and the site's natural beauty and symbolic geometrical designs. A casual sojourn to stroll the grounds and admire the scenery is permitted free of charge, and resident clergymen will not inflict "pocket proselytizing" on you.

The Wayfarers Chapel fetches a glimpse of unique architecture, a chance to gain insight into one of the world's minor but attractive religions, and a picture-perfect spot for contemplation. Other wayfarers will be encountered but, unless you've chosen a day of special service, you'll be able to stake out a corner of solitude for yourself for awhile.

Grounds open daily during normal daytime hours. Visible from Palos Verdes Drive South, the chapel is well-marked and easy to reach along the southern coast of Rancho Palos Verdes on the peninsula south of Los Angeles. If the habitually congested freeway network is not abnormally clogged, you should be within a half-hour to an hour of most anything in the Los Angeles area.

COLORADO

THE MILE-HIGH GRAVE IN THE MILE-HIGH STATE

There's a mountain in Chattanooga, Tennessee where you can see seven states on the proverbial "clear" day that never seems to be there when you're visiting. During the Civil War, the "Battle Above the Clouds" was fought on it, and it's called Lookout Mountain.

But there's another Lookout Mountain just as striking in Golden, Colorado...and with a much more challenging drive. The paved Lariat Trail, summoning an army of horseshoe turns and hairpin and double hairpin curves, one after another, relentlessly climbs the mountain, often with no guard rails.

The summit surveys the cities of Golden and Denver and Mount Vernon Canyon, Clear Creek Canyon, and 14,264-foot Mt. Evans. Colorado's 6,800-foot-high average makes it the highest state in the union, and only two other states - Alaska and California - have higher mountains. Lookout Mountain rises to 7,375 feet and its pulloffs overlook purplish peaks and clear streams cutting watery furrows through canyon bottoms.

A 22-foot statue of Christ - the Sacred Heart pose - clings to a side of the mountain near Mount Vernon Canyon at the Mother Cabrini Shrine where 370-some steps scale a hill, leading visitors on a pilgrimage to the statue. Named for America's first canonized saint, the shrine is open daily, free, from dawn to dusk.

A buffalo herd, interesting if you've never seen one but modest compared with those to be seen in Wyoming and South Dakota, grazes on a hill near Exit 254 of Interstate Highway 70. Denver pays the herd's keep as a tourist novelty.

But the ultimate destination is the grave at the mountain's highest point. It holds the remains of the frontier icon known as Buffalo Bill. How did a man born in Iowa and who lived in Nebraska and founded a city in Wyoming while touring throughout the world come to be buried atop a Colorado mountain?

Born William Frederick Cody, he rode a Pony Express circuit when barely a teen-ager, once enduring 322 miles on a score of horses over a 24-hour period to deliver mail, and went on to scout for the cavalry and kill buffalo as a contractual meat supplier for railroad construction crews. In this last capacity, he slew dozens of buffalo a day, a skill that won him his soubriquet. He killed an Indian in a one-on-one encounter that made him famous. Dime novels written by his colleague, publicist, and flack Ned Buntline extolled his merits, created his legend, and made him a household name in the last quarter of the 19th century. In the 1880s, he assembled actors, real cowboys, Indians like Sitting Bull, and expert riders and shooters like Annie Oakley and toured America and Europe with "Buffalo Bill's Wild West and Congress of Rough Riders of the World". The show played 30 years and made more than a million dollars a year at its zenith.

He became a state legislator in Nebraska, using the "Honorable" prefix that went with it while declining to attend any of the sessions, and served as the judge advocate general of Wyoming. He held an honorary colonelcy in the National Guard, and Theodore Roosevelt called him "an American of Americans." During the peak of his fame, he was the most recognizable person in America. More than anyone else, he presented the myth of the Wild West - with its simplistic good guys versus bad guys theme - to the American public, popularizing oversimplifications that later became the staple of Hollywood movies.

His great wealth evaporated in improvident financial ventures and reliance on unscrupulous promoters, partners, and loan sharks. Performing in others' shows to make money, he endured arthritis and rheumatism and eventually needed someone to help him mount a horse. The public never viewed that part of his decline and still revered him when he died in 1917 in his sister's Denver home.

More than others, Cody - and Ned Buntline, who made him famous - crystalize the colorful yet phony Wild West imagery that still lives on. If not as heroic as his character in the dime novels and films, Cody still was a good horseman, marksman, and explorer who parlayed an adventurous disposition into huge success as a scout, hunter, and showman. Unlike so many of his contemporaries, he was more virtuous than dastardly and generally stands head and shoulder-length hair above so many of the other ethically hermaphroditic legends of the Wild West.

He was buried atop Lookout Mountain's highest elevation, a site he had supposedly chosen on his deathbed (according to his widow). Some 25,000 people either attended the funeral or visited the gravesite that day.

In later years, the town of Cody, Wyoming, which he founded and where he also reputedly wished to be buried, attempted to reclaim the body. Denver resisted the challenge to remove its tourist draw and exhumed his coffin, dug down 20 feet, repositioned the casket in a three-inch-thick vault, covered it with more than 60,000 pounds of concrete, and enclosed the plot within a steel fence. A plaque laid into the stone and cement memorial marker atop the grave lists the names and birth and death dates of Cody and his wife and a brief epitaph ("AT REST HERE BY HIS REQUEST") that provides the final exclamation point on the message to the good people of Wyoming that they can look, but not touch.

Denver also built a showcase for the mementos of Cody's life and located the Buffalo Bill Memorial Museum just yards from his grave. Its exhibit rooms portray Cody, a strikingly photogenic man with flowing hair, upturned mustache, cascading goatee, wide-brimmed Stetson hat, and beaded, fringed buckskins, in hundreds of paintings, posters, and photographs. The museum displays a lock of his hair, collections of his saddles and bridles, his elaborately crafted show costumes, dioramas illustrating his exploits, and sections highlighting Western art and Native American costumes and culture.

Though normally charging admission, the museum sponsors several annual days celebrating important dates in Cody's life and premiering new exhibits, on which Colorado residents get in free. The museum turns festive in July for a Buffalo Bill Days celebration and in December for a holiday commemoration. It is open daily during daytime hours. A rooftop observation deck brings the western Rocky Mountains, Denver, and the eastern plains into view...on a clear day, of course.

The Lariat Trail drive and stops at the Cabrini Shrine, the buffalo herd, and Bill's grave, as well as grabbing a bite and shopping for souvenirs at the Pahaska Tepee, adjacent to the museum, can take a half-day. Golden awaits at the bottom (near the intersection of U.S. Highway 6 and 19th Street); you can catch a free guided tour of the Adolph Coors Company brewery or visit one of several museums dedicated to Colorado railroads, geology, pioneering, or hostelry. Heritage Square, a theme and amusement park and Victorian shopping village, is nearby. Also close are Denver's museums, shops, and restaurants and Blackhawk's gambling casinos.

CONNECTICUT

-SHAY

SHERLOCK'S HOME

It looms high above the Connecticut River, its stone and concrete buttresses, parapets, and promenades enticing visitors with the heart-pounding entrancement of a Gothic castle out of Mary Shelley or Bram Stoker. On a gloomy day or when the sun fades beneath the horizon, the towering hulk appears eerily majestic, even threatening with its dark recesses, hidden corners, and balconies whose cold, jagged stones seem to drip icicles from their bottoms.

Surely, Dracula's ghost must haunt this foreboding mansion. Surely, Frankenstein's monster must have stalked the bartizans and peered menacingly through the open windows of this aerie less than 10 miles - as the bat flies - inland of Long Island Sound. But this is neither Transylvania nor Bavaria. This is merely Gillette Castle State Park near Hadlyme in south-central Connecticut. The mansion, called simply Gillette Castle, was built from 1914-19 when it was more romantically known as "The Seventh Sister" in reference to its location atop the southernmost hill in a series of seven such rises above the eastern shore of the Connecticut River.

The inspiration behind the construction of the castle was William Gillette, today an obscure stage actor. In his day, however, Gillette, a former architecture student, became a pre-eminent playwright and accomplished actor as famous as the Barrymores. The son of a United States senator, he gained extraordinary renown in playing Arthur Conan Doyle's fictional sleuth Sherlock Holmes more than 1,300 times on the stage between 1899 and 1932. Holmes' familiar sartorial accouterments - the deerstalker hat, Inverness, and tapered calabash pipe - spring from Gillette's characterization.

The distinguished thespian was a true eccentric. Tall, thin, handsome in his youth, with a stern face and aquiline nose, he became widowed in 1888 and chose not to remarry in nearly half a century of subsequent life. He listened to Frederic Chopin compositions on his player piano and regularly served alcohol to guests, though he himself rarely joined them. He collected art - landscapes and seascapes - and once amassed over 100 canvases. For three decades, he sailed the Atlantic coastal waters on a 140-foot luxury yacht - usually alone, save for a Japanese servant and one of his cats. A creature of the theater and its habits, he breakfasted at 11, lunched at 3:30, and dined at 8, even when relaxing at the castle.

He spent well over a million dollars - a fantastic sum then, even for a millionaire (which his acting and writing talents had helped him become) - on purchasing 120 acres of land and constructing his estate. He placed his hand on every phase of the operation.

The mansion resembles a medieval Rhennish fort with its battlements, crenelations, and apertures. It rises to five stories in places from a natural rock formation, and solid granite forms the foundation walls, anywhere from two to five feet thick. A grand stone porte-cochere leads to a hidden recess and a large oaken door that opens into the entrance hall.

Gillette insisted that no piece of metal, even a nail, be left exposed to prevent the magnetic conduction of electrical current during a lightning storm. Because of that idiosyncracy, objects usually crafted from metal are fashioned of wood, leather, or glass.

The living room assumes gargantuan proportions - 50 feet long, 30 feet wide, 19 feet high - and sports a grand staircase that leads to subsequent floors, side rooms, and hidden staircases.

Gillette held several affinities, including a fondness for cats, whether sculpted, etched, painted, or slinking around on all fours. At one time during his 18-year occupation of the house, he kept dozens of feline images scattered throughout and 17 real ones roaming at will; they remain (all except the live ones, that is) in virtually every corner to delight modern visitors.

The castle contains two dozen rooms - more than ample for its single occupant - and 47 doors, all designed differently and some equipped with obscure locking mechanisms whose secrets only he fathomed.

Among the built-in eccentricities are: hidden bathrooms; a wall between the balcony and bedrooms that hangs from rafters and never quite touches the floor; wooden handles, in place of switches or push buttons, to flick electricity on; a sculpted wooden icicle, suspended, pendant-like, above the living room, that, when pulled, released up to 7,000 gallons of water into the main pipe, rendering the house fireproof; a study intended to resemble Sherlock Holmes' fictional digs at 221-B Baker Street, complete with violin; an indoor waterfall in the conservatory where Gillette kept his pet frogs; a board beneath the dining table that, when pressed by foot, emitted no discernible noise yet still signaled the butler; another secret panel that, when pressed just right, turned an innocent-looking cabinet into a well-stocked liquor bar; a sequence of mirrors within his hidden private chamber and in a neighboring balcony that allowed him to observe his guests in the living room below without himself being seen.

An avid pleasure boater and motorcyclist, Gillette also nurtured an intense fondness for railroads. He constructed a small-scale working railway system on his grounds that included three miles of narrow-gauge track, switches, turnouts, stations, tunnels, and rolling stock that could carry 35 guests at a time. A speed demon who frequently appeared before judges because he rode his cycle in excess of 70 miles per hour, he startled his guest passengers by taking curves at the train's top 20-mile-per-hour speed with no attempt to apply the brakes. The railroad setup has since gone to an amusement park, but his "Grand Central Station" terminus for his "Seventh Sister Shortline" can still be seen.

Having no direct heirs, Gillette expressed concern over what would happen to his palace after his death and included instructions in his will for his executors "to see to it that the property did not fall into the hands of some blithering saphead who has no conception of where he is or with what surrounded."

Sometime after Gillette died in 1937 at 83, Connecticut's State Park and Forest Commission took over the estate and has since maintained it as a recreational park and museum to one of America's unique eccentrics who lies buried in the Hooker family cemetery in Farmington, Connecticut.

The park generally opens Memorial Day and closes Columbus Day for daily visitation; thereafter, it is open only on weekends till the Christmas season. Hiking and picnicking facilities are offered during daytime hours. A moderate admission is charged. Because of its proximity to the coast, you might see anywhere from a couple dozen people to a couple hundred, depending on whether you pick an off-day or a holiday. The grounds and house usually require at least an hour or two of time.

Halfway between Hartford and Mystic Seaport, the castle is north of Interstate Highway 95 and then north on State Highways 156 or 9. From 156, take State Highway 82 west to State Highway 148, Hadlyme, and the castle. From 9, take 148 east to Chester and a car ferry that crosses the Connecticut River in full view of the imposing structure on the hill.

A SUBTERRANEAN PRISON

It commands a hill on Newgate Road west of East Granby in Connecticut's Hartford County, appearing very much a deserted fortress, a castle in disrepair.

A writer of another century once commented: "The appearance of this place forciby reminds the observer of the walls, castles, and towers, erected for the security of some haughty lordling of the feudal ages; while the gloomy dungeons within its walls, call to remembrance a Bastile...."

But looks are deceiving. No soldiers ever defended this point, no monarch ever sat on a throne within. In fact, what catches your attention at surface level is only the visible tip of the iceberg. What lurks beneath is far more interesting.

What today is known as Old New-Gate Prison and Copper Mine began in 1707 as America's first chartered copper mine, the Simsbury Copper Mine. Private companies, free whites, and black slaves all mined its ore. Generations later, after mining had stopped because of the high cost of transporting the ore to England for smelting (a procedure mandated by England in America's colonial days) as well as for other financial and business reasons, it became the new nation's first state prison and a detainment center for captured Loyalists (Americans who supported the British in the Revolutionary War).

It opened as a prison in 1773, taking its name from New-Gate Prison, an infamous incarceration center in London, England. Prisoners originally mined copper ore but soon shifted to nail manufacturing, shoe cobbling, and other trades of the day when authorities realized that mining copper provided the inmates with the exact tools so useful in attempting escape.

Its most dramatic moment came on May 18, 1781, near the end of the war, when 28 prisoners rebelled and fled their dungeon, killing one guard and wounding six others. Only a dozen of the escaped prisoners managed to elude pursuit beyond a few days.

After the end of the war, New-Gate remained an internment complex for burglars, counterfeiters, and horse thieves until September 1827 when it closed. The remaining inmates of the more than 800 who had endured internment over the years of the prison's operation wound up in a new correctional facility in Wethersfield. And New-Gate slipped into disuse, mined only sparingly for its still-unrecovered copper ore in succeeding years until it closed for good, only to eventually reopen as a tourist attraction and historical curiosity.

It achieved notoriety in its day, in part because it jailed its inmates in damp quarters well below the earth's surface. Edward Augustus Kendall, a British traveler passing through New England in 1807-08, blanched at viewing American men (New-Gate later included women as well) living in the darkened bowels of the earth, in jagged holes originally clawed from the rock in search of precious metal. "...the subterranean cells in this prison...are rather adapted to convey horror to a transitory visitor, than to occasion any particular misery to those who become their inhabitants," he wrote in 1807. "A human visitor will console himself with this reflection; but he will still call in question the rectitude of the persons by whom those inhabitants are placed there under a very different intention...." He described the life of a New-Gate inmate as "burdensome and miserable" for convicts who became "ferocious" because they were "treated precisely as tigers...in a menagerie."

Today, visitors may tour the tiger pen - the museum, information center, and, best of all, the ruins of the old copper mine and prison. The above-ground stone wall, zigzagging skyward in an uneven line of upturned angles and roofless bricks, surrounds a guardhouse, a chapel, four-story cellblocks where women stayed, and an old well no longer in use. A 20-foot vertical ladder, the original entrance, descends to the nearest shelf of the mine and the quarters where prisoners lodged in darkness and which they left each morning at 4 a.m. to begin their daily toil in the workshops above. The daring 1781 mass escape utilized this ladder after the ringleaders had first secured the services of a colleague up above who opened the hole's cover.

A modern staircase, installed in 1972, replaced the ancient ladder and affords today's visitors easier access to the prison labyrinth - formerly the passages through which miners traveled on their way to compartments to dig ore. Though damp, with a temperature hovering constantly somewhere in the mid-40s, the tunnels are well lit and marked so visitors can follow a one-way sloping path in a clockwise fashion as they peer into individual cubbyholes where humans once slept in wooden berths long since gone.

The path descends about 65 feet through an ore shaft, a well that provided both water and air, a drainage system, and a network of side pockets and tunnels so tight that visitors must duckwalk or crawl through the scant space between floor and ceiling. One tunnel in particular reeks of claustrophobic nightmares. Chipping its way underneath a low ceiling, it veers off into a hidden alcove offering no communication with the rest of the labyrinth. A hook, pounded into the rock floor, remains, its loop rising above the surface as a reminder of how inmates often spent their days in the damp unlit bleakness of solitary confinement, shackled to the cold rock ground.

Informational markers provide details of life in the mines that once extended hundreds of feet in all directions. At the ore shaft and drainage tunnel, the easternmost point on the underground loop tour, prisoners once lifted copper ore 65 feet to the surface and removed water that had penetrated crevices in the rock and trickled into the mine via the drain. The area also provided a popular escape route. The very first inmate, John Hinson, fled the prison shortly before Christmas 1773 by climbing out through the shaft with help from his girlfriend, while subsequent detainees enlarged the drainage ditch and burrowed their way to freedom.

Uniformed employees of the Connecticut Historical Commission operate New-Gate today as an historical site. They defend the penal excesses as not unduly harsh and insist that prisoners, even if handcuffed and collared while toiling from 4 a.m. to 4 p.m. in the forges behind the walls up above, yet retained the option to earn money for themselves by using those same forges to produce similar products they could sell to customers on the outside. They maintain that food for the prisoners was adequate and warded off starvation, unlike so many other jails of the day. They also contend that the underground cells, though hardly comfortable, actually offered both cool respites from the summer heat and warmer temperatures than surface lodging in the bitterly cold, subzero winters and, furthermore, permitted discourse between fellow inmates.

Visitors can tour Old New-Gate in an hour or two free of encountering great numbers of other tourists at the remote site on 115 Newgate Road, just north of State Highway 20 and west of East Granby between Interstate Highway 91 and U.S. Highway 202 in north-central Connecticut. Hours are limited - daytime, Wednesday through Sunday and holidays, mid-May through October. A moderate admission is charged, and a gift shop is maintained. Old Viets Tavern, the house of New-Gate's first warden, Captain John Viets, sits across the street from the entrance to the complex.

The state capital of Hartford, with its shopping districts, historical museums and houses, and gardens and galleries, is only 15 miles away.

Though not as severe as Georgia's infamous deathtrap prison camp at Andersonville or as imposing as California's virtually escape-proof Alcatraz, New-Gate still serves up a harsh reminder of prisons of days gone by. Many a man, imprisoned there only because he had the misfortune of being captured in combat, seldom saw the sun as he lived out the days of his captivity in a dark pit beneath the earth's skin that nature had intended as a receptacle for minerals, not men.

A caveat of sorts: those suffering from claustrophobia will want to avoid the self-guiding underground tour; others, especially the young and adventurous, will find it fascinating.

DELAWARE

AMERICA'S FIRST CRY OF CONSCIENCE

He was born the same year as George Washington.

When his father died in 1760, he inherited dozens of slaves and a plantation. The slaves cultivated the farm's corn and wheat crops, but the thought of one people in eternal bondage to another bothered his Quaker conscience.

He became a lawyer and an ardent champion of political and human rights even before the revolution that sundered America's ties with England. Under the guise of "a Farmer in Pennsylvania," he wrote essays indicting England for its unjust taxation of the American colonies. He also wrote "The Liberty Song," a tune that became very popular throughout the young nation. He grew as famous as Washington and John Adams and Thomas Jefferson, and his stirring writings gained him a reputation as "The Penman of the Revolution."

But when the others decided to break relations with the mother country, he equivocated because his conscience considered hostilities not the right answer. He refused to sign the Declaration of Independence in 1776, a stance that alienated his fellow Founding Fathers.

Yet he remained an American patriot and supplied provisions to the militia, even participating in the Battle of Brandywine. Pro-British Tories raided his Delaware home.

Throughout a distinguished career, he became a member of Delaware's colonial and state assemblies, a member of the Continental Congress and numerous conventions, the president of the state of Delaware, a signer of the Articles of Confederation and the

Constitution of the United States, and a governor of both Pennsylvania and Delaware.

Possessor of one of the greatest minds of the early republic, he was also one of its most talented spokesmen.

He lost three of his five children in infancy and left his plantation home, the scene of so many of his memories, to accommodate his wife's desire to live closer to her Philadelphia roots.

He was a wealthy farmer owning six plantations and 5,000 acres...and a deeply troubled conscience. An inheritor of slaves, an owner of slaves, he viewed slavery as an odious degradation of mankind. Only a year after the Declaration of Independence, he had decided he could no longer condone slavery and drafted a contract completely freeing his slaves in 21 years; in the interim, they would continue in his employ in exchange for food, clothing, shelter...and pay - a revolutionary concept. But his conscience still bothered him and, in 1785, he freed everyone with absolutely no conditions, long before Washington, Jefferson, and other enlightened minds - slave owners all - set about grappling with that moral issue.

He died on Valentine's Day in 1808 at 76 and was buried at the Friends Meeting House (4th and West Streets) in Wilmington, Delaware.

Today, John Dickinson has nearly been forgotten in the trample to honor our more famous Founding Fathers.

The house his father built in 1740, the house in which he lived before settling in Wilmington to appease his wife, still stands, in reconstructed form, as the John Dickinson Plantation in central Delaware. Both the kitchen and the 1793 addition he built survived an 1804 fire that burned the interior of the house. He built anew within the brick exterior. Visitors now tour that second domicile, restored and reconstructed for modern preservation. The site includes several personal possessions (his chair, razor, belt buckles, cradle, dining plates, and a teapot he received as a wedding present). Costumed guides present 20-minute tours of the house, addition, and kitchen.

The visitor center shows a 14-minute film, "The Peaceful Rebel," professionally executed by Video Dialog Productions, along with brief exhibits. A book rack and gift shop are included.

The grounds contain Samuel Dickinson's (his father) grave and a half-dozen reconstructions of typical farm buildings and log quarters of the day.

Admission is free, and total touring time is usually an hour. Delaware State Museums, Division of Historical and Cultural Affairs manages the site which is open weekdays (except Mondays and state holidays), during daytime hours, and Sunday afternoons (except in January and February, when it is closed).

The plantation is six miles south of state capital Dover along U.S. Highway 113 and then a short distance off Kitts Hummock Road. Signs are provided.

Area attractions include Dover and its historic colonial sites, museums, and Dover Air Force Base, as well as the coastline with its natural wildlife refuges, recreation areas, and beaches.

John Dickinson's home sees about 7-10,000 visitors annually, more than a fair amount by 1776 standards. But the Founding Father with a conscience, who took unpopular stands in difficult times, deserves better.

FLORIDA

A DESERTED ISLAND WITH TOURS AND A FESTIVAL

The cacophonous sounds of fierce shrieks, musket reports, and shattering glass roused the island's 45 inhabitants from their deep sleep around 2:00 in the morning of a brand-new day, August 7, 1840.

Jacob Housman, who owned the island, and his wife Elizabeth Ann suddenly awoke to find their paradise invaded by marauding Caloosa (or Calusa) Indians. Still in their sleeping togs, they ran for their weapons, only to find their front door broken into. Petrified, they scrambled out another way and hurried barefoot across the sharp, cutting coral. Frantically peeling off their night clothes, they plunged into the cold water and swam to one of their boats near the wharves. Getting into the boat, they quickly fled to a naval schooner anchored nearby.

Henry Perrine, a noted diplomat, physician, and botanist, who had lived on the island not quite two years as part of a mission to introduce tropical plants to southern Florida, stealthily hid his wife and three children in a half-submerged crawlspace that held turtles under the dock outside their dwelling, a passageway connected to the house by a secret trap door. They sat in the enclosure, concealed by rock walls, water up to their necks, turtles all around them, as Indians ran along the dock directly above.

The senior Perrine approached the Indians, told them he was a doctor, treated them to drinks at his bar, and tried to reason with them. His family heard his death yell.

Thirteen-year-old James Sturdy woke from his slumber on his mother's porch at the first report of musketry. Making for a warehouse, he secreted himself in an underlying cistern only to be boiled to death when the flames collapsed the building overhead.

The Mott family raced to an outhouse behind their dwelling. The Caloosas broke into the enclosure, wounding the father, dragging the mother outside to be slaughtered and scalped, flinging an infant into the Atlantic Ocean. Another young child, a little girl, perished when the Caloosas slammed a hunk of wood against her body.

The marauders stripped the island of every valuable and burned every building but one to the ground. Everything went up in smoke - the warehouses, the docks, the 30 homes and cottages, the slave quarters, a hotel and dry goods store, repair shops, the public square, the streets, the transplanted tropical plants and trees. The United States and the Seminole Indian tribes of Florida had been waging war against one another for years, and Jacob Housman had incautiously said he would capture or, better yet, kill every Indian he could find for $200 a head. The Caloosas had gotten word of his offer.

From the safety of the schooner to which he and his wife had fled, Housman folded his arms across his chest, smoked a cigar, and watched his island empire erupt in flames and smoke. "There goes $200,000," he said.

A shrewd businessman and unethical opportunist, Housman never financially recovered from the tragedy and perished in an accident at sea less than a year later.

Indian Key, his island paradise, never regained its former prominence either.

Exactly when the first man tamed the island is anyone's guess, perhaps thousands of years ago. Surviving artifacts found in the area indicate a human presence 2-3,000 years before the days when Christ strode the earth. The man who opened Florida to the whole world, Juan Ponce de Leon, may or may not have been the first of his race to stop on the island in 1513.

Members of both the white and red races used the island as a base for trading posts and as a cache for goods salvaged from shipwrecks on the nearby reefs. At one point in the days when European imperialism still stretched to the New World, Caloosa Indians swooped down on an island, supposedly Indian Key, where shipwrecked Frenchmen had taken refuge and slaughtered them all. Buccaneers and riffraff briefly flitted about the island with the deep-water harbor in the late years of the 18th century and early years of the 19th.

Renowned naturalist John James Audubon hunted and sketched birds there in 1832. Earlier that same decade, Housman had bought the island and used it as headquarters for his wrecking business. He not only put Indian Key on the map, he lobbied the state government to name it as the Dade County Seat (in those days, Dade County covered nearly the entire southern half of Florida). During its tenure as county seat in those pre-Miami times, Indian Key bustled, becoming, along with Key West, one of the two most important cities in the state's southern portion. Housman imported dirt and covered the island's jagged rock surface. He landscaped the isle, beautified it, and enticed customers. Two hundred people worked for him either as employees or slaves during Indian Key's busiest days.

The 1840 depredation killed Indian Key politically. In time, people returned to the island to farm or build a shipyard or run a fishing concern or smuggle goods, but the isle never recaptured its former glory. Hurricanes pummeled it in 1935 and 1960, rendering it increasingly uninhabitable. Florida bought it in the early 1970s and entrusted its care to the Department of Natural Resources which offers three-hour boat tours most days of the week.

Indian Key is totally uninhabited today and probably will remain so. A small 10-acre oval mound of coral limestone and one of the tiniest of the hundreds of isles (keys) off Florida's southern mainland, it sits three-quarters of a mile south of U.S. Highway 1 (Florida's famous bridge-speckled Overseas Highway) about midway along the crescent of keys between Key Biscayne to the east and Key West to the west.

Figuring out why no one lives there is easy. The island has only a half-dozen or so "streets," although that term overly dignifies them. The thoroughfares are dirt paths, about a yard wide and hemmed in tightly on both sides by Mexican sisal and other tropical vegetation, intersecting each other at frequent intervals. Wooden posts with simple street names (Second Street, Third Street, Fourth Street) stand at the more major crossroads. A state-built observation tower, dock, and shelter complement the island's amenities. That's it. No picnic benches or tables, no houses, no food, no indoor plumbing, no outdoor plumbing, for that matter.

Yet Indian Key is probably the only uninhabited island anywhere in the world that sponsors its own festival: historical re-enactors staging a raid on the island, complete with musketry and cannonfire; historical talks and tours of the island's surviving cisterns, remnants of building foundations, and the site of Housman's grave (the body was stolen decades ago by vandals); stationary exhibits and displays about the island's history and archeological excavations; unusual food like "Key Limeade" (lime-flavored lemonade), conch salad, and conch fritters; the ubiquitous T-shirt stands; and an opportunity to stroll the island and read about a dozen historical markers or watch the ocean's waves as they roll in against the rocky shore or wave at boats or jet skiers as they skim by the shore's edge.

If you attend the two-day festival, usually the first weekend in April, you park along the highway and take a complimentary boat ride from the boat landing at Indian Key Fill (mile marker 78.5) to the dock at Indian Key. No admission is charged. Everything but the food you eat and the souvenirs you buy is free. The event is funded by a number of state and municipal sponsors, including the Florida State Park Service, the Friends of Islamorada Area State Parks, the Islamorada Chamber of Commerce, and the Monroe County Tourist Development Council. The festival draws several thousand.

If you journey to Indian Key at any other time of the year, either in your own boat or via the pay boat run by the Department of Natural Resources (for information, call 305-664-4815), you will encounter no other visitors. Call the above number or the Islamorada Chamber of Commerce (305-664-4503 or 800-FAB-KEYS) for more information on any particular year's festival.

The guided tour provided by the state lasts a few hours. If you visit during the festival, figure on at least a half-day and several rounds of Key Limeade to quench the sun's fire.

If you need more things to do to fill up your week or weekend in that part of the state, turn yourself loose in Islamorada, just northeast of Indian Key, one of the major cities along the Florida Keys, with shops, restaurants, and sightseeing attractions.

A patch of a grassy slope: all that separates you from him.

"DARLING" GATORS UP CLOSE

Visitors seldom come to Florida's Sanibel Island for a chance to gawk at gators up close. In recent years, Sanibel has become a mecca for snowbirds and sunworshippers because of its alluring stretches of Gulf of Mexico beaches, exotic malls and gift shops, and proximity to the mainland (only 20 miles from the heart of Fort Myers and a shade over 160 from Orlando and its megaentertainment complex. But if standing in line for hours to see the Magic Kingdom and Epcot Center begins to pall and the warm sand beaches along the coast seem too crowded, there are gators just waiting at the J. N. "Ding" Darling National Wildlife Refuge.

Laying claim to the northern half of Sanibel and encompassing some 5,000 acres of wetland, the refuge delivers a slice of the Everglades milieu. It dates back to 1945 when it came into existence as a migratory bird sanctuary and indigenous wildlife center.

The refuge is named for Jay Norwood "Ding" Darling, a political cartoonist for the Des Moines Register, a Pulitzer Prize winner, and a conservationist who spearheaded the Bureau of Biological Survey, the predecessor of the U.S. Fish and Wildlife Survey. Reeling from watching land development eat away huge portions of waterfowl habitat, he served as chief of the bureau in 1934 and 1935 and led the campaign to establish what is now well over 400 wildlife sanctuaries and refuges throughout the United States.

He conceived the idea of a stamp whose sales would fund the purchase of waterfowl habitats. On March 16, 1934, Congress enacted the Migratory Bird Hunting Stamp Act, mandating waterfowl hunters to buy and carry the stamps every season. He designed the first stamp himself. Profits from sales of the so-called "Duck Stamps," released every year for constantly escalating prices, helped acquire waterfowl habitat land. The annual issues have become highly collectible, earning over $350 million which has been used to salvage over four million acres of wetland.

The site consists of several observation points, two canoe trails through wildlife clusters amidst red mangrove forests, and three walking trails, ranging from a third of a mile to four miles in length. The five-mile drive through the unspoiled mangrove swamp, forming the heart of the refuge, is the easiest and most popular way to tour. The roadway cautions drivers to proceed at a 15-mph clip. Visitors traveling at that speed and stopping periodically at the dozen or so recommended pulloffs can breeze through in an hour.

Taking your time, however, packs rewards. Animals and birds indigenous to this terrain tend to often blend into the background of their surroundings. Even a quick drive through will yield views of some of the white ibises, the common moorhens, and yellow-crowned night-herons that poke around the vast expanses of marshland. But a more leisurely pace, in which you venture out of your car and quietly perch at water's edge, will deliver far richer sightings. Patience and silence will inevitably provide not only views of countless red-shouldered hawks and yellowthroats, but also roseate spoonbills burrowing food from mud flats with their spatulate bills.

You may sight a brown pelican, expanding its seven-foot wing span, cruising around 20 miles per hour and skimming the water for another meal - about four pounds of fish a day - and fully one half of its bodily weight. Or a great egret methodically rummaging through shallow water in search of a fish or crab or frog or snake to dine on. Or a double-crested cormorant or an anhinga, submerged for more than a minute, finally breaking the surface of the water, tossing its catch up in the air and gulping it down, head first. Or a kamikaze osprey dive-bombing a fish from a height of 100 feet.

Best of all, the refuge guarantees several examples of the one animal everyone wants to see when in Florida. The Bailey Tract walking tour allows you to stroll by them in abundance. And the western half of the drive places you so close you might be tempted to reach out and touch their backs as they slumber half-submerged in watery ruts along the side of the road. Resist the urge. Stay behind the picket fence that affords the only real barrier between you and them. The law prohibits feeding alligators. Those that have been fed by humans in the past have lost their natural reticence and have become more forward. When hungry, they have been known to amble up to humans for a handout. And even a tame alligator cannot differentiate a piece of fish or meat from the hand that holds it.

Most gators you see will measure from six to eight feet in length and will amble at 10 mph on land when sufficiently motivated. If you encounter one on the road, remain at least 15 feet away or, better yet, in your car.

You may also see baby gators, with or without their mothers, under the protection of aquatic plants or grass. Though they are cute, their jaws can easily snap human fingers off.

Directly descended from the era of dinosaurs, alligators trace their lineage back 35 million years and one time roamed America from North Carolina to Florida and as far west as Texas. Today, they thrive in Florida's fresh-water lakes, rivers, canals, and marshes and some salt-water channels. On land, they equal a human's speed for a short distance; in the water, they can outswim him. They also serve several ecological purposes: they use their swimming patterns to open up water flow in channels impeded by weeds; they dig water ponds or "gator holes," providing shelter and friendly habitats for birds and mammals who move in when they move out; and, though it sounds harsh, their snacking on weak, sickly prey ensures the survival of healthier members of various species.

The refuge offers no camping or picnicking facilities (they are to be found elsewhere on Sanibel) because the primary emphasis is to introduce people to a natural setting where wild flora and fauna coexist with a minimal amount of human interference. Many of the species, though threatened and endangered, can still be enjoyed in their natural habitat by a quiet stroll on the boardwalk that wends through the mangroves to the tidal flats. And an unending number of birds, fish, crabs, insects, raccoons, and otters will be your companions if you tread softly on your sojourn in their world and leave it in precisely the same condition you found it in. A visitor's center at the entrance includes exhibits and souvenir items.

The refuge occupies a tropical barrier island that may have first seen man as early as 300 B.C. European colonists discovered it in the mid-1500s, and settlers raised agricultural crops on it three centuries later. By the 1930s, it had become a magnet drawing tourists to its white sand beaches and benign weather.

For a memorable experience that marries tranquility with nature, leisure with wildlife, spare a few hours for the refuge and get to know an alligator closer than you ever thought possible. A moderate entrance fee entitles you to stay as long as you want during daylight hours. The refuge is open from sunrise to sunset, and site employees recommend the five-mile drive at low tide or near sunrise or sunset for maximum exposure to the citizens of the swamps.

The refuge can be reached from Fort Myers by taking McGregor Boulevard south to a toll bridge connecting with Sanibel. Once across the causeway, take Periwinkle Way to Palm Ridge Road which soon becomes the Sanibel-Captiva Road. Then watch for signs...and gators.

GEORGIA

AMERICA'S CONCENTRATION CAMP

Manifest destiny and westward expansion helped make America great in the 19th century, stretching the young nation from coast to coast across the entire breadth of the continent.

Unfortunately, there were people along the way, and their ancestors had lived on that land for centuries.

Native American Indians became an endangered species the moment the first white Europeans landed on the North American continent.

Though many memorials and museums throughout the country attest to the culture, lifestyle, and legacy of Indians, none conveys the emotions of shame, regret, and loneliness resultant from the treatment of Indians better than the New Echota Historic Site in Gordon County, Georgia, a once-prosperous Cherokee town reduced by white avarice to little better than a concentration camp.

On December 29, 1835, the United States government signed the Treaty of New Echota, corraling a small fraction of agreeable Cherokees into putting their names on a document relinquishing their nation's natural sovereignty over all their ancestral lands east of the Mississippi River, a huge chunk of real estate. Some 100 Cherokees actually signed the document; 15,000 other tribesmen protested its validity, labeling it fraudulent and petitioning for its nullification. All to no avail. The government ordered all Cherokees to migrate west of the Mississippi to land that would be theirs "forever." To induce them to go within two years, the government ignored any crime committed against them - thievery, rape, murder.

The government also ordered in the military to prod them

even faster. Some 15,000 Cherokees left their native land in 1838 on what history would later shamefully record "The Trail of Tears" - a forced 1,000-mile exile from Georgia to Arkansas and beyond. The journey continued into 1839, consuming thousands of victims who died from malnutrition, disease, exposure to harsh elements, and broken spirits.

In December 1838, with thousands of Cherokee exiles only halfway through their exodus, President Martin Van Buren told Congress, "Their removal has been principally under the conduct of their own chiefs, and they have emigrated without any apparent reluctance." Balm for the wounds of sensitive politicians. The truth proved far harsher.

On January 26, 1839, the "New York Observer" printed the firsthand account of "A Native of Maine, traveling in the Western Country:"

> ...we fell in with a detachment of the poor Cherokee Indians...a severe fall of rain... heavy wind. With their canvas for a shield... the cold wet ground for a resting place... multitudes go on foot - even aged females, apparently nearly ready to drop...traveling with heavy burdens attached to the back... frozen ground...muddy streets...no covering for the feet...they buried fourteen or fifteen at every stopping place...ten miles per day only on an average...downcast dejected look... the appearance of despair....

Ironically, the government forced the Cherokees, of all Indians the most totally Americanized, to endure this death march. The Cherokees...who manufactured cloth, spun and wove, cultivated crops, printed newspapers, legislated councils, courts, and laws, founded Christian churches and schools, even adopted the United States Constitution as the model for their own version.

The story survives at the New Echota Historic Site in words and images that subtly weave themselves among the blades of grass on the broad acres now standing where a flourishing civilization once lived.

Markers relate the sad chronicle…like the one near the site of the New Echota stockade - "one of about 25 built at various points in the Cherokee Nation for use as prisons," where people, herded together against their will in the shadows of their homes, suffered and died for no reason other than the incompatibility of the races to get along together:

> …On May 26, 1838, the round-up began as 7,000 soldiers forced the Cherokees to the stockades…where food was poor, water often short, and there were no provisions for sanitation. Disease soon raged…and by October, almost 2,000 had died. Hundreds more would die on the "Trail of Tears"….

Another marker near the entrance to the grounds refers to the suicidal treaty forced upon the Cherokees.

A leaflet distributed to visitors as a self-guiding map of the complex also unflinchingly details the betrayal and subsequent removal of the nation.

The museum showcases a 15-minute slide program that follows the ill-fated community through its zenith as a bastion of white-styled civilization to its decline as a holding pen, a detainment center, as close to a concentration camp as white America ever produced. The program's final moments recount the "injustices that man sometimes bestows upon his fellow man," as images of a banished and vanished race emerge: the callous splitting apart of families in the holding stockades; weary survivors, haggard in appearance, bereft of spirit, trudging onward through a devastating winter on a death march to a strange land not of their choosing "with the sky for a blanket and the earth for a pillow," in the words of eyewitness Private John Burnett; the deafening silence now engulfing the ghosts of New Echota, leaving behind a legacy of lives stopped in mid-breath.

Yet New Echota also celebrates Indian achievement. Markers, museum displays, and a scattering of carefully preserved and restored 19th-century dwellings and reconstructed structures bear witness to the village of New Town that arose from the forests of New Echota in 1819 and the seat of government for the nation that centered around New Echota in 1825. The Cherokees practiced agriculture at New Echota, growing vegetables, fruit, and cotton and raising livestock. The Cherokee bicameral legislature enacted laws, and its supreme court interpreted them...all at New Echota. The official New Echota newspaper, the "Cherokee Phoenix," the first Indian newspaper in the country, printed its items in both Cherokee and English and was distributed throughout the nation and even to white America and England.

The reconstructed printing office runs off complimentary facsimiles of the front page of the newspaper's first issue for visitors who take the guided tour of the restored and recreated buildings.

Staff members lead tours several times each day at regular intervals. Visitors who arrive between tours and lack the time to wait can take an easy self-guided tour of the grounds. Whether solo or guided, the tour - and a visit to the museum - will take at least an hour. The walk through the fields is easy, although the paths receive direct sunlight; expect the blazing Georgia heat in the summer.

New Echota State Historic Site lies just off U.S. Interstate Highway 75, east of Calhoun, and is open daily (except Monday) during customary daytime hours (Sunday's hours are abbreviated and during the afternoon). A modest fee covers both admission and tours.

The tufted carpet and rug outlet centers of Dalton are 20 miles north, and the sprawling Civil War battle sites of the Chickamauga and Chattanooga National Military Park are 45 miles north. Chattanooga's Lookout Mountain, shared by Georgia and Tennessee, is also nearby.

Georgia's Department of Natural Resources and its Parks and Historical Sites Division operate New Echota - open fields stretching out to an encircling wilderness, vast flatlands broken only by occasional trees and a few buildings. Excursions and school groups sometimes visit. Otherwise, the grounds may be singularly empty.

Don't expect tepees and bonfires and dripping scalps. New Echota serves history, not Hollywood hokum. Expect instead to see fleeting images of a vanished civilization that deserved a better fate.

New Echota today is a ghost town. No Native Americans live there; few even come to visit. Despite an honest evocation of the Indian community and what occurred there, both noble and shameful, New Echota remains a white man's tourist attraction. It is a moving, educational celebration of Native American civilization, culture, and achievement and an indictment of white lust for land.

You may be chagrined at how civilized and gentle "savages" could be. You may also wince at how savage "civilized" Americans could be to a people whose main crime happened to be the culture and skin into which they were born.

That is the message of the lonely fields of New Echota...a silenced legacy, wordlessly blowing over the grasses, wafted along by the winds of a shattered destiny.

THE SHRINE TO A DEATH THAT STOPPED THE WORLD

The April Thursday began much like all other days in that rural part of Georgia 60-some miles south of Atlanta.

The portraitist added more color, more lines with each dab of paint on the canvas. The subject tended to his business as he sat at his revolving-top table. An invalid, he rarely walked, rarely even stood up. He had already perused that day's newspapers and mail.

The portraitist had completed her subject's face. The suit and cape he curiously wore over his dress jacket remained to be limned. A splotch of gray on either side of the ears served as the only break in the blandness of the white background.

The picture candidly displayed its subject's haggardness, his age. Gone was the effervescence typified by his usual jovial smile. Gone were the rounded cheeks, the meaty jowls, the fleshy dewlap. Gone also was the trademark pince-nez, replaced by furrowed-out trenches beneath his eyes. Gone also the color in the hair. Though surprisingly fuller and thicker than it had looked in recent years, it had turned gray under the weight of the years. The face looked every bit its 63 years of age. Yet, ironically, the image on the canvas displayed a sensitive dignity; the man had never looked more handsome.

The painter continued her work.

And then came the moment that transfixed time. The subject groped for his forehead, muttered softly, "I have a terrific headache," and then slumped over in his chair.

The time was 1:15 p.m.; the day, April 12, 1945; the place, Warm Springs, Georgia; the artist, Elizabeth Shoumatoff. The painting became famous as "The Unfinished Portrait." America was four months into its fourth year within the global tilt called World War II. And the President of the United States of America, the Depression-era president, the wartime president, the only president many Americans had ever known, had suddenly died of a massive cerebral hemorrhage.

In the history of the 20th century, only three events have traumatized Americans to their very souls, united them in great tragedy and sorrow, made them stand dead in their tracks: the Japanese bombing of Pearl Harbor; the assassination of John F. Kennedy; and the death of Franklin D. Roosevelt, the 32nd President. Every teen-aged and adult American alive on April 12, 1945 could vividly recount years later where he was when he heard the news of FDR's death and what feelings pierced his psyche as sharply as the burst of pain that had shattered Roosevelt's brain and ended his life.

Long before Americans ever heard of other presidential retreats - John Kennedy's Hyannis Port, Lyndon Johnson's Pedernales River ranch, Richard Nixon's San Clemente, George Bush's Kennebunkport - FDR's Warm Springs vacation home captured the nation's imagination.

The former state legislator, assistant secretary of the Navy, and vice-presidential candidate came to Warm Springs in 1924, a crippled man in body and spirit. The polio that had rendered his legs useless three years earlier and kept barraging his normally indefatigable buoyancy prompted him to journey to Georgia where reputedly wonderful things had happened to fellow polio sufferers. Native Americans had congregated at the site of the perennially warm springs centuries before white colonizers had given it its current name. The springs had served yellow fever sufferers in the 18th century, and the site had turned into a summer health spa the following century. Roosevelt basked in the year-round 88-degree warmth of the pool of healing water flowing from the rocky base of Pine Mountain. It never cured his affliction, but it rekindled some feeling in his stone-dead lower limbs, enabled him to simulate normal locomotion with the assistance of crutches, invigorated a moribund will to live.

The energized patrician lawyer drew a metaphor from the curative power of the warm springs and the community that had arisen around them. He acquired a newfound ambition, one tempered with the desire to extend healing of body and spirit to the suffering, despondent specks of humanity throughout the country. The specks became throngs in a few short years when the stock market crash of 1929 ushered in a massive economic depression the likes of which the nation had never seen, a rampaging beast that destroyed fortunes and futures and pitted the face of an entire generation.

By 1933, FDR had become one of the most energetic presidents the nation had ever produced and a leader who tackled the woes and miseries of the masses head-on.

He returned to Warm Springs 40 more times in all, sometimes for a day, other times for several months at a clip to rejuvenate his atrophied legs. Staying in various cottages for the first few years, he moved into a newly constructed six-room house in 1932, the year of his election to the presidency. The modest building came down in history as the Little White House, and Roosevelt the President visited it 16 times, including the final fateful one. While there, he constructed policies that later led to the bank holiday that froze deposits to prevent assets from disappearing in the economic free fall and signed the Rural Electrification Administration bill.

Closed after FDR's death in memorial tribute to the nation's longest-serving president, the Little White House, presently administered by the Georgia Department of Natural Resources, now welcomes visitors. The house, museum, and grounds display a number of relevant items: the haunting, unfinished portrait of a president about to die; the brown leather armchair in which he sat when the hemorrhage exploded within his head; the maple bed on which he died shortly thereafter; the sideless wooden wheelchair, seldom photographed during his presidency, in which he sat during private moments; the guest house where his long-time romantic interest and secret companion, Lucy Mercer Rutherford, stayed and from which she was quickly ferried away after his seizure; the servants' quarters and the garage with his specially built dark blue 1938 Ford convertible - with hand-operated controls and the "FDR1" license plate; the swinging bump gate entrance to the grounds, through which FDR passed countless times on his joyous and occasionally high-speed drives; the touching graffiti on the kitchen woodwork - "Daisy Bonner cook the first meal and the last one in this cottage for the President Roosevelt" (immortality etched in pencil by a domestic justifiably proud of her footnote in history); the living room fireplace with the same wooden logs that suddenly went out on April 12, 1945, never to be rekindled.

The Little White House is a shrine to a sudden death that cast an awesome pallor over America.

Time has eerily stood still at the cottage, and visitors are transported back to 1945...just moments after the death. Nothing has been changed. People now up in age who remember Roosevelt's death relive that awful moment when they visit the house. Those who cried as his cortege processed through the streets of the nation's capital or as the train bearing his flag-draped coffin slowly rolled along hundreds of miles of track through the country he loved may dab at their eyes once again, so vivid are the memories, so vibrant the displays.

Those who do not remember FDR may be surprised at the unpretentiousness of the spartan cottage with its simple wooden paneling and furniture.

Just east of the cottage, the museum shows a film of FDR's years at Warm Springs. In never-before-seen footage, "A Warm Springs Memoir of Franklin D. Roosevelt" presents graphic imagery of how difficult everyday life was for the famous polio victim. Seldom photographed in his wheelchair and always publicly seen standing up and leaning on a railing or cane for support, his baggy trousers camouflaging the heavy leg braces he always wore, the FDR of this film frolics in the therapeutic waters of Warm Springs with fellow polio victims and relaxes on the ground with them. The images are a little shocking; the man who epitomized vitality and strength for troubled Americans with ringing words of self-assurance ("The only thing we have to fear is fear itself") could not even cross his legs or move them an inch without lifting them first with his hands.

A set of leg braces worn every day by Roosevelt - sturdy, heavy, confining enough to prevent near-dead legs from buckling under a six-foot-two-inch, 200-pound frame - helps focus on the daily reality of the affliction.

Many of the treasured gifts that Roosevelt received from kings and commoners alike and some of his possessions fill the display cases, but nothing can speak as eloquently as the wheelchair, the braces, the leather sitting chair, his final bed, and the mesmerizing portrait of a man in his last hours. Perhaps most vivid is the famous photograph of Graham Jackson, reputedly FDR's favorite musician, playing "Going Home" on his accordion, while his eyes flood his face with tears as he bids farewell to the president's funeral train as it leaves Warm Springs on its final trip across American soil.

Opened to visitors in 1948, the Little White House area also contains a bubbling memorial fountain and a walkway that threads its way through symmetrical files of the flags and native stones from all 50 states and the District of Columbia. A gift shop, snack bar, picnic facilities, and Dowdell's Knob - the Pine Mountain Range's highest pinnacle and FDR's favorite picnic site - are available. The famous pools where FDR and lesser-known victims took therapy are closed but may be viewed as historical sites. Near the outdoor pools is the Roosevelt Warm Springs Institute for Rehabilitation, the current center for patients with a variety of disabilities that emerged from the Georgia Warm Springs Foundation polio treatment center founded by FDR in 1927.

Also in the vicinity are the old train depot where FDR entered and left, the Franklin D. Roosevelt State Park situated on the side of a CCC (Civilian Conservation Corps) camp funded by Roosevelt's New Deal economic recovery acts, and several memorials to him at or near the various cottages where he stayed prior to construction of the Little White House. The community of Warm Springs, depending so much on the magnetism of FDR for its livelihood, hit upon hard times following his death. Since resurrected, it presents tourists with dozens of craft and specialty shops and restaurants in its village mall.

Touring the Little White House and affiliated Roosevelt sites in the area can take a half-day. A moderate admission is charged, and the site is open daily during daytime hours. Warm Springs is on Alternate U.S. Highway 27 in Meriwether County. Look for signs for the Little White House, which is just southwest of the town off State Highway 85W.

HAWAII

HAWAII'S ST. VALENTINE'S DAY MASSACRE

Valentine's Day of 1779 dawned ominously for the gentle yet indomitable 50-year-old Englishman whom history would call its greatest explorer as he prepared to step aboard the longboat that would transport him across Kealakekua Bay to the safety of his seafaring vessels.

This was his third globe-girdling exploration, and he had already charted much of the hitherto unknown Pacific Ocean and penetrated the Antarctic Circle. Just a year and a month earlier, he had become the first known western explorer to set foot on the Sandwich Islands - what we today call Hawaii. He had previously given nearly a decade to navigating and charting many of the islands anchoring the South Pacific Ocean, opening them up for discovery, trade, and conquest en route to achieving his mission - a connecting route with the Atlantic Ocean via the Arctic. The natives of Kauai, on which he had landed, had treated him well, freely exchanging food staples for anything made of metal, a manufactured product they lacked.

A year later, unable to locate his intended northern passage, he had returned, but to a different Sandwich Island, the largest and easternmost, what we today call Hawaii, with its sheltered inlet midway down its western coast. The natives who greeted him at Kealakekua Bay in January 1779 echoed the same warmth the Kauaians had bestowed on him a year earlier. Thinking him the god Lono - who in their mythology was to appear on a floating island - they feted and honored him. As luck had it, the explorer's arrival coincided with the natives' annual celebration honoring Lono, the god of the harvest. Their mistake was understandable. The men of the expedition, to their joy, found a paradise of food, drink, gaming, and sexual indulgence.

The crew remained half a month, sowing the seeds of both good will and venereal disease, then set sail for other islands. But a storm damaged one of the ships and forced its return to Kealakekua Bay. Conditions had changed, too. The festival to Lono had ended, replaced by a social custom that temporarily closed the harbor to traffic. The sight of a battered "floating island" coming in to port when the bay was officially closed to all commerce destroyed the notion that the explorer was really Lono. Misunderstandings followed. Some of the crew's possessions were stolen. The explorers thought of kidnapping a chief to use as leverage in regaining their pilfered material. Violence flared. And the white leader decided he had best leave the island as quickly as possible.

As the white captain was about to splash through the shallow water to his waiting longboat on Valentine's Day, a native made a hostile gesture. It triggered a general melee. Shots rang out. A native whacked the captain's head. More natives came forward and pummeled him and knifed him as he fell into the water. They hacked his body apart.

Later, when a truce had halted the bloodletting, the natives returned to the sailors the remnants of the great captain, including a severed head, devoid of its skin (and hair, which the young warrior and future monarch Kamehameha reputedly carried away as a trophy). The crewmembers consigned the bodily parts to the open sea in the bay and left.

The descendants of those murderers are fellow Americans today - Hawaiians. And Kealakekua Bay, where Captain James Cook met his watery end, is now a favorite spot for snorkelers and scuba divers.

A monument marks the putative spot of his death on the north end of the bay, but no roads approach it, making it impossible to see for anyone except snorkelers who take a chartered boat to the site, swimmers who cross the bay from Napo'opo'o Beach County Park at the southern end, or hikers who use a primitive, unmarked trail down from the highway.

About 10 miles south of the popular Kailua-Kona tourist centers, Kealakekua Bay stretches a mile, north to south, along an historical and underwater parks and marine life conservation district. The bay separates the isolated cove where the marker has been placed from Napo'opo'o Beach County Park. An intervening high mountainous cliff wall blocks a land route from the beach, leaving expert swimmers the prospect of swimming a mile of often fatiguing, choppy bay water to reach the monument. If such is your plan, you can reach Napo'opo'o Beach by turning west on Middle Keei Road from Highway 11 near the town of Captain Cook.

The other possible way to see the monument is via a relatively short but strenuous hike. Turn south off Highway 11 onto Napo'opo'o Road. A short distance farther along, a tenth-mile or so, a secondary road (which may or may not be paved) veers off to the right.

Begin your hike at this point. Park your car or arrange to have others pick you up later and begin walking along the auxiliary road. A few dozen yards ahead, near a gate to private property, turn left and thread your way through high grass on a seldom-used trail that will probably look it. At times, the path will widen to accommodate a jeep or all-terrain vehicle. At other times, you'll barely be able to see a foot's width through the high jungle-like growth of grass and trees that will dwarf anyone short of an NBA center. You may think you're lost, but it will probably just seem that way. Look to your flanks for the reassurance of a stone wall; if you fail to see the parallel rock walls, it may mean only that the thick tangle has overtaken them. Don't panic, and remember your ultimate destination lies southwest (or to the left).

At length, the trail will become more traditional and you'll spot the coastline and the bay. The trail will descend more steeply as it negotiates a swath of broken lava rocks and uneven stone fragments embedded in the slope of a hill. When you level out at the bottom, you need to hike to the left through a dense forest to the monument.

The hike only encompasses a couple miles, but its severe conditions make it seem longer. The trail affords little shade and no water; novice hikers should be forewarned. If you choose a scorching day, as we did, wear proper clothing and bring a canteen of water. The sun will fry you, the heat will sap your energy, and the tough terrain will wear you out. Though a baby hike for experienced hikers, step by step, it proved as enervating a journey as anything else we experienced in Hawaii (and we marched across some of the world's most demanding trails).

The monument itself, a graceful white obelisk near the water's edge, technically belongs to Great Britain which erected it in tribute to its distinguished native son. The plinth includes the following tribute:

> IN MEMORY OF THE GREAT CIRCUMNAVIGATOR, CAPTAIN JAMES COOK, R N., WHO DISCOVERED THESE ISLANDS ON THE 18TH OF JANUARY, A. D 1778 AND FELL NEAR THIS SPOT ON THE 14TH OF FEBRUARY, A.D. 1779. THIS MONUMENT WAS ERECTED IN NOVEMBER AD 1874 BY SOME OF HIS FELLOW COUNTRYMEN.

A chain link rope and thick stanchions surround the monument. A nearby marker says the jetty was constructed by Australia "IN MEMORY OF CAPTAIN JAMES COOK RN THE DISCOVERER OF BOTH AUSTRALIA AND THESE ISLANDS."

Yet another marker lies submerged near the shore but under water. It says:

> NEAR THIS SPOT CAPT. JAMES COOK WAS
> KILLED FEBRUARY 14, 1779 ORIGINAL

TABLET DEDICATED AUGUST 18, 1928 BY COOK SESQUICENTENNIAL COMMISSION.

Several feet of water have reclaimed that part of the shoreline in the decades since 1928, and the marker is generally not visible.

Other hikers are rarely encountered. You're more likely to see a cruise ship entering the bay, a swimmer stroking his way across the water, or a raft docked alongside the jetty. Snorkeling within the sheltered cove is permissible. And if you just elect to sit on the dock, you will oversee the bay sandwiched in between cliffs and the broad ocean.

The monument stands at the far edge of a long-gone village formerly called Ka'awaloa. The cliffs above hold caves formerly used as burial crypts. Rumors suggested that parts of the mutilated remains of James Cook wound up in one of the caves.

The return hike, all uphill, winds generally to the right.

The hike and a brief stop at the monument will occupy a few hours. Taking time to tarry longer or swim or snorkel can provide a full day's diversion. The site affords no picnic facilities, but you can easily eat at the dock if you bring food with you and the thought of Cook's butchery doesn't disturb you.

Should you decide to change into swimwear, remember there are no change rooms; you'll have to use the great outdoors. The forest around the monument provides ample privacy for a quick change, if no one is around. Also, consider that, as tempting as it may be to trek down to the monument in swimwear and sandals, the terrain is too rough to accommodate such minimal protection. And though the site is generally empty, be wary of leaving valuables untended, if you are alone.

Area attractions include: the major shopping and tourist hub of Kailua-Kona; Kealakekua, a few miles north of the bay, with shops, restaurants, and a free tour of a macadamia nut factory at a local Mrs. Fields cookie franchise; the town of Captain Cook; and the Pu'uhonua O Honaunau National Historical Park, an ancient place of refuge for criminals and lawbreakers, a few miles south of the bay.

And if you want to pursue the James Cook saga further, journey to Waimea on the southwestern coast of the island of Kauai. A plaque in Lucy Wright Park off Ala Wai Road marks the site of the intrepid adventurer's first landing on the Hawaiian Islands in January 1778. A statue of him, a version of the original by Sir John Tweed erected in England, stands in the center of town less than a quarter-mile from the landing site on Highway 50. And the town celebrates the seafarer every year during the last weekend in February with a festival offering food, games, and music...and no one gets killed.

A JOURNEY TO HEAVEN... AND INTO HELL

When American writer Mark Twain first saw it, he shrank back in disbelief. "I felt like the Last Man, neglected of the judgment, and left pinnacled in mid-heaven, a forgotten relic of a vanished world."

Imagine beholding this "vanished world," as Mark Twain did. Then imagine doing something he never did - entering it. Imagine walking through the stratosphere, high above the clouds. And strolling a desolate, uninhabited moonlike surface, crunching the grit of black cinders afoot. And entering a volcano from the edge of its crater. Imagine being on top of the world and then walking down through clouds to be lost amidst giant cinder cones, mountains of towering mystery. Imagine periods of utter silence, with no trace or sound of any life around you, and then, suddenly, bursts of howling winds. Imagine the bright sun one minute and the spattering rain the next. Picture an expanse of mountain and valley, alpine desert and volcano, grassland and cinderfield.

At times, it may seem like Mars or Pluto, but it's very much of this earth...Haleakala National Park on the Hawaiian Island of Maui. More specifically, it is a descent into the innards of what will alternately seem like Heaven and Hell.

Many tourists come to Haleakala (pronounced Hah-lay-ah-kah-LAH) to glimpse its famous sunrises or bicycle down its dozens of miles of winding roadway. That's what tourists do, but it's not what Haleakala is about.

To experience Haleakala in all its humbling splendor, you have to do more than snap a picture of the sun coming up behind it or ride down a paved road from its summit. You have to venture into its bowels by entering its mouth, snaking your way down into its pit, and letting its winds and rain ruminate you at will. It can smack of torture and agony at times; it will also reward you with an everlasting memory.

Haleakala - the "House of the Sun" - is unlike few places on earth. Its topography, at times unremittingly bleak, at times a painter's palette of subtle and vibrant shades, suggests a world of mystery and weird sensations. You may even get momentarily lost on the little-trodden cinder sands of the conservatively marked trails that weave through the maze, but even the gripping panic will tingle you - the hypnotic power of Haleakala bouncing you around the tracings of its turf.

For all its stark unearthly beauty, Haleakala is nothing more than the depression of a volcano. Its crater is about seven and a half miles long and about a third as wide, for a total circumference of 21 miles. It descends more than 3,000 feet from topmost rim to floor bottom. Individual cinder cones within the crater rise hundreds of feet from the sloping floor, breaking the evenness of the valley. To many, it resembles the Grand Canyon of Arizona. But it is far more gloomy and moody, until the volcanic flora suddenly appear, astounding you with their shape and color, against the backdrop of the silent cinder dunes, changing color at the slightest vagary of the sun. And like the Canyon, Haleakala resulted in part from the erosive movement of water - but an ocean, not a river. The buckling of plates along the ocean floor started the job, then rainwater created streams and waterfalls to complete it.

But Haleakala is also a volcano whose lava explosions formed the island of Maui. The Hawaiian Islands are not actually islands, but rather the expansive peaks of a connected mountain range far beneath the surface of the water. Haleakala's highest point thrusts 10,023 feet above the surface of the Pacific Ocean, but its lowest point, visible only to denizens of the deep, reaches down to the ocean floor an estimated 26,000 feet (about four and a half miles).

Last erupting sometime around 1790, Haleakala is earth's largest dormant volcano. It is not extinct; it can blow again. The cinder cones that pock the pit of the crater, forming dunes within the greater dome, are giant heaps of spent material spewed upward by previous explosions.

Western man first encountered it in 1828 when three missionaries wrote: "We stood on the edge of a tremendous crater, down which, a simple misstep would have precipitated us, 1,000 or 1,500 feet. This was once filled with liquid fire, and in it, we counted sixteen extinguished craters."

Today, the full threatening majesty of Haleakala can be experienced as the missionaries and Mark Twain never could have. The Halemau'u Trailhead, at 7,990 feet of elevation, takes you on a downward path through shrub and along a 2,000-foot-thick lava wall that forms the western edge of the crater. Shortly after the trail yields its easterly direction, a series of switchbacks begins the serious descent 1,350 feet to the floor of the crater. A dense cloud cover often enshrouds the view of the cinder cones, two miles to the south, and the winds whip at your face as you round a corner of the corkscrew. Grasses, shrubs, and ferns - including the 'ama'u whose youthful fronds emit a bright reddish color - accompany you along the narrow trail.

The descent ceases when you reach the bottom - the 6,640-foot mark, 2.9 miles into your adventure. A mile-high zigzag course through grass varying from ankle-high to thigh-high conducts you to the Holua Cabin, one of three within the crater built in the 1930s by the Civilian Conservation Corps. You walk just east of the Leleiwi Pali, the western wall of the crater, a portion of which you have descended. A quick glance at the wall provides a magnificent view of the enormity of the crater you have just entered and the huge Ko'olau Gap - a break in the northern wall of the crater.

At the 3.9-mile mark, you come across the Holua Cabin and perhaps your first flock of nenes (pronounced "nay-nays"), Hawaiian geese, brown and white with diagonal streaks ringing their necks. Brought back from near-extinction, they are Haleakala's most ubiquitous inhabitants. They are friendly and will often follow you, sensing the possibility of a handout (always frowned upon because free food tends to make the recipients human-dependent and skews the natural order of things). Though Haleakala hosts a variety of animals, you are likely only to encounter nenes and a few scattered members of your own species.

From the cabin, well below the clouds, you may get your first unobstructed view of the cinder cones to the south and, beyond them, the southern crater wall.

The Halemau'u Trail now takes a southeasterly track, affording glimpses of cloud-shrouded Hanakauhi, nearly 9,000 feet of symmetrical lava.

The Silversword Loop features the heaviest concentration of perhaps the most aesthetic plant God ever created - a perfect circular porcupine-like plant found only on the isles of Maui and Hawaii and a feast to behold with its slender silver, white, and aqua tubules. Some may be in bloom; you'll recognize them by their high stalks, sometimes stretching up to eight feet, of yellow blossoms with purple centers. How anything so delicate could spring from a black cinderfield always amazes. Native Hawaiians call the silversword "ahinahina" ("gray-gray"). It lives in its spiked porcupine ball five to 20 years, then sprouts hundreds of blossoms on its cactus-like barrel stalk. A few months later, the entire plant withers, droops, and dies. A cousin of the sunflower and the daisy, the silversword may have emigrated to Hawaii from forebears whose seeds traveled the air across the Pacific Ocean from the western hemisphere.

The most foreboding part of the hike now welcomes you. You pick your way through a minefield of debris - black rock-like particles, formerly molten lava ejected out of an active volcanic vent with enormous pressure and then thrown to earth to cool and harden. The ejecta assume all shapes and sizes, from large blocks requiring several people to lift to minute ash particles that give the ground the consistency of crunchy sand. If the sun is out or the temperature is high, you'll feel as though you're walking on a frying desert with black sand instead of white. The terrain resembles a battleground, a wasteland, with no sign of life. Unless the sky is blue, you'll feel you've entered a world of black and white. Though unbearably dismal, it's an unforgettable plunge into a barren world; astronauts trained here in preparation for moon landings.

The terrain becomes even bleaker as you wind around a cinder cone called Halali'i to Kawilinau (the Bottomless Pit), a sunken hole 65 feet deep, in the shadow of Hanakahui - 8,900 feet of rugged majesty, bathed in pastel reddish browns and steel grays and, with its cloud cap, appearing like Everest itself.

The trail then draws you around more cones and gives you a dilemma: either proceed farther east on the Halemau'u Trail, gradually descending 1,000 feet over about two and a half miles to the Paliku Cabin, the easternmost sentinel overlooking the vast expanse of the Kipahulu Valley (a tangle of rainforest trees, vines, and shrubs that drops 6,000 feet to the 'Ohe'o Pools and the Pacific Ocean near where aviator Charles Lindbergh lies buried just off park lands); or go south on a level patch of bushy grass and desert flowers to the Kapalaoa Cabin, a much shorter route that shaves off the five-mile round trip to Paliku and back.

From Kapalaoa, the ominously named Sliding Sands Trail takes over, serving as your Yellow Brick Road for the final 5.8 miles back to the top of the crater. At first the walk is level as you traverse the flat land between the southern rim and the cinder mounds. Rain can pelt you at any point, and the sun can feel like a load of concrete as you trudge through the black sands. You'll encounter more silverswords, and the cinder cones will take on the pastel hues they're famous for, brownish red patches reflecting the oxidation of iron and pale yellow shades emanating from a sulphuric presence, both resulting from the mineral detonation spawned by the volcanic eruptions.

The crater floor will also bleed color - reds, oranges, yellows, and greens - from the squat grasses and shrubs that stipple the cinderbed like freckles.

At length, you pass a junction of trails, a crossing of paths; the one to the right takes you north to the Holua Cabin and the ascent up the Halemau'u Trail; the one straight ahead takes you west along the Sliding Sands Trail. If you take the latter, the quickest at this stage, you'll still have four miles and nearly 2,400 feet in elevation to go before you reach the western rim of the crater.

Halfway up the Sliding Sands, a side trail swerves to Ka Lu'u o Ka 'O'o. If you avoid the detour and just push straight forward, you'll walk directly through the misty vapors of the clouds, a sensation that must be experienced to be understood.

The final stretch brings you to the top of the trailhead at 9,780 feet. From here, a short walk along the paved Haleakala Highway takes you to the Pu'u 'Ula'ula, at 10,023 feet, the highest point in the park.

The route described is the most taxing; we chose it specifically for that purpose. The National Park Service recommends doing the converse (descending the steep Sloping Sands Trail and exiting via the Halemau'u Trail). Doing it the way we did it, however, intensifies the drama and saves the best for last. We skipped the jaunt to Paliku Cabin but did everything else: about 15 miles in fewer than eight hours including breaks to rest and refill canteens (and regroup when we got momentarily lost) and pauses to take 100 photographs. If you descend one way and ascend the other, be aware of one problem: about five or six miles of pavement (Highway 378, the Haleakala Crater Road) separate the two trailheads, and you might wish to have someone drop you off at one point and pick you up at the other. You might also wish to just leave your car in one parking lot and go down and come back the same trail.

If you decide to descend to the bottom, be aware of certain basics also. Don't go all the way to the bottom if you've never hiked this sort of terrain before. Keep in mind that the winds and rain of Haleakala can chill you as easily as the sun can bake you. Temperatures vary drastically from day to day...and often hour to hour. Carry sufficient water - the cabins can replenish your supply - and high-protein, high-energy food; a jaunt down into the depths is not the time to try out that new 1,000-calorie-a-day diet you've been aching to go on.

Rangers provide a number of tours throughout the 27,200-acre park, including a Sliding Sands walk and a Cloud Forest hike, none of which can equal the intensity and challenge of descending yourself. Talks about the site also occur throughout the day at the Summit Building. A visitor center operates at the Sliding Sands Trailhead.

Park estimates place Haleakala's annual visitation at more than a million. But 90-some percent of them only come for the sunrise or to cycle down the road or to visit the Kipahulu area on Highway 31 which skirts its southeastern end by the 'Ohe'o Pools and Lindbergh's grave. None of those visitors has truly seen Haleakala.

Dare to be different. Postpone the luau (they're a dime a dozen on any of the Hawaiian Islands). Skip the Road to Hana (everyone does it; it's no more scenic than any other coastal drive anywhere in the world; and the curves become irksome after several hours, when you realize there's no quick way back). Even if you can only do a portion of the route we mapped out, you'll enter an alien world you'll never forget and have an experience virtually no one else you'll ever meet can match.

The approach to Haleakala, secluded in the Makawao eastern bulb of the island, presents another challenge. The park entrance crowns a 27-mile drive uphill along the Haleakala Highway (Highways 37, 377, and 378), nearly two-thirds of which consists of two lanes of sinuous curves and loops. The 27 miles - supposedly the shortest span covering so great a rise in elevation anywhere in the world - will take a while.

The usual National Park entrance fee is charged - good for seven days. The park contains no lodging, dining, or service amenities, but they can be found elsewhere, including Pukalani and Kula on Highway 37. Camping facilities are available at the Holua and Paliku campgrounds within the crater, as well as at Hosmer Grove campground at the top and at 'Ohe'o Stream campground near Kipahulu. To reserve a cabin (one of those within the crater, as previously mentioned), write in advance (Cabin Reservation Request, P.O. Box 369, Makawao, Maui, Hawaii 96768). Detailed trail maps are available at the park's visitor center. If you're interested in riding into the crater on horseback, call (808-667-2200).

A WALK ALONG THE CLIFFS WHERE MOVIES ARE MADE

Hurricane Iniki did a number on it in September 1992, with wind gusts roaring by at 160 mph, inflicting $2 billion of damage in the worst hurricane to alight on any of the Hawaiian Islands in the 20th century. But natives of Kauai brim with enthusiasm at the prospect of their "Garden Isle" returning to its normal state.

The fourth largest of the eight Hawaiian Islands, Kauai is the one least visited among the major four (Hawaii, Kauai, Maui, Oahu). It is also the least inhabited of the quartet. Rather oval-shaped, it stretches about 25 miles north and south and 33 miles across and accommodates 50,000 residents. According to professional photographers and most impartial experts, Kauai (mainlanders pronounce it "Ka-WHY," but native Hawaiians prefer "Ka-WAH-ee") is the most wildly beautiful of the islands because of its lush greenness, fertile valleys, and audaciously high coastal mountains.

Those same high mountains constitute the main reason so many film crews journey there. "South Pacific" utilized Lumahai Beach and Hanalei Bay for its Bali Hai backdrops. "Raiders of the Lost Ark" and the 1976 version of "King Kong" also used the same northern coastline. The 1966 epic "Hawaii" took advantage of the stunning mountains rising sharply from water's edge. Elvis Presley's "Blue Hawaii" and exterior shots for the "Fantasy Island" television show were filmed on Kauai. The recent "Honeymoon in Vegas" used its southern coast. And Steven Spielberg was shooting location scenes for "Jurassic Park" when Iniki struck in 1992.

Kauai is generally a casualty of seven- or 10-day three-island tour package vacations. But if you're looking to shy away from crowds and still have shopping and luau opportunities while taking in some of the most awe-inspiring scenery anywhere in the world, Kauai is your best bet.

The dead center of the island, Mount Waialeale, at more than 5,120 feet, is the wettest spot in the world with something like 480-plus inches of average annual rainfall, which means you may get wet if you hike in that area. Lush Pacific islands become lush because of rain; water makes for colorful and thick vegetation.

Despite that, Kauai offers the usual tourist draws: snorkeling, surfing, boogie boarding, fishing, golf, tennis, shopping, eating, etc.; Waimea Canyon, the "Grand Canyon of the Pacific;" Wailua Falls, twin jets of water cascading over an 80-foot cliff; and the Fern Grotto, a popular site ever since it was used in a Presley movie.

But the most breathtaking sights on the island are among the least seen - the mountains, where the movies are filmed. Head for the Na Pali coast, quite possibly the most majestic vista anywhere in Hawaii. Jagged, thrusting mountains extend about 20 miles along the northwestern shore. Monumentally high, they are deeply furrowed, from cliff to water's edge, as if some god ran his fingers from top to bottom down a huge piece of modeling clay. Clouds can sometimes obscure their view from above. But on a clear day, they present a rainbow of pastel colors set against the vivid blue of the ocean.

Few people see them because they are difficult to reach and because they are best viewed from either a boat at sea or a helicopter hovering overhead (boats tend to be more economical than the pricey whirlybirds). Both can be obtained easily in the island's cities, and information on prices, times, and other logistics are contained within the free island information magazines available at the airport and car rental offices everywhere.

To see the Na Pali coast up close without paying for either of the above options, drive as far north as you can on Highway 550 (the Kokee Road) and check out the views from the lookouts near the end of the thoroughfare: Kalalau Lookout and Puu O Kila Lookout. Both provide sweeping views 4,000 feet down through the irregular grooves of the Kalalau Valley. Clouds may interfere, but you can always try to outlast them. On a sunny day with clear skies, the valley will be awash with greens, pinks, and purples that instantly explain why filmmakers come here for background shoots. The unceasing ocean rolls on, blue wave after blue wave slapping against the distant shore. Tourist helicopters fly beneath you as they move over the giant creases and folds of the Na Pali mountains that flank the valley. You may also spot a cruise ship approaching from the north.

For veteran hikers, a fairly easy loop affords impressive views of a portion of the coastline. The Nualolo and Awaawapuhi Trails, the former about 3.75 miles long, the latter 3.1 miles in length, bring you to the edge of precipitous cliffs overlooking their respective valleys far below. The views can be spectacular, if the clouds, sun, and elements cooperate. The 2.1-mile Nualolo Cliff Trail joins both trails together close to their overlooks. If you're pressed for time, opt for the 6.2-mile round trip Awaawapuhi Trail. You may come across yellowish guava fruits along the way. They're free and highly touted for both their availability and niacin and Vitamin C content. They also generally taste like lemons and yield very little fruit for the work expended extracting the pulp from the dozens of seeds each one packs.

Some of the world's most demanding and rewarding hiking trails are also on Kauai. To actually walk across the mountains of the Na Pali coast, drive as far west on Highways 56 and 560 as you can (Ke'e Beach). From there, begin hiking the 22-mile round trip Kalalau Trail, one of the toughest pristine stretches in the world. The bad news is you'll be fording streams and traversing slippery rocks that move when you step on them. The good news is you'll start seeing the beauty of the Na Pali coastline very soon after you start the trek, making the rest of the rigorous maneuver entirely optional.

"Na Pali" means "the cliffs," and so they are, as they majestically separate five distinct major river valleys - Milolii, Nualolo, Awaawapuhi, Honopu, and Kalalau. Old Hawaiian civilizations once flourished there; goats live there now, which provides an inkling of their mountainous seclusion.

The Kalalau Trail is commonly considered the toughest in Hawaii and one of the world's most rugged. The accolades are justified. You'll see some of the world's most gorgeous scenery unfold before your eyes as you round a curve or descend a path. But you'll have to work for it. This is not a trail for the novice. Massive cliffs, bright green valleys, brilliant flowers, picturesque waterfalls and pools, and rolling swells of Pacific teal alternate with mud, slick rocks, boulder-strewn streams with overhead guide ropes strung from one side to another, slippery fallen leaves from the kukui and ohia trees, toppled trunks, and beaches with sudden surfs and counter currents. But if you make it all the way and back, you'll have the satisfaction of conquest. Permit camping is allowed. No commemorative "I Hiked Na Pali" T-shirts are available. The entire hike will take a full day, more if you decide to camp; travel as lightly and carefully as you can.

Regardless how you see the Na Pali coastline, you will see the best Hawaii has to offer in a way few visitors do. A lifetime of memories will be your reward.

IDAHO

WHERE THE SUN STILL RISES OVER BLOWN-OUT BRAINS

Born to an Illinois doctor in 1899, he grew up to be intensely handsome, talented, and congenial. He eschewed college for an immediate career in journalism. During World War I, he drove Red Cross ambulances and won the rather dubious distinction of being the first American wounded in Italy.

He wound up falling for the nurse that tended him. But after she jilted him, he married an American years older than he in 1921, a woman whose father had committed suicide. Later that same year, the couple moved to France where he worked as a foreign correspondent and short story writer. He also dabbled in novels.

The marriage ended in divorce, and he remarried in 1927. The following year, his father committed suicide.

For the next three decades and through two more marriages, he pursued his writing career, living alternately in the American West, the Florida Keys, and Europe. He took African safaris and reported on Spain's civil war, traveled the world, hunted for big game and fished for trophy-size catches, and yielded to the pleasures of the senses while concurrently being a father to his children and a friend to his associates.

In 1939, while he was in Idaho, a friend died. He composed and read a eulogy at the funeral, a tribute that included the following words:

> Best of all he loved the fall.

> The leaves yellow on the cottonwoods,
> Leaves floating on the trout streams.
> And above the hills,
> The high blue windless skies.
> ...Now he will be a part of them forever.

During World War II, he again worked as a journalist, reporting on D-Day and the European theater. He also sailed the waters off Florida and Cuba in search of Germans who might be looking for inroads to the American mainland.

He spent time in the western states, Florida, and Cuba and won a Pulitzer Prize in 1953, a Nobel Prize the following year. He became world-famous and often entertained and was entertained by the intellectual elite.

He endured inner pain and doubt in his later years. A life of unfettered food, drink, and gambling plagued him with high blood pressure. His tax situation bothered him. His years in Cuba, then on the brink of a revolution that was to turn the country Communist, as well as his lone-gun spying off the coast of Cuba during the war and his involvement with the Spanish Civil War had aroused FBI suspicions and he was monitored.

He underwent electroshock therapy for depression, in part caused by a rash of deaths among family and friends and in greater part fomented by a marked diminution in his physical and mental health. He had once written "...better to die in all the happy period of undisillusioned youth, to go out in a blaze of light, than to have your body worn out and old and illusions shattered."

He grew agitated, paranoid, fearful, guilt-ridden. Worst of all, he had trouble stringing words together into sentences, his bread-and-butter livelihood. He broke down in tears when the words would not come. He began aimlessly wandering the Idaho house he used as his self-imposed exile, a shotgun in his hands.

On Sunday morning, July 2, less than three weeks shy of his 62nd birthday, he awoke early, before his wife. He reached for a double-barreled shotgun he had favored for pigeon hunting. Walking to the foyer of the house, the man considered by many the greatest American writer of the 20th century propped the butt of the shotgun against the floor, placed both barrels against his forehead, and blew his brain out of his head.

In between his 1899 birth and tragic 1961 death, Ernest Hemingway had written some of literature's most cherished classics: "The Sun Also Rises," "A Farewell to Arms," "To Have and Have Not," "For Whom the Bell Tolls," "The Old Man and the Sea."

The twin communities of Ketchum and Sun Valley, more famous for their location just east of 9,150-foot Bald Mountain, the scene of some of America's most storied skiing experiences, curiously retain his memory, but almost anonymously. Book stores stock his works, local schools and universities sponsor various discussions and seminars, and the name "Hemingway" graces an elementary school. But otherwise, you'll have to diligently search for vestiges of the last place the great writer called home.

U.S. Highway 75 spears its way through Ketchum, which Hemingway first visited in 1939. Coming from the south along the highway, named Main Street in Ketchum, you first notice the Ketchum Korral at 310 South Main Street, to your right (or east). Hemingway stayed there several times in the 1940s when it was known as the MacDonald Cabins. Tourists can still book rooms there.

The Ketchum Cemetery lies on the east side of Highway 75 slightly less than a half-mile north of its intersection with Sun Valley Road, the major intersection in town. Though no directional marker is present, Hemingway's grave is relatively easy to find. An evergreen copse of four pines in the center rear of the cemetery pinpoints the location of the flat stones that cover the graves of Hemingway and his fourth wife. Both stones contain only names and birth and death dates; Ernest's stone often carries a lone flower or two strewn across its breadth, testimony to the presence of an admirer or sentimentalist. You are unlikely to encounter other visitors during your stay.

To locate Hemingway's last house, the domicile in which he blasted mortal life into immortal legacy, proceed north past the cemetery to the intersection with Saddle Road. The house, which the Hemingways obtained in 1959, is currently not open to the public. After Hemingway's widow's death in 1986, the state's Nature Conservancy acquired the property as well as 14 surrounding acres of the Hemingway Preserve. The house is rather block-shaped with two stories rising above a basement garage; four large windows, two on each floor and occupying much of its front side, and a balcony are its prominent features. It can be seen from either of two vantage points: proceed north on 75 a few hundred yards past the aforementioned intersection with Saddle Road and alongside a golf course to your right and a residential subdivision to your left, stop the car and peer off to your left (west) at a hill that rises above all the houses (Hemingway's house will appear by itself about a third of the way up the hill); or, again facing north, turn left onto Saddle Road at its junction with 75, turn right onto Northwood Way, stop your car just past Northwood's intersection with Blue Grouse Way, and again look to your left.

Three other prominent Hemingway sites await visitors. Return south along 75 to Ketchum's main intersection and turn left onto Sun Valley Road.

The Christiania Restaurant, near Sun Valley Road and Walnut Avenue, is one of the dozens of eateries Hemingway frequented during his many stays at Ketchum before his final move there in 1959. It was a particular favorite of his, a table in the southwest corner being his special place. He ate his final meal there with his wife on the night of July 1, 1961.

Farther up Sun Valley Road, in Sun Valley itself, is the Sun Valley Lodge which decorates some of its corridors with pictures of Hemingway. The author usually reserved Suite 206 during his several stays in the lodge and worked on "For Whom the Bell Tolls" while there. The suite can still be rented.

Still farther up Sun Valley Road, 2.6 miles from its intersection with Highway 75 in Ketchum, is the Hemingway Memorial, easy to miss for the uninitiated. A small wooden signpost on the right identifies the spot simply as "Hemingway Memorial." A short trail leads from a pulloff to a semicircular stone bench by the side of a narrow stream. A fallen log and a few gingerly steps take you to the other side of the brook. A bronze head of Hemingway, sculpted by Robert Berks, tops a stone pedestal and cemented cairn surveying the Trail Creek valley and a golf course. Aspen and willow help isolate the monument from its recreational surroundings and lend an air of natural solitude. A plaque holds the same inscribed words that Hemingway wrote and read for the funeral of his friend in 1939.

The sculpted head, parallel to the stream, faces on a bit of an angle to the east rather than peering at the people who journey down the hill to view it. It seems a strange orientation until one recalls the direction in which "the sun also rises."

The towering miner:
transcending the day the sunshine died.

THE DAY THE SUN WENT OUT ON THE SUNSHINE

At midday, May 2, 1972, the vice president and general manager of the Sunshine Mining Company spoke before corporate stockholders at an annual meeting in the resort town of Coeur d'Alene, a popular northern Idaho tourist and vacation haven, a city that blossomed around one of America's most scenic bodies of water.

The report to the stockholders was impressive. The Sunshine Mine had extracted seven million ounces of silver the previous year, fully a sixth of the nation's total silver production. And 1972 figured to be even better.

The Sunshine Mine had dominated domestic silver production throughout much of the 20th century, repeatedly yielding more silver than any other American mine. Eventually, in 1978, it was fated to unearth its 300-millionth silver ounce and overtake even Nevada's fabled Comstock Lode as the country's largest-ever silver producer.

Things boded well for the Sunshine, America's wealthiest, largest, and deepest silver mine, as its executive officer addressed the stockholders that Tuesday in May by postcard-pretty Lake Coeur d'Alene.

Yet even as he gave the stockholders the good tidings, fewer than 50 miles away and unbeknownst to him, his miners were dying by the dozen, trapped thousands of feet below the surface of the earth: Foreman Robert Warren Bush, 46, the father of four, the grandfather of six; Donald K. Firkins, 37, a former state Jaycee vice president who had been named one of America's 10 best vice presidents; W. L. Goos, 51, a World War II army staff sergeant who had won the playful nickname "Cat" because he had survived more than a dozen car accidents and a slew of mining mishaps, including a week stuck in a collapsed Montana mine.

Many of the miners were related. Like William R. Delbridge, 55, and his son, Richard Delbridge, 24, and Richard's cousin, Michael James Johnston, 19.

Elmer Kitchen, 54, a 27-year mining veteran, and his son, Dewellyn, soon to turn 32, a five-year contract miner at the Sunshine, had never worked together at the mine. But on May 2, father and son ironically died together at the 3,100-foot depth level.

Some were barely out of their teens, others were creeping toward retirement. But destiny careened blindly through the Sunshine mine that day. They died at their work stations in the dank bowels of the earth, some with the tools of their trade still clutched in their lifeless hands. Others died at their lunch places, huddled together, half-eaten sandwiches strewn by their sides.

"Cat" Goos died at the 3,400-foot level, apparently trying to save fellow miners after having managed to ascend from the 5,400-foot level where he had been working... expending his ninth and final life.

They died where they had been trapped, wedged between hard rock a half-mile or more beneath the open air: Clarence Lee Case, 54, and his 23-year-old son-in-law, Donald James McLachlan; Custer L. Keough, 59, a 17-year Sunshine veteran, a father, grandfather, and great-grandfather who would have been 60 on Christmas Day.

As the Sunshine Mining Company stockholders had sipped coffee, smoked cigarettes, and heard encouraging news about the future of their investments, a fire had begun in an abandoned chamber at the 3,400-foot level in the Sunshine Mine. It wasn't supposed to happen in hardrock metal mines; the Sunshine held silver, not coal. Yet flames eagerly ensnared timber beams and woodpiles, creating a one-two knockout punch of suffocating smoke and carbon monoxide gas that, fueled by the mine's ventilating system, shot through the narrow tunnels and alcoves of the underground maze in billows of death.

At the surface, smoke erupted from the main ventilation shaft as if lava from a volcano. Officials immediately shut the mine down and began evacuation procedures.

But under the surface, on countless levels as far down as a mile, 100 miles of corridors spewed forth in all directions. Of the near-200 men below, about half managed to scurry to the top and reach safety within an hour. But toxic fumes overcame many others as they desperately fidgeted with lifts, hoists, and elevators that would never get them to the surface in time.

Back at the top, rescue efforts intensified. Officials, engineers, and entrapment specialists worked tirelessly. Relatives and friends embraced one another, fretted, wept, and prayed.

The hours became days. Several dozen bodies were retrieved. Distraught family members sang hymns: "He Is Able to Deliver Thee;" "Love Lifted Me." Clergymen hovered everywhere. "We should give praise to God for the heroics, praise a man who went back in the mine after he was out...to help others and didn't return," said the Reverend John Sanford of the United Church of Christ. The wife of one of the missing miners peered into the rain one day and observed, "The whole world is crying for us." President Richard Nixon sent condolences and pledged assistance.

A ray of hope emerged on Tuesday, May 9, a week after the fire had begun, when two miners were found, 14 pounds lighter and bearded, at the 4,800-foot level. They had subsisted for a week on clean air emanating from a bore hole, a supply of water, the uneaten lunches of some of their dead comrades, stamina, prayer, luck, and an unwillingness to die.

But they were the only miners to walk out. By Thursday night, May 11, rescuers had located the corpses of the last unaccounted-for miners.

The Sunshine Mine fire claimed 91 lives, becoming one of the worst American mining disasters of the 20th century and the most casualty-ridden hardrock mine tragedy since 1917.

It is commemorated today in two locations along Interstate Highway 90 in northern Idaho: the Wallace District Mining Museum at 509 Bank Street in Wallace; and the Sunshine Miners Memorial, about eight miles west at Exit 54.

The museum displays various drills and mining tools, ore samples, mining reconstructions, videos, photographs, and the world's largest silver dollar (150 pounds, a yard in diameter) in recounting the story of the Coeur d'Alene Mining District, the world's richest silver lode, responsible for over a billion ounces in a century of production. The museum reserves a corner for the Sunshine disaster and includes a cross-section model of the mine, explaining how the flame-infested tunnels had to be sealed from oxygen and deluged with a "slurry of water and sand" and quoting the Bureau of Mines' belief that "spontaneous combustion of refuse near scrap timber" probably ignited the inferno. It also holds a binder brimming with contemporary newspaper accounts of the tragedy. The museum charges a nominal fee and is open daily (except major holidays and mid-fall to early spring Sundays) during the daytime (and into the evening during June, July, and August). It can be visited within an hour, excluding a perusal of the binder.

Exit 54, two miles east of Kellogg, leads to the unusual monument to the 91 victims. Sculptor Ken Lonn's twice-life-sized steel statue of a heroic miner, jack-leg drill upraised, stands against a rocky backdrop just north of the highway. A semi-elliptical walk wraps around the rear of the statue and leads to plaques listing the victims and recounting their memory in poetry. More than 50 individual marble markers, laid in cement blocks, complete the other half of the enveloping ellipse in front of the statue and along its flanks; some markers bear individual victims' names, while others are dedicated to "All Miners" or "Our Miners." Planted trees grow all around them. Flowers often lay strewn by the markers. It is heart-tugging and somber, nearly a cemetery in appearance. An historical marker tells the tragic events. Directly south of the memorial, Big Creek Road meanders 2.2 miles to the actual Sunshine Mine, scene of the accident and still a major silver producer.

The Kellogg-Wallace area is the heart of Idaho's Silver Belt with mines, related museums, and historical buildings everywhere. Wallace conducts the Sierra Silver Mine Tour. Kellogg has skiing and summer recreation. And Coeur d'Alene boasts of all manner of recreational activities and outlet shopping.

But for an enduring memory even years later, nothing can top the resolute statue of the miner and the trees that tower in tribute to 91 lives lost the day the Sunshine went down.

ILLINOIS

THE BEATIFIC BAHA'I BEHEMOTH BY THE LAKE

In 1844, a man named Mirza (Siyyid) 'Ali-Muhammed of Persia, a descendant of Muhammad, proclaimed himself the "Bab" (meaning "door," as in the gateway through which the "Promised One" would channel his grace). He founded a new religion, an offshoot of mainstream Islam that predicted the return of the 12th successor to the great prophet and messenger of God, Muhammad. His new religion was called the Babi faith.

Reaction was less than enthusiastic, and, in 1850, he met his earthly end in front of a firing squad.

Two years later, one of his disciples, Mirza Husayn-'Ali, also known as Baha 'u'llah ("The Glory of God"), realized while in a Tehran jail that he was the messenger referred to. A series of exiles followed until 1863 when, in Baghdad, he publicly announced his identity. He spent the rest of his life promulgating his faith and spreading its tenets in letters.

Today, it is called the Baha'i faith and, though numerically small, it extends around the world. About 5 million Baha'i adherents (contrasted with 1.6 billion Christians and 1 billion Islamics) currently live, according to recent estimates. But the relatively few believers, though strongest in Asia and Africa, disperse throughout 120,000 places in more than 200 sovereign and nonsovereign countries, more nations than any other sect except Christianity. They operate from 18,000 local spiritual assemblies (their version of community churches) and more than 160 national spiritual assemblies (governing bodies).

They believe in the supremacy of a genderless God, the creator of all matter, and hold Abraham, Krishna, Moses, Zoroaster, Buddha, Jesus, the Bab, and Baha 'u'llah (and others yet to come) as equal prophetic messengers who, while reflecting the universality of a single timeless God, still address the specific needs of the eras in which they appear. They profess that man, the noblest of all God's creations, must heed God's word, as interpreted by the messengers, to attain harmony and that he should further promote peace, unity, equal rights, mandatory education, service to others, and an international secondary language while rejecting anything that polarizes or isolates classes - slavery, affluence, formal priesthood and monasticism, and bigotry.

Specifically, a Baha'i must believe in the teachings of Baha 'u'llah and the interpretations of his successors, pray daily, fast for 19 days in one annual stretch, and forgo alcohol, tobacco, mind-altering drugs, and extramarital relations. Baha'is embrace no formal churches, clerics, or sacraments but subscribe to selective fast and holy days (not surprisingly, days of special significance to the Bab and Baha 'u'llah). Their temples offer no formal preaching but rather the reading of scriptures from various religions.

Though the religion is relatively new and rarely understood, one of its basic doctrines - "The earth is but one country, and mankind its citizens" - has appeal.

But you don't have to be a Baha'i to journey to Wilmette, Illinois on the western shore of Lake Michigan, just north of Chicago, to tour the Baha'i House of Worship, an elaborate domed temple rising more than 100 feet skyward at the center of a precise circle of symmetrical gardens and pools.

An estimated five million visitors have pilgrimaged to the ornate portals of the first Baha'i temple in the West (and one of only seven, thus far, in the world) since its completion. All Baha'i temples have nine (the most significant number in the Baha'i world) sides and are noted for their radiant beauty and architectural symmetry. The first American Baha'i temple arose in Wilmette because of a high concentration of the faithful in that area in the early 20th century, when a temple was first contemplated. Construction began in 1920 and finished three decades of painstaking labor later.

Nine sides, each with an arched door and recessed windows, rise above white stairs surrounding the temple. Nine more sides with windows and brilliant white tracery surmount the nine bottom facades as setbacks. A dome, resembling sculpted lace, crowns the whole, lending uniformity amidst palatial splendor - nine sides, distinct yet equal, rising to unite in one all-encompassing unit. Quartz and white cement give the building its solid white purity. A steel superstructure provides support.

The dome measures 90 feet in diameter and 46 feet in height on its exterior. The interior stretches 138 feet from the auditorium floor past a pair of balconies to the center of the dome and holds nearly 1,400 upholstered chairs symmetrically arranged. A simple wooden podium, equipped with a microphone, stands where an altar might logically exist. Potted trees and flower urns surround it. Behind the podium, a veil camouflages a spiral staircase, flanked by columns, that remains closed to the public.

The interior intersperses columns with epigraphs taken from the writings of Baha 'u'llah and receives natural illumination from numerous windows and nine sets of brass lights mounted on pillars.

The outside structure bears further inscriptions overlooking bed after bed of impatiens, hosta, marigolds, roses, rhododendron, day lilies, begonias, ivy, bleeding heart plants, and hosts of other varieties of flowers hemmed in by rows of perfectly sculpted evergreens and circular pools with fountains, subliminally planting the seeds of the symmetry, balance, and harmony that underscore the faith's essence.

Beneath the great temple, a visitor and information center distributes free literature, shows a slide presentation, employs wall panels to posit questions and answers on Baha'i tenets, and displays a seven- by 25-foot four-panel tapestry crafted by Vickie Hu Poirier to symbolize in text and image the harmony of mankind with God. A book store, a library of information on the Baha'i faith, rest rooms, administrative offices, and classrooms fill the remainder of the basement.

Members of the community greet guests at the door and temple entrance and answer questions while refraining from applying social pressure. Visitors may sit politely during daily 12:15 p.m. services (15-30 minutes of scripture reading and chanting from Baha'i members in the temple) and freely tour the site at other times. The temple is open from 10 to 10 daily from May through September (otherwise during daytime hours). There is no charge.

Viewing the temple and slide program and walking along the grounds for photographs and solitude can take an hour. Those with a quickening interest in the Baha'i faith or its architecture might wish to prolong the visit. People filter in and out throughout the day, but there's always lots of space for privacy and serenity.

The temple occupies the grounds by the intersection of Sheridan Road and Linden Avenue in the southwestern corner of Wilmette.

THE CAVE
WITH SKELETONS
IN ITS CLOSET

In the early years of our country's history, shortly after the Revolutionary War but long before paved highways crisscrossed the nation and long before roadside motels turned up in every city, people who journeyed to the great western wilderness often depended on the hospitality of any homesteader they chanced to come across or, just as often, trusted on a clearing in the woods or a natural earthen shelter on a riverbank to provide temporary rest.

On the banks of what is now southeastern Illinois where the Ohio River cuts its way through America's heartland, a natural protective rock with a built-in cavern offered welcome relief from the elements and a place of seclusion, safety, and rest.

Ancient Indians had used the cave and its surrounding woods for burial mounds. The first documented white man to visit it came in 1729. A Frenchman named de Lery, he called it "Caverne dans le Roc" ("Cave in the Rock"). The name stuck. Decades later, the great American naturalist John James Audubon stayed in its hidden recess while traveling the countryside.

Thousands of travelers seeking new lives for themselves out west or taking their goods to downriver markets on rafts and crudely constructed boats passed by over the decades.

In 1799, a pair of young romantics - the details lost to the ages - visited the cave as a break from the rigors of their travels. They walked atop it and rested somewhere high above its great mouth and looked at the river far below.

Suddenly, the first serial killers in United States history sprang from their cover and viciously pushed the lovers off the cliff.

During those early days, that incident was typical of the infamous Cave-in-Rock, the haunt of opportunists who saw a chance to make an easy buck by staking out the place and offering lodging, food, barter, liquor, card games, conversation, and even prostitutes. But all too often, the travelers got bopped over the head or knifed in the gut, then robbed of their valuables.

Cave-in-Rock's most nefarious period came in the late years of the 1790s and continued into the first couple decades of the 19th century when a succession of robbers infested it and pounced on innocent travelers. One of the most famous was a Revolutionary War veteran turned criminal named Samuel Mason who led a loose confederation of thieves in the 1790s and used a sign on the riverbank advertising liquor and games to lure the unwary to his trap.

The most dangerous thugs who took up temporary residence within the cave were Micajah and Wiley Harp, a pair of psychopathic killers who used the cave in 1799 in the middle of a swath of terror that claimed dozens of victims - dead and mutilated men, women, children, and the elderly in Tennessee, Kentucky, and Illinois. In addition to tossing the young lovers from the heights, the Harps also once got hold of another traveler, stripped him, tied him naked to a horse, and shoved both animal and man off the cliff to their deaths.

Civilization and law and order finally rooted the criminals out of the cave for good in the 1830s. Human skeletons, reputed victims of the murderers, turned up in and around the cave, and counterfeit coins and the materials to make them also surfaced.

Inch for inch the most dangerous cavern in America, the cave is now the gemstone of the 150-acre Cave-in-Rock State Park, a mile-long strip of turf just northeast of the tiny town of Cave-in-Rock in Hardin County.

Formed by erosion from the Ohio River, the arched cave is 25 feet high, semicircular at its opening, and measures about 55 feet wide by 160 feet deep, according to state park statistics. A narrow vertical notch cuts through the floor of the opening, allowing visitors a passageway into the cool interior. The floor rises gradually on an incline farther back, eventually leading into a hollow chamber where the floor and ceiling round to meet each other. A side chamber, dark and often wet, leads intriguingly off to the right, but goes nowhere.

Birds fly in and out. People wander in to check it out but don't stay long because there are no amenities within the cave. Graffiti, names, and initials, some of them historic, mark the walls and ceiling. But otherwise, the hole is the same as it was 200 years ago, only considerably safer.

Occasionally, passing barges can be seen from within by peering through the cave's mouth. The boulder-strewn water's edge lies only a couple dozen feet farther down, and, at times in the past when spring rains have bloated the Ohio, rowboats have entered the cave (which might explain some of the initials written into the rocky ceiling).

Portions of the Walt Disney television program "Davy Crockett and the River Pirates" were filmed at the cave during the mid-1950s, and, in the early '60s, the star-studded "How the West Was Won" theatrical release used parts of the area for its segment on river piracy.

A modern state park has arisen around the cave. Picnicking and camping activities take place atop the surrounding 60-foot-high bluffs. A restaurant, lodges, and cabins occupy the high ground east of the cave, overlooking one of America's longest, most important commercial waterways. Fishing, boating, and hiking are allowed. Colorful names ("Buzzards Roost," "Pirates Bluff") for some of the vantage points and trails recall the cave's former infamy; but, strangely, no historical markers commemorate the cave's dark secrets, and the park brochure's narrative provides the only clue of past villainy.

Neighbored by the Shawnee National Forest of southern Illinois, the park remains open year-round, although some facilities may close for inclement weather.

Its namesake village affords lodging, restaurants, and a couple modest souvenir and craft stores. Cave-in-Rock also hosts its annual July Frontier Days, including a staged battle between river travelers and the cave's denizens of darkness. Elsewhere in Hardin County are museums and historic sites, old iron furnaces, Indian mounds, and 160-foot-high Tower Rock, the highest promontory above the Ohio River and a U.S. Forest Service camping and recreational site three miles west of the cave.

Of related appeal to those interested in 19th-century river piracy are quick side trips: the Ford's Ferry site, two miles east of the cave along the river, where lawman James Ford surreptitiously operated a criminal network until his assassination; Hooven Hollow, about seven miles northwest of the cave off State Highway 1, where counterfeiters operated out of Bixby Cave; and Battery Rock, about six miles northeast, where human "river rats" used an outcropping at a U-shaped flexure of the Ohio to spot approaching flatboats and signal their colleagues back at the cave. Only local roads connect these sites; visitors should seek directions from knowledgeable residents of Cave-in-Rock.

Hardin County is rural and small. State Highway 1 approaches Cave-in-Rock from the north. And if you're entering from Kentucky, State Highway 91 brings you to the Cave-in-Rock toll ferry which will get you across the narrow river in just a few minutes. The rather considerable price (about $5 per vehicle during the early '90s) offsets scores of miles you would have to travel by using the nearest bridges. The ferry operates from dawn until about 5:30 p.m. or so.

THE GODS' ROCK GARDEN

Blame it all on Mother Nature.

In her random capriciousness, she took earth, leavened it with wind and water, and cooked it over eons of time under varying temperatures.

Some 300 million years ago, when man was not even a gleam in evolution's eye, the earth rumbled, creating an east-west fault in today's southeastern Illinois. Then, 200 million years later, the earth belched again, further rupturing that part of the planet. About a million or so years ago, melted glacier water from a gigantic ice sheet that blanketed about 90 percent of current Illinois flowed south, eroding hills and enlarging valleys of pounds sandstone that an ancient river had deposited 300 million years earlier.

Rivulets, rain, and wind gusts added their own finishing touches. Water, which had been trapped in crevices and ledges, froze, expanded, and then splintered parts of the rock.

Finally, man entered the picture, stumbling across the strangely contoured rocks in the bluffs of southeastern Illinois and calling the region "The Garden of the Gods."

During the Civil War, southern sympathizers who suffered the misfortune of living in Illinois, a northern state, formed a secret organization they called "Knights of the Golden Circle" and met by night in a cave in the bluffs near the site.

And today, other men come to this garden to see Anvil Rock, a rock that resembles a blacksmith's anvil. And to slide through Fat Man's Squeeze. And to walk on the wooden boardwalk that overlooks the valley as it wends through irregularly shaped rock columns with reddish-brown patches, rings, streaks, and raised patterns of swirls and coils that look like bas relief maps. And to check out Devil's Smokestack and the Tower of Babel. And to troop over to Camel Rock, a formation with that animal's head, neck, and hump (more daring souls descend the bluffs and then the hump, cross the neck, and scale the head, a stunt not recommended for the casual visitor).

The Garden of the Gods is one of the best of the six dozen recreation areas within the 260,000-acre Shawnee National Forest which sprawls across much of southern Illinois. An easy half-mile flagstone-path and wooden-boardwalk combination encompasses the rocks artfully wrought by Mother Nature in her infinite (and "finite," for she is ever changing) wisdom. Two dozen picnic and camp sites, eight miles of nature trails, and a geological exhibit are also included.

A million visitors a year pass through various parts of the Shawnee National Forest, but only a handful venture to the little-known Garden of the Gods. It occupies the southeastern niche of Saline County near its junction with Gallatin, Hardin, and Pope Counties. The nearest fair-sized cities are Eldorado, Harrisburg, and Marion.

INDIANA

THE TOMBSTONE WITH LIPSTICK PRINTS

He was no giant, no legend, no hero during his life...only a small 5'8" mortal who swore like a trooper and reeked of cigarette stench.

He was a mischievous lad who, testing a theory that ducks excrete salt pork nearly as fast as they swallow it, tied a piece of the meat to a fishing line and fed a succession of the animals, only to wind up with a line of ducks strung together, beak to anus, quacking discomfort.

He once publicly urinated in front of hundreds to overcome his nervousness.

He posed for pictures in a coffin and later said the lid squashed his nose when it was down.

Rumors, whether true or not, said he was bisexual, even homosexual, and enjoyed having cigarettes extinguished on his chest.

He drank often and intemperately and, when drunk, was capable of beating his girlfriends.

He anguished over his prostitute-like homosexual encounters yet superficially dismissed them as "free meal tickets."

He was a psychological question mark, an emotional loner who lived with relatives after his mother died and who grew up crying over her grave and sleeping with the ribbon from her funeral wreath under his pillow.

He was athletic and devastatingly handsome with thick eyebrows, bushy light hair that shot upward from his scalp and rolled back in golden-tufted waves, and a penetrating stare dripping with dreamy sensitivity that made him one of the 20th century's greatest sex symbols.

He plowed his expensive silver Porsche Spyder 550 racing machine into a Ford sedan that had veered into his lane in Cholame, California on Friday, September 30, 1955, at nearly 6 p.m., two hours after having received a speeding ticket and only minutes after continuing to drive faster than 100 mph.

He was an actor on the cusp of becoming an icon of rebellious discontent, conflicted emotions, and unbridled sensuality. His death made him a legend. He was 24 years old. He was James Dean.

Few people have enjoyed as much celebrity after their deaths as James Dean. Even silent screen legend Rudolf Valentino, whose 1926 death at the height of his popularity had produced unparalleled mass hysteria, is today a forgotten footnote.

Time may enact a similar sentence on James Dean. But, four decades after his death, his cult appeal is as pronounced as ever. Perhaps the circumstances of his demise help perpetuate the legend: he perished behind the wheel of a speeding car on his way to a place where he was to participate in a car race; the impact of the crash nearly decapitated him. Perhaps his age is a factor: a wild youth who burned quickly and brightly and died before old age, diminished talents, vanishing appeal, and self-indulgence could strip away his luster.

Were he still alive today, James Dean could get senior citizen discounts anywhere. Many of his longest fans are either dead of old age or retired. Yet his name lives on, and devoted followers still journey to his Indiana hometown to sense the gravitational pull of his roots and visit the cemetery to photograph his tombstone. And the romantically obsessed, clinging to ingrained, self-induced fantasies too personally wedged into their psyches to purge, stoop to kiss the stone that bears the chiseled dates of his mortality.

His three major films - "East of Eden," "Rebel Without a Cause," "Giant," classics all - continue to sow the seeds of his legend.

How else to explain the fans, some never even alive when Dean died, who yank souvenir ears of corn from stalks in a field opposite the house in which Dean grew up - ears of corn that Dean never saw? Will the corn be consumed in some silent, teary ritual, kernel by kernel, or will it be allowed to wither and dry, a talisman of unfathomable memories?

How else to explain the visitors who tear blades of grass from the front yard of the home in which he lived, grass that Dean's feet never trod? Is the reel image of the man actually that real?

How else to explain the New Yorker who pilgrimaged to Dean's hometown nearly every year since his death and claimed to have seen one of his films more than 2,000 times in the 1950s and 1960s (before videotape), a staggering average of one viewing a day for nearly six straight years?

Such is the idolatry given a guy who leapt to legend primarily because he had the pure bad luck to die tragically while barely beyond adolescence.

Fairmount, Indiana, population 3,000, holds James Dean's corpse, his legacy, and the essence of his mystery. It also supports a small cottage industry dedicated to preserving the mementoes and memories of the idol.

The Fairmount Historical Museum at 203 East Washington Street contains a dozen rooms of local historical interest. But visitors go there for the two rooms of Dean paraphernalia: his baby and teen-aged clothes; high school items; his hand and foot impressions laid in cement when he was about 10; his prized black and yellow Czechoslovakian hometown motorcycle and the Triumph cycle he rode in Hollywood; movie clothing, scripts, and so forth; racing trophies and his pit pass; awards and plaques; his handwritten phone numbers for movie people - actress "Liz Taylor," director "George Stevens," and "Heda Hopper" (the acerbic gossip columnist who spelled her first name with a double consonant; Dean was not an accomplished speller). The museum fills an historic house, includes a gift shop of Dean souvenirs, and operates during customary daytime hours (abbreviated on Sunday) from March to November. A modest donation is charged, and, surprisingly, no photographs are allowed.

The James Dean Gallery and Gift Shop at 425 North Main Street, about a half-dozen blocks northwest, focuses on Dean's Hollywood days. Its seven rooms of varying size showcase what a brochure calls "the world's largest collection of memorabilia and archives" on Dean: hundreds (perhaps thousands...who can count?) of lobby cards, paintings, photos, magazine covers, books, records, cardboard cutouts; a fence prop from "Rebel Without a Cause;" a doorknob from a New York City hotel closet which bears his prints from his 1952 stay there; a menu signed for a fan in a restaurant a week before his death; more trophies and plaques; a pastel portrait of him by artist Tony Lucev which fell to the floor, its glass shattering, exactly one year to the minute after Dean himself had died; a half-hour video of Dean's screen test, rarely seen segments from his early TV work, and some amusing outtakes. The gallery also has a gift shop, maintains the usual daily daytime hours (except Thanksgiving, Christmas, and New Year's), charges a moderate admission, and allows photographs.

Fairmount bills itself as the "Home of Distinguished People," and historical markers throughout the town trumpet its alumni who lived there and then moved away to become famous: Jim Davis, creator of "Garfield;" Phil Jones, a network newsman; Robert C. Sheets, director of the National Hurricane Center; and Mary Jane Ward, author of the best-selling novel "The Snake Pit."

But Fairmount's only real attraction is James Dean. And his gravesite delivers the single largest emotional jolt. The most significant day in Fairmount's history occurred on October 8, 1955, when 3,000 people mobbed Park Cemetery to witness the interment of the actor's broken body. The cemetery completes Fairmount's trilogy of tributes to its native son. A short trip north of the gallery along Main Street (and continuing on the road as it crosses State Highway 26) leads to the graveyard. Turn left (west) onto the cemetery's entrance road and drive past a memorial to the actor and continue a short ways north and west. The grave is visible to the right (east) of the inner cemetery road, just south of a paved circle. Flowers will usually surround the pink granite stone bearing his name and birth and death dates. Lipstick prints and phrases of love will impregnate both sides. It is the second stone on the site, the badly chipped original having disappeared in 1983. By the time you visit, perhaps even a third stone may be in place.

The Fairmount Historical Museum honors Dean with an annual Fairmount Museum Days/Remembering James Dean three-day tribute during the last weekend in September that includes a Dean look-alike contest, antique car show, bicycle tour of the Dean sites, grand parade, and showings of his films.

And a 600-plus-member "We Remember Dean International" fan club is active at P.O. Box 5025, Fullerton, CA 92635.

Unless it is a Dean anniversary, only scattered visitors will be encountered at any of the sites. Touring both museums and the cemetery will take a couple hours. If you're a Dean devotee, you may also want to see Fairmount's more peripheral tourist attractions: the old high school where he attended classes (Vine Street between Madison and Jefferson Streets, a few blocks southeast of the Historical Museum); the Fairmount Friends Church where his funeral service occurred (corner of Mill and First Streets, three blocks northwest of the museum); Marvin Carter's Motorcycle Shop where Dean bought his first bike in 1947 (just north of the cemetery on Sand Pike, as Main Street is there known); the Back Creek Friends Church where he attended services as a youngster during the church-going phase of his life (just north of the cycle store); and the Winslow farmhouse where he lived during his adolescence (north of the church).

And if you want to immerse yourself even more fully in the life of a talented, introspective, self-absorbed, untrammeled youth whose death leapfrogged his handful of achievements and catapulted his legend into immortality, drive 10 miles north of Fairmount on State Highway 9 for a plaque at Fourth and McClure Streets in Marion which commemorates the site of his birth.

Fairmount is about 60 miles northeast of Indianapolis along State Highway 26, five miles west of its intersection with Interstate Highway 69 in southern Grant County. It has restaurants but no lodging facilities.

CRIME TIME IN NASHVILLE

It will not be everyone's cup of gin, but the graphic little museum in Nashville, Indiana captures the essence of the man it commemorates in shocking black and white photographs and full-size wax figures of gore and bloody death. Three cramped rooms purport to collect 90 percent of all known artifacts reflecting the sensational, sleazy, and skewed life of America's infamous "Public Enemy Number One."

The museum stands out like the staccato burst of a clip fired from a Thompson submachine "Tommygun" in a quaint tourist town brimming with ski enthusiasts, festivals, whole blocks of craft shops, and aromatic restaurants and bakeries, a town where a small train ferries visitors through tree-lined streets, where traffic is slow and horn blasts rare, where streams of shoppers surge along the sidewalks.

It recounts the career of an average child born to average parents in Indianapolis in 1903. Rather homely, with an unprepossessing grin, ski nose, and high straight forehead, the child showed ordinary qualities. But early in life, he turned sour. His marriage lasted only a few years. He enlisted in the Navy, then deserted. He stole a car at 20, attempted store robbery at 21, and did a term in the state reformatory until being paroled at nearly 30.

With his newfound freedom fresh in his nostrils in May 1933, he turned seriously to crime, using the bank robbery tricks he had gleaned from his more accomplished correctional colleagues. Sometimes alone, other times with friends of a like mind, he hit bank after bank in Indiana, Kentucky, Ohio, Iowa, Wisconsin, and South

Dakota and raided the munitions arsenals of three Indiana police departments. His take amounted to about a million dollars (an astronomical sum then) in scarcely more than a year.

Evading FBI traps and attacks, he was captured in Arizona in January 1934 and remanded to an Indiana jail on robbery and murder complicity charges, then escaped from a supposedly foolproof facility by bulling his way past guards with a drawn pistol (either a toy fashioned from wood or a real smuggled pistol). FBI agents finally caught up with him on July 22, 1934, outside Chicago's Biograph Theater, and shot him without warning.

John Herbert Dillinger was never the mastermind of his gang, only a key member in a confederacy of criminals who shared bank robbing responsibilities, yet he received the notoriety. Evidence indicates he only killed one person, if that.

The John Dillinger Historical Wax Museum displays relics that trace his career: childhood photos and items; newspaper headlines emblazoning his name during his 14-month ride into infamy; wanted posters and police bulletins; a letter from FBI agent Charles B. Winstead certifying his role as the person who fired the bullet that killed Dillinger in the alley outside the Biograph at 2433 N. Lincoln Avenue, as well as a .38 Colt worn by Winstead when he slew the thief; the purported .22-caliber Mossberg Brownie four-shot pistol that served as Dillinger's hidden weapon; a collection of his guns, including the carved wooden barrel he supposedly used in escaping jail; his 1933 Essex Hudson Terraplane 8, his favorite escape vehicle, affording him 83-mph speed and capable of going from zero to 60 in a then-impressive 14.4 seconds; and the good luck rabbit's foot he gave to a newspaperman in January 1934 with the prophetic words, "You may as well have this...my luck's running out anyway."

Nearly two dozen realistically molded wax figures stand at alarming attention behind glass cases around the museum: Dillinger and one of several girl friends, a married woman named Mary Evelyn "Billie" Frechette; his cronies, Russell Lee Clark, John Hamilton, Charles Makley, George "Baby Face" Nelson, Harry "Pete" Pierpont, and Homer Van Meter; Rita Polly Hamilton Keele, another girl friend, posed alongside his actual, original tombstone - chipped by souvenir fanciers and acquired by the museum in exchange for a new one; famous law officers of the day; other assorted gangsters; and Anna Cumpanas Sage, the mysterious "woman in red," a brothel madam who tipped off the FBI in a deal to ward off deportation, the woman who made the fatal ambush possible - her wax figure sits against a brick wall, a facsimile of the original wall in the alley where Dillinger died, with the same anonymous verse chalked on it as on the original:

> Stranger, stop and wish me well,
> Just say a prayer for my soul in hell,
> I was a good fellow, most people said,
> Betrayed by a woman all dressed in red.

The two most glaring figures show Dillinger in death: his bloodied corpse on a morgue table; and his body laid out in its cheap cloth coffin, the tear in the flesh of his upper right cheek caused by one of Winstead's bullets still visible.

Other bizarre tidbits abound: morgue photographs of Arizona Donnie Clark "Ma" Barker, Charles Arthur "Pretty Boy" Floyd, Baby Face Nelson, Bonnie and Clyde, and others; an anatomical model of the inside of Dillinger's head, showing the path the fatal bullet traveled; a cutaway view of Dillinger's grave showing why the corpse is virtually unreachable (following a threat to steal the body, authorities reopened the grave, sunk the coffin deep, and covered it with layers of earth leavened with concrete slabs); the wicker body basket used to carry his remains to a hearse from the Cook County Morgue; a death mask of the criminal made by students in the morgue; the button-fly trousers he wore when he was gunned down, with his faded blood visible on the pocket; and his last items, found on his body (disguise glasses to conceal his face, a watch with a photo of Polly Hamilton, a cigar, Colt automatic pistol and ammo clip, and $7.70).

ARCANE AMERICA

Dillinger witticisms adorn the walls:

- "Maybe I'll learn someday, Dad, that you can't win in this game."
- "I don't smoke much. And I drink very little. I guess my only bad habit is robbing banks."
- "I'm for (Franklin) Roosevelt all the way. And for N.R.A. (National Recovery Act). Particularly for banks."
- "A jail is just like a nut with a worm in it. The worm can always get out."

Beyond the gore, the museum evokes period charm in its nooks: newspapers and license plates of the '30s; a Burma Shave billboard, that classic icon of Depression-era roadway advertising; posters and stills and a video of the last movie Dillinger saw ("Manhattan Melodrama," a gangster film with Clark Gable); endless recordings of Bing Crosby, Jimmy Durante, and radio music and shows of the day.

In a breezeway outside the museum (a portion of the bottom floor of the Homecrafters Mall at the corner of W. Washington Street and S. Honeysuckle Lane), "Dillinger: The Man and the Myth," a documentary, plays continuously, free for the viewing.

The museum advises patrons of its unusual displays in its brochure ("The John Dillinger museum was created to preserve a very real, if regrettable, part of American history.") and warns visitors at the entrance about its "violent nature," admitting children under 12 only with an accompanying adult. Two criminologists (ex-FBI agent Barton N. Hahn and former Pinkerton detective and current author and Dillinger authority Joseph M. Pinkston) own the museum. A modest fee is charged. Normal daytime hours are in effect from March through November and when weather permits otherwise. A small gift shop sells items of interest to students of crime.

Viewing the video and glancing at the exhibits might eat up

an hour or two; reading everything contained on the museum's walls will require a day.

Nashville is the seat of Brown County on State Highway 46, about 40 miles south of Indianapolis.

And if you want to see the grave of John Dillinger (pronounced by him with a hard "g"), a man much of his contemporary public considered a dashing Robin Hood because of his wit and habit of only robbing banks (and not depositors at them), go to Crown Hill Cemetery at 700 West 38th Street in Indianapolis, where 23rd President Benjamin Harrison, poet James Whitcomb Riley, author Booth Tarkington, and three vice presidents repose. Dillinger keeps them company in section 44, adjacent to Boulevard Place. A small stone, rising just inches from the ground, remembers his name and birth and death years but tastefully declines to mention the cumulative loot from his heists.

IOWA

BRIDGES ON THE WAYNE

It was the birthing ground for one of America's mightiest legends and one of literature's biggest tear-jerkers. And it doesn't seem to matter much that the legend turned his back on the place early in life or that the backdrop for the novel's star-crossed lovers doesn't look that romantic in real life.

Without them, Winterset, Iowa would be a small, anonymous American town too many miles removed from the interstate to see any visitors. But with them, it becomes a surprising tourist stop.

Thirteen-pound Marion Robert Morrison was born May 26, 1907 in Winterset. But he didn't remain long. His pharmacist father developed tuberculosis before the child was 10, and the family moved to California where the boy grew up to be 6'4" John Wayne, one of the world's most recognizable actors. And Winterset is also the seat of Madison County which lays claim to a sextet of covered bridges that author Robert James Waller turned into his smash 1992 best-seller "The Bridges of Madison County."

First, the Duke. In 1910, when young Marion Robert Morrison was just three, the family moved elsewhere in the county, leaving Winterset for good. A subsequent move to southern California allowed the boy to grow up under the eye of Hollywood notables who noticed his physique and good looks, signed him to a contract, changed his name to a more rugged one, and watched him become a celebrity, a superstar, and finally a myth through a succession of films - "Stagecoach," "Red River," "Sands of Iwo Jima," "The Searchers," "The Alamo," "True Grit" - that established him as the nation's ultimate hero and patriot. Directly after his 1979 death, Congress gave him its highest civilian medal. His passing made headlines throughout the world, and columnists feted him to tributes usually reserved for heads of state. To many, he is still "the great American."

Winterset remembers him. One of its major streets is called John Wayne Drive and carries his image on its signs.

His birthplace home, a modest five-room bungalow at 224 South 2nd Street, dotes on him. Though Wayne never had any memories of the house, it recalls his memory in every corner of the foyer, kitchen, parlor, reception room, and bedroom with period furniture bulging with Wayne photographs, movie posters and lobby cards, literature, paintings, a letter he sent to Winterset in 1973 requesting copies of his birth certificate, and one of several black eye patches worn in his Oscar-winning "True Grit" role (the patch contained a thin gauze center which permitted vision while giving the illusion it didn't).

Binders invite comments from visitors: "Were you in any John Wayne movies?"; "What is your favorite John Wayne movie? story? experience?". Solicited letters carry tributes to Wayne from the likes of Ronald Reagan, James Stewart, Maureen O'Hara, Lucille Ball, and Bob Hope. Color pictures of the most famous tourist to visit the site - President Ronald Reagan during a November 3, 1984 campaign stop - decorate the house (he got in free; you won't).

Tours depart the adjacent visitor center about every half-hour. The guides blame the prohibition of indoor photography on a stipulation of Wayne's estate and chalk the scarcity of personal Wayne memorabilia up to the estate which, they say, still has most of his items "tied up." They also add the estate has assured them that Wayne's surviving horse, Dollar, will be stuffed upon death and shipped to the birthplace.

Dedicated in 1982, the site sees about 30,000 visitors a year and charges a modest fee. Tours are short, but you can look around leisurely afterward. The visitor center stocks items relevant to Wayne's world. It opens daily during normal daytime hours.

Then there are those bridges, immortalized beyond their scenic worth by the throbbingly romantic pages of Robert James

Waller's runaway first-novel hit and a subsequent film. The book centers around a passionate, haunting affair between a middle-aged photographer on assignment in Madison County and a slightly younger unsatisfied housewife who guides him to the bridges. Though the romance fulfills her as nothing before, she remains with her family. Both lovers later die, the bittersweet memories of their love tugging at their hearts.

The former math, economics, and management professor at the University of Northern Iowa put Madison County on the map with his soaring romantic prose, also setting himself up in a writing career that allowed him to chuck his teaching post.

Following the book's initial popularity, tourists descended upon Madison County to see the nature of the bridges that so personified the fictional romance that transcended time and space. As the novel settled into its historical niche, visitation inevitably subsided.

Madison County's six bridges, all well over 100 years old and on the National Register of Historic Structures, are all that remain of 16 such spans. Their physical appearance cannot match the lofty lyricism of Waller's novel; they were originally built for utilitarian purposes - to shelter roadways over water. But if you'd like to see them and let your imagination run wild, they are in Winterset and its environs.

Imes Bridge, the oldest (dating to 1870), is the most attractive primarily because of its location behind a fence-enclosed lawn and a handsome sign proclaiming it the "GATEWAY TO THE BRIDGES." It crosses Clanton Creek off County Road G50 in St. Charles, southeast of Winterset and about a mile west of Interstate Highway 35.

The Cutler-Donahoe Bridge, built in 1870-71, is the easiest to reach, having been moved to Winterset's City Park at the intersection of South 9th Street and East South Street in 1970.

The Holliwell Bridge, a few miles southeast, is the longest. A barricade blocked access to it during our visit. From the intersection of East Court Street and John Wayne Drive in Winterset, go

1.5 miles east; at a "T" intersection, turn right onto a gravel road; bear left at the first "Y," bear left again and, 1.7 miles beyond the above-mentioned "T," turn right; the bridge is visible at the end of the gravel road, spanning Middle River.

To reach the Cedar Lake Bridge, a few miles northeast of Winterset, go .5-miles east on State Highway 92 at its intersection with U.S. Highway 169, then turn left on an unmarked county road and proceed 1.8 miles; at a fork in the road, turn left - the bridge is there. Built in 1883, it originally crossed nearby Cedar Creek but was moved in 1920.

The Hogback Bridge, constructed in 1884, crosses North River about five miles northwest of Winterset. At the State 92-U.S. 169 intersection, go north on 169 1.5 miles; then turn left on County Road G31 and proceed 1.5 miles; turn right and go another 1.5 miles until you encounter a loop and see the bridge.

The Roseman Bridge, also known as the Haunted Bridge, is the one most identified with the novel's lovers. It dates from 1883 and crosses Middle River. Take State 92 west of Winterset about 8 miles until its intersection with County P53 (also called Macksburg Road); turn left (south) and generally go in a southeastern direction through one "Y" intersection and to another; at the second "Y," turn right to the bridge.

Seeing all the spans will take several hours; you may encounter a lone car or two doing the same thing, although we had the bridges to ourselves on a summer Friday.

During October's second full weekend, Winterset also hosts a Covered Bridge Festival with an antique car parade and show, a bus tour of the town and bridges, and the usual accouterments. The town has historic buildings, an historical museum, an art center in a house that formerly hid slaves on the underground railroad, and recreation areas and parks. It is southwest of Des Moines, at the intersection of U.S. Highway 169 and State Highway 92, about a baker's dozen miles west of Interstate 35.

KANSAS

Concrete Christianity: Dinsmoor's view of the crucifixion.

AN UNHOLY GARDEN OF EDEN

It may be the greatest misnomer on the North American continent. It is also one of the most bizarre places you'll ever see in your life. And its grand finale, artfully saved for last by tour guides who appreciate its impact, may repel you.

The self-styled "Garden of Eden" in north-central Kansas is anything but a sylvan idyll. It is instead the inspiration and work of one of America's most unique, eccentric, and - some would say - semi-demented creative spirits. The Garden of Eden is more a Biblical allegory twisted awry than a place of tranquility and beauty. And the so-called "Rock Log Cabin Home" it encompasses is no traditional log cabin home, not in construction, not in style.

The complex is the handiwork of one S.P. Dinsmoor, Civil War veteran, architect, sculptor, homespun philosopher, self-promoting entrepreneur, and perhaps the quirkiest eccentric you never heard of.

Born March 8, 1843, in Ohio, S.P. Dinsmoor spent three years in the uniform of the North in the War Between the States, in his words, fighting "in eighteen big battles besides skirmishes" and witnessing "the capture of Lee, and in every fight I was in we either captured or run the Johnnies."

He migrated to Illinois in 1866, farmed and taught school, and, in 1870, in perhaps the first overt manifestation of the weirdness that was to dominate his later life, married Frances A. Barlow Journey...while both were astride horses. He relocated to Lucas, Kansas 18 years later and, except for a brief sojourn in Nebraska, remained in Kansas the rest of his life. He built his "Cabin Home" in 1907 when he was a robust 64 and then began the various sculptures destined to flesh out his Garden of Eden.

In the meantime, he became a father and grandfather. His wife died in 1917, when he was 74. Still brimming with energy and the fire to blast his detractors who suggested he was a bit too old for such things, he married his Czechoslovakian servant, Emilie Brozek, in 1924, when he was a spry 81, she a callow 20. The second marriage produced offspring as well. And Dinsmoor went on until his own death in 1932, just shy of 90.

The tour of Dinsmoor's Cabin Home is interesting but unspectacular. Considerably less than a mansion, it exudes a homey, plain, rustic modesty that seemingly matches its creator's penchant. The limestone rock, cut along the fashion of actual logs and notched as it would be in a log cabin, encloses 11 rooms, a bathroom, three halls, a couple closets...and a cave. Cement, California redwood, pine, and oak contributed to the effect.

But once outside in the grotesque Garden of Eden, with its striking figures wrought by their artist in unremitting homeliness, the tour takes a turn southward to Hell. The concrete statues and artwork evoke nightmares out of Dante's Inferno or Goethe's Faust.

Retired from farming, the disabled soldier worked like a demon in the final quarter-century of his life, fashioning patriotic, bellicose, Biblical, and, above all, sardonic imagery that appalls as it mesmerizes. By 1927, five years before his death, the sculptor had utilized more than 113 tons of cement, the equivalent of more than 2,270 sacks, by his own reckoning. The cement assumed the shape of fencing, trees, strawberry and flower beds, grape arbors, sidewalks, porches, pools, even a remarkable seven- by four-foot American flag, reputedly the first ever woven from concrete, in full red, white, and blue colors, with appendant tassels, rippling nearly straight out from its perch atop a cement tree. "I think it would be a great advantage to the government if they would put up cement flags...over lighthouses and other places where a permanent flag is wanted," he once mused. "It would stand out in plain view in all kinds of weather and could be seen where a cloth flag could not be seen."

The actual "garden" of Eden, a portion of the greater work, rises west of the house - "The most unique home, for living or dead, on earth," in Dinsmoor's words. But don't expect any symbols of salvation, for that was not his style. Yard-high letters spell out the phrase "GARDEN OF EDEN" because, as Dinsmoor explained, "I could hear so many, as they go by, sing out, 'What is this?'" No wonder.

The finished work is a marvelously jaundiced view of creation. The women, from Eve to Cain's wife, are voluptuously bare-breasted but bizarrely proportioned. Wearing only a loincloth to cover her ventral nakedness, Eve is cursed with hips wide enough to give birth to an entire species - perhaps the precise point of Dinsmoor's metaphorical caricature. A snake deposits an apple in Eve's outstretched palm. Adam (facially, an exact replica of Dinsmoor himself) steps on another snake as he holds Eve's free hand. Dinsmoor explained:

> The other snake didn't have any apple, so Adam got hot about it, grabbed it, and is smashing its head with his heel. That shows the disposition of man. If he doesn't get the apple there is something doing. And the Bible says, the heel of the seed of the woman shall smash the serpent's head, or something to that effect.

A horned skeletal devil lurks overhead with upraised pitchfork poised to ever threaten mankind.

The Cain and Abel tableau is partially menacing. Having been brained by his jealous brother, Abel lies sprawled on his back, limbs askew, looking like a victim of a Holocaust concentration camp. Cain and his bare-bosomed wife run away, "a 'possum hanging down over Cain's head to eat lunch with...." Dinsmoor commented:

> Now, when people are standing around here on the side walk as we are, and I am in the house, and feel all right, they

will hear voices away over there where that angel is, saying, "Cain, you son-of-a-gun, where is your brother Abel?" Cain's answer nowadays would be, "Damned if I know. Am I my brother's keeper?" Now that is all Scripture except the flourishes. I put them in, because when I was building this they accused me of being bughouse on religion. I am bughouse good and proper, but not on religion, perpetual motion or any other fool thing that I cannot find out one thing about.

You be the judge.

Nearly everything is askew in the world according to Dinsmoor. Above the fishpond, a concrete snake rears up, jaws agape, ready to pounce on an unsuspecting waterfowl.

The north side displays Dinsmoor's cynical outlook to its fullest. A soldier - the Civil War may have influenced Dinsmoor's perceptions more than any other stimulus - shoots at an Indian who readies himself to fire an arrow from his bow at a dog who is treeing a fox who has his eyes set on snatching a bird about to devour a worm that is himself eating a leaf - "modern civilization as I see it. If it is not right I am to blame, but if the Garden of Eden is not right Moses is to blame. He wrote it up and I built it."

In another bit of stinging cement satire, Dinsmoor poses a female - threatening in her appearance, selfishly greedy in her posture - leaning over to catch the soldier in her marital grasp, as the tentacles of the monopolistic business trusts that Dinsmoor loathed entwine around her: "And here is the girl after the soldier. I know that is right. I was a soldier once myself. They are after the soldiers today, but she does not know that the trust has got her around the waist with one claw...."

Then there is the crucifixion tableau; only the central figure nailed to the concrete tree is not Christ, but Labor. And the perpetrators are the Banker, the Lawyer, the Doctor...and, yes, the Preacher. Dinsmoor scathingly opined:

The Preacher is saying to this poor fellow crucified, "Never mind your suffering here on earth, my friend, never mind your suffering here, secure home in heaven for A-l-l E-t-e-r-n-i-t-y and you'll be all right." ... He knows nothing about Eternity and that he does know if he knows anything.

Sympathy for the downtrodden masses is a recurrent emotion in Dinsmoor's outdoor art. His Goddess of Liberty scene depicts the female freedom figure spearing the symbol of his hated trusts while a man and woman saw off the trusts' underpinnings.

Throughout the grounds, Dinsmoor's concrete figures are sculpted nearly as awkwardly, disproportionately, and surrealistically as Pablo Picasso's famed canvas characters. Whether the result of genius or puerility, the sculptures - classic examples of Gothic, primitive, or folk art, according to the slant of the observer - embed themselves within the psyche, for good or bad. It's difficult to leave the Garden of Eden without lingering images flitting through the crevices of the mind.

Apparently fond of animals - or, at least, of observing them in confined spaces - Dinsmoor also built enclosures for eagles, pigeons, owls, badgers, and coyotes. The specially constructed compartments remain, minus their long-departed inmates.

Perhaps an engaging conversationalist, certainly a man of strong opinions, Dinsmoor entertained guests, most of whom paid to glimpse the details of his world. As part of the package deal, he dined them at his alfresco "visitors' dining hall" - an open-sided pavilion with picnic tables. "Over 1,000 visitors have eaten dinner at my tables and not one has ever complained of their grub," he commented in the 1920s, "something I don't think any hotel man in Kansas can boast of."

The guided tour ends with a trip into the locked pyramidal mausoleum built by Dinsmoor for his first wife and himself. Eccentric to the very end, Dinsmoor constructed a special coffin for himself, made entirely of concrete and glass. The guides tastefully refrain from commenting on any of the details locked within the dark vault. They simply advise you that, alone of all the nooks and crannies within the grounds, the mausoleum's interior is off limits for photographs. They then open the door and switch a flashlight on. How long you stay in the mausoleum is determined by your tolerance of the macabre. It is the unquestionable highlight of the tour, diminishing everything that has gone before. It is also the stuff of many a nightmare.

The formal tour lasts about a half-hour or so, depending on how long you elect to remain in the mausoleum. Once done, you are free to wander the grounds among the statuary as long as you desire.

The Garden of Eden holds a National Register of Historic Places designation. The usual museum-historic home admission is charged, and tours are available from March through November during daytime hours. The site is well-marked in Lucas at 2nd and Kansas Avenues, about 15 miles north of U.S. Interstate Highway 70. From 70, take State Highway 232 north to the intersection with State Highway 18, then turn west onto 18 to Lucas and follow signs.

Rounding out a full day's activities in the area can include stops at the old army post at Fort Hays, the cowboy town of Hays where Wild Bill Hickok briefly served as sheriff and which now has a number of museums showcasing antique cars and natural history, St. Fidelis Catholic Church - the immigrant-inspired Cathedral of the Plains - in Victoria, and the Kansas Barbed Wire Museum in La Crosse - all within 100 miles of the Garden of Eden.

Other tourists may arrive during your stay, but your tour is likely to be a private one. All the better for trying to comprehend a saturnine man with a satiric sense of humor.

"Some people know they are going to heaven and those they do not like are going to hell," he wrote in his mid-80s. "I am going where the Boss puts me. He knows where I belong better than I do."

A trip to the Garden of Eden is a journey into the markedly different, odd realm of S.P. Dinsmoor. It is also a date with Dinsmoor himself who is, unlike his cement legacy, somewhat the worse for wear...as becomes hauntingly evident.

THE GHOST TOWN OF THE UNBURIED

They are there before your eyes, 146 bodies compressed in their death crouches, just as when buried: fetal posture, legs folded at the joints and drawn close to the torso, arms either folded up and brought toward the face or drawn downward by the sides. The flesh has long since disappeared, and the bones are lacquered for preservation. They appear brown and shiny and seem to have solidified into their background, a part of the dirt upon which they rest. They lay close by one another on pillows of earth that have been left standing as islands surrounded by paths that excavators have dug. Some skeletons are incomplete, some fully intact. All are marked and clinically identified, for they are now museum pieces, uncovered by archeologists for the edification of 20th-century sightseers. Devoid of personalities, they are now relics, conversation pieces, artifacts to be studied and photographed and gawked at.

Welcome to the Indian Burial Pit in central Kansas.

A handmade sign, one of several inside a shelter constructed over an excavated hole in the ground, says in rudimentary language:

> IN THE SUMMER OF 1936 WE FOUND IN THE
> FIELD SOUTH OF THIS BURIAL, A PRE-HISTORIC
> INDIAN VILLIAGE (sic). 12 EARTHEN LODGES
> HAVE BEEN FOUND. 2 HAVE BEEN EXCAVATED.
> OVER 75 YEARS AGO - THE PIONEER IN DIGGING
> HIS CAVE TO LIVE IN - FOUND SOME BONES -
> SUPPOSEDLY INDIANS - WE, IN HEARING OF

> THIS STORY - STARTED DIGGING - FINDING THE REMAINS OF ONE SKELETON - LEAVING IT AS WE FOUND IT - REMOVED THE EARTH FARTHER - WE FOUND MORE. NOW HAVE THE REMAINS OF 146 PEOPLE IN THE ORIGNAL (sic) POSITION. THESE PEOPLE LIVED FROM 500 TO 1000 YEARS AGO. WE ARE STILL FINDING SKELETONS OUTSIDE THIS BUILDING.

Other handmade signs present the fruits of the excavations, the facts obtained from the uncovering of what is billed as the "Largest Prehistoric Indian Burial Pit in the Middle West:"

- Most bodies were interred "headed" south.
- A man buried in the middle may have been a chief because he, alone of all others, was laid to rest with a "stone for designative mark."
- Many skeletons are six feet, indicating a tall race.
- And:
  > "IN REGARDS TO THE HUNCHBACK AS IT IS LEGANDARY (sic) HISTORY THAT THE ABORIGINES DID NOT LET A DEFORMATIVE LIVE BUT THE CRIPPLE THAT HE WAS EVEN IN THOSE DAYS OF PRIMITIVE MAN MIGHT WE SAY THAT HE WAS THE MEDICINE MAN OF HIS TRIBE OR DICTATOR BUT AFTER DEATH THINGS WERE DIFFERENT HE WAS LAID TO REST ON HIS LEFT SIDE HEAD TO THE WEST FACING NORTH LOOKING OVER HIS PEOPLE"

Another sign by the hunchback, who apparently suffered from arthritis and rickets as well, invites us to observe his spinal curvature and the dimensions of his lower jaw.

We know nothing of this man, whom archeology has introduced to us, this creature suddenly reappearing in skeletal structure, other than what he suffered from. What of his personality, his character, his aspirations? What motivated him? What was his name?

One skeleton - number 65 - lies in the typical fetal position, arms folded before her chest, legs drawn up to meet them. A sign identifies her as a "LARGE FEMALE ADULT." Who was she in life? Did someone ever love her? Did she love someone? Was she someone's wife, someone's mother? Did anyone mourn when she died? It's impossible to tell from the contorted tangle of bones.

Another skeleton casts a deeper pall. Resting near the presumed tribal chief, farther down, lower than most others nearby, the bones are arranged in a way that seems unnatural. The person rests on his stomach, arms close to his sides and tucked tightly in, face reposing on its right side, eye sockets vacant, teeth bared. This is not a human pose; it is the posture of death itself.

These are not human beings anymore; they are but shards of shattered humanity, their flesh putrified, their bones petrified. They inhabit the innards of a city of the dead, a city where bodyless skulls peer from the grave...where signs point out a teen-aged girl with a "WELL SHAPED SKULL" and "BEAUTIFUL TEETH"...where pottery, clamshell necklaces, and ceremonial objects remain intact long after the people who owned them decompose...where our ancestors now look at us with vacant stares of death.

In recent years, Americans of Indian descent have petitioned the government to stop violating the revered repositories of their ancestors.

The Indian Burial Pit unwittingly dredges up tough questions. Is knowledge of the past as important as reverence for the dead? Is it excavation...or desecration? If the act of dying is man's most intimate moment, surrendering his entire life all at once to human mortality, should the residue of that life be displayed through the ages? How would you feel with thousands of eyes scrutinizing your naked bones or those of a loved one?

Either way, echoes from the Indian Burial Pit resonate within oneself for years to come.

The Indian Burial Pit is at Price Brothers' Farm on the former U.S. Highway 40, a few miles east of Salina and south of Interstate Highway 70; watch for signs. A moderate admission is charged, and the attraction is open daily during daytime hours. The enclosure is hot in the summer, and walking around the perimeter of the pit while looking down into the cemetery can be stifling, which (along with the ethical dilemma posed by the site) may affect the time you spend. An average self-guiding tour usually lasts a quarter-hour. A small gift shop with low-brow souvenir items adjoins the pit.

Nearby sights include: Rock City, a collection of large, odd-shaped rocks to scamper over; Abilene, a juvenile-geared Wild West town reconstruction; and the Eisenhower Center, preserving the boyhood home and presidential library of Dwight Eisenhower, as well as a museum dedicated to him. He is also buried on the grounds...but his bones have not yet been unearthed for public viewing.

KENTUCKY

A MUSEUM TO A CHICKENMAN

It's hard to take seriously a man who devoted his life to chicken. But when the man becomes a legend, it's a different story.

The nemesis of chickens worldwide, the man fryers would love to roast, Colonel Harland Sanders, even years after his death, remains an international icon for good fowl food. He founded Kentucky Fried Chicken (now called KFC and, since 1986, a subsidiary of PepsiCo) and coined one of the most familiar catch phrases in American history, even if "Finger-lickin' good" pales alongside "With malice toward none, with charity for all."

And in Kentucky, the man who turned chicken cutlets into cash cows, metaphorically speaking, is golden. On the first floor of an ornately columned white mansion at 1441 Gardiner Lane in Louisville (KFC's international headquarters), a plushly carpeted, track lighting-equipped museum pays tribute to good old-fashioned American business sense.

A 25-minute film produced by Alfred Viola and written by Cherney Berg plays fequently in the anteroom. And though parts of "Portrait of a Legend," consisting of interviews with Sanders when he was 75, provoke titters (for example, Tom Glazer's catchy song that links Sanders with Daniel Boone and Davy Crockett as pioneering trailblazers), the film lays the legend of the cooking colonel who overcame a poverty-stricken birth in southern Indiana in 1890 and became an aggressive Kentucky entrepreneur.

Only five when his father died, he learned cooking from his mother so he could help her raise himself and his two siblings. He made his first loaf of bread at seven and carried it three miles to show his mother as she worked in a canning factory. He left school in the sixth grade because he couldn't deal with algebra (his teacher "started mixing the numbers and the alphabet together"). A succession of jobs followed: army service in Cuba; train fireman; insurance salesman; streetcar conductor; ferry operator. A service station stint led to his experimenting with providing food for his trucker customers. He managed a motel and restaurant.

Then one day, in the early 1930s, the man whose mustache and goatee would later turn as white as his hair, hit upon a concept that was to eventually enshrine him in the pantheon of poultry: he began doing chicken in a pressure cooker, succeeding where others had failed. He added a delectable blend of seasonings, his vaunted "11 different herbs and spices." And with the help of keen marketing skills, his Corbin, Kentucky chicken and country ham business gradually became known as the best restaurant between Cincinnati, Ohio and Atlanta, Georgia.

Around age 65, when a new interstate highway routed traffic away from his business, he took his food on the road, selling the recipe to restauranteurs. Franchises followed, and the honorary colonel (who had been inducted into the Order of the Kentucky Colonels in 1935) became the king of capons.

The poultry industry loved him for his contributions to chicken consumption in an age when Americans preferred red meat; the Southeastern Poultry & Egg Association named him its "Man of the Century" in 1979 and the National Restaurant Association once gave him an award in the form of a wire chicken that has laid a golden egg and flaps when a button is pressed.

The museum takes a straightforward look at its honoree: a life-size statue of Sanders in his trademark white Palm Beach suit and black string tie which made him look neat and "stand out;" photographs ranging from his childhood to his international personal appearances (at his peak, the peripatetic poultry patriarch logged more than a quarter-million miles annually); humanitarian awards (he donated most of his earnings to university scholarships and charities for the young and the afflicted).

A 10-minute gem of a videotape shows five vintage, funny American TV commercials for his product, a pair of Japanese TV ads, and snippets from TV interviews in which he relates how he improved his mother's old chicken recipe and expresses amusement at being told he is more recognizable than the current U.S. president.

The exhibits flesh out the business profile of a man who received half a dozen honorary doctoral degrees and whose portrait Norman Rockwell painted, of the man who sold his multi-million-dollar business in 1964, was appointed Kentucky's Ambassador of Good Will in 1972, and presided over the museum's opening in 1978 from an office he kept on the same floor.

Many of the novelty artifacts jog the memory: an original "Bucket-O-Chicken" (minus its load, of course); a "Barrel-O-Chicken," the greasy paper container that held enough pullet pieces to please "'10' normal appetites;" an original individual dinner (chicken, mashed potatoes, and roll) box with its now-embarrassing side panel containing the lyrics and bar music to Stephen Foster's "My Old Kentucky Home" ("The sun shines bright in the old Kentucky home, 'Tis summer, the darkies are gay").

Recordings augment displays showcasing one of his original pressure cookers, which turned out chicken chunks crisp on the outside and tender and moist on the inside in seven minutes, and one of his many all-white suits (he bought a half-dozen new ones every year, heavy English wool for the winter, lighter blends for the summer).

The museum is free and usually sparsely attended. Even watching the film and video, you can tour in less than an hour. The hours correspond with a normal first shift, Monday through Thursday, and are limited on Friday to the morning. The facility is closed holidays and weekends.

To reach the museum, take Exit 15 (Newburg Road) from Interstate Highway 264 East. At the intersection of Newburg Road and Bishop Lane, turn right and proceed about a quarter-mile, then turn right onto Atkinson Drive which takes you to Gardiner

Lane. Park in the visitors' lot and enter through the front, past a bust of Sanders done by his daughter Margaret in 1971 and presented to him by KFC employees and franchisees on his 81st birthday. A receptionist will guide you to the museum. Unfortunately, no complimentary chicken is served, although you'll seem to smell it while you tour, if you visit at the right time (a functioning kitchen exists below the museum, and the aromas waft upward).

Sanders died in Louisville on December 16, 1980 and is buried about four miles, as the crow flies, north of the museum in Louisville's Cave Hill Cemetery, the resting place of Revolutionary War hero George Rogers Clark. From the museum, take Newburg Road north into Louisville proper. Continue as the road becomes Baxter Avenue. At the intersection of Baxter and Broadway, turn right to enter the cemetery. The grave is in Section 33, near the easternmost portion, and set back from the road. A bronze bust of Harland Sanders, also done by daughter Margaret, occupies the center of a columned monument resembling the side of a Greek temple.

Famed for the Kentucky Derby at Churchill Downs the first Saturday in May, Louisville also has mansions, an art center, a zoo, research centers, a planetarium, and a host of museums commemorating the Derby, state history, international art, the railroad, and science.

THE COKE CAPITAL OF KENTUCKY

In 1886, Georgia pharmacist John Styth Pemberton created a syrup. That same year, Frank Mason Robinson, who worked as a bookkeeper for Pemberton Chemical Company, gave it a name - Coca-Cola - and spelled it in its distinctive Spencerian script. Also that year, Jacob's Pharmacy in Atlanta sold the first batch of Coke. In 1888, Asa Griggs Candler traded $2,300 for the uncontested rights to the product. Four years later, he founded the Coca-Cola Company in Atlanta.

Today, Coca-Cola is headquartered in Atlanta; so also is the world's largest collection of Coke artifacts.

So how does the Bluegrass State enter the picture?

Well, in 1901, production of the carbonated beverage had spread to Kentucky, and Fred S. Schmidt began managing a Louisville bottling plant. The plant moved over the years, but the descendants of Schmidt still make the stuff at a modern facility two miles northwest of Elizabethtown along U.S. Highway 31W. And the Schmidt Coca-Cola Memorabilia Museum owns and exhibits the largest private collection of Coke items anywhere in the world.

The Schmidt family allows free access to the plant and production line and, most tasteful of all, the help-yourself Coke counter service in its attractive lobby, where koi swim in a manmade pool surrounded by ferns and plants beneath a mural of stained glass mosaics.

The self-guiding tour conducts visitors along an elevated platform overlooking several production line phases. Informational plaques along the way identify what you see happening at blurring speed: an H&R 120 valve filler depositing soda in 12-ounce aluminum cans at the rate of 1,350 a minute; a "Carbo Cooler" that "proportions syrup and water," cools the mix, and carbonates it; a can warmer that ensures the containers reach room temperature prior to packaging; several other fillers that pump the soft drink into five-gallon containers, 16-ounce glass bottles, and 2-liter containers; a bottle washer that does what it promises to do; and electronic bottle inspectors that guarantee no deficiencies. The production area is clean, efficient, and noisy. You may or may not see "the real thing" being processed; the plant makes myriad other carbonated beverages as well.

The elevated gallery leads to a museum and huge warehouse where at least hundreds of thousands of bottles of various soft drinks stand in towering stacks of cases awaiting shipment.

The museum charges a modest fee and presents a light-hearted look at Coke's early days: portraits and information on Coke's founding fathers and its initial merchandising as a medicine (a turn-of-the-century clock proclaims Coke as "The Ideal Brain Tonic Delightful Beverage Specific for Headache - Relieves Exhaustion"); sheet music for "My Coca Cola Bride," a 1907 ditty that claims Coke "'Twould quench the thirst ev'n of a fish," and whose back cover calls the drink "a delightful palatable & healthful beverage...for business and professional Men students wheelmen athletes...the favorite drink for Ladies when thirsty & weary despondent...."; other mementos of a more innocent time that push Coke as a "temperance beverage" for people whose work necessitates "Sustained Brain Effort or Continued Muscular Exertion;" information on the genesis of the drink (the coca leaves of South American shrubs and the nuts and fruits of tropical African cola trees); a huge reconstructed soda fountain, complete with mannequins, once displayed at the Columbian Exhibition of Chicago in the 1890s.

A glut of Coke-related items takes you down memory lane: three dozen red metal coolers and soda dispensers of all sizes and shapes; an old Coke billboard from a barn; old-fashioned six-packs, each a quarter plus deposit; advertising posters and magazine ads spanning the years from World War I to Vietnam; the familiar hourglass bottles; case upon display case of unrelated merchandise that nonetheless advertised Coke, including such oddball items as metal swastika key rings, thimbles, candy and gum, and fly swatters.

Space permits only a third of the museum's holdings to be displayed at any time. Plans call for a larger facility, one that will include actual delivery trucks.

The whole site can be toured in a half-hour to an hour weekdays, except major holidays, during normal daytime hours. Visitation averages 35,000 annually. A small gift counter adjoins the museum. And the ever-popular lobby soda fountain dispenses cupfuls of complimentary carbonation: Classic Coke, Diet Coke, and one or two other flavors, generally including a non-cola. You may slake your thirst at will.

A nonprofit corporation founded to preserve and showcase classic bits of advertising reflecting America's passion for one of the most universal drinks, Schmidt's Museum willingly accepts donated items.

Elizabethtown is slightly more than 40 miles south of Louisville along Interstate Highway 65. It also has the Brown-Pusey Community House (a restored stagecoach inn) and Lincoln Heritage House (a house Abraham Lincoln's father helped build). Two other places associated with Lincoln are nearby: his birthplace, a national historic site, a dozen miles southeast and below Hodgenville; and his boyhood home near White City, 15 miles southeast. And Bardstown, with its historical and whiskey museums and "The Stephen Foster Story" outdoor musical production, lies 25 miles northeast.

LOUISIANA

THE WORLD'S LONGEST BRIDGE OVER WATER

Twenty-four miles of stone and steel suspended over a body of water Mother Nature never intended man to traverse in such fashion - the longest bridge ferrying highway traffic over water anywhere in the world.

And it's probably not where you think. It's not California's famous Bay Bridge, connecting San Francisco with Oakland, not Florida's Sunshine Skyway, linking St. Petersburg with the Bradenton area. Nor is it Virginia's Chesapeake Bay Bridge Tunnel, spanning the waters that commingle when the Chesapeake Bay bleeds into the Atlantic Ocean.

Surprisingly, it's the Lake Pontchartrain Causeway in Louisiana, north of New Orleans, which dwarfs all other over-water bridges. Buttressed by pier clusters every few yards, it consists of two northbound and two southbound lanes, each span separated from its mate by yards of rippling water. Regularly spaced crossover pulloffs connect the pairs of opposing lanes and are wide enough for sightseers to temporarily park in or take photographs; fishing is not allowed.

On a foggy or hazy day, it's possible to reach the midpoint and not see land anywhere, as though you're out to sea; although on most days, you'll be able to glimpse a bit of Chinchuba or Mandeville to the north and New Orleans to the south.

The majority of the causeway's traffic stems from daily commuters, shaving time and miles off travel along the circuitous ring of interstate highways that tightly encircles the oval lake. The fee is extremely modest ($1 per vehicle, each way, in the early '90s) for such a long span, probably the cheapest per-mile ride in America.

Simple in design and construction, the bridge hovers close to the water, only occasionally rising and falling to allow the passage of sea vessels. It also opens a little north of midsection to permit tall-masted ships to pass. From the air, the bridge looks like two thin parallel lengths of string. It came up in little more than a year, reaching completion in the summer of 1956 at a cost exceeding $50 million.

Traffic moves briskly at 55 mph, and the pulloffs are generally empty. Emergency phone hookups stand at frequent intervals.

Fewer than 10 miles northwest of New Orleans' French Quarter, the causeway attracts only a small percentage of the millions who party in the city annually. Riding over water for such a long period is a different experience...and a sedate one seemingly worlds removed from the boisterous hedonism of its big city neighbor.

To reach the bridge from New Orleans, exit Interstate Highway 10 in Metairie at Causeway Boulevard and follow the signs. To get to the causeway from the north, exit Interstate 12 at Chinchuba and Mandeville.

THE VALHALLA OF PIRATES AND WITCHES

She was born in New Orleans in 1794, when Louisiana was not even an American possession. A free mulatto, she lived at 1020 St. Ann Street in the French Quarter of the city and gave up hairdressing for voodoo, a cult practice that mixed religious symbols with black magic, mysticism, and ritualistic entreaty to the gods. She took on clients and concocted potions to bring them good fortune and wreak vengeance on their enemies.

Her rituals often involved decadent dancing with snakes and pairs of scantily attired couples whose gyrations often led to uninhibited sex in front of her patrons, generally the wealthy and socially prominent. The revelers frequently partook of alcohol as well as animal blood. The police never intervened because they believed in her ability to foretell the future and bring either good luck or bad luck with her incantations.

Supposedly intelligent, she apparently indulged in the excesses of her profession only to provide her customers with the lusty shocks they wanted. She reportedly gave birth 15 times and also tended the sick. Rumor said she embraced Catholicism in her advanced years and lived to renounce her past. She died in 1881 at 87.

Her name was Marie Laveau, New Orleans' fabled "Voodoo Queen." Today, her remains reside in one of the Crescent City's most fascinating and least visited corners, one of its many aboveground "cities of the dead."

The graveyards of New Orleans are intriguing, foreboding, and historic. Some graves carry memorial plaques, others are unmarked and unornamented. Some crypts have fine statuary and architecture, others are decrepit eyesores. They honor pirates and poets, governors and ghosts, the famous, infamous, and anonymous.

With a 35-foot altitude and a water table a yard or less underneath the surface of the ground, New Orleans depends heavily on levees to contain the rampaging waters of the Mississippi River when they occasionally rise higher than street level. The city also needed to protect its dead and centuries ago began the custom of entombing within above-ground vaults. Though modern technology has alleviated the problem of moisture-packed earth, New Orleans' cemeteries continue to rely on traditional entombments with a nod to the past.

The crypts vary in size from single units partially or wholly above the earth to family temples with access steps, side urns, and peaked roofs with cornices, entablatures, and statues and even mass-production mausoleums 100 or more feet long and stacked four-high.

The oldest cemeteries are just northwest of the French Quarter: St. Louis Cemetery Number One fills the space between Basin, Conti, Treme, and St. Louis Streets; St. Louis Cemetery Number Two lies a few blocks farther north, just east of the Bienville Street-North Claiborne Avenue intersection. The largest, Metairie (or Lake Lawn) Cemetery, occupies a large area across Interstate Highway 10 from Greenwood, Cypress Grove, and other cemeteries, just east of the New Orleans-Metairie border and southwest of City Park. And St. Louis Cemetery Number Three, a popular destination for tour buses because of its accessibility, crops up between Esplanade Avenue and Desaix Boulevard, just east of City Park.

St. Louis Number One contains several notable crypts: Paul Morphy (1837-1884), a chess wizard, the Bobby Fischer of his day, considered the world's greatest, the conqueror of a Hungarian champion when he was all of 13; Etienne Bore (1741-1820), New Orleans' first mayor and the first person to market granulated sugar;

Bernard deMarigny deMandeville (1785-1868), a seminal politician in early city history; Clarice Duralde Claiborne, the young wife of William Charles Cole Claiborne, American governor of Louisiana, who died at 21 in 1809 before her husband could help Andrew Jackson and Jean Laffite defend the city against the British invasion. Historical plaques identify their crypts.

No one knows where Laffite himself is buried. But one of his trusted henchmen, Dominique You, lies in a crypt in St. Louis Number Two. A smuggling buccaneer like Laffite, You served honorably during the Battle of New Orleans, received a pardon for his piratical activities, then lived as a swaggering hero till his 1830 death. The New Orleans Archdiocesan Cemeteries restored his tomb in 1977 and today it is the cleanest crypt in its row. The inscription on his tomb calls him an "INTREPID WARRIOR" who "COULD HAVE WITNESSED THE ENDING OF THE WORLD WITHOUT TREMBLING."

Governor Claiborne is entombed within the Metairie Cemetery on Metairie Avenue in Section 12. Steps lead to the crypt, and a cross rises above the semicircular hump at its apex. A stone summarizes highlights in the life of the Virginian who served as a Tennessee politician, became territorial governor of first Mississippi and then Louisiana, and then became a state governor and U.S. senator before his 1817 death at 42.

The same cemetery memorializes 20th-century Louisiana historian and scholar Stanley Clisby Arthur in a crypt north of Avenue B in Section 94.

The most remarkable crypt - actually crypts - purports to hold the bones of Marie Laveau in St. Louis Number One. Her three-tiered Greek Revival crypt in the southern section of the graveyard carries a plaque explaining the "NOTORIOUS 'VOODOO QUEEN.'" But more noticeable are the "X"s plastered across the facade, across the inscriptions to the tomb's occupants, and even across the historical plaque, the work of modern occultists who believe her spirit still wanders the earth, haunting the city where she worked her miracles and waiting to be summoned into service by the scratching of "X"s that will rouse the human will that slumbers within the tomb. Some visitors deposit flowers, candles, religious objects, vases, and coins at the shrine; others take objects, usually particles of plaster, chipped paint, and soil from surrounding plots for their own cult use. The "X"s are inscribed with colored pencil or crayon or paint, occasionally blood.

To add to the mystique, Laveau actually may be entombed in a smaller twin-tiered sepulchre farther west and along the wall, next to Conti Street, a little south of deMarigny's crypt. Though unmarked, the telltale "X"s crosshatching the entire front indicate that Laveau's followers believe she secretly rests inside.

The newer cemeteries and those farther away from the French Quarter are clean and well-kept. Crypts in the shape of mosques, temples, even European palaces with porticos and sculpted arches straddling classical columns populate them. Others, particularly St. Louis Numbers One and Two, show their age. Crypts are often crumbling heaps of mortar and brick, their inscriptions long gone, their inhabitants long forgotten. A plaque near the northern boundary of Number One minces no words:

> PROBABLY THE OLDEST EXTANT WALL VAULTS, A TYPE OF BURIAL FACILITY SINGULAR TO NEW ORLEANS, THIS ROW OF CRYPTS SEPARATED THE PROTESTANT AREA FROM THE MAIN AREA OF THE CEMETERY. AS FAMILIES DIED OUT OR MOVED AWAY, TIME AND THE UNRELENTING ELEMENTS TOOK THEIR TOLL.

The cemeteries are open daily during daytime hours. Only the one on Esplanade Avenue, Number Three, with its venerable Creole family crypts, is likely to attract busloads of tourists.

The National Park Service, operating from an information center at 527 St. Ann Street, east of Jackson Square, conducts 90-minute walking tours of Number One, including both Laveau vaults. The center opens daily during normal daytime hours.

Once completely safe, Numbers One and Two are considered questionable today. A plaque near the front gate of Number One warns:

> VISITORS ARE WELCOME BUT ENTER THESE PREMISES AT THEIR OWN RISK. NO SECURITY NOR GUARDS ARE PROVIDED AND THE NEW ORLEANS ARCHDIOCESAN CEMETERIES DISCLAIMS RESPONSIBILITY FOR THE PERSONAL SAFETY OF VISITORS AND THEIR PROPERTY.

New Orleans cringes under some of the highest per-capita murder and crime rates in the nation. The cemeteries have narrow alleys, irregularly shaped crypts, and angular heights that create a world of hidden crevices and paths more familiar to local pickpockets than first-time visitors. We visited all the cemeteries, including Numbers One and Two, a number of times and alone; we saw no one and lived to tell of it. But Number Two lies amidst project housing, and fate is better left untempted. If you go to any of the cemeteries with a small group and stay together, you should be safe.

Since virtually no one comes to New Orleans for its graveyards, you will have a world of ageless architecture and forgotten humanity to yourself. The world-famous food, jazz, and all-night revelry await you in the French Quarter.

MAINE

THE DESERT
THAT ATE A FARM

Some 6,000 years before the birth of Christ, in the most recent Ice Age, a glacier moved across a portion of northeastern North America. Churning up the earth's surface, rearranging the topography, it left sand and mineral deposits as souvenirs - the makings of a desert.

Then, over the thousands of years, vegetation sprouted and covered the sands.

Sooner or later, man entered the picture. He learned to talk. And migrate. And farm.

Finally, in the years after the Revolutionary War, William Tuttle began operating a 300-acre farm near modern Freeport, Maine. He grew potatoes, vegetables, and hay, cultivated apples, and herded. He and his family kept busy but neglected to rotate crops, depleting the topsoil. The Tuttles also cleared much of the land, selling the lumber to neighboring railroads, and turned their herds loose to graze. They unwittingly eroded the soil over a secret desert hidden beneath them, and the cattle chewed the grass down to its roots.

With nothing but mineral-poor soil remaining as a cover, the underlying sand poked through the surface and began seeping out. It took over completely in short time, creating a living desert, overwhelming vegetation and small trees, and knocking the Tuttle farm out of business. It spread throughout the acres. Winds eventually were to create sand dunes as high as 50 feet.

The Tuttles and others who inherited or bought the old farm did the only thing they could with the failed farmland: turn it into a tourist attraction, the Desert of Maine, an actual desert in one of the least likely places, just a few miles away from the Atlantic Ocean.

Today, the desert can be toured via a motorized, canopied wagon with a narrated tour. Along the way, you come across trees partially buried by the shifting sands, moss and clay beds, a section of colored sands, and the highest point overlooking a 70-foot drop to the desert floor. Of particular interest is the site of a spring house, built along a stream in 1938, that is now under more than two dozen feet of sand.

The tours are educational and folksy and depart every half-hour. Afterward, visitors can walk across the hot sands or through the cool shade of the tree-lined nature trail on one side of the desert.

Markers provide information on this most unlikely of deserts, and a museum housed in the 1783 barn, the only pre-desert building still standing, collects sands from deserts around the world, colored sand paintings (including the world's largest), farm implements, and clippings documenting the 20th century's use of the desert for films and tours.

The desert's residents include raccoons, foxes, porcupines, skunks, rabbbits, deer, moose, squirrels, and chipmunks (and once a black bear who escaped from confinement and went on the lam in the desert), but you'll most likely encounter only others of your own species.

Bearing the same attributes of most of the world's larger and more famous deserts, the Desert of Maine can move about a foot a year (the rate at which the blowing sands approach adjoining non-desert territory); but as the desert piles up more sand in different areas, new vegetation crops up at about the same rate elsewhere, keeping the size fairly constant. The desert supposedly contains over 100 different sand tints, most brilliantly seen after rainfalls, and sand artists create vials of various designs in an adjacent shop.

A gift store sells average-priced admission tickets and finished sand artwork. A campground and picnic area are only yards away.

The Desert of Maine is well marked on Desert Road, off U.S.

Interstate Highway 95, just west of Freeport. It is open daily from early morning till dusk, from mid-May to mid-October. Historic Freeport, the city of L. L. Bean, boasts of more than a hundred outlet stores.

MARYLAND

THE HOUSE WHERE A BABE WAS BORN

He was the greatest figure in all of sports, a giant, a blazing meteor slicing through a constellation of luminous stars making up the firmament of America's first great age of celebrity idolatry. He became more beloved than world leaders. The term "superstar" had yet to be coined, but it easily could have been minted for George Herman Ruth.

In the minds of millions who saw him play or heard of his prowess with a few pounds of lumber in his hands, "Babe" Ruth will always be associated with New York, where he spun the threads of a legendary lifestyle as easily as he launched home runs into orbit for the Yankees in the stadium christened "The House That Ruth Built."

Yet this human deity had humble origins. And Baltimore, not New York, claims him as its native son. The house where he lived during his mischievous childhood is now gone, fittingly enough displaced by left center field in Oriole Park at Camden Yards, the home of baseball's Baltimore Orioles.

But his grandparents' home at the intersection of Dover and Emory Streets, a couple blocks to the northwest, is still around, having been converted into a shrine to the "Bambino" and a museum to Maryland baseball and the Orioles. It became a National Historic Landmark in 1973 and opened as a museum a year later.

A simple, uneducated man with a kindred outlook on life, Babe Ruth was revered in his lifetime for his 714 career home runs, including 60 homers in 1927, both baseball records long after Ruth's 1948 death. Revisionist sports historians note that he was a problem child, an adulterer, a self-absorbed glutton (a typical meal included half a dozen hot dogs, a half-gallon of beer, and a quart of ice cream). Museum staffmembers maintain the actual wiener count often reached 18 at a sitting and verify that his favorite food was smoked eel. His admirers say he donated time and resources to orphans and the underprivileged. His detractors call them effortless gestures from a self-indulgent slob.

Still, the man, so often larger than life, elevated the sport to the same status. And some say the history of baseball really means the history of Babe Ruth.

The Babe Ruth Birthplace and Baseball Center, at 216 Emory Street, in the heart of Baltimore's historic district, is an homage to Ruth. Most of his historic baseball artifacts are in the Baseball Hall of Fame in Cooperstown, New York, but Baltimore's version is not exactly an orphan with its collection of bats and balls associated with him.

And a few items deliver emotional appeal, revealing the human legend of Ruth in a way that Cooperstown's largeness precludes.

There is the ball Ruth gave Jake Giser on August 11, 1929 in Cleveland in a trade for the one Giser had earlier that day caught - Ruth's 500th career home run, at a time when no one else had hit 500 home runs. Ruth signed the substitute ball for Giser: "Received in exchange for my 500th homer. Babe Ruth."

There is the display case devoted to Johnny Sylvester. Young Johnny was 11 in 1926 when he fell from a horse and came down with bone marrow inflammation. Given a poor prognosis for recovery, Johnny received an autographed ball from Ruth on October 5 with a promise that the Yankee slugger would hit a home run for him the next day in the World Series. True to his word, Ruth walloped a trio of homers. When Johnny received the ball bearing Ruth's promise and then heard that Ruth had knocked three round-trippers, he miraculously recovered. Ruth visited the boy on October 11 and said, "He's some kid...I'm glad my hits helped him." Johnny went on to graduate from Princeton in 1937 and became a 25-year corporate president. He died in 1989. The ball Ruth signed for him is exhibited.

There is the school hymnal found at St. Mary's Industrial School in Baltimore with its inside cover message: "George H. Ruth, worlds worse singer - worlds best pitcher."

George H. Ruth may not have been the world's best speller, but he was well on his way to becoming one of the premier pitchers in baseball (92 wins, 44 losses; 2.24 ERA; 486 strikeouts) when the New York Yankees converted him into an outfielder to fully capitalize on his penchant for hitting prolific and prodigious home runs. More than anything else, including his .342 batting average and 2,873 hits, Ruth is noted for his home runs. An alcove of the museum devotes itself to the 14 (at this writing) major leaguers who joined the exclusive 500-home run club.

Two films (one on Ruth's life; the other a folksy collection of pages from Ruth's scrapbook illustrating, in rare home movies, private and public moments in his life) alternately play in the little theater within the main shrine room which holds many of his mementos. The films show Ruth as a superman of sport, a boisterous clown, a Herculean blend of profligacy and power, and - in his last few months - a slowly dying 53-year-old shell, ravaged by a throat cancer that aged him 20 years, rasping out his thanks to a world that had not forgotten him, a pitiful specter, a symbol of a perceived invincible era suddenly forced to pay for its run in the sun.

The museum has some nice touches. A wall bears 714 plaques, one for each of his career home runs, each containing information on when and where that home run was hit. Baseball bats become rail posts on the staircase that ascends to the room where Ruth was born on February 6, 1895. An upstairs exhibit explains how baseball bats are made (40- to 50-year-old white ash trees in Pennsylvania and New York, noted for their "tough, hard wood with whip and resilience," are felled, split apart into 40-inch billets, seasoned for a year, and then shaped into bats; each tree becomes approximately 60 bats).

One room carries the Maryland Baseball Hall of Fame and displays artifacts of its famous native sons, including major leaguers Jimmie Foxx and Al Kaline. A larger room houses the history of the Baltimore Orioles. The oldest baseball in Maryland, dating back to sometime around 1870, a single-stitched relic fashioned from a leather sheath and looking as old as the pharaohs, also is on display.

Current years have seen annual attendance rise upward of 50,000. That figure may dramatically balloon with anticipated changes. A $3.3-million expansion will quintuple the current size. And another building, currently a warehouse a short block south, will combine with the current house to form the projected Babe Ruth Museum Baseball Center. A huge entrance lobby, videowall, 380-seat lecture hall, 220-seat banquet hall, baseball timewalk, rooftop restaurant, and interactive computer and laser displays are planned.

The museum is currently open daily, but with fluctuating hours: 10 a.m.-4 p.m. most of the time; a later closing hour during spring and summer; a still-later closing hour when the Baltimore Orioles are playing a couple blocks away. A moderate admission is charged, and a parking lot is available one block north on Pratt Street, just west of Emory. If you like baseball and the Babe, you'll spend hours watching all the videos and reading all the statistics.

A RAVEN'S GRAVE, A PLOTTER'S PLOT

Two of America's most saturnine figures lie in separate Baltimore cemeteries within two miles of each other, as the raven flies. They never knew each other, but they had much in common.

Both lived considerable portions of their lives elsewhere, in other cities of the East. Both were free spirits and gifted artists, the one a poet, the other an actor. The poet became as famous for a melancholy, lugubrious, decadent lifestyle. The actor, one of the foremost tragedians of his day, saw his artistic fame eclipsed by the most dramatic single moment of his century.

Both died alone, young, and tragically: the poet by the bottle and the disease it had wrought, the actor by the bullet of a soldier.

Edgar Allan Poe wrote some of the best-known poems and short stories in the American literary canon: "The Raven," "The Cask of Amontillado," "The Pit and the Pendulum," "The Mystery of Marie Roget," "The Fall of the House of Usher." His works radiate nefarious shadows of malignancy, evil, torment, and disfigured human relationships. If any 19th-century body of American work is sardonically skewed from the mainstream, it is Poe's.

The man himself was odd-looking, ungainly, at times pathetic, at other times nearly frightening. He acerbically castigated his artistic contemporaries, dressed in dark clothing, and drank to excess. He died at 40 on October 7, 1849 of any of several possibilities: concussion caused by hitting his head in a drunken fall, cirrhosis, rabies, or pneumonia coupled with brain congestion. He had earlier that month been discovered, confused and bumbling, on a Baltimore street and been taken to a hospital to die in a delirious, hallucinogenic state.

John Wilkes Booth was the son of Junius Brutus Booth, one of America's finest stage actors. With striking good looks and a commanding presence, he became a popular entertainer and idol. He carried a number of photographs of ladies and was betrothed at the close of the Civil War.

He had everything going for him...but one thing. A secret southern sympathizer throughout the war, he could not abide the thought of the Confederacy going down to defeat. With the war obviously and irretrievably lost, he plotted to kill the President of the United States, the hated northern leader. He engaged a coterie of conspirators, formulated plans, and carried them out to their tragic conclusion. Several years shy of his 30th birthday, he put a bullet into Abraham Lincoln's brain on April 14, 1865 and wound up taking one himself less than two weeks later with his dying words "Tell mother, tell mother. I died for my country."

They both ended up in Baltimore graveyards, Poe in Westminster Cemetery at the southeast corner of the intersection of Fayette and Greene Streets and Booth in the mammoth Green Mount Cemetery to the northeast.

An air of mystery surrounds both interments. Poe was originally buried in the eastern portion of the cemetery that contains the graves of a Baltimore mayor and several soldiers and officers of the Wars of the Revolution and 1812. A stone currently stands on the site of his first burial where he lay undisturbed from October 9, 1849 to November 17, 1875. His most famous verse - "Quoth the Raven, 'Nevermore'." - adorns the top of the tombstone.

On that latter date, his remains were unearthed and moved to the entrance of the burial ground, the northwest angle. He is now buried under a tomb that bears his likeness and contains the names and life dates of himself, his wife (whom he married when she was barely a teen-ager and who died in her early 20s), and his mother-in-law. An historical marker on the outside wall maintains the tomb was "constructed in part with pennies collected from Baltimore schoolchildren." Indeed, pennies and other coins often lean against a ledge of the tomb under Poe's visage, a tribute to the enduring appeal of an author who has fired the imaginations of generations of scholars and bohemians alike.

The grave swirls in controversy. Some students of Poe claim the body buried beneath the tomb is not Poe's. They say the wrong skeleton was exhumed in 1875. They reason thusly: the first grave never had a tombstone; one was ordered but accidentally damaged before emplacement; a substitute never came; the one tombstone that marked the Poe family's plots vanished, throwing the entire network of graves into confusion; Poe's coffin was oaken, lined with lead, and bore a brass plate; the one exhumed in 1875, nearly fallen apart, was made of mahogany, contained neither lead nor brass, and yielded a 5'10"-skeleton (Poe was two inches shorter) wearing buckled shoes of an earlier period and a swatch of leather around the neck indicative of a soldier's collar. These proponents suggest the skeleton is, in fact, Private Philip Mosher, who died during the War of 1812 and was supposedly buried in a mahogany coffin. Poe authorities debunk the theory as rubbish.

Further adding to the mystery is the appearance every year on his birthday, January 19, of a Poe devotee who steals into the cemetery during the night and anonymously gifts Poe's ghost with a bottle of cognac or liqueur and either a rose or a bouquet of them. Though many people have stood vigil on that date over the years, they have reportedly either grown tired or fearful during the ghoulish watch and left before the phantom appeared, creating a creepy scenario entirely to Poe's liking. Then in 1990, photographer Bill Ballenberg employed a hidden camera, infra-red equipment, and a remote control to photograph a man, wearing a hat and with a scarf wrapped around his lower face, kneeling at the grave at 3 a.m. In subsequent years, vigilant observers have seen a male figure at the grave.

Poe reputedly often traipsed through the cemetery's hundred-year-old vaults (replaced by an adjoining church built in 1849). Some believe Poe used the sojourns to conjure up creative ideas;

others think the macabre author occasionally slept in one of the vaults.

Booth was secretly buried in the family plot at Green Mount Cemetery alongside his illustrious father. An obelisk serves as family tombstone. Its obverse features a left profile of Junius Brutus Booth nearly encircled by a laurel wreath and the words "IN THE SAME GRAVE WITH JUNIUS BRUTUS BOOTH IS BURIED THE BODY OF MARY ANN, HIS WIFE, WHO SURVIVED HIM 38 YEARS." The reverse carries the family name and the names of the children, including "JOHN WILKES," in a vertical column. It is the world's only monument to the memory of Lincoln's assassin.

The Booth plot occupies Lots 9 and 10 in the Dogwood Section (the south central portion of the cemetery), close to Hoffman Street. The cemetery office, just north of the intersection of Greenmount Avenue and Hoffman Street, provides maps. The Booths share eternal space with over 60,000 people, including notables like philanthropist Johns Hopkins, Confederate General Joseph E. Johnston, poet Sidney Lanier, and CIA director Allen Dulles. The cemetery identifies Booth on its roster of famous people as an "actor." His exact grave is not marked but is near the obelisk. You will stand over it and not realize it.

Fans of Poe may also want to tour the Poe House at 203 Amity Street, a few blocks northwest of his burial ground in a questionable neighborhood. It has irregular hours and delivers the same message as other Poe homes scattered throughout eastern cities. You might want to steer clear of the cemetery at dusk; its maze of tombstones, barrel-roofed vaults, and narrow passageways will look twice as eerie.

Both gravesites can be done in an hour; few, if any, other visitors should be encountered.

MASSACHUSETTS

THE REAL ADAMS FAMILY

There are two quintessential "Addams" (or "Adams") families: the one with Gomez and Morticia, Uncle Fester and Lurch who live in cartoons, TV shows, and movies; and the other one from Quincy, Massachusetts.

The latter clan may have been, through the generations, the most accomplished family in American history. No other family has produced a father and son who both became American presidents or a woman who became the wife of one president and the mother of another.

John Adams, the Second President (1797-1801), was the first to occupy the White House and the one to live the longest - 90 years and eight months. Prior to his presidency, he had been a delegate to the Continental Congresses, a drafter and signer of the Declaration of Independence, a foreign commissioner and minister, and a vice president. He lived more than 25 years after his presidency and deeply loved his wife, his "dearest friend," until the day she died. He died in Quincy, the town of his birth, on the 50th anniversary of the Declaration of Independence and during the presidency of his son.

Abigail Smith Adams was one of the nation's most intelligent, educated, and articulate first ladies. She gave birth to five children and witnessed the death of three in her lifetime. She became her husband's constant support and his conscience. The first audible voice for equal rights in the history of the United States, she urged her delegate-husband in March 1777 to "remember the ladies and be more generous and favorable to them than your ancestors." She gently pointed out to him that "all men would be tyrants if they could" and promised that women "will not hold ourselves bound by any laws in which we have no voice or representation."

John Quincy Adams was born in Quincy, where his father was born and where both his parents died. A scholar and lawyer like his father, he became an overseas diplomatic minister, senator, secretary of state, and the Sixth President of the United States (1825-29). The first of only a handful of chief executives to resume a distinguished public career after his presidency, he became a congressman, championed important issues, and received the affectionate sobriquet "Old Man Eloquent." A paralytic seizure struck him down at his congressional desk, and he died, uttering, "This is the last of earth. I am content."

Louisa Catherine Johnson Adams, during her term as first lady, offered a hospitality only glimpsed in previous administrations. She suffered the trauma of seeing three of her four children die in her lifetime and followed her husband's passing by four years. She joined him - and her in-laws - in the family crypt in the Adams Temple (the United First Parish Church).

Quincy enshrines the entwined lives of America's forgotten first family.

The Adams National Historic Site protects the three houses most singularly connected to the Adamses: the John Adams birthplace home, now more than 300 years old and where he wrote the first of his renowned letters to the lady who was to become his wife, is at 133 Franklin Street; the house in which John Quincy Adams was born, built in 1767 when he was born and the setting for the drafting of the Constitution of Massachusetts (which became the prototype for the U.S. Constitution), is at 141 Franklin Street; and the house most commonly associated with the Adamses, Peacefield, is at 135 Adams Street.

A Georgian clapboard mansion, Peacefield served four generations of Adamses. Dating to 1731, it became the focal point for the family from 1788 to 1927. The house holds the furnishings and artifacts that made post-presidential life bearable for both presidents (Thomas Jefferson defeated the elder Adams in his bid for re-election; Andrew Jackson did the same to the younger Adams): period furniture and heirlooms; an 18th-century garden; a carriage house; and a 14,000-volume library.

As historic and beautifully furnished as George Washington's Mount Vernon, Jefferson's Monticello, and Jackson's Hermitage, it receives nowhere near their visitation figures. The parlor has a unique four-sided love seat. The study, where John died, holds the upholstered chair in which he suffered his fatal seizure. The bed in which Abigail died still rests in her bedroom. The congressional desk at which John Quincy endured his fatal paralytic stroke now reposes in the library. Other generations of accomplished Adams descendants, including writers and historians, also lived in the house, adding their own individual legacies.

Elsewhere in Quincy, at 1306 Hancock Street, the United First Parish Church holds the Adams pew and plaques to the memory of the distinguished quartet. The undercroft, available to visitors with a church escort, contains an iron-gated room in which four sarcophagi - two each in either of a pair of alcoves - bear their earthly burdens. Nowhere else in America can visitors see and touch the side-by-side crypts of two presidents.

A new visitor center is nearby in the Galleria at President Place on Hancock Street.

A modest admission is charged for all three historic homes. The sites are open daily, mid-April through mid-November, during the day. Tours are conducted frequently. The church gives free tours daily, except Sunday, from Memorial Day to Labor Day, and otherwise by appointment (call 617-773-1290). Donations are accepted.

All four sites are within a mile or two of each other and easy to reach; they will take a few hours to tour. Quincy is just east of Interstate Highway 93, fewer than 10 miles south of central Boston. Once in Quincy, look for signs for the Adams sites...and a glimpse into the lives of two of America's most underappreciated presidents.

Potholes: large and small; some with still water;
others with roaring cascades.

FLOWERPOTS AND POTHOLES

Many thousands of years ago, a primeval glacier scraped across the northwestern Massachusetts terrain. Grinding millstones and swirling whirlpools lent their abrasive helping hands and, voila, potholes emerged from the granite. Today, dozens of potholes near the Deerfield River - some six inches in diameter, others several yards, and one, the world record holder, 39 feet across - stipple the earth with pockmarks that collect water from falls of varying heights cascading down the slope of the outcropping.

In the 18th century, Mohawk and Penobscot Indians freely roamed across the geological phenomenon known as Salmon Falls.

Then in 1908, across the river at a small community, a five-arch concrete bridge was built to allow a trolley to cross the Deerfield. Not wide enough to handle automobiles, the 400-foot bridge shut down with the trolley in 1928. Some time later, Mrs. Walter Burnham suggested beautifying the nonfunctioning span by planting dirt beds along its sides and stocking them with flowers and shrubs. The Shelburne Falls Woman's Club sponsored the task, and the bridge became the Bridge of Flowers. Today, a namesake committee tends its upkeep with financial help from the fire district (which owns the bridge), the towns of Buckland and Shelburne, the Woman's Club fundraisers, and donations.

A yard-wide gravel path slices through the parallel flower beds on either side of the bridge. You can walk across the bridge in a couple minutes, but you might want to tarry a bit longer and check out the explosion of color all around you. The bridge is open from May to October. During summer nights, lights illuminate the walkway until 10:30 p.m. Donations are accepted, and you might encounter a volunteer working on the flowers.

Just southeast of the bridge, you'll find the nation's largest single collection of potholes. Descending to them requires normal agility. Nature has sculpted some of them into smooth bucket-seat depressions. Waterfalls keep the water churning over the ledges and gurgling into some of the holes, creating private wading pools for swimmers. A street-level observation area affords an overall view of the potholes for those who might choose not to go down.

The bridge and the holes are in Shelburne, a few miles west of Interstate Highway 91 and along Massachusetts' Mohawk Trail (State Highway 2), a 55-mile road closely following a centuries-old footpath used by the Pocumtuck Indians before they were wiped out by New York's Mohawks in the vendetta violence that often marked relations between Native American tribes. The road and its environs include historic towns, arched and covered bridges, a towering Indian statue, the Hoosac Railroad Tunnel and a museum to the corridor and the 200 workers who died digging it, a natural bridge, the state's highest peak, craft shops, ski facilities, campgrounds, restaurants, state forests, and festivals.

Both the bridge and the potholes can be done at your leisure as part of the Mohawk Trail experience.

MICHIGAN

MICHIGAN'S MOTORIZED MUSIC MECCA

Man has been fascinated with mechanical music since he first learned to harness melodies to motors.

One of the country's better collections of mechanical music exists in the appropriately named Music House on the shores of the East Arm of Grand Traverse Bay in northern Michigan.

An average admission gets you a lengthy guided tour (well over an hour) of a place that is part museum, part entertainment palace, and part wistful nod to yesteryear.

The narrative is loaded with "bore and stroke," a term we lifted from a plaque describing the technical mechanics of a ship's engine in New Orleans. But not to worry. Chances are when your guide tells you that the Regina Orchestral Corona Model 34 music box, an 1899 product of the Music Box Company, Inc. of Rahway, New Jersey, runs by coil springs that trigger the changing mechanism and holds 27-inch-diameter steel discs, double cones, and more than 170 tongues, you'll probably only remember the John Philip Sousa march that blares out of it. And when you hear all about the Style RX Coin Piano with mandolin, violin, and flute pipes, made by the Link Piano Company, Inc. of Binghamton, New York to play 15 tunes coded on 300 feet of continuously rolling perforated paper, you'll probably only marvel at how it somehow managed to emerge unscathed from the 1907 fire that roared through San Francisco and destroyed the house it was in.

The Music House preserves vintage examples of mechanical music, painstakingly restored, if necessary, in reconstructed settings of area landmarks. The Regina Corona occupies a niche in the recreated general store formerly standing in Acme, a couple miles south. The reconstructed Hurry Back Saloon, once of 116 East Front Street, Traverse City, features a completely stocked soda fountain with mechanical music machines on either end. A hidden alcove holds a portion of the reconstructed neighborhood Lyric Theater and the Reproduco Piano Pipe Organ, manufactured by the Operators' Piano Company of Chicago for silent film accompaniment, and the Violano-Virtuoso, a violin and keyboard combination made by the Mills Novelty Company of Chicago, that the 1909 Alaska-Yukon-Pacific Exposition labeled "one of the eight great inventions of the new century," now just a bodacious bit of bric-a-brac.

Piano nickelodeons, fed by vacuum pipes and the perforated paper rolls so familiar to earlier generations, and steel disc music boxes stand alongside Wurlitzers and reed organs. The Aeolean Duo-Art Weber Reproducing Piano of the 1920s plays "Rhapsody in Blue." The Bruder Mechanical Band Organ, a 1913 product of Waldkirch, Germany, used to bellow its music loudly above crowd noise high atop a Wildwood, New Jersey amusement pavilion.

The largest piece, the Amaryllis Mortier Dance Organ, fills the loft above the saloon with its hardwood facade, metal and wooden pipes, decorative domes, murals, gold and silver leaf trim, balustrades and columns - 18 feet high, 30 feet across. Manufactured by Theofiel Mortier in Antwerp, Belgium in 1922, it was one of a thousand constructed from 1908 to 1930 to entertain in exquisite ballrooms or in touring programs. Only 100 remain, and most of them have been altered. This one has been restored to its exact appearance when it graced the Victoria Palace in Ypres, Belgium. A large handheld flywheel used to operate it (an old true-to-the-period electric motor now does), and its 97-key organ plays folding, perforated cardboard music books - waltzes, foxtrots, polkas, and standards of the '20s. Its pipes and percussive parts simulate the full-bodied sound of an entire orchestra at top volume.

When the formal tour ends, you are free to either tailgate another tour or venture into other corridors of the old refurbished farm complex to see dozens of vintage televisions, radios, vacuum tubes, transistors, transceivers, receivers, diamond-tipped styluses, music posters and sheet music, organs and organettes, pianos and piano rolls...and such relics as organs on canopied surreys, 1920s phonographs built to look like miniature grand pianos with trumpet-like speakers...and bits of information, like how inventor Thomas Edison expanded upon an audio device designed by Frenchman Leon Scott de Martinville to produce the first functioning phonograph and demonstrated it in 1877, only to shelve it for 10 years because it was considered too frivolous.

One wing displays the evolution of the juke box: a 1939 Rock-Ola Luxury Light-up, made by David C. Rockola, the biggest-selling juke of the pre-World War II era; a 1941 Rock-Ola Spectravox Tunecolumn, built to stand in the center of a ballroom and cast colored lights at the ceiling; a 1946 Wurlitzer Model 1015 with color animation, three-dimensional plastic casing, and signature tubes that ferried "bubbles" all the way to its arched top; and a 1948 Seeburg Model 148, colloquially called the "trash can," with its blonde wood-grained metal cabinet.

A working juke box plays any of dozens of vintage hits for a quarter; sitting chairs are interspersed throughout.

Visitation is 20,000 a year, and most people spend a couple hours. The season runs during daytime hours from May to October, and special programs are conducted through December. An elegant gift shop sells mechanical music recordings, related items, and fine crystal, china, and porcelain.

The Music House is on the bay side of U.S. Highway 31, a mile or two north of its intersection with State Highway 72 in Acme. Ten miles west, around the southernmost loop of Grand Traverse Bay, is Traverse City, home of the annual National Cherry

Festival in July in honor of the area which reputedly grows nearly a third of the world's cherry crop. The area sports water and snow activities, scenic bay drives, and specialty shops and restaurants.

THE WOODWORKER WHO USED WOOD OTHERS WOULDN'T

Sometime around the end of the 19th century, Hortense Brown, an Ohio schoolmarm born around the close of the Civil War, began teaching young Raymond W. "Bud" Overholzer, born one year shy of a quarter-century later, in a rural Paulding County school.

The two apparently hit it off quite well. And though history has not recorded the details, at some point or other, Hortense must have thought she could teach young Bud something more than mere reading, writing, and 'rithmetic. They married.

In the early 1920s, when Bud was in his early 30s, he brought his middle-aged bride and widowed mother with him to Lake County, Michigan, a rural west-central part of the state where tall stands of pines reign supreme. The education Hortense gave him must have been basic, for he settled into a career that looked like that of a self-employed outdoor roustabout. He guided fishermen to area streams where trout swam in abundance, guided hunters to thickets where they could stalk deer, and stuffed their kills, if they wanted flesh-and-bloodless mementoes.

At length, he harnessed his whittling skills to plans for a unique museum built in a wilderness cabin of white pine that would hold handmade furniture made exclusively from pine remnants - roots, knots, and stumps that loggers couldn't use in Michigan's lumber business. It became a pastime that filled nearly all his spare time in the final three decades of his life.

Slowly, painstakingly, functional furniture that doubled as rustic works of art emerged from the sweat of his brow when applied to nature's refuse. Three months of effort every year for three decades of his life produced over 200 articles made entirely of wood, natural materials, and glue - no nails, no screws - and fashioned either by hand or by the crudest of non-mechanical tools like wire brushes. The compartment doors and drawers of his woodwork hinged together, swung around, or pulled open by the natural interaction of hand-carved wooden pegs and auger holes. Raw deer hides substituted as bed springs, and the tips of white pine trees became bed posts; deer hair filled a mattress, wild duck down a pillow.

A giant 700-pound white pine stump - after a year of masterly handiwork - whittled down to a striking 300-pound single-piece table with naturally gnarled legs and with built-in openings serving as unique shelves.

He combed the forests for odd-looking remnants that could transcend nature's compost heap. In his hands, a single massive continuous root became a chair.

Another such unusable part of a tree turned into a poker table with a drawer for cards and shelves for beverages…and matching chairs each with a tray for playing cards and gaming chips on its left. A huge twisting root, six and one-half feet by seven feet, framed a rough oval-shaped window.

Overholzer (the Teutonic name fittingly translating into "upper wood") used a knot to construct a vase, hollowing it out to its very bottom - a burdensome task for which the word "knotty" seems to have been invented. He constructed a ponderous settee on a single pivot point so his teacher-turned-homemaker wife could tip it on end to dust. He also threw in decorative finishes - one of his trademarks - whenever possible, like a sculpted bird perching on a bottom beam.

An estimated 70 tons of fieldstone make up the chimney; astute eyes might be able to pick out specific random designs that reputedly resemble a turtle, an owl, an ear, and bells. The root-hewn mantel set against the chimney holds aloft a weird fanlike root that carries all 26 letters of the alphabet in its veinous interlacing network - if you look hard enough. A rustic rocker contains just the proper balance of symmetrically arranged roots to rock 55 - and exactly 55 - times each time it is put in motion. Candelabra made from knots and twists of root decorate tables.

A thorough outdoorsman, Overholzer designed a 12-rifle gunrack that rotates on wooden roller bearings and sports shelves for ammunition. He also fashioned a table with a hollow leg - a perfect alcove for a secret bottle of liquor.

He began showing his unique furniture in the mid-1930s. Then in the early '40s, he bought 28 acres of white pine land along the Pere Marquette River, just south of Baldwin in southern Lake County, and constructed a cabin large enough to serve as both workshop and repository for his increasing output. He drew his inspiration from the adjoining river, designated one of the country's wild and scenic streams. He worked in the basement of the so-called "Shrine of the Pines" main cabin. The finished work wound up on display in the large continuous room upstairs - a stone chimney along its west wall and, on the east, a loft (with a 10-step staircase from a tree killed in a forest fire and held together by dozens of auger holes and pegs).

Roots of various shapes frame the irregular windows (rough ovals, rectangles, triangles, and semicircles). Like everything within it, the building is completely natural, even to the strip of rawhide that serves as the latch string on the front door, the pine knot that becomes the door handle, and the thatch that formerly covered the roof.

Oddly enough, though the cabin appears to have been constructed as an outdoorsmans' lodge (with the gunrack, card settings, and Overholzer's taxidermic prowess adorning various walls and balconies), no one ever used the place. The furniture pieces are as virginal as when his fingers buffed them with resin and pitch to a natural (no artificial shellacs or varnishes) finish. He even turned a deaf ear to automobile magnate Henry Ford who once offered him $50,000 for the 300-pound table alone...this in an earlier day, when $50,000 nearly ensured a complete life of ease.

Though hidden in a rural part of Michigan, the Shrine of the Pines gained regional celebrity, and Overholzer displayed his creations to those who came calling till his death in 1952 at 62. His widow then ran the place with assistants until she died seven years later at 93.

Today the site is operated by Shrine of the Pines, Inc., a local non-profit organization. Guided 20-minute tours of the expansive show room occur as often as visitation warrants - daily, from May through October, during normal daytime hours. A moderate fee is charged, undoubtedly to meet the operational costs and recompense the young but enthusiastic school-age guides who demonstrate the legacy of a man whose "three ideals," according to his widow, were that every creation he carved from the rough "had to be done by hand from Michigan white pine, had to be useful, and must cost nothing."

Tucked nicely away on the banks of the Pere Marquette in Marlborough (two miles south of county seat Baldwin on State Highway 37), the house receives about 12,000 visitors during its five-month season, according to employees...or somewhat fewer than 100 a day; long lines should not be a problem. An adjacent gift shop, formerly called the "widow's cabin" in reference to Hortense Overholzer's residence there following her husband's death, sells souvenirs and white pine crafts and houses an historical museum. A series of nature trails winds along the river where Overholzer's cremated remains were scattered, fulfilling his desire to return to the soil that in time produces the majestic pines with which he so entwined his life (his wife was disposed of more traditionally - burial in an Ohio cemetery).

The average length of visitation time, including the tour, is less than an hour. The rest of the day can be devoted to pursuits that ordinarily draw people to the Manistee National Forest, which includes the Shrine of the Pines - water-related activities running the gamut from swimming to fishing, pleasure boating to canoeing. In winter, snow pursuits are popular. The nearest big cities are Ludington (where French explorer and missionary Jacques Marquette died in 1675), 35 miles to the west, and Big Rapids, about the same distance southeast. Both offer shopping, dining, and lodging; and Ludington throws in public beaches, museums, and a reconstructed village.

The Shrine of the Pines is not the sort of attraction that will haunt you for years to come. But viewing artistry drawn from nature's scrap heap is nice. Not every man is fortunate enough to have a legacy that outshines his life.

MINNESOTA

AMERICA'S GREAT MISSISSIPPI RIVER HERO

Though his grandfather was a Swedish legislator and his father a congressman from Minnesota, the boy showed no signs of following in their footsteps. He grew up in Washington, D.C. and attended prestigious private schools like Sidwell Friends but preferred to spend his time at his family's Minnesota home during summer recess, lying on his back in the grass, studying scudding clouds and dreaming of flying the brand-new flying machines so he could enter their white puffy world.

His parents grew distant - the congressman and his wife (a Michigan dentist's daughter who had taught high school chemistry before marriage). Their only child wound up spending more time with the mother, becoming her companion and defender, oddly shaking hands with her before retiring each night. He favored the inventiveness of his maternal side and tinkered constantly when he wasn't going through the motions of his formal education. He grew to be nearly 6'3" and all of 130 pounds.

He ran the family farm in Minnesota as a teen-ager, gave college a try, then chucked it for aviation. He took his first airplane ride and flying classes at 20 in 1922. He spent five years piloting airplanes, barnstorming throughout the country, walking on wings and doing parachute stunts, and eventually settling down as a commercial mail pilot based in St. Louis, Missouri.

Then in 1927, he did what no man had ever done before, essentially a daring stunt. America lionized him, the media tailed him, mothers named children after him, kids tried to emulate him. A proud nation feted him to a 48-state tour. Crowds demanded to hear him speak. He met the erudite daughter of a career politician and married her after a courtship that thrilled the nation. He fathered a child to America's delight.

And then the hero's world imploded in tragedy. Someone stole and murdered his baby. He went to Europe to live and began preaching isolationism, an unpopular tenet on the eve of America's entry into World War II. In a September 11, 1941 speech at Des Moines, Iowa, while the Holocaust was gearing up in Europe, he made anti-Semitic remarks, criticizing Jewish influence in motion pictures, the press, and government.

He managed to make amends by flying 50 combat missions for America in the war. And he went through a profound inner change. Where once he had extolled the benefits of air travel, he recoiled in horror at the devastation that airplanes had inflicted. For the rest of his life, he spoke of conservation and the natural order. Intensely private, introspective, sensitive, eccentric, he wrote extensively and won a Pulitzer Prize in 1954. He moved to Hawaii and lived the remaining years of his life in private, except when traveling on behalf of conservation efforts. He died of cancer on August 26, 1974, at 72, in his Hawaiian home.

He was buried overlooking the Pacific Ocean on Maui's southern coast. No embalming fluid preserves his body. His bones lie in the Palapala Hoomau Congregational Church burial ground next to those of apes - someone's pet gibbons. Goats roam across the top of his grave and eat the nearby flowers placed in his memory.

Many places contain bits of the life of America's great flying hero, Charles A. Lindbergh, who flew his silver single-engine monoplane, "The Spirit of St. Louis," from New York to France - 3,600 miles - alone and nonstop in 33.5 hours on May 20-21, 1927: Detroit, Michigan, where he was born; nearby Dearborn, which has his motorcycle; Washington's Smithsonian Institution, which owns his famous plane; and Hawaii, which claims his bones. But the Charles A. Lindbergh House in Little Falls, Minnesota, his boyhood home, and its adjacent history center possess the most complete and personal summation of the American legend.

The interpretive center clusters exhibits and mementos of Lucky Lindy's life on three inclined ramps, and exhibit boards recount the history of his ancestors. Among the relics are: the aft wing beam, altimeter, and part of the horizontal stabilizer from his first plane, a Curtiss JN-4D "Jenny" leftover from World War I; a large wall map of the country used by the young traveler to register his journeys from childhood through 1926, with his differently colored lines designating individual modes of transportation (red for airplane, green for boat, blue for motorcycle, solid black for car, dotted black for train); a list of the equipment he carried on his historic flight (two flashlights, a ball of string and another of cord, hunting knife, quartet of red flares, matches, large needle, air raft with pump and repair kit, two air cushions, hacksaw blade, and a little food); a large picture of him in his older years paired with one of his telling observations ("...if I had to choose, I would rather have birds than airplanes.").

One display compares his monoplane with a typical modern 747 to provide an idea of how minimal his protection was when he flew over thousands of miles of icy water in the darkness, in the mist, in the clouds, in the fog, in the uncertainty of going where no one else had gone, with ice overtaking his plane's wings and drowsiness creeping over him. His monoplane measured 27 feet in length, compared with a 747's 230-plus feet; it weighed 2,150 pounds, excluding fuel, contrasted with a 747's 357,000 pounds; it soared along at a maximum 124.5-mile cruising speed, less than a fifth what a 747 can do.

A room showcases vintage products marketed to capitalize on Lindbergh's popularity. A monitor periodically plays a 20-minute video of a 1984 David McCullough "Smithsonian World" interview with his widow, Anne Morrow Lindbergh, herself an accomplished author and aviatrix.

The first-floor theater rotates a 20-minute narrative of Lindbergh's life with videos on various local immigrant and ethnic groups.

Lindbergh attended the dedication of the interpretive center on September 30, 1973 and spoke to the guests along the banks of the adjacent upper Mississippi River.

The Lindbergh house, built in 1906 on the site of a previous home, adjoins the center. The Lindberghs left the house vacant when they moved from Little Falls in 1920. Then, when Lindbergh became a hero in 1927, souvenir hunters nearly stripped the house. The Lindbergh family donated the house, farm, and land to the state in 1931. The Minnesota Historical Society later acquired it and, with the state, made it a memorial. Lindbergh donated many of his personal possessions and suggested how the house should be refurbished to reflect its original appearance.

Half-hour guided tours of the house occur throughout the day and point out the hole in the kitchen wall where the young Charles squirreled away his toys, the slash marks on the kitchen floor he made when he cut wood into kindling, the daring dress (its hem scandalously above the ankle) worn by his mother Evangeline at a White House ball during Woodrow Wilson's administration, the bed he slept on within the screened-in porch overlooking the Mississippi, the dining room where he hatched chickens in an incubator, the spinning wheel he won at auction for a dollar for his mother, and the living room with his collection of metal soldiers, Indians, and animals.

The tour concludes in the basement with two cars owned by Lindbergh: a 1916 Saxon he had once driven to California; and a 1959 Volkswagen he used to eat and sleep in while traveling (the cans and packages of food that Lindbergh had with him when he donated the car in 1973 remain on the front seat).

The guides flesh out the tour with amusing tidbits: his favorite cookie was the plain sugar butter cookie; he was buried only hours after his death, according to his wishes, dressed in his work clothes, wrapped in a Hudson Bay blanket, and planted in a coffin made from eucalyptus wood.

The so-called "Moo Pond" (adapted from a Chippewa word for "dirty") that he built for ducks to drink from in 1919 still stands alongside the house. His original inscription remains chiseled on its side.

The Charles A. Lindbergh House and History Center lies within Lindbergh State Park on the west side of the Mississippi and in the center of the state, just south of Little Falls on Lindbergh Drive (County Road 52). It is open daily, from May until Labor Day, during normal daytime hours; otherwise it is open only weekends. A moderate fee is charged and includes admission to the house and interpretive center and sometimes complimentary punch and cookies. Viewing everything, videos included, takes a couple hours; studying Lindbergh and the forces that made him one of the most complex, gifted, and intriguing men of his time doubles your time. A book store and gift shop and well-maintained rest rooms serve the 25,000-40,000 annual visitors.

If you visit during the summer, watch out for droves of mosquitos. Either wear repellent or plan not to stay outside long. If the pests are on a sabbatical, either of the quarter-mile or two-thirds-mile loop trails will take you along the former gardens, trees, growth, and animal dens along the river that Lindbergh frequented as a child.

Across Lindbergh Drive on land formerly part of the family's 110-acre farm is the state park - 328 acres of hiking and skiing trails, campsites, and water opportunities. Little Falls' shops, restaurants, and recreation areas are just north.

JOURNEY TO THE CENTER OF THE TURF

You trudge up a loaf-shaped hill in central Minnesota and enter a darkened elevator. It takes you 630 feet straight down into the earth's innards. The door of the cage opens deep within the earth, and you plunge into a world of utter darkness punctuated only by occasional lamps. The temperature is a cool 50 degrees.

You stumble through various rooms where miners once extracted ore with dynamite and drills. You enter cavities chiseled deep within the earth's guts, alcoves called "Dog Hole" and "Man Rise." The Explosive Room, where dynamite charges were stored, still carries warnings in several languages to warn the foreign-speaking immigrants who worked the mine; but, as your guide tells you, problem was half the immigrants couldn't read in any language.

Your guide tells you that iron ore still remains in the area but lies untapped because ore can be more cheaply imported from countries without labor unions. He tells you that, in the pre-union days, miners sometimes worked 16- or 18-hour days for miserable wages. He gives you a feeling for how safe the miners' hard hats were: "Made you feel real comfortable with a million tons of rock above your head."

You walk the dark paths 630 feet below the surface until you come to the engineer's office. Then the tour ends, and the guide opens a door and you find yourself outdoors, on a paved path, with the sun directly overhead.

Things are not what they seem to be at Croft Mine Historical Park. The mine you just toured was no mine at all, just an above-ground simulation built into a small hill. The elevator only took you a couple dozen feet at a creeping pace. Air conditioning provided the 50-degree coolness.

America has a number of either abandoned or working gold, copper, ore, and coal mine tours. But the Croft tour, just north of Crosby in Crow Wing County, is not one of them; it's all make-believe.

There once was a real Croft Mine...directly underneath the fake one recently built into the low hillside.

In the 1880s, Cuyler Adams established a residence a few miles east of the Mississippi River in central Minnesota. While surveying his land, he unwittingly discovered iron ore - the 80-mile-long Cuyuna Range (named, in part, for him and his St. Bernard, Una). In 1903, his mining company began digging into the ground. The following year, the men struck a lode. The first of more than three dozen Cuyuna Iron Range mines started in 1905. Shipment tonnage soared. Communities sprang up around Crosby, the flagship town, and frame cottages, called "Honeymoon Row," housed the immigrants drawn to the mines. During its heyday, the Cuyuna led America in the production of manganiferous iron ore.

In time, the Croft Mine came up, not far from Honeymoon Row. It shipped nearly two million tons between 1915 and 1934.

But eventually the Cuyuna mines closed, victims of more economical mining alternatives and the development of taconite, a low-grade iron ore. Most of the Croft's buildings and equipment were removed in 1977. The Croft Mine Historical Park opened in 1980, then closed for more thorough restoration, and reopened in 1989.

Today, the park consists of an accurate restoration, a half-hour guided tour heavy on technical "bore and stroke" information and generally seasoned with humor, and a gritty museum of mining artifacts in the mine's old Dry House, where miners once congregated after resurfacing. A gift shop sells basic items involving mining.

The so-called "Beaver Pond," about halfway between the Dry

House and the underground simulation, resulted from ground water seeping in when the mine was dynamited after its closing. Maybe beaver are there; we saw flies, ants, and annoying mosquitos. Beyond the Dry House are the original smokestack, the foundations of several structures, and more than a dozen signs explaining the importance of the mine and the Cuyuna Range. A nature trail winds back to the entrance, passing the since-flooded mine shaft and Cuyler Adams' original house and outhouse, as well as the last of the four-room Honeymoon Row cottages still around, all of which have been moved to the park for permanent display.

The state currently administers the park, which also includes a small children's playground and picnic tables. It is open daily during normal daytime hours from Memorial Day to Labor Day; special allowances are made for group tours during the rest of the year (218-546-5466 or 218-546-5625). A moderate fee is charged for the simulation tour; the buildings, grounds, and museum are free.

Though visitation is slight (7-8,000 a year), the park presents a realistic look at the rugged day-to-day lives of miners and throws in a lot of information on mining in America. An average visit might take an hour or so. The only warning: beware Minnesota's mosquitos; they're fierce and persistent.

Crosby lies on State Highway 210, 15 miles northeast of Brainerd. The mine is on the northern outskirts of Crosby; from the center of town, proceed north on 2nd Avenue, then west on 8th Street (George Spalj Drive), or simply follow the signs.

Those interested in mining might want to consider either the Cuyuna Range Historical Museum in Crosby's former Soo Line Depot on Hallett Avenue or, farther away, Ironworld USA, a sprawling theme park and interpretive center on Minnesota mining along State Highway 169 in Chisholm, 100 miles northeast.

The Brainerd-Crosby area teems with lakes and their usual activities, antique and specialty shops, and the Paul Bunyan Center and Lumbertown USA amusement theme parks.

MISSISSIPPI

A HUMBLE PALACE FOR THE LITTLE KING

In the middle of the Depression, the man fated to become an American music institution, a legendary performer, and a cult idol for a generation was born in a two-room shack in the Deep South. Fifty-eight years to the day later, the United States Postal Service honored him with a commemorative stamp, the most widely ballyhooed one ever issued and an instant collectible.

Elvis Presley, the King of Rock and Roll, the hip-swinging, karate-chopping singer-showman who parlayed a striking physical presence and a resonant baritone voice into a career that made him a millionaire many times over and sank deeply into a lifestyle that dragged him into the abyss of drug dependence, food binging, and emotional roller coaster rides, first saw the light of day in Tupelo, Mississippi.

The house in which he was born and spent his early childhood years is still preserved with some changes. The original house afforded no running water and contained only three windows. Today, the plankboard house has largely been built over, though it does conform to the original rectangular shape built by his father.

Visitors who journey to the eastern part of the city to tour the house on Elvis Presley Drive (known as Old Satillo Road before Presley became famous) are struck by its smallness. The 30-foot by 15-foot house's twin rooms are still there, one behind the other lengthwise, as they were when the Little King was born; most of the furnishings, however, are period replacements. Restored by Virginia Boyd in 1971, the house conveys the image of the confinement of little Elvis' world before he took to warbling. Gone are all traces of both the outdoor pump that provided water for Vernon and Gladys Presley and their son and the outhouse that the little prince in waiting used (imagine what that collectible would be worth today!).

The style of the house is the so-called "shotgun" because of its narrow rectangularity. The small family slept, dressed, relaxed, ate, and talked within the compact compartments. Though cramped by today's standards, such rooms often accommodated much larger families during the Depression.

There is more to the site than the house. A brick wall surrounds the rise on which the house stands, showcasing the freshly mown lawn and giving the place an elevated dignity. Spotlights illuminate the house at night, and shrubbery, plants, and seasonal flowers border it. Paved walkways intersect the various buildings, including a tennis court, swimming pool, and picnic area, within the 15-acre Elvis Presley Park and Youth Center. Beautifully landscaped lawns and gardens blossom where fields once grew. The Elvis Presley Center, a museum and gift shop offering the usual Presley paraphernalia, occupies an attractive brick, glass, and wood edifice in the rear. A state historical marker proclaims the "BIRTHPLACE OF ELVIS PRESLEY" in front of the house:

> Elvis Aaron Presley was born Jan. 8, 1935, in this house, built by his father. Presley's career as a singer and entertainer redefined American popular music. He died Aug. 16, 1977, at Memphis, Tennessee.

You can also get married in the adjoining Elvis Presley Memorial Chapel (or Chapel of Memories), a stained glass, carpeted temple of tranquility and reflection "built with donations from his fans and friends around the world" and suggested by Presley as his choice for a Tupelo memorial. Hundreds of people have wed there since its August 17, 1979 dedication.

The house is a shrine to the droves of people interested in Presley. He lived there until moving as a youngster to Memphis with his family. The birthplace became a landmark shortly after the young crooner shot to stardom with his recordings of "Hound Dog," a rough-edged screamer, and "Love Me Tender," a gentle ballad with romantic lyrics set to a popular melody that had stood the test of time. Some of the take from Elvis' performance at the 1957 Mississippi-Alabama Fair and Dairy Show went to furthering the development of the birthsite.

Since the official 1971 unveiling of the house, both hours and visitation have increased. The site currently opens during normal daytime hours every day except Sunday (when it opens only during the afternoon). Separate admissions are charged for the house (modest) and museum (average). Touring usually takes an hour or so; and, if you want to get hitched in the chapel, reservations are necessary (601-841-1245).

The site sits in northeastern Mississippi, about 100 miles southeast of Memphis. U.S. Highway 78 takes you to Tupelo; exit on either Veteran's Boulevard or Main Street and follow signs.

Though the site will have visitors (about 100,000 annually), it will not have the hordes who descend on Presley's Graceland home in Memphis (unless you drop in on an anniversary of either his birth or death).

While in Tupelo, don't miss the McDonald's restaurant, across from the Tupelo Mall (one of several malls in a city famed for its upholstered furniture manufacturing), where Presley photos, paintings, and memorabilia adorn every available inch of wall space. You can also have a cheeseburger, one of his favorite meals, in his honor.

In the immediate vicinity are the Civil War Tupelo National Battlefield just to the south and the site of a Chickasaw Indian village just to the north. Fifteen miles north of the Indian village is Brices Cross Roads, another Civil War battlesite. And Memphis and Graceland are just a couple hours away.

AMERICA'S FIRST INTERSTATE HIGHWAY

It was the Route 66 of its day, America's first interstate highway, the quickest, most direct way to travel.

It was the Natchez Trace, a legendary network of roads in the annals of American transportation that connected Nashville, Tennessee with Natchez, Mississippi and also went through a small part of Alabama in a day when no other road stretched over so many hundreds of wilderness miles. At its peak, it provided cheap travel between the important frontier settlement of Nashville and the key river trading center of Natchez, second in importance only to New Orleans farther down the Mississippi.

The trace never amounted to more than its name implied - a swampy, insect-infested rut worn into the soil of the then-unspoiled American frontier forests, wide enough for a horseman or two abreast or a couple travelers afoot.

As a word, the "trace" came from a French term for "track," or "trek," or "line of footprints." As a path, it derived from prehistoric Native Americans who developed it, undoubtedly following the lead of the buffalo and deer who initially had trampled brush and small saplings to the ground in moving from one place to another. These trailblazing men used the path on their daily hunt for provisions. With the progression of civilization, hunters began packing their crops to barter with other hunters a hundred or more miles distant. In those long-ago days, the trace consisted of trails crisscrossing the continent.

Eventually, white men came, the Spanish and French explorers of the 16th and 17th centuries. By 1800, it had become the nation's most important frontier road. Postriders traveled it daily delivering mail from one corner of the frontier to another. Traders and planters from back east floated their goods downriver to New Orleans, then, their saddlebags stuffed with money, rode or walked it back home (their crude boats couldn't easily go upriver in those pre-steam days). Drawn to the prospect of rich merchants with money to burn, bandits utilized the heavy forests flanking the trace as camouflage and freely victimized and murdered in those lawless years. Then the military moved in, widening the road to accommodate wagons and providing a measure of safety. The Tennessee Militia used the road during the War of 1812, its commander, Andrew Jackson, during one especially rigorous movement, earning his famous sobriquet "Old Hickory" from the hickory trees alongside the trace.

Steam travel in the 1820s allowed two-way traffic on the Ohio and Mississippi Rivers and doomed the trace to the status of a local road. It enjoyed a brief renaissance when Civil War troops used it in the 1860s but shortly thereafter fell into permanent decline. Paved roads cut across it and paralleled it; landowners converted parcels of it into crop fields.

Historians and preservationists on the municipal, state, and national levels sought to mark the location of the long-since disappeared trace in the 20th century. Beginning in the 1930s, the National Park Service has constructed a paved two-lane highway somewhat adjacent to the old trace, at times exactly shadowing the path, at times swinging five or more miles in either direction for topographic or traffic considerations. Roughly 90 percent of the road is complete over some 450 road miles between Natchez and Nashville.

Some modern travelers attempt to drive the entire distance of the Natchez Trace Parkway; others follow only a small portion. Some parts of the parkway are connected by detours that deviate from the actual route, but frequent points of entrance and exit and intersecting highways allow easy on-and-off access. The parkway uses a milepost system starting with its southern terminus at Natchez. You can, of course, drive it in either direction.

An exhibit shelter at mile marker 8.7, northeast of Natchez, welcomes you to the highway with maps, textboards, and a glimpse of an actual section of trace just west of the road. It appears as a patch of mown grass between trees.

At mile 10.3, Emerald Mound, the second largest Indian temple in the country, appears. At 12.4, you see Loess Bluff, a dramatic example of the erosion of Ice Age volcanic topsoil (loess). At 15.5, you come across Mount Locust, the only surviving, restored roadside inn from the trace's heyday.

Mile 40 brings you to the exit for Port Gibson, a strategic Confederate town whose quaint homes Union General Ulysses S. Grant declared "too beautiful to burn" during the Civil War. Mile marker 41.5 leads you to a stretch of original trace remarkably preserved and yards below the humps of earth that border it. Leafy trees, roots partially exposed, shoot skyward. Spanish moss decorates the bower like tinsel on a Christmas tree. It perfectly captures the essence of the trace that confronted travelers 200 years ago when any sudden snap of a twig in the stillness of the night could mean a prowling animal, a hopping bird, or a marauding villain. If you stop at no other spot, stop at this one to see the trace for what it was.

Around mile 67, the parkway intersects with State Highway 27 which goes about 20 miles west to Vicksburg and its antebellum mansions, the scene of the Civil War's most famous siege.

The parkway may still be incomplete for a 12- or 15-mile stretch around Jackson, Mississippi's capital, when you travel. If so, the interstate highway network will detour you to the resumption of the road.

At 104.5, you encounter another deeply worn section and the site of Turner Brashears' Stand, the common term for a motel of the day, one of more than four dozen such inns that stretched for nearly 500 miles to cater to travelers.

Mile 128.4 identifies Doak's Stand, another "motel," where, in 1820, American commissioners, led by conquering hero Andrew Jackson, signed a treaty with the Choctaws that amounted to one of the biggest land grabs in white American history.

The town of Kosciusko's welcome center at 159.9 contains information, courtesy of the chamber of commerce. Two more segments of original trace occur at 198.6 and 221.4.

Mile 266 takes you to the parkway visitor center and headquarters, just north of Tupelo, a major detour for Civil War battlefields, shopping, and Elvis Presley's birthplace. It is open daily during normal daytime hours and dispenses information, exhibits, and souvenirs. Another original section and some unknown Confederate graves lie at 269.4.

At mile 308.9, you cross into Alabama for its share of the road. Its most important stops are: exhibits on Chickasaw Chief and inn owner Levi Colbert at 320.3; and the Colbert ferry site, where Levi's kinsman George took travelers across the Tennessee River for inflated prices, at 327.3. A couple dozen miles east are the quad cities of Florence, Muscle Shoals, Sheffield, and Tuscumbia, Wilson Dam, Tennessee Valley Authority facilities, water recreation, and Helen Keller's birthplace.

The parkway leaves Alabama for its final run through Tennessee at 341.8. More examples of the sunken trace occur at 350.5.

An old trace drive, two and a half miles parallel with an original section, crops up at 375.8.

Mile 385.9 produces the Meriwether Lewis Park with camping and picnicking facilities and the grave of the co-leader of the 1804-06 Lewis and Clark Expedition, an accomplished man who was found nearby in 1809, a bullet in his head and brains oozing from his shattered forehead. A presumed suicide, he was buried near the site. A purposely unfinished circular shaft, broken at its top, marks his grave.

Additional sections of original trace, one driving, one walking, occur at miles 401.4 and 403.7, respectively.

The end of the parkway, proposed at mile 450, just south of Nashville, is presently still short of that goal.

The Natchez Trace Parkway is designed to be a leisurely alternative to high-speed highways; expect to drive no faster than 50 mph. Rural countryside will be your near-constant companion.

Deer and smaller game frequently bound across the roadway. If you hike a hidden trail or pitch a tent, be alert for fire ants, poison ivy, and rattlesnakes, copperheads, and cottonmouths; they're possible, though not necessarily likely.

The stops listed above are only some of the sojourns available along the parkway. Scores of interpretive signs, history and nature exhibits, periodic ranger stations, living history demonstrations, campgrounds, hiking trails, picnic areas, historical sites, and dozens upon dozens of cities with lodging, dining, and shopping are all nearby. Gas is available at Jeff Busby at mile 193.1 and near most of the exits.

Mississippi contains more than twice as much parkway as Alabama and Tennessee put together and some of the best sights.

If you intend to drive along the entire parkway and see a good share of the attractions, you'll need several days, perhaps a week or more. But even a quick day jaunt can provide a good study of frontier life, an excursion into the past with a quick escape to the present in a matter of minutes. There is no charge to use the road.

MISSOURI

THE ROOT OF JESSE

America's greatest legendary bandit was born on September 5, 1847 to a Baptist minister and his six-foot bride. He eventually grew to be nearly as tall as his mother and lived in Missouri, a border state that produced both Yankees and Rebels in the Civil War. The boy's loyalties took after his mother's, and, when 16, he joined a wanton Confederate guerrilla unit led by "Bloody Bill" Anderson, a name not bestowed in haste. The boy just wanted to get back at the North for attacking his house and roughing him and his mother up, glossing over the fact that the Federals had attacked to retaliate for inexcusably harsh raids on civilians that his Southern-leaning brother had participated in.

After the South lost the war, the juvenile delinquent decided to turn full-time to crime. He may have been involved in what became the first daytime non-war bank robbery in America (Liberty, Missouri; February 1866). An 1868 hit on a Russellville, Kentucky bank also implicated both him and his brother. Bank robberies continued, but he always denied complicity in carefully crafted letters to Kansas City and St. Louis newspapers run by John Newman Edwards, an ex-Confederate who eagerly explained the perpetrators of the bank jobs as only modern Robin Hoods (Edwards probably ghosted or edited the letters himself).

In July 1873, an Iowa train robbery cast suspicion on the brothers. Bank, store, train, and stagecoach thefts in Alabama, Mississippi, Tennessee, Kentucky, West Virginia, Arkansas, Texas, Kansas, Nebraska, Missouri, and Iowa followed. If the brothers didn't commit them all, they did their fair share.

Still, the partisan press exonerated them, fabricating stories about how they'd financially help widows and only rob from men whose hands weren't calloused and redistribute the wealth they acquired to the needy poor.

Lawmen saw it differently. Pinkerton detectives closing in on the brothers wound up dead. In January 1875, Pinkerton agents lobbed incendiary devices into the boys' homestead, hoping to get the brothers. But the boys weren't home, and the bombs only killed the brothers' nine-year-old half-brother and shattered their mother's arm.

Things got even hotter the following year. A captured trainrobber fingered the brothers. Then in September, the bandits met their match in attempting a bank robbery in Northfield, Minnesota. The townspeople fought back and killed or captured every robber but the two siblings, who spent the next few years living under the cloak of aliases in other states.

Public opinion finally turned away from the brigands when more robberies and related killings occurred and Missouri became known as "the bandit state."

Allan Pinkerton, the founder of the famous detective agency that bears his name, considered the reputed ringleader brother "the worst man, without exception, in America. He is utterly devoid of fear, and he has no more compunction about cold-blooded murder than he has about eating his breakfast...."

In July 1881, Missouri put a $5,000 bounty on each brother.

And then, on April 3, 1882, "That dirty little coward who shot Mr. Howard...laid poor Jesse in his grave."

Jesse Woodson James, the robber of a half-million dollars in two dozen raids, masquerading as Thomas Howard at a house he rented in St. Joseph, Missouri, lay dead with a bullet fired from fellow gangmember Robert Ford, intent on collecting bounty money.

Jesse's mother knew of her son's criminality but excused it. She planted his remains in the southwest corner of the yard adjacent to the house in which he had been born. She feared that curiosity seekers might flood the place or that unethical scoundrels, similar in nature to her late, lamented son, might dig up the body and exhibit it at sideshows. That gave her an idea. She began a cottage industry, greeting visitors, telling them her reminiscences, extolling Jesse's merits, whitewashing his villainy with tales of how the North had driven him to crime by its shameful treatment of him, expounding on how the real thieves were the railroad magnates and bankers, and showing them the house and her son's grave…for a price, of course. She also sold pebbles from Jesse's grave for two bits each and, when the supply dwindled, simply took more from a creek.

Jesse's wife died in 1900 and was buried in the town cemetery. Two years later, Jesse himself was unearthed and placed alongside her in Mt. Olivet Cemetery. The coffin fell apart when lifted, leaving loose parts of the body in the original grave.

When the mother died in 1911, brother Frank (who had surrendered, been acquitted of all crimes in one of the West's biggest legal travesties, gone straight, and started his own Wild West show) took over the farm and continued showing the homestead to the curious for a price.

The house remained in the family till 1978 when the county bought it and restored it. Clay County stocked it with relics of its most famous resident and reopened it. Also in 1978, an excavation team dug into the old plot where Jesse had originally been buried and where his coffin had broken open and found bone fragments, a swatch of hair, and a bullet theorized to be the very one that had laid him low.

Today, you, too, can pay to see the house that spawned a great American cheat. Revisionist evidence suggests that Jesse, his brother, and other gangmembers more or less acted in concert with shared responsibilities, with each member free to stay or leave, as he saw fit, and that Jesse may not have been the great criminal mastermind behind the robberies anymore than anyone else was. But he was handsome and young and got good press (a plus in any racket) and had the good grace to die young (a bigger plus in any legend).

The house contains interesting artifacts for those interested in America's famous robbing hood: a portion of the original 10-foot gravestone obelisk with only the "SSE W. JAM" left from his name, thanks to souvenir hunters; the boots he wore when killed; his .45-caliber Colt pistol, the last weapon he had worn before death; his final cartridge belt; a portion of the coffin handles from his original casket; the room in which he was born; the original kitchen where the Pinkerton bomb had torn his mother's arm off; and the location of his first grave.

Open daily during normal daytime hours, the farm operates a mile or two east of Kearney on State Highway 92 and then north on Jesse James Farm Road. Signs point the way. A moderate price is charged. A visitor center and souvenir shop are enclosed. The farm also presents outdoor theatrical presentations on the life of Jesse James on August weekends.

The grave lies within Mt. Olivet Cemetery in Kearney, just a few miles southwest of the farm. A flat stone, even with the ground, marks his grave ("JESSE W. BORN SEPT. 5, 1847 ASSASSINATED APRIL 3, 1882") and that of his wife. It cannot be seen from a distance but, if you see anyone else in the cemetery, chances are it will be at his grave. His mother and stepfather are interred nearby.

The house attracts a fair trickle of visitors, the grave far fewer. Both sites can be done in a couple hours (more if the outdoor drama is included).

If you want to steep yourself in Jesse lore, try the Jesse James Bank Historic Site in Liberty, about seven miles south of Kearney, reputedly the James boys' professional debut. The original wood floor supposedly contained a victim's blood stains. When either the stains disappeared or the flooring was replaced, an enterprising curator simply poured chicken blood over the new floor (Jesse would have loved it).

Northwest of Kearney, St. Joseph has the restored Jesse James Home, where he was killed, at 12th and Penn Streets.

And that's not all. Stanton, Missouri, a bit more than 250 miles southeast of Kearney by the shortest highway route, contains Meramec Caverns, where James hid out, and - hold on to your Stetson - the Jesse James Wax Museum, which presents the fascinating but largely discredited theory that someone else took the bullet for Jesse and the real McCoy holed out in retirement under an assumed name until 1951 when he died at 103. Believe it or not!

THE BOTANICAL GARDEN THAT PLANTED ITS FOUNDER

Botanical gardens tend to look the same - beautiful floral patches, winding walkways around ponds, streams, and waterfalls, bridges, gazebos, arbors, boathouses.

But there's one just a notch different.

It's America's oldest botanical garden, dating to 1859 when founder Henry Shaw, a St. Louis businessman with bucks, opened it to the public. It also has the nation's oldest constantly open public greenhouse. Its herbarium and library rank among the largest and best on the planet. Its twin rose gardens have been voted America's best. A scented garden uses braille to communicate with blind visitors. It owns the largest Japanese garden anywhere in the world (except in Japan, of course). It sports a sunken 90-foot-square maze of yew hedge and arborvitae for the adventurous to negotiate. Its bulb-like centerpiece, the Climatron, is the world's first public greenhouse encased within a geodesic dome. Statues and sculptures pop up everywhere, including in the Waterlily Garden where sensual figures gyrate explicitly. It's a National Historic Landmark...and a cemetery where Ferdinand von Miller's heroic sculpture of a man in deathly repose surmounts the actual crypt of the garden's creator.

It is the Missouri Botanical Garden in St. Louis.

It encompasses 79 acres which can be traversed through paved paths or on an electric tram, enclosed and heated during the winter, with half-hour narration. Benches and seats, drinking fountains, and rest rooms are scattered throughout to ward off St. Louis' notorious sticky summer humidity.

If you walk, you first encounter Spoehrer Plaza with Latzer Fountain and its shooting water jets. A dense concentration pulls you east: the flowers and pools of the John S. Swift Family Garden with Emilio Greco's statue "The Bather," a sinuous seductress; the camellia-bearing Linnean House, built by Shaw to honor botanist Carolus Linnaeus; the entwined "Three Sturgeons," the work of sculptor Sirio Tofinari; the trellises and shaded arbor near the Scented Garden, where an entire row of benches provides restful views and ample shade; the Shoenberg Fountain displaying Gerhard Marcks' "Three Graces."

From there, individual gardens take over, spotlighting hosta, roses, bulbs, and whatever is in season.

A gazebo encloses the memorial to Shaw at his gravesite, just north of his home, Tower Grove House, built in 1849 and laden with Victorian belongings. The maze, an herb garden, and another Shoenberg Fountain are nearby.

Turning west, the English Woodland Garden, with its azaleas, dogwoods, and wildflowers, provides a prelude to the largest section within the grounds, the 14-acre Seiwa-En ("garden of pure, clear harmony and peace") Japanese Garden, scenic and isolated, with its lake, tributaries, waterfalls, islands, and arched bridges.

The Shapleigh Fountain invites you to sit within it as it nearly surrounds you with thin rods of jet-driven water shooting upward and splashing back to ground, all the while keeping you dry.

The Climatron is a natural tropical rainforest, minus the rain, and with 2,000 varieties of plants between two greenhouses, each with a differing climatic theme.

There are also: a demonstration vegetable garden with practical tips; an experimental propagation greenhouse; and an azalea-rhododendron garden. The research repository museum, administration building, research and production greenhouses, and Lehmann Building (holding the library, herbarium, and working staff of botanists) are generally not available to visitors.

The Ridgway Center, its massive arched entrance rising high, includes the Gardenview Restaurant, a souvenir shop, a floral hall and displays, a gallery, and an auditorium. Concerts, lectures, special productions, and family programs occur frequently. Picnic facilities are available at Tower Grove Park, adjacent to the garden. Touring usually takes a couple hours.

The Missouri Botanical Garden operates daily, except Christmas, during normal daytime hours (which expand to dusk from Memorial Day to Labor Day). A modest fee is charged and that is waived if you visit Wednesday or Saturday before noon; Shaw's house and the tram cost a little extra.

The garden is bounded by Shaw Boulevard and Tower Grove, Magnolia, and Alfred Avenues, about five miles west of the Gateway Arch. U.S. Interstate Highway 44 takes you near it.

MONTANA

THE MOUNTAIN PASS WHERE HEROES PASSED

Monday, August 12, 1805 - the most satisfying, momentous day thus far on a journey that history has recorded as the greatest exploratory mission ever undertaken on the American continent.

A 30-year-old white man, dressed in weathered frontier garb, drank eagerly of the cool waters in the middle of no man's land. He took up his pen:

> thus far I had accomplished one of those great objects on which my mind has been unalterably fixed for many years, judge then of the pleasure I felt in allying my thirst with this pure and ice-cold water... here I halted a few minutes and rested myself.

He gathered his three companions and pushed on:

> after refreshing ourselves we proceeded on to the top of the dividing ridge from which I discovered immense ranges of high mountains still to the West of us with their tops partially covered with snow. I now descended the mountain about 3/4 of a mile which I found much steeper than on the opposite side....

The journalist was Meriwether Lewis. His companions were George Drouillard, Hugh McNeal, and John Shields. They were the first white Americans to go beyond the territorial limits of the newly acquired Louisiana Territory...the first white Americans to cross the Continental Divide...the first white Americans to actually stand on the exact spot where the American waters go in opposite directions, those on the western slope flowing to the Pacific Ocean, those on the eastern side descending to the Atlantic (theretofore, no white American had ever seen western-flowing water).

The men were tired, grizzled, and bedraggled, as they had been most every day since starting their epic journey across the continent in May of the previous year, yet they exulted in reaching the 7,339-foot elevation of Lemhi Pass on the Continental Divide.

The Corps of Volunteers for Northwest Discovery (today known simply as the Lewis and Clark Expedition) had been commissioned by President Thomas Jefferson to explore the great unknown western part of the continent in search of geographical and scientific knowledge and a water route to the Pacific Ocean, with an eye on future westward expansion. Reaching the divide high atop the Bitterroot Range of the Rocky Mountains presented Lewis with a symbolic milestone no white American had ever achieved. It also ensured speedy access to the camps of the Shoshone Indians where Meriwether Lewis and William Clark, his partner, hoped to obtain horses to aid in their crossing of the Rockies.

Today, Lemhi Pass sits atop the divide on the very border of Montana and Idaho. But in Lewis' day, there was no Montana, no Idaho, just virgin wilderness and unpolluted waters, broken only by sporadic Native American villages. After journeying up the Montana side to Lemhi Pass, Lewis and his advance party descended the steeper Idaho side, finding and persuading Shoshones to return with them via the pass to join the main white party under Clark still miles back in Montana. The Shoshones agreed, and Lewis and his entourage reunited with Clark on land now under the waters of Clark Canyon Reservoir off Interstate Highway 15 in Montana. There, the Shoshone chief, Cameahwait, met his long-lost sister, Sacajawea, in Clark's party. Her presence helped the transaction for the needed horses, and the Lewis and Clark Expedition continued on to the Pacific Ocean, returning in triumph in September 1806, after a massive exploration of more than 8,000 uncharted miles across the great American western wilderness.

Today, visitors can retrace the expedition's footsteps along Lemhi Pass in the leisure of their cars. Take Local Highway 324 west at Exit 44 of Interstate Highway 15 (at Clark Canyon Dam, about 17 miles south of Dillon, in southwestern Montana). A memorial by the intersection marks the approximate site where Lewis reunited with Clark and Cameahwait with Sacajawea (the more proper, but seldom-used, spelling of her name substitutes a "g" for the "j").

Highway 324 goes through only one populated area on the way to Lemhi Pass, the tiny hamlet of Grant. Shortly thereafter, an historical marker commemorating the Lewis and Clark Expedition stands near the intersection with a local road unfit for vehicles larger than cars, pickups, or jeeps. Turn right onto this road and proceed two miles to a sign for the Sacajawea Memorial Camp. Continue along the road 4.3 more miles to a sign for a private ranch. Keep driving past the cows and ranch buildings along the unpaved road, passing a sign listing Lemhi Pass and the Idaho State Line as three miles distant. You'll crest Lemhi Pass 5.8 miles after passing the ranch sign (and 12.1 miles after having left the intersection with Highway 324).

A number of historical markers atop the Continental Divide explain the historical significance of the spot you've just driven to, a pass which Native American hunting parties traversed in search of buffalo long before the advent of white explorers, a pass used by later generations of trappers and farmers, a pass the Red Rock-Salmon Stagecoach Line rumbled through, at the risk of being upended or held up, in the closing decades of the 19th century. A quarter-mile loop trail, wide enough for a car, leads to the Sacajawea Historical Area, a picnic ground with tables, toilets, a short hiking trail, a visitor registry book, and historical markers including one that recounts, in Lewis' words, how "two miles below McNeal had exultingly stood with a foot on each side of this little rivulet and thanked his god that he had lived to bestride the mighty and heretofore deemed endless Missouri."

Depending on the time of day, you may see full-racked deer bounding across the wooden poles, set along the divide in cheval-de-frise fashion, unwittingly crossing from one state into another. If the sun is just right, you'll get a spectacular view of the Bitterroot Range as it drops down into Idaho just yards from where you stand.

If you have the time and inclination, cross over into Idaho and descend a precipitous, narrow, unpaved "backcountry byway loop" road that hugs the mountain's edge and takes you 13 miles, past more historical markers and an Indian burial ground, to Tendoy at Idaho Highway 28 (do not attempt Lemhi Pass at night or with over-sized or fishtailing-prone vehicles). More historical markers and memorials recalling the Lewis and Clark Expedition and Sacajawea's birthplace are along 28, just a few miles north of Tendoy.

Driving along the entire pass on both sides will take a couple hours, allowing for stops for historical markers, pictures, and a brief stay at the Sacajawea Historical Area on the Montana side. The Montana approach to Lemhi Pass is about 160 paved road miles west of Yellowstone National Park by way of U.S. Highway 287, Montana Highways 287 and 41, and I-15.

Lemhi Pass will allow you to retrace the steps of some of the most storied and stalwart adventurers ever to stride across the globe. And, if you like solitary rides to hidden places with a hint of danger clinging tightly to winding curves of mountain trails, Lemhi Pass will imprint its legacy onto your memory forever.

NEBRASKA

THE ROCK OF THE AGES

The Indians called it "me-a-pa-te" ("hill that is hard to go around"). To the white pioneers moving west in search of fur, gold, a promised land, or a new beginning, it was "The Lighthouse of the Prairie" and "The Gibraltar of the Plains." Alfred J. Miller, who sketched it in 1837, its earliest known artistic rendering, termed it "an immense fortification."

But its primary name came from Hiram Scott, who went west on a fur-trapping expedition. He died sometime before 1830 close to the towering mountain of clay and sandstone. Rumor had it that the party left him behind when he became incapacitated, and he traveled 60 miles back east to the rock which they had all passed earlier so he could be buried atop its high summit. Those who found his corpse rendered him a small degree of immortality by conferring his name upon the tall butte. The marginally literate nature of many of the pioneers caused the term to be recorded without the possessive apostrophe, and it is still known as simply "Scotts Bluff."

The Oregon Trail, actually a collection of parallel routes covering 2,000 roughhewn miles of middle and western American terrain, the longest road in the history of mankind, slipped by its south side. From the 1840s to the 1860s, an estimated 350,000-500,000 pioneers crossed under its southern shade.

The first white eyes to view the 800-foot-high bluff above the North Platte River may have belonged to fur trappers working with John Jacob Astor, the first American fur king, who siphoned a fortune from the mountains and streams of the Northwest. His associates passed the bluff during Christmas of 1812.

In years to come, other trappers and traders passed the impenetrable rock, followed by wagoners, horsemen, footwalkers, mail couriers, Mormon emigrants, United States cavalrymen, stagecoaches, and, above all, the Oregon Trail pioneers. For the hundreds of thousands of Americans heading west, the dramatic natural formations along the North Platte - Courthouse Rock, Jail Rock, Chimney Rock, and finally the sweeping breadth and towering might of Scotts Bluff - became welcome landmarks signaling the end of the great central plains portion of their journey and the beginning of the Rocky Mountains part.

Today, Scotts Bluff is a national monument, a 14-million-year-old relic of an age long gone, one battered into oblivion by the erosive effects of constant wind and water. A hard, protective caprock, akin to concrete in toughness, covers much of the top of Scotts Bluff, sealing its more delicate underlayers of sandstone and siltstone from much of the force of erosion, protecting the bluff's height, transforming it into a giant among its neighbors on the plains.

Encompassing 3,000 acres, Scotts Bluff National Monument is reached by a paved road that cuts along the flank of Eagle Rock (the sheer bluff most readily visible from the bottom), then ascends the bluff via three tunnels before reaching a parking lot halfway between short, level walks leading to the north and south overlooks. The Saddle Rock hiking trail provides an alternative route to the top, matching the roadway's 1.6-mile length.

At 4,649 feet above sea level, the north overlook glimpses the surrounding grooved Badlands hills, the North Platte River, and the neighboring towns of Scottsbluff(spelled as one word), Terrytown, and Gering.

Even more scenic, the south vantage point presents a stunning panorama of the backside of Eagle Rock, the hiking and driving trails, the Wildcat Hills, South Bluff on the other side of State Highway 92 (paralleling the Oregon Trail), and Dome, Crown, and Sentinel Rocks...and, in the distance, the approximate area of Mitchell Pass where the Oregon Trail crept under the very shadow of the western side of Eagle Rock...and the spindly spire of Chimney Rock, 20 miles southeast...and the Great Plains...all from God's perspective, a sky-high view the pioneers never saw.

The wind is extremely stiff at this height, but the sight is worth it. You might even imagine a train of covered wagons, braving the hardships of months of rigorous travel under the open sky, coursing through the flat plain between the rocks, as the travelers relentlessly crawl west, suffering, enduring, breaking down, and sometimes dying of rampant disease and Asiatic cholera on their way to Oregon's free land, Utah's religious tolerance, and California's gold.

A visitor center at the origin of both the driving and hiking routes features exhibits on the Oregon Trail, natural landmarks of the Nebraska panhandle, and works of western painter and photographer William Henry Jackson. A gift shop is included.

An hour can accommodate the drive and a quick stop at the visitor center, but you may want to actually walk along the ruts of the old Oregon Trail, 200 yards west of the visitor center.

You'll most likely not see much wildlife, although prairie dogs, gophers, squirrels, deer, coyotes, foxes, and snakes live in the bluff area.

A word about snakes. Scotts Bluff contains three varieties, only one of which (prairie rattlesnake) is poisonous. They seldom frequent established hiking trails, preferring instead the brush or tall grass off to their sides. Generally, poisonous snakes are afraid of people and will retreat at their approach. Should you meet up with any belly crawler, the best thing to do is stop in your tracks and let the creature slither away. Should the snake advance toward you (extremely unlikely, unless you have provoked it), gradually back away.

Scotts Bluff can center a much longer vacation in Nebraska's most picturesque corner. Chimney Rock and the other natural formations are within 35 miles southeast; the North Platte National Wildlife Refuge lies a dozen miles north, and the Agate Fossil Beds National Monument is 30 miles farther up. You can catch a covered wagon out to the base of Chimney Rock and then eat a more-or-less authentic chuckwagon western dinner under the stars. Lake Minatare State Recreation Area is 10 miles northeast of Scottsbluff, and the Wildcat Hills State Recreation Area is 10 miles south of Gering. Gering hosts its Oregon Trail Days during the third week in July, and Scottsbluff and Gering combine for an Old West Balloon Days & Old West Weekend in October. The Western Nebraska Antique Car Rally holds its Sugar Valley Rally in early June when pre-1943 clunkers whiz by the venerable old landmarks.

The visitor center and driving road are open daily during daytime hours. A per-vehicle fee is charged. Visitation is steady, but not overwhelming. A day at Scotts Bluff or a weekend in the area might give you a better appreciation of Nebraska, an underestimated state many tourists believe only a connecting link in traveling between the East and the West.

NEVADA

SILVER...WITH A SLIVER OF SPIELBERG

Visitors to Nevada often think its nickname - "The Silver State" - refers to the coins they just lost at the casinos. But what Nevada taketh away (in the form of endless nickels and quarters in the slots), it first gaveth (in the form of the Comstock Lode).

The story of Nevada is the story of silver, and it goes back to 1859 when W. P. Morrison picked up some black rocks gold miners had unearthed and cast aside as useless. He had them assayed in California and found them rich in silver. For the next two decades, silver was king in Nevada, prompting a California senator to decry in 1873, "We have more silver than we want. Nevada appears to be getting ready to deluge the world in silver."

A U.S. branch mint began operations in Carson City, the state's capital, in 1870. When it closed nearly a quarter-century later, it had produced $50 million in coins.

Today, that same mint building is part of the Nevada State Museum: canceled coin dies, ingot molds, and money bags; bullion wagon; complete Carson City U.S. mint collection; silver service minted from Nevada silver and given by the state to the U.S.S. Nevada battleship; reconstruction of a 19th-century Nevada silver town with an animatronic prospector providing narration; and the Carson City Mint's six-ton Coin Press No. 1, built in 1869 and still working.

Even though the museum focuses on silver, its other exhibits prove even more eye-catching. Elsewhere on the first floor are the J. W. Calhoun Changing Gallery and extensive displays of stuffed wildlife that once roamed the state or flew above it, the modest species (godwit, grebe, egret, weasel) mounted alongside the mighty ones (black bear, bobcat, mountain lion).

Nevada's ichthyosaur fossil welcomes guests up the staircase to the second floor where they come across a junior Jurassic Park. The Hall of Regional Geology peeks into the Precambrian, Paleozoic, and Mesozoic Eras, among others. A ramp leads to a hidden Devonian Period shocker where a ferocious six-foot-long eel-like eusthenopteron gnaws on a fish it has impaled on its teeth.

In the spacious room devoted to the Cenozoic Era, a towering, fearsomely tusked 50-year-old imperial mammoth, who died 17,000 years ago in Nevada's Black Rock Desert, seemingly battles a large dinosaur-like Ice Age horse who inhabited Nevada's Pyramid Lake area 25,500 years ago. Though they never saw each other in real life, they provide great contemporary theater.

Another room studies the archeology of Nevada's Great Basin with exhibits on toolmaking, prehistoric missile weapons, dioramas on pueblo culture, and an astonishingly vivid Great Basin Indian camp scene, a massive and realistic centerpiece.

Finally, in the basement, visitors exit the museum by snaking through a replica of an underground silver mine, following an ore car track as it negotiates sinuous turns that suddenly present full-figure tableaus of miners at work and cutaway views of ore veins that highlight crystals of scheelite and calcite with the press of a finger on a panel. Kids love the underground simulation, and it's a clever way to end a tour of a multifaceted museum that promises a lesson on Nevada's silver connection and then peppers the brew with a dash of Steven Spielberg adventure and a touch of Walt Disney whimsy.

The museum attracts 100-150 people a day during its daily (except major holidays) operation (normal daytime hours) at 600 North Carson Street, four blocks north of the capitol building. A moderate admission is charged for the couple hours you're likely to spend. A large book store awaits you before your final descent into the underground mine.

A small, visitor-friendly town, Carson City packs in a lot of museums: the State Capitol; the State Railroad Museum; the Stewart Indian School Museum; the Carson Brewery Arts Center; the J. D. Roberts House; the Supreme Court Building; Amuseum of Northern Nevada (for the children); the Warren Engine Company No. 1 Fire Museum; and the Historical Home District, including the house used for "The Shootist," John Wayne's final film. All are within easy walking or driving distance and will occupy two or three entire days at a cost under $20.

Or, if you'd prefer to return some of your pocket silver to its original owner, you could simply leave the Cenozoic Era and the underground mine, turn south, and walk a short block or two to the Nugget or Cactus Jack's.

NEW HAMPSHIRE

WHERE AMERICANS LIVED...2,000 YEARS BEFORE CHRIST

In the early decades of the 19th century, Jonathan Pattee surveyed his share of the family tract, a small granite hill too rocky to do much with. He built some rustic structures on it, tended to his livestock, and lived there with his family about 25 years. A local history book, now nearly 100 years old, described Pattee's estate as "...a wild but beautiful spot among rough boulders and soft pines, about which the most weird and fantastic tale might be woven...." He lived over a collection of stone-lined caves and oddly shaped rocks protruding in a sort of ritualistic pattern from the earth.

Eventually Pattee died, and his house burned down in 1855. Many of the hill's stones and rocks wound up carted off, destined for construction use elsewhere.

The entire hill returned to a state of nature, and neighboring people occasionally picnicked there. William Goodwin bought the vandalized hill in the 1930s and studied its unusual surviving formations. He theorized the site might be far older than anyone had ever realized.

Then in the 1950s, Robert E. Stone acquired the land. He cleared it and painstakingly studied it and called in experts.

What they found suggests that Jonathan Pattee may have unwittingly homesteaded on the very site of America's oldest manmade construction.

The English at Jamestown? The Pilgrims at Plymouth? The Spanish at St. Augustine?

No, it was only a mystery people, well-versed in astronomy and megalith construction, who built a fair facsimile of England's Stonehenge on a hill outside North Salem, New Hampshire well before the English, the Pilgrims, and the Spanish, well before Christopher Columbus and the Vikings, well before even Christ (by about 2,000 years).

Today, it is billed as a "giant megalithic astronomical complex." Though not as big, monolithic, or impressive as Stonehenge, it is equally mysterious and important.

It possesses a chamber, once referred to as the "Tomb of Lost Souls"... and another one called the "Oracle," with two passages, a so-called "secret bed" (a cavity large enough for someone to ease into and hide in), wall carvings, a flat stone presumably used for sacrificial offerings, and a stone-lined natural "speaking tube" extending from the interior to the sacrificial ledge. More important, a row of unusually shaped large monoliths rings the central living complex and contains stones that directly line up with sunrises and sunsets during solstice and equinox periods and other important ancient days. The systematic arrangement of stones over 30 acres makes it one of the continent's largest ancient astronomical calendar sites and very possibly its oldest.

Radiocarbon dating of excavated implemental artifacts indicates an age of 4,000 years. Experts conclude the ancient people who rearranged the surface of the hill by moving multi-ton sculpted boulders into precise settings belonged either to a civilization endemic to North America or one that migrated from Europe. Research continues at the site.

A self-guided tour starts at the visitor center-gift shop-snack bar and wends through three dozen stops, culminating in a modern gazebo-like platform which explains the astronomical alignment of the surrounding ring of rocks. A complimentary, richly detailed tour guide map is handed out to further amplify what you see.

Reading every note on your guide, locating its corresponding point, and studying the precise celestial information as you walk along the outer ring will take a couple hours, time you may not have, especially if the mosquitos are thick. The essence of the site can be grasped in a much shorter walking tour combined with a few moments of study in the mosquito-free visitor center where you can view "Puzzles in Stone," a good 10-minute film, and see inscribed stones removed from the area.

America's Stonehenge, as it is called, appeals more to the scholarly armchair scientist and the naturally inquisitive. Kids enjoy running around the rocks, but that's not their purpose.

The site is open daily from May through October and on weekends during April and November. The hours vary slightly through the months but generally correspond to customary daytime hours. The slightly above-average admission charge, worth it if you stay for a couple hours, contributes to "the preservation and further research" of the privately owned site. About 30,000 visitors stop each year.

America's Stonehenge is in North Salem, a little northeast of Nashua, in southern New Hampshire. State Highway 111 intersects with Haverhill Road which, in turn, leads south to the entrance.

The heart of Boston is only about three dozen miles south.

THE FINAL MISSION OF SANDY SLOANE

Sanderson "Sandy" Sloane had a simple dream, the universal dream of every man. He dreamed of building a house for himself, his wife, and his small son. He selected a site atop Halo Hill, just north of Rindge, in southern New Hampshire, a site that offered a view of Grand Monadnock Mountain and Mount Kearsarge and even the Green Mountains of neighboring Vermont. He dreamed of growing old there with his family.

Sandy Sloane had only one problem. World War II was on, and he had a job to do. Still, he kept the dream alive. "Do not touch anything until I return," he wrote home, chafing at the delay.

Sandy Sloane was an airplane pilot with many flights under his belt. He had only one more mission to fly.

On February 22, 1944, 27-year-old Second Lieutenant Sanderson Sloane piloted the B-17 Flying Fortress Bomber "Peg-O-My-Heart" over Koblenz, Germany. It was the last thing he ever did.

Another tragedy awaited his widow. Their only son, Sandy, Jr., born on October 21, 1943, died not long after his father.

The home that Sandy Sloane envisaged for himself and his family remained unbuilt. And Halo Hill remained empty, except for its stand of pine trees.

Sandy Sloane's parents, Douglas and Sibyl Sloane, decided to erect a memorial to their son where his house would have been, a place of worship and tranquility atop Halo Hill. Even before anything permanent could be constructed, the first service occurred on August 26, 1945.

Gradually, word got out and donations came in. The memorial became the Cathedral of the Pines, a roofless outdoor altar in the midst of the towering trees. An act of Congress in 1957 transformed it into a national war memorial to America's war dead, male and female, military and civilian.

The Altar of the Nation overlooks the Garden of Remembrance and the countryside that so enthralled Sandy Sloane. Farther down the hill, the Mother's Chapel and the St. Francis of Assisi Chapel highlight a winding, semicircular paved trail below the altar. A stone monolith carries the inscribed Ten Commandments. Another holds the St. Francis Prayer. The Memorial Bell Tower, with its Tree of Life fountain, bell peal, and quartet of bas relief bronze tablets sculpted by Peter Rockwell from drawings done by his father Norman, honors all female war dead. The Hilltop House Museum shows a film and provides information about the site and has an indoor chapel. Another museum farther down the hill displays an eclectic mix of donated military and religious items and pictures. A cemetery of flat stones and highly personal epitaphs lies by trees and evergreens.

And Sandy Sloane and his young son, never to know each other in life, now rest together for all eternity in an affectingly private section beneath the stone pulpit.

The Altar of the Nation is a simple, rustic altar comprising stones donated from every state and from both unknown and highly prominent people, including seven American presidents, and cemented together with soil from Mount Zion in Jerusalem.

The donated stones, pebbles, petrified wood and dinosaur bones, glass, and so forth that make up the altars, pulpits, lecterns, and rail posts throughout the grounds nearly tell the story of mankind in their disparate geographic origins: the Normandy beachhead of the D-Day invasion; General George Patton's Luxembourg grave; Korea and Vietnam; American Indian mounds; Plymouth Rock; Abraham Lincoln's Kentucky birthplace and his Illinois tomb; Hawaiian volcanoes; the New Orleans battlefield; the Hermitage; the Roman Colosseum and catacombs; the birthplace of Joan of Arc and the grave of the Marquis de Lafayette, both in France; the Parthenon; the Rock of Gibraltar; the White House; an Incan temple in Peru; the Temple of Diane in Ephesus, Turkey, one of the ancient world's seven wonders; Hitler's Bavarian mountaintop retreat in Berchtesgaden; Hiroshima; the Great Wall of China; the Sea of Galilee; the Grand Canyon; the crematorium at Birkenau, Poland; Napoleon's tomb; St. Patrick's grave; King Tut's tomb; the Statue of Liberty.

A flagstone laid by George Washington at Mount Vernon is there. So also is some four-billion-year-old Canadian basalt, the solidified lava known as the "Rock of Ages," the earth's oldest-known stone.

The Cathedral of the Pines invites congregations to hold their services on its grounds for special occasions; and visitors are always welcome. The cathedral also receives, courtesy of surviving relatives, flags that formerly draped the coffins of loved ones killed in action; the flags are flown at half-mast on the birthdays of the people they honored in death.

Wooden backless benches make up the pews and hold some 2,000. Religious and patriotic services frequently occur, including a 9:15 a.m. ecumenical service every Sunday, from May to October. Musical programs highlight the summer. Weddings, christenings, bar and bat mitzvahs, and burials also take place (call 603-899-3300 for details).

A visitor center sells related gift items and souvenirs. The Cathedral House, a converted old farmhouse with bed and breakfast rooms, also hosts receptions, retreats, and social affairs (call 603-899-6790).

Per-vehicle donations are suggested upon entering the grounds because the shrine is a non-denominational, non-profit foundation receiving no government support, but no pressure is exerted. Though most everything is outdoors, indoor church rules apply: smoking, eating and drinking, pets, and improper attire are not allowed within the cathedral portions of the compound; a separate picnic area is provided.

The 400-acre site is a little west of center in southern New Hampshire, about five miles from the Massachusetts border and just north of Rindge. It is open daily from 9 a.m. to dusk, May through October. Free guided tours are available; self-guided tours usually last a half-hour to an hour.

Mount Monadnock, Temple Mountain, Annett State Forest, Miller State Park, and innumerable hiking, skiing, and outdoor activities are all nearby.

The flies and humidity can be intense in summer, and the chill and breezes are noticeable in the fall. But if the timing is right, the Cathedral of the Pines can be a wordless place of poignancy and serenity, a place where you might get to know your God a little better, and a place where you might even see a vision of Sandy Sloane embracing his family in the clouds, high above the pines he once longed to call home.

NEW JERSEY

THE MINIATURE KINGDOM THAT KILLED ITS KING

He lies in a grave atop the summit of a cemetery on the western side of State Highway 31 in Washington, New Jersey. A simple flat stone crowns his grave. Its inscription tersely lists his name and his dates of birth and death - all that the limited space on the stone and the financial resources of his widow could afford.

He began life in another land in 1923. At age seven, he assumed the demanding work ethic that was to serve as his hallmark when he apprenticed at the family department store in Holland, painting lampshades and building miniature houses to complement toy train sets. After school, the boy logged hours in his father's basement workshop, his food arriving by dumbwaiter so he wouldn't have to leave the family factory.

At 15, he quit school and the oppressive regimen at home, taking to the road, exchanging his paintings and handiwork for lodging and food.

A teen-ager embroiled in the full weight of World War II, he returned to Holland and joined the Dutch underground in the fight against fascism. His facility with painting and detail made him valuable in combating Nazism. He became a forger, faking passports and papers for Jews to use in fleeing Adolf Hitler's ever-widening program of genocide against an entire race. He put his acquired collection of German military uniforms to use in commandeering food for his fellow countrymen.

After the war, he turned to music, fashion design, education.

He gained a doctorate in math and an architectural degree.

Ultimately, he settled on architecture. He built hotels, restaurants, and municipal buildings. He designed a town in Saudi Arabia, a pair of Mideast harbors, and a portion of a bridge in Nigeria.

He found his greatest fame in small-scale models, however. He built Madurodam - a microcosmic version of Holland on three acres of outdoor ground at The Hague. He also constructed Mini-Mundus in Austria and Swiss-Miniatur in Switzerland and another miniature world - eventually destined for America under the name Miniature Kingdom - at Valkenburg, Holland. Monaco's Prince Rainier and the Shah of Iran commissioned him to create splendid miniatures for their private collections.

He arrived in America in 1974, a failed marriage behind him and with deep resentment of his country for having sued him over the rights to Madurodam. He signed a five-year contract with what is now Six Flags Great Adventure of Jackson, New Jersey - a thematic entertainment park - to exhibit his Miniature Kingdom. When the contract expired, he and his second wife moved the village to its present location and built a 13,000-square-foot castle-like building to house it.

Plagued in those years by lung and kidney failure, hooked up to a dialysis machine for two years - the result of 40 years of inhaling the fumes of the materials and chemicals used in fashioning his miniature masterpieces - he opened the exhibit to the public in December 1983.

He succumbed to his fatal ailment less than a year later on August 2, 1984.

His widow - Trudy Baumann Thuijs - has struggled ever since to stay afloat, saddled with the enormity of having to pay his astronomical medical bills. She has operated the Miniature Kingdom - his greatest legacy - ever since to diminished crowds (most people are not aware of its location far afield from the state's popular shore resorts and casinos and the New York City spillover suburban sprawl that so characterizes northeastern New Jersey).

On clear days and when the trees have not grown thick foliage to obstruct the view, the cemetery and the exhibit can be seen, one from the other. The creator and his creation, artist and artistry - a stone's throw from one another for all eternity.

The Miniature Kingdom - a poor man's tour of Europe - is the greatest legacy of Arthur Thuijs (pronounced "Tice") on American soil. Some three dozen major settings, some containing numerous interconnected set pieces, surround the exhibit room and rise from four massive islands within. Each building, built to precise scale (one half-inch of model equaling one foot of actual edifice) and created only after extensive surveying and photography sessions at the actual locations, required some three to 18 months of labor with Swedish masonite, lead, copper, wood, plastic, stone, brass, glass, and high-gloss enamel - with weatherproofing precautions included to accommodate outdoor display.

Though the artist's fondness for Dutch and German architecture peeks through everywhere, the exhibit succeeds in glimpsing quaint corners of Europe: "The 12 Apostles" or "The 12 Weavers Houses" of Schonberg, Poland, dating to 1214; Amsterdam's centuries-old Dutch Canal Houses; London, England's 1710 Georgian House; Belgium's monument to the monumental Battle of Waterloo where 226 steps scale a summit to a 15-foot-high lion ("built by the people of Belgium out of 10,000,000 baskets of sand over 100,000 corpses of horses and men who fought the battle on June 18, 1815 when Wellington and Bluchner met at Napoleon's 'La Belle Alliance,'" as the explanatory card proclaims); a pair of modern Swiss hotels; and a hotel on the French Riviera, complete with ersatz sand and a plethora of sunbathers - all sartorially and facially different.

The most imposing scenes highlight the center islands: Stuttgart, Germany's Castle Lusthouse, a theatrical, art-galleried complex with restaurants, that delighted patrons from 1587 until 1900, when fire consumed it; the New York City harbor of the 1700s, where three-masted tall ships ride at anchor, docked along the wharves for their cotton, tobacco, and wine cargoes to be unloaded and sold at market; Moscow, Russia's famed Kremlin and

Red Square with three spired cathedrals and half a dozen imposing towers.

Thuijs' attentiveness to detail manifests itself throughout. When Stuttgart's Castle Lusthouse burned down, the architectural renderings perished as well. Thuijs devoted years of archival research among arcane manuscripts and venerable books, ferreting out any clue to the original plans. The finished product so entranced the experts that the University of Stuttgart petitioned to obtain it for its museum.

Ten thousand handmade fake hyacinths, painstakingly crafted from gravel, glue, wire, paint, and plastic, rise as colored sentinels in the flower fields surrounding Holland's "spider" windmill.

The incredible Counts' Castle of Flanders in Ghent, Belgium, spanning nearly a millennium, oozes the reeking stench of battlefield fire, oil, sweat, and blood. The most dramatic setting of the entire display, it sends an attacking army sloshing through the mud to press a spirited siege of one of history's most impregnable forts. Wheeled battering rams, semicircular head-to-foot shields of stockade pickets, projectile-hurling catapults, and massive movable wooden attack towers all push relentlessly forward. Footsoldiers square off against equestrian knights who gallop across the courtyard to augment the defense of the outer wall. Thuijs' war imagery throbs with the guts and gore of a medieval battle royal.

But the stately 10-foot-tall Neuschwanstein Castle and eminence on which it reigns in splendor, perhaps more than any other single Thuijs creation, captures the essence of olden Europe. Though relatively new (the castle arose in 1869 in Fussen, Germany), this most majestic of the string of castles erected by King Ludwig II of Bavaria is the universal symbol of a Cinderella castle; tall, angular, buttress-laden towers with appendant turrets crowd the sky in a profusion of splendor. The actual Neuschwanstein has served as backdrop in many motion pictures because it embodies everyone's conception of what a castle should be. Those who have visited the real article near the Austrian border will experience instant nostalgia at Thuijs' handiwork and almost imagine they're back in Bavaria as they stroll around the gargantuan model, complete with switchback approach to the castle entrance...and all to the strains of Strauss waltzes filling the cavernous interior from a behind-the-scenes tape player.

An air of consummate craftsmanship gently floats over the interior, rather dark save for spotlights illuminating the buildings. Each of the kingdom's 2,000 people were sculpted and painted. Trees grew from electrical wire, leaves from steel wool with painted sawdust glued on.

Houseboats ply the waters of the Dutch canals. Hundreds of cheese balls await purchase at outdoor markets. Scores of lampposts illuminate the streets of Europe. And two LGB Lehmann passenger trains endlessly girdle the recreated villages, towns, and ports on journeys without departures and destinations, effortless trips spanning the ages.

The thousands of buildings, ships, vehicles, people, animals, trees and flowers, and stationary items required more than 100,000 actual hours of labor, considerably more than a decade of round-the-clock, 24-hour-a-day, everyday effort. The exhibit is valued at more than a million dollars. If some of the figures appear somewhat artificial, stilted, or obviously crafted, it is because the buildings they are juxtaposed against so closely resemble the real structures upon which they are modeled.

Trudy Baumann Thuijs, the artist's creative assistant and widow, manages the Miniature Kingdom. She speaks emotionally of her husband's craftsmanship, of how he "never rested...seldom slept...and worked himself to death," breaking the skein of generational longevity that had made both his father and grandfather nonagenarians. She maintains the museum in memory of a master craftsman who never knew when to quit and who paid the price with an abbreviated life, leaving behind a legacy of beauty, culture, and romance, all in miniature.

The Miniature Kingdom is open most days from April through November and takes an hour to tour adequately and intelligently. Children enjoy running through the aisles between the islands and up and down the ramps, but the museum is designed for adults and older adolescents who appreciate artistry; smaller and more rambunctious children are best left behind. A moderate admission fee is charged.

Informational textboards interspersed among the various buildings along the avenues of the exhibit explain the history of each historic structure, providing behind-the-scenes commentary on the construction of each miniature facsimile. And, for 50 cents, visitors can purchase a four-page flyer that duplicates the precise text of every board and serves as a keepsake.

The miniature kingdom is just south of Washington, on the west side of State Highway 31, about halfway between Interstates 80 and 78. It can be part of a day that includes the Delaware Water Gap National Recreation Area 20 miles to the northwest.

To confirm current operating schedules, a call is advisable: 908-689-6866.

THE BURNING SANDS OF SOUTHERN NEW JERSEY

"Down in southern New Jersey they make glass," wrote the poet Carl Sandburg. "By day and by night, the fires burn on in Millville and bid the sand let in the light."

Sandburg's lines from "In Reckless Ecstasy" are everywhere in Wheaton Village in Millville where they mix sand, lime, and soda ash, fire it, and then shape it into glass.

There is more to New Jersey sand than beaches and boardwalks. The presence of fine silica sand, water networks, and forests in southern New Jersey transformed the region into a hotbed of glass manufacturing: over 200 separate operations since 1739; 20 today.

A blend of authentic and reconstructed 19th-century houses and shops, Wheaton Village not only makes glass, it makes it before your eyes.

The T. C. Wheaton Glass Factory, named for Doctor Theodore Corson Wheaton, a physician, pharmacist, and founder of the T. C. Wheaton Company glass manufacturing firm, is an exact replica of Wheaton's original 1888 glass factory. Today, it provides three daily 20-minute demonstrations of glass manufacture with narration: 500 pounds of sand, lime, and soda ash (called "batch") are heated to 2,600 degrees in a furnace fire for 14 hours, then cooled to 2,000 degrees; blobs of batch are gathered onto blowpipes and rotated and shaped by artisans blowing small amounts of air into the pipes and rounding the edges with rods and paddles; and, when the blobs have been fashioned into the desired shapes, they are returned to annealing ovens for tempering (gradual cooling and hardening).

The village's premier attraction, however, remains the 20,000-square-foot Museum of American Glass, one of the country's largest collections of glass. Nearly a dozen period and thematic galleries display a dazzling assemblage of color and shape: an 1829 grand harmonicon, a musical instrument of two dozen wine glasses of alternating size, played by filling the glasses with water and then rubbing the rims (Ludwig von Beethoven actually composed music for the instrument, such was its appeal once); stained glass; Avon figural bottles; chandeliers and hanging lamps; iridescent carnival glass, the "poor man's Tiffany," created by spraying metallic salts on pressed glassware when still heated; Dorflinger glass; milk bottles; pressed glass through the decades; glass miniatures; marbles from akro and agate to cat eyes and clearies; patent medicine bottles; punch bowls and soda bottles; Mother of Pearl and Coralene, Craquelle and Overshot; and the world's largest bottle, at 7'8" and 188 gallons, authenticated by the Guinness Book of Records and blown at Wheaton Village in 1992.

The Special Exhibit Gallery contains changing displays of gorgeous glass artwork.

Every object is identified, and the text often fascinates:

> - Germany invented the marble in the 1840s, but America dominates its production;
> - Ancient Mesopotamia (modern Iraq) invented glass in 2,000 B.C., and Syria (today's Palestine area) discovered the blowpipe in 50 B.C.;
> - Proprietary medicine manufacturers often chose not to patent their concoctions because that required listing the ingredients, opting instead to contrive
> "some catchy trade name" and then register the trademark, thereby hiding the fact that their nostrums usually consisted primarily of water and alcohol;
> - Unprocessed sand contains natural colorants (iron) which produce aqua-colored glass; other metallic oxides must be blended into the batch to produce clear or differently colored glass.

The Crafts and Trades Row consists of separate shops offering pottery, woodcarving, and lampworking (creating glass objects from glass tubing and cane roasted over a small lamp flame for pliability) demonstrations.

The rest of the village includes original tinsmith and print shops with relics on display, an authentic 19th-century one-room schoolhouse, and a row of attractively reconstructed shops selling sundry items. Glasswork wrought by area artists ranges from easily affordable souvenirs to one-of-a-kind artworks well into four figures.

The grounds include a playground, a serene lake with flocks of Canada geese and a duck or two, and an above-water gazebo with entrance bridges (and occasional summer concerts). The Wheaton Village Special Excursion half-scale mini-locomotive departs the 1897 Palermo Train Station at lakeside every half-hour between 11 a.m. and 4 p.m. for a three-quarter-mile round trip ride. Flower gardens, shrubbery, gaslight-type lampposts, and tree-lined lanes are scattered throughout the 88-acre complex.

Wheaton sponsors special exhibits and weekends, concerts, festivals, and art, antique, and car shows throughout the year.

The village is open daily (except during January through March, when it closes Monday and Tuesday) during customary daytime hours. An average entry fee is charged for a single person, a well-discounted fare for a family.

You can easily spend three hours at the village and still not see all the objects in the museum. A restaurant and lodge are on the premises. Visitation will be hundreds on busy days and just handfuls on others.

The village is in Millville, near the intersection of State Highways 55 and 49, halfway between Atlantic City to the east and Wilmington, Delaware to the west.

A nice break from the beaches, Wheaton Village illustrates the heights man can achieve with sand when he is not lying and frying on it.

NEW MEXICO

BULLETS, BLOOD, AND A BOY NAMED BILLY

It began with bad blood over control of a money market.

Forgettable names like L. G. Murphy, James J. Dolan, John H. Riley, and Thomas B. Catron, owners of a general store appropriately called "The Big Store," controlled much of Lincoln County in the Territory of New Mexico in the 1870s, including lucrative contracts providing beef cattle and produce to the U.S. Army and Indian reservations. They also had many of the territorial administrators and legislators in their pocket, and lawmen protected them.

But another business faction chafed under such monopolistic competition: John S. Chisum, the wealthy owner of the largest cattle herd in America; Alexander A. McSween, a local lawyer; and John H. Tunstall, a young English merchant. They sought to get their slice of the pie. Tunstall opened up his own general store in Lincoln. And in 1877, Tunstall, McSween, and Chisum became officers of the Lincoln County Bank.

Both sides tried to hamstring each other whenever possible.

Then in February 1878, angry words, court orders, newspaper accusations, and warrants gave way to violence when a posse organized by Lincoln County Sheriff William Brady, a Murphy and Dolan man, killed Tunstall.

In typical vendetta fashion, the Tunstall faction responded in kind. Dick Brewer, a Tunstall foreman, formed an illegal posse that captured two of Tunstall's killers.

Brewer guaranteed the captives' safety. But when he was out of sight, two posse members murdered the captives and one of their own when he attempted to intervene.

The infamous Lincoln County War was under way.

One of the murderers became notorious. A teen-aged loner with a blind loyalty to anyone who befriended or employed him and who variously used the names Antrim, Bonney, or McCarty, he had briefly ranched, herded sheep, bused tables, and rustled cattle. At 17, in Arizona, he had killed Francis Cahill when the latter had labeled him a "pimp;" the youth merely called his taunter a "son of a bitch" and shot him. He then fled to New Mexico and wound up in Tunstall's employ.

In April 1878, the teen and his criminal coterie killed Sheriff Brady from ambush. Then in July, they participated in a gun battle with the Murphy-Dolan faction at McSween's home. McSween died in the gunfire.

Soon thereafter, Murphy died and Dolan went bankrupt, effectively ending the economic rivalry. But the criminal gang went on, and the violence continued. The juvenile killer and his comrades remained on the shadowy side of the law, stealing and selling cattle the next two and a half years.

Apprehended by the new sheriff of Lincoln County in December 1880, the youth escaped jail in the town of Lincoln the following April, killing both jail guards along the way.

In mid-July 1881, the sheriff tracked him northeast to a Fort Sumner homestead. And in the darkened bedroom of the ranch around midnight, in the early moments of the 14th, Sheriff Pat Garrett fired a bullet through or near the heart of the 21-year-old killer named Billy the Kid.

Ironically, Billy became a hero in death, a mythical figure, less sinner than sinned against. Some said he was gentlemanly, kind, proper. Others responded that he was only a petty thief and psychotic killer, an ill-mannered boor, a punk who killed compulsively and who befriended only mental cases like himself.

His killing count became of paramount importance, as if to justify his legend: anywhere from four to 21.

And the early movies didn't help, portraying him sympathetically under the guise of matinee idols Robert Taylor and Paul Newman.

His contemporaries described him as a buck-toothed manchild, a pleasant sort fond of singing and dancing when he wasn't killing, about 5'8" and 140 pounds, with the hint of a mustache desperately trying to poke through.

His legacy lives on in books, films, and the popular imagination...and in two small towns in New Mexico.

With a population of about 75, Lincoln, the former hub of the Lincoln County War, carries almost as many historical markers as it does residents. U.S. Highway 380 (Main Street) splits it in half and has a spate of memorials.

With the 10,000-foot-high peaks of the Capitan Mountains looming in the background, the north side of the road includes: the Historical Center, a museum of county artifacts; the Torreon, a thick tower designed as defense against Apaches which instead provided shelter for "Murphy's sharpshooters;" Tunstall's store; the site of the McSween home, now an open field, where Alexander McSween, holding his Bible and praying, perished in tongues of flame while Billy the Kid, six-gun blazing, bolted out of the inferno; and a marker to "OLD LINCOLN TOWN," mentioning the graves of Tunstall and McSween, Lincoln's most famous martyrs.

The south side is equally historic: an outdoor amphitheater that stages annual re-enactments of Billy's escape from the Lincoln jail; Dolan's home; the site of the house of J. B. Wilson, a justice of the peace who arranged a secret meeting between Billy and Territorial Governor Lew Wallace (a Civil War general who also wrote a book called "Ben Hur" in his spare time); and the old "Big Store."

A two-story adobe structure once owned by Murphy, the "Big Store" became a courthouse and jail, the same one from which the Kid escaped on April 28, 1881 while awaiting his execution in his upstairs cell. Though handcuffed and shackled with leg irons, he somehow got a pistol and startled jailer James Bell with it. As Bell ran down the stairs, Billy plugged him dead. Still on the second floor, the Kid took a double-barreled shotgun from the office, raced back to his opened cell, and took a position by the northeast window. When the other jailer, Bob Ollinger, who had been eating across the street, popped into view, Billy yelled, "Hello, Bob" and then leveled a blast at him. Ollinger fell, and Billy rushed out on the front balcony, firing another round at the body. Violently breaking the shotgun on the porch, he hurled it at the dead Ollinger, swearing, "Take it, damn you! You won't follow me anymore with that gun!" He danced around the porch, laughed, and removed his manacles, as terrified onlookers stayed back and allowed him to skip town.

The building is now a museum to the war that swirled within and around it. It preserves the original corner where the killer was confined, the window through which he fired his first shot at Ollinger, the porch from where he pumped the second shell, and the staircase where he killed Bell. Framed glass protects bullet holes within the wall at the foot of the stairs; an adjoining plaque identifies the holes as "believed to have been made by the shots fired by William Bonney...." A flat stone outside the courthouse marks the spot where "ROBT. M. OLLINGER DIED...KILLED BY BILLY THE KID."

The town's historic buildings, sites, and markers make up the Lincoln National Historic Landmark. Tours operate daily, during daytime hours, from March to mid-September (call 505-653-4372 or 505-653-4025 for times the rest of the year). An average admission is charged; touring all the museums and houses will take an hour or two. Visitation is normally slight. If you want to see Lincoln come alive, visit during the first weekend in August when the Last Escape of Billy the Kid Annual Pageant offers a re-enactment, parade, food, and arts and crafts exhibits.

And 135 highway miles northeast of Lincoln lies Fort Sumner and Billy's bones. The glitzy Billy the Kid Museum at 1601 East Sumner Avenue, a bizarre assortment of "60,000 relics," including virtually any item the founder managed to acquire, whether it contained local significance or not, is not really a museum about Billy the Kid, although it might be worth a look. The grave is nearby.

A locked wrought iron cage protects the remains of a severely chipped tombstone marking the graves of three "PALS" - Tom O'Folliard and Charlie Bowdre, who died violently in December 1880, and William H. Bonney, who died likewise a half-year later. Another marker confined within the cage identifies the plot's principal occupant as "THE BOY BANDIT KING. HE DIED AS HE HAD LIVED. 21 MEN TO HIS CREDIT."

A nearby historical marker tells how the chipped stone was stolen in 1950, recovered in 1976, re-stolen in 1981, found again later that year, and finally "reset...in 'iron shackles' May 30, 1981."

From time to time, history buffs offer "evidence" that Billy is not buried in the grave, that he worked out a deal with Pat Garrett, and then retired elsewhere in the country to live well into the 20th century under an alias. Recent computer checkups, comparing facial characteristics, however, have exposed all the would-be Billys as impostors. Some accounts have also placed the Kid's grave nearby in an unmarked plot.

The house in which Billy died, owned by Pete Maxwell, no longer survives, but the site can be viewed at the nearby Fort Sumner National Monument.

The grave is free for the viewing. The museum is not. An hour will easily take care of everything. Crowds should not be a problem.

Lincoln is 57 miles west of Roswell, the major city in that part of New Mexico, on U.S. Highway 380.

To reach Fort Sumner from Roswell, go north on U.S. Highway 285 and then State Highway 20; then follow signs on U.S. Highway 60 in Fort Sumner.

If you want to track the trail of the Kid in both places, start early in the day and expect a full day, including travel time.

And decide for yourself whether he had the "face of an angel...soft voice of a woman...blue eyes of a poet," as Ygenio Salazar, who knew him, described him. Or whether he was "no better and no worse than the other boys of his age," according to Mary Richards, who taught him at school. Or whether he was "not handsome, but he had a certain sort of boyish good looks....always smiling and good-natured and very polite and danced remarkably well," in the words of Paulita Maxwell, Pete's sister and the Kid's reputed girlfriend. Or whether "He ate and laughed, drank and laughed, rode and laughed, talked and laughed, fought and laughed, and killed and laughed," as Pat Garrett, who killed him, said.

NEW YORK

THE BUCKING BRONCOS OF BROOME COUNTY

It may be the only place in the country where you can still get a free ride...and then another one...and another still...and yet get nowhere when you're done.

Broome County owns a herd of horses, 300 in all, free for the riding, over and over again. But they're not just any horses. They're painted ponies...colts of the carousel...merry-go-round mares.

Broome County owns the largest collection of carousels, per-capita, anywhere in the world. It also owns the world's only free collection of carousels. Six carousels in all, with a total of 300 mounts (296 horses, two dogs, and two wild boars). For upwards of threescore years, Broome's 25 dozen wooden animals have been going around in circles, roaming its pavilion pastures, a herd strung out nearly 10 miles across the heart of the county, thundering to a calliope cadence, bounding to the beat of the band organ.

Carved by woodcrafters for the Allan Herschell Company, the sculpted steeds strode into Broome through the generosity of the paternalistic patriarch of the Endicott-Johnson Shoe Company, one of the country's largest shoe manufacturers for the first half of the 20th century. A resident of the county in which his shoe empire thrived, George F. Johnson endeared himself to his community by doling out gifts left and right: public parks, swimming pools, tennis courts, bowling alleys, libraries, a golf course, and the six carousels that never took a cent in return. As a child, the philanthropist had been denied a carousel ride for lack of a nickel. He vowed it would never happen again. True to his word, Johnson and his family lassoed 300 horses in slightly more than a dozen years beginning around 1920 and entrusted them in perpetuity to the county's corral, with local municipalities having jurisdiction over the carousels within their boundaries.

In one form or another, carousels date back at least several centuries. In practicing for jousting matches, 17th-century Frenchmen mounted wooden horses attached to a central wheel that spun on an axis. A version of this surfaced in America's early years. And shortly after the Civil War, German immigrant George Dentzel reputedly concocted a merry-go-round of wooden horses in a park; a live animal, generally a horse, connected to the contraption, put it in motion by walking in circles.

Then in the early 1880s, Scottish immigrant Allan Herschell, an inventive tinkerer, harnessed a steam engine to the slow-moving carousels then popular, and an entertainment inspiration was born. A few years later, Great Britain came up with a gadget that permitted the horses to slide up and down on poles as they revolved around a center core. Herschell then vaulted to the forefront in the competition to produce carousel horses. The Herschell-Spillman Company and later the Allan Herschell Company continued to churn out American carousel animals, first wooden and then aluminum, until 1970, when the Chance Manufacturing Company acquired the firm and began making them from fiberglass.

The wooden mounts of the "Golden Era," generally the 1890s to the onset of the Depression, are today prized for their handiwork, antiquity, and scarcity. In their most prolific period, they included a vast menagerie of animals (horses eventually were to prove the most popular), expertly crafted, sometimes with anthropomorphic features (jewelry, hats, belts, snakes, even human heads), and with each animal hollowed out to keep its weight at about 125 pounds. Where formerly 10,000 wooden carousels arose from American factories and 3,000 revolved in American cities, today only some 100-200 still operate in the country. In recent decades, as many as 10-20 carousels a year have gone out of existence, sold to antique dealers who chop the collections apart and sell individual horses as novelties.

The first of Broome's six carousels arrived in 1920 when George F. Johnson bought a 60-horse unit from Herschell for Ross Park in Binghamton, the county seat. The merry-go-round featured a pair of chariots (permitting people desiring a less strenuous ride to sit back and avoid the risk of saddle sores), a 51-key Wurlitzer military band organ, and five dozen horses in rows four deep, moving up and down ("jumping").

Other carousels followed: a 36-mount unit with landscape paintings on the interior rounding boards and hand-stenciling on the sweeps (Highland Park in Endwell); a 60-horse, two-chariot pavilion, complete with Wurlitzer and landscape and seascape murals (Binghamton's George F. Johnson Recreation Park); a smaller unit, comprising 34 horses, two baroque chariots, carved scrollwork on the rounding boards and avian and floral figures in the crown center (West Endicott Park in the Town of Union); and a 36-horse, two-chariot pavilion with scroll designs on the rafters, beveled posts, and paintings of cartoon characters (George W. Johnson Park in Endicott).

The king of Broome's carousels and one of the largest ever made sits in Johnson City's C. Fred Johnson (or "CFJ") Park. Encased within a two-story-high, 18-sided pagoda, the carousel harnesses 18 rows of four horses each, a ponderous herd of 72 in all, to a crown center displaying twin tiers of alternating oval mirrors and pastel landscapes ablaze with lights. Glass jewel-encrusted saddles twinkle as lights splay upon them, and mirrors pick up the refracted rays of color. Calliope music floods the cavernous interior. A circular corridor coils nearly around the latticed chain-link fence separating the carousel from an outer walkway with benches.

Experts consider Broome's carousels unparalleled in the country for a number of reasons. They have been, are, and will remain free of charge, virtually unheard of anywhere else where admissions are routinely charged. They represent the nation's highest per-capita concentration; Portland, Oregon, far more populous, has recently bought and shipped in more carousels than Broome's six. Except for one, Broome's carousels remain standing exactly where first emplaced, giving the county five of the nation's reported 13 still on their original sites. All Broome's carousel horses "jump" on the poles that impale them at midsection; most other carousels feature jumping horses only on the inner portions. And the only remaining Herschell carousels containing four horses across each row are those in Broome.

Directional signs to the nearest carousel crop up throughout the county, and boards proclaim Binghamton the "Carousel Capital." Plastic standing carousel horses, in prancing stance, with appropriate brass poles, and bolted to the pavement, adorn Binghamton's Court Street in the heart of its downtown section. Silk banners with carousel logos hang from light poles. In addition to its carousel, Ross Park also hosts the Carousel Museum, a repository of information, photographs, and artifacts; admission is free.

Though science has yet to discover it, riding a mechanical wooden horse in circles is the greatest, purest thrill in all of life. Broome County delivers that thrill in spades, absolutely free, with no waiting. The carousels open Memorial Day and close Labor Day, operating daily until dusk.

Experiencing the grand slam, all six carousels, is possible but will require a good half-day. Though Broome County is not excessively congested, one municipality blends into another with no apparent distinction, often confusing visitors. Directional markers for the carousels, as of this writing, appear geared more for locals than for tourists arriving in the county for the first time who don't know their way around.

Binghamton is the county seat and the hub where Interstate Highways 81 and 88 connect with State Highway 17 (soon to be Interstate 86), all major thoroughfares. Anyone entering Binghamton is likely to come in via one of those high-volume arteries. The following is a suggested route for encompassing all six carousels, moving east to west through the county.

- Ross Park Zoo carousel: from Interstate 81 (near its junction with Highways 88 and 17), take Exit 4S south to Binghamton;

pass a sign for "downtown;" ascend an overpass above railroad tracks and remain on it as it curves right; follow signs for Route 434 west to Vestal and turn right onto a ramp that crosses a bridge above the Susquehanna River; eventually the route leads to a stop light; turn left at the light onto S. Washington Street; proceed one block and turn right onto Vestal Avenue; go two blocks and turn left onto Park Avenue; drive along Park Avenue .8-miles; turn left onto Morgan Road for about .5-miles; turn right into the zoo's parking lot; the carousel is on zoo premises (though the carousel is free, the zoo charges an admission).

- George F. Johnson Recreation Park carousel: leave the zoo parking lot and turn left onto Morgan Road; return to the Park Avenue intersection and turn right; turn left onto Vestal Avenue and go one block to a stop light; turn right onto Pennsylvania Avenue and take a quick right ramp designated "business district;" proceed through a stop light intersection and veer to your left on an overpass that takes you across the same Susquehanna River; at your first stop light intersection after crossing the river, turn left onto Hawley Street; follow Hawley as it curves right to Court Street; turn left onto Court, cross the Chenango River on a level bridge; after crossing the river, Court Street becomes Main Street; follow Main Street for .9-miles to Beethoven Street; turn left onto Beethoven; at .4-miles, turn left into a parking lot for your second carousel.

-C. Fred Johnson Park carousel: leave the Recreation Park parking lot and turn right onto Beethoven; at Main Street, turn left, proceeding 1.1 miles to a stop light intersection at Lester Avenue; turn right onto Lester and go over a viaduct; after descending the viaduct, you'll encounter a stop light intersection; the king of Broome carousels is on your right.

- Highland Park carousel: return to Main Street via Lester Avenue; turn right onto Main and proceed straight through (do not become alarmed when Main Street enters a non-urban area and becomes a 55-mph highway); after 3.6 miles beyond the Lester Avenue junction, turn right onto a ramp for Hooper Road; at the crest of the ramp, turn right and drive 1.6 miles on Hooper Road; turn left into Highland Park for your fourth carousel.

- George W. Johnson Park: from Highland Park, turn right onto Hooper Road and follow it for 1.4 miles; at a stop light intersection with Watson Boulevard, turn right; after 1.7 miles, you'll come to an intersection with Oak Hill Avenue; turn right onto Oak Hill and go up one block to an intersection with Witherill Street; the fifth carousel is to your left.

- West Endicott Park carousel: reverse your direction on Oak Hill Avenue and drive beyond its intersection with Watson Boulevard; go through a railroad underpass and get into the left lane; at a stop light intersection at North Street, you have three choices (left turn, zigzag straight, or right turn); take the zigzag straight road which becomes Madison Avenue; follow Madison .4-miles to Park Street; turn right onto Park and go one block to Jefferson Avenue; turn left onto Jefferson and drive one block to the intersection with Main Street; turn right onto Main; after 1.2 miles, you'll come across a stop light intersection with Page Avenue; turn right onto Page; .3-miles later, turn left onto Maple Street; the sixth carousel is on your right.

The carousel sponsors award souvenir prizes to visitors who complete the circuit.

Broome County is in southern New York along the Pennsylvania border, about equally distant between Syracuse to the north and Scranton and Wilkes-Barre (Pennsylvania) to the south. If you want to spend a few days in the general area, consider a trip to Cooperstown, the home of several museums including the Baseball Hall of Fame, or the Finger Lakes Region with its wineries and boating. Both are fewer than 100 miles away, the former to the northeast, the latter to the northwest.

THE TREASON THAT SHOCKED THE NATION

In the pitch blackness of the moonless night shared by September 21 and 22, 1780, at the foot of a mountainous range on the western banks of the Hudson River, one of the most distinguished generals ever to wear an American uniform met an ambitious, handsome, genteel British officer.

It would be the most profound moment of their lives. It set in motion a train of events that doomed both men, one to the hangman's noose, the other to eternal exile.

The American was Benedict Arnold, called the best fighting general of the Revolutionary War, a favorite of his commander-in-chief, George Washington.

The Briton was John Andre, a provincial major, the adjutant general of the British Army, and a personal favorite of the British commanding general in America.

They talked in utmost secrecy, with no lanterns or bonfires to betray their presence, in a thicket of fir trees a little up the hill, but not far from the water's edge. They talked of treason. Benedict Arnold offered to turn over the important garrison of West Point, which he commanded, along with its complement of soldiers, to the British in exchange for money, safety, and a British officer's commission. John Andre was the agent sent to broker the deal.

War was going on at the time, and both men placed themselves in jeopardy: Arnold, because he was conducting treasonous transactions against the country he had sworn to defend; Andre, because he was engaged in suspect activity with his sworn enemy on enemy soil.

It was America's most famous case of treason, before or since. Had it succeeded, it might have changed the complexion of the Revolutionary War.

But hitches developed. Andre could not return to his base the way he had come, via ship, and was forced to make his way through enemy lines in disguise, which made him technically a spy, carrying documents that incriminated Arnold as a traitor.

On September 23, the unthinkable happened. Andre was caught on enemy land with Arnold's papers. The plot had been discovered. Arnold managed to escape by the skin of his teeth but left America and became an outcast for the rest of his life. Andre underwent trial as a spy, was found guilty, and was hanged on October 2, bringing the fruits of their midnight meeting to a dramatic and tragic conclusion.

The scene of their benighted encounter is a desolate stretch of beach in Haverstraw in Rockland County, north of New York City. The site of Andre's death is farther south at Tappan.

The main artery cutting through Haverstraw, U.S. Highway 9W, contains an historical marker entitled "TREASON SITE" west of the approximate site where "On the Hudson shore below a boulder marks the place where General Benedict Arnold and British Major John Andre met in the dead of night."

If you want to reach the boulder, you'll have a much tougher go of it. Mark off two miles south of the Nyack Hospital Health Care Center on 9W in your car; then turn east (toward the river) .2-miles on an acutely angled road across railroad tracks to a sign for the Tilcon plant; take a sharp dogleg to the right for .7-miles through the Tilcon quarry on a riverside road and along a narrow residential road; proceed .1-miles on an even narrower road through trees and thick vegetation until you reach a tiny semicircular pull-off on the left.

The adventure has just begun. Cars and bikes can go no farther. Just south of the pull-off and toward the river is a narrow dirt path that may or may not be clearly outlined. Descend the path 70 or so normal walking steps; then follow the trail to the right until you reach the rock-strewn shore of the Hudson; go 300 roughly estimated steps along the shore and around a bend to a waist-high boulder etched with "ANDRE THE SPY LANDED HERE SEPT. 21. 1780." Andre disembarked from his rowboat at this approximate site, scaled part of the hill, and met Arnold somewhere above the boulder.

The last leg of this trek can be tricky. Slippery stones and fallen tree limbs may impede your footing. And if the water is at high tide, the boulder may be partially submerged, making you either wade the water or tackle the pricker-rich hillside above the water line. If you decide to follow this route, don't wear good clothes. The view of the Hudson from this point is good, and the setting is just a little eerie, particularly at dusk. Do not expect to meet anyone else there.

The trip to Tappan is much easier. Proceed south on 9W beyond Haverstraw and transfer to State Highway 303; continue south about a dozen miles to Tappan.

That small community holds an historical marker at the site of the Reformed Church (corner of Main and Washington Streets) where Andre was tried, another marker along the nearby hill on which he marched to his execution, and a tombstone at the site of his hanging and initial burial (Andre Hill). His remains currently repose in honor in Westminster Abbey in London, England.

The nearby DeWint House (Livingston Avenue and Oak Tree Road) contains memorabilia of colonial and revolutionary times and artifacts of Washington and Andre. It's most famous for headquartering Washington on numerous occasions, most notably in September and October of 1780 when the commander regretfully signed Andre's death warrant there and, lamenting what he felt was a necessary but unfortunate step, refused to watch as the tragic victim went stalwartly to his death. It is free and open daily during usual daytime hours.

The most touching memorial to the gallant romantic and poet whose death brought forth tears from the hundreds of onlookers is the former Mabie's Tavern, since rechristened "Old '76 House"

(Main and Washington Streets), now a restaurant. Though the structure where he was imprisoned awaiting his execution has been done over, it remains an intriguing renovation and invokes Andre's memory. Revolutionary era reprints, portraits, weapons, and assorted items on the walls recall the feel of the times. A portrait of Andre peers into the dining room from the fireplace mantel. The decor is nice, and the food is good. It is primarily a dinner restaurant (call 914-359-5476 for information and hours).

Fewer than 20 miles apart, both sites can be done completely in a day. Haverstraw has restaurants and specialty stores. Tappan, smaller and quainter, has a number of historic homes and a couple craft stores. Together, with the overriding specter of Arnold's and Andre's tragedy looming in the background, they present a haunting picture of a single moment, frozen in time, and the consequences it held for a poet-artist-soldier who won hearts with his charm and a brave, determined warhorse whose lone miscalculation cost him his honor and rightful place in history.

BENEATH THE PEEL OF THE BIG APPLE

Nathan Hale regretted he only had one life to give for his country in 1776 when he was hanged there as a spy. George Washington retired from the military there in 1783. Washington Irving, who would later create Ichabod Crane and Rip Van Winkle, was born there that same year. Alexander Hamilton, who graces the 10-dollar bill, lived there...and died there, too, in 1804. President John Tyler cut out from the White House and got married there in 1844. Newspaper editor Francis Church wrote, "Yes, Virginia, there is a Santa Claus" there in 1897. The Titanic never arrived there in 1912. Fighting Father Duffy, the Catholic chaplain of World War I, cleaned up the gangs there until he died in 1932.

Manhattan...New York City...the Big Apple. It's more than just the Statue of Liberty, Macy's, Broadway, cab drivers from Hell, rude people, and the world's filthiest subway. It's also a treasure chest of buried significance, an appetizing stew of delectable morsels of history, society, and culture tucked in hidden recesses within the overwhelming steel canyons.

Manhattan may have witnessed more remarkable moments of human achievement, good or bad, than any city in the world. And it has recorded many of them for posterity. But they tend to get lost in the maze of monolithic skyscrapers and two or three million people saturating an island 13 miles long and two miles wide, and you have to look for them.

Way down south near the tip of the island stands Fraunces Tavern (54 Pearl Street by Broad Street), an 18th-century tavern still serving lunches and dinners. But it's more significant as the place where George

Washington, yet to become president, relinquished his military career as commander-in-chief of the Continental Army on December 4, 1783. The second-floor room where he embraced his officers in word and gesture can still be seen. So can a museum on the third floor of the neo-Georgian brick building. Both are available for a moderate fee weekdays during the day and Saturday afternoons.

Bowling Green (junction of Broadway with Whitehall and State Streets), just a few blocks away, is now a park. But it used to be a parade ground when the Dutch controlled the island and spoke of it as Nieuw Amsterdam. Peter Minuit allegedly palmed $24 worth of trinkets and cloth off on the Indians in exchange for the island there in 1626. Bowling Green is also famous for a riot that occurred on July 9, 1776. The Declaration of Independence had just been read to Manhattanites and it spurred them to yank down a gilded lead equestrian statue of British King George III (which they themselves had erected during happier times a few years earlier). You can still see the wrought iron fence that surrounded the green in the 1770s. Each spear formerly held a small crown at its top; the crowd broke the crowns off when they downed the statue.

Nearly opposite Bowling Green at 1 Broadway (corner of Broadway and Battery Place) is a plaque identifying the site as the former Archibald Kennedy House where Washington headquartered in 1776 in the early days of the Revolution. When Washington moved out, the British high command moved in and stayed until 1783.

At the approximate site of 9 Broadway stood a house that hosted a number of important British officers during the war. The most famous was Benedict Arnold who used it as sanctuary after betraying America and defecting to the enemy.

At 39-41 Broadway, a plaque marks the site of the Alexander McComb House, the unofficial second "White House" in American history. The first capital of the Constitutional United States was not Washington, D.C., but Manhattan, and Washington lived in the spacious house that once stood on this site for six months during 1790. The very first "White House" stood at 3 Cherry Street, a site now lost forever under the Brooklyn Bridge.

Farther up Broadway, at its intersection with Wall Street, sits Trinity Church, Manhattan's first Anglican parish. In its adjoining cemetery are: steamboat pioneer Robert Fulton; statesman Albert Gallatin; War of 1812 naval hero James Lawrence; and Alexander Hamilton, the first Secretary of the Treasury.

One block east (junction of Wall, Broad, and Nassau Streets) is the Federal Hall Memorial. Originally the site of City Hall, where freedom of the press was challenged in the 1735 "seditious libel" case of John Peter Zenger, it later became Federal Hall, the scene of the first presidential inauguration (Washington's on April 30, 1789) and the location of the very first Congress of the United States; the Departments of State, Treasury, and War, the Supreme Court, the federal court system, and the proposal for the Bill of Rights all came about there. Though the original building is gone, the present Greek Revival structure houses a free weekday museum. A larger-than-life statue of Washington by John Quincy Adams Ward stands at the approximate site and height where the real Washington stood when the American presidency came into existence.

Three blocks north of Federal Hall is 57 Maiden Lane, the site of the house where Thomas Jefferson, the nation's first Secretary of State, lived. And James Madison, another future president and the "Father of the Constitution," lived at what is now 19 Maiden Lane.

Northeast of Maiden Lane, at 131 William Street, America's first internationally renowned author, Washington Irving, was born on April 3, 1783. The house is now gone.

The entrance to South Street Seaport (Fulton Street) holds the Titanic Memorial Lighthouse, originally created to mourn the victims of that ship's 1912 sinking and placed high atop the roof of the Seaman's Church Institute farther south on the island. When the organization relocated in 1968, the lighthouse was dismantled. Eventually, it wound up at the seaport.

West of William Street, at the intersection of Fulton Street and Broadway, six blocks north of Trinity Church, is St. Paul's Chapel of Trinity Church which contains an enclosed pew area where Washington attended services as president. It is open most days during daytime hours. The east porch of the exterior holds the crypt of Major General Richard Montgomery, a Revolutionary War commander and one of the highest-ranking American officers ever killed in combat.

A few blocks north of St. Paul's at the intersection of Broadway and Murray Street is City Hall and City Hall Park. A heroic statue of Nathan Hale stands west of City Hall, on the approximate site of Bridewell Prison, built by the British in 1776 to hold American prisoners. Frederick MacMonnies executed the statue...and the British executed Hale, either at that spot or at one of two or three other suspected locations on the island. City Hall contains a museum of founding father portraits and artifacts. It is free and open weekdays for a few hours on either side of noon. The surrounding park features numerous plaques, monuments, and statues.

On the northwestern fringe of Greenwich Village, a plaque adorns the house at 82 Jane Street, formerly the William Bayard House site, where Alexander Hamilton died on July 12, 1804, still holding a bullet in his torso from a duel he had fought the day before with Vice President Aaron Burr.

Milligan Place (east of Jane Street and off Avenue of the Americas around West 10th Street) once enjoyed a splendid reputation as a picturesque winding way. Turn-of-the-century guidebooks extolled its quaintness. Today, it is a shadow of its former self, more properly a private alley than a thoroughfare.

The Episcopal Church of the Ascension occupies the northwest corner of Fifth Avenue and 10th Street. It came up in 1841 from an English design by Richard Upjohn. On June 26, 1844, 10th President John Tyler, a Virginia widower, married Julia Gardiner, a New Yorker, there - the first wedding of a sitting president. After his term in office, Tyler supported the South during the Civil War.

A bust of Washington Irving, a Manhattanite for much of his life, rests in front of a high school named for him at the corner of East 17th Street and Irving Place. Another of the city's hundreds of plaques honors his home at 47 Irving Place.

The grave of Petrus Stuyvesant, the Dutch Governor-General of New York in olden days, is ensconced in St. Mark's Church-in-the-Bowery. A bust of old Pegleg Pete, who scurried about his island empire on one sound leg and a prosthesis, also stands in the churchyard at the junction of Second Avenue and Stuyvesant Street. The current church is Manhattan's second-oldest surviving public building, dating to 1799, and reposes where the venerable old Dutch master erected a family chapel in 1660.

Theodore Roosevelt, the 26th President, was another native Manhattanite. A facsimile of his Victorian birthplace now stands on the spot at 28 East 20th Street (between Broadway and Park Avenue South). The National Park Service now runs the place and charges a modest admission. It is closed Mondays and Tuesdays and open the remaining days during daytime hours.

The picturesque Church of the Transfiguration, colloquially known as "The Little Church Around the Corner," sits nearly obscured by towering trees overwhelming 1 East 29th Street. Completed in 1856, the Episcopal Church achieved fame as the "Actors' Church" in the days when actors still went to church. According to folklore, the rector of a neighboring church refused to provide a funeral for an actor and told the inquirers to try "the little church around the corner." It is open daily during the day.

A profile on a plaque on Seventh Avenue and 44th Street recalls Eugene O'Neill, "America's greatest playwright," who was born in the Barrett House on that site in 1888.

Times Square (junction of 42nd Street, Seventh Avenue, and Broadway) is well known. Duffy Square (four blocks north between Broadway and Seventh) is not. The Times Square Theatre Center (TKTS) discounted theater ticket operation usually obscures its view. But if you can look beyond the huge lines of people awaiting tickets, you might get a glimpse of Charles Keck's statue of Lieutenant Colonel Francis P. Duffy, the Roman Catholic chaplain of the "Fighting 69th" World War I Division famed for waging war on street gangs in nearby Hell's Kitchen. He resided at the Church of the Holy Cross on 42nd Street. You might also see another statue, Georg Lober's version of Tin Pan Alley composer George M. Cohan who penned "Give My Regards to Broadway," among other standards.

Many famous and affluent tenants have lived within the Dakota Apartments at Central Park West (between 72nd and 73rd Streets) through the years. A luxurious palace when built in 1884, it took its name from the Dakota Territory because both the territory and the apartment complex then had a reputation for being beyond the mainstream of civilization. Since 1884, however, Manhattan's throbbing pulse has enveloped the Dakota Apartments, outside of which, in December 1980, former Beatle and rock icon John Lennon was gunned down.

Eight-year-old Virginia O'Hanlon lived at 115 West 95th Street in 1897 when she wrote the editor of the New York Sun, asking if there was a Santa Claus. "Yes, Virginia...," Francis Pharcellus Church responded in his famous editorial of September 21, 1897, "He exists as certainly as love and generosity and devotion exist." The little girl grew up to become Virginia O'Hanlon Douglas and died on May 13, 1971. Her four-story red-brick rowhouse still stands.

The Hamilton Grange National Memorial (287 Convent Avenue, between 141st and 142nd Streets), in the Manhattanville-Harlem section, marks the final home of Alexander Hamilton. Its current location is two blocks south of where it originally stood. The immediate area is no longer considered safe to walk in. The National Park Service operates the house and recommends traveling to and from via car. The Federal house cherishes a few original Hamilton possessions and William O. Partridge's statue of the hero of the early republic. It is open during daytime hours.

A spinoff of Trinity Church, the Chapel of the Intercession stretches out between Riverside Drive West, 153rd Street, Amsterdam Avenue, and 155th Street in Washington Heights, north of the Grange. Its adjoining cemetery holds the remains of several notables: painter-naturalist John James Audubon; Alfred Tennyson Dickens, the son of British novelist Charles Dickens, who died in Manhattan while preparing to attend a ceremony honoring the centennial of his father's birth; Eliza Bowen Jumel Burr, Aaron Burr's second wife; John Jacob Astor, the millionaire who died a watery death aboard the Titanic; and the "Father of Christmas," Clement Clarke Moore, the author of "A Visit from St. Nicholas" (since 1911, parishioners have laid wreaths on his grave and recited prayers in his memory in a Christmas Eve procession with lanterns).

Farther north, at 1765 Jumel Terrace (near Edgecombe Avenue and 160th Street), is the Morris-Jumel Mansion. Anchoring the highest point in Manhattan, a promontory in Washington Heights near the southern end of Highbridge Park, the Georgian-Federal house carries an illustrious pedigree. Originally constructed in 1765 for Roger Morris, it served as headquarters for Washington during the battle of Harlem Heights in 1776 and afterward for the British. In 1810, Stephen Jumel, an aristocratic French wine merchant, took over the house. In 1833, his widow, Eliza Bowen Jumel, married former Vice President Aaron Burr, Alexander Hamilton's killer, in its front parlor. It is the oldest extant residence in Manhattan. The marriage room (America's first-known octagonal room), Washington's office, and Burr's bedroom and office desk are all displayed. Madame Burr's bedroom sports a single bed Napoleon once reputedly owned. An original milepost outside the mansion, proclaiming New York City 11 miles to the south, demonstrates how the city has expanded northward in the last two centuries. Like the Grange, the mansion is within an area considered iffy (although we walked to and away from it without incident). It is open during daytime hours daily except Monday and Tuesday; a moderate fee is charged.

These are just a sampling of Manhattan's out-of-the-way curiosities. Scores more are scattered throughout the city that never shuts down.

You will rarely encounter others at these sites. If you do, they may be there for other reasons; for example, Trinity Church is an active parish with liturgical and musical services.

And some words of caution. All the above sites cannot be seen in a single day. You should select a reasonable agenda that includes frequent breaks for rest, food, and rest room necessities. Keep in mind that walking Manhattan is not easy because of its pounding pavement, heavy pedestrian and vehicular traffic, and constant stop-and-go pattern occasioned by stoplights at most intersections and taxis that career through streets even a second or two after stoplights have turned red. Though inexpensive and generally quick, Manhattan's subways are frequently dirty and crowded and, at times, subject to agonizing delays; the stations are unbearably stuffy in summer. Buses require exact change - no dollar bills - and often come equipped with surly drivers (our apologies to the courteous ones). Taxi bills can mount up, especially if you're going from one end of town to another just to read a plaque. Forget driving your car; parking is very difficult, and other drivers will make quick sport of you. Your best bet is to get a good map of Manhattan, carve out a comfortable game plan, and see the sights the old-fashioned way - by putting one leg in front of the other; use subways for quickly traversing long distances.

Lodging is fairly expensive, but bargains can be had. Food abounds everywhere and runs the complete gamut in both price and quality.

You will not find public rest rooms as such, often even in fast food places; employees are told to tell patrons that there are none or that they're closed for repair. Finer dining establishments and hotel lobbies provide them. Large department stores do, also.

Finally, it is a regrettable fact of contemporary life that all big cities are not as safe as they used to be decades ago. Most of the sites described in this chapter are safe. Still, be cautious and alert with handbags, wallets, and valuables. With a proper degree of foresight and precaution, Manhattan can still be a great place to visit.

Marie Beatrice Nemcek (hatless) with her mother and sister, July 4, 1934, at Trudeau in front of the famous statue of the sanitorium's founder by Gutzon Borglum (who later went on to bigger things at Mount Rushmore).

THE RESORT WHERE PEOPLE CAME TO DIE

Scottish author Robert Louis Stevenson, reeling from tuberculosis, stayed there from October 3, 1887 to April 16, 1888, hoping it would help him feel better. While there, he wrote portions of "The Wrong Box" and "The Master of Ballantrae" and dined with the widow of George Armstrong Custer.

A young Branch Rickey came there in the winter of 1908-09. He survived and went on to become a baseball coach, manager, and general manager. Forty years after wintering there, he gained immortality by sponsoring Jackie Robinson, the first black man in major league baseball.

Christy Mathewson, who won the third-highest number of games of anyone who ever played professional baseball, came in 1920, his pitching career over, his illness not. He died there on October 7, 1925, at age 45, a victim of tuberculous pneumonia. In 1936, he was posthumously elected to the Hall of Fame in its first year along with Babe Ruth and Ty Cobb.

Thea LaGuardia arrived in mid-1921. Her devoted husband took a train from New York City every three weeks to spend time with her. Frail and dispirited, she died later that year at 27. Her husband Fiorello later became the most beloved mayor in New York's history.

Manuel Quezon, the president of the Philippines, died there in 1944.

Bela Bartok, Hungary's most distinguished composer, suffering from a tubercular diagnosis that proved to be leukemia, composed his most famous opus - Concerto for Orchestra - there from

August 15-October 8, 1943. He returned the next two summers for the air, then went to New York City to die on September 26, 1945.

Actors came, too - Veronica Lake, Conrad Nagel - usually quietly, so no one would notice their ailments. And the unknown came, also, especially those with money who could afford the expensive care.

It was a matter of life or death back then, for tuberculosis was America's deadly killer, a contagious disease that panicked anyone who had it...or anyone who knew someone who had it. Some patients came there hoping for a cure...and lived long lives afterward. Others also came hoping for a cure...and the local cemeteries hold their shattered dreams.

The place was beautiful Saranac Lake, the "City of the Sick," nestled in New York's Adirondack Mountains. During its heyday, it was the most famous tuberculosis sanatorium in the nation.

In 1884, Dr. Edward Livingston Trudeau, stricken by tuberculosis, founded the Adirondack Cottage Sanitarium, later to become simply the Trudeau Sanatorium. It was a little city for the more than 15,000 patients it treated through the years. At its peak, it included nearly three dozen cottages, a medical center, a laboratory, a pair of infirmaries, an administration building, nursing quarters, a library, a workshop, an interdenominational chapel, a recreation pavilion, and a post office - all capable of serving more than 200 patients at a time.

Trudeau's cure for victims in the early stages of pulmonary tuberculosis was simple: constant medical supervision, including artificial pneumothorax and pneumoperitoneum; and bedrest on screened-in porches exposed to the pure Adirondack air, even in the dead of winter. Those showing signs of recovery participated in arts and crafts projects, business and electrical classes, and music, painting, and drama activities.

Some patients never recovered and gasped their final breaths from the hospital bedrooms. Others not only prospered on the fresh air cure but found romance with fellow patients at 1,650 feet above sea level on a sheltered side of Mount Pisgah with majestic views of New York's highest peaks.

Marie Beatrice Nemcek came there during the 1930s at the tender age of 18. Known as the "Baby of Trudeau" because she was the youngest patient at the time, she fully expected to die and never again see her family. She lost a boyfriend when he found out she had the dreaded disease. But after almost a year at Trudeau, she returned home to find another boyfriend. She later married him, gave birth to one of the authors of what you're now reading, and lived to return to Trudeau three times as a visitor in her 60s and 70s.

Dr. Trudeau also founded the Saranac Laboratory, the nation's seminal research lab dedicated to tuberculosis. He was elected the first president of the National Association for the Study and Prevention of Tuberculosis, the forerunner of the modern National Lung Association. He died in 1915, famous and beloved. His great-grandson Garry became the Pulitzer Prize-winning creator of "Doonesbury."

Most of Saranac Lake followed Trudeau's lead. Individual homes within the village turned over their rooms for patient care. Robert Louis Stevenson, who remained sickly all his life and died of a stroke in Samoa in 1894, stayed at the Andrew Baker cottage (Stevenson Lane), now a museum holding America's largest collection of his artifacts (July to mid-September; daily, except Monday; day hours; modest fee). Bela Bartok resided at 30 Park Avenue and 89 Riverside Drive. Christy Mathewson stayed at 36 Church Street and 21 Old Military Road. Other cure centers came up on the outskirts to meet the needs.

The discovery of streptomycin reined in much of the lethalness of tuberculosis and also spelled the end of the cure cottages. Once the nation's prototypical bedrest and fresh air sanatorium, Trudeau closed in 1954.

A visit to Saranac Lake today can conjure memories of a tubercular's way of life.

The old Trudeau site now belongs to American Management

Association. Though trespassing is not allowed, AMA has been liberal in allowing former residents and interested parties to tour the grounds. Visitors should first secure permission from AMA (P.O. Box 319, Saranac Lake, NY 12983 or 518-891-1500). Though some buildings have been razed, most of the "city within a city" is intact. To reach the site, drive north on either Park Avenue or Bloomingdale Avenue and look for the AMA signs.

The Trudeau Institute, a research lab complex dedicated in 1964 to infections, cancer, and parasitic diseases, currently has two links to the old sanatorium: the "Little Red," a 14-foot by 18-foot cabin that was the nation's first tuberculosis cure cottage; and a 1918 statue of Dr. Edward Trudeau taking the bedrest cure, sculpted by Gutzon Borglum who later went on to chisel four presidential faces out of a South Dakota mountain. Ranked among the finest in the nation for "high-impact medical research," the hilltop center commands a spectacular view of Lower Saranac Lake and can be reached by taking State Highway 3 west of town to the intersection of Algonquin Avenue and then driving a short way west along that street.

Other cure center sites still exist, but in new incarnations. The National Variety Artists' Lodge, later the Will Rogers Memorial Hospital, is now the Will Rogers Castle Point Resort Condominiums at 1 Will Rogers Drive. The Ray Brook Sanatorium, a few miles southeast on State Highway 86, is currently the Adirondack Correctional Facility.

The house at 105 Main Street, formerly Dr. Trudeau's home, is now a medical office. The waiting room which once served as his office currently houses historical artifacts. Visitors are welcome. Saranac Lake is loaded with former cure cottages, easily recognized by their porches, still attached and often screened.

Historic Saranac Lake, a preservation organization, relentlessly pursues placement on the National Register of Historic Places of virtually every cure building still standing and has spearheaded three recent reunions of tubercular survivors.

Saranac Lake sponsors park concerts, fairs and festivals, field days, and athletic competitions and races throughout the year. Its famous annual winter carnival occurs during the second week in February. The crowning achievement is a fireworks display over the huge "Ice Palace," generally comprising 60-foot turrets and more than 700 tons of ice on Lake Flower in the heart of the village. The festival dates to 1897 when Dr. Trudeau initiated it to lift the morale of his patients.

Lodging and restaurants are plentiful throughout the area. Easy to drive around in, Saranac Lake is at the very core of the high Adirondacks deep in upstate New York. Nearby attractions include: abolitionist John Brown's home and grave in North Elba; Santa's Workshop at North Pole; Whiteface Mountain Observatory; cascading Ausable River at High Falls Gorge; and Lake Placid.

THE SUNNY SIDE OF THE SEA

The distinguished man of letters and traveler, beloved on both sides of the Atlantic, took pen in hand late in the 1830s and wrote a message to his friend, the President of the United States:

> I had hoped before this to see you at my little Dutch cottage on the Hudson. Whenever you are in this quarter, and can steal a little interval from the "Cares of Empire," come up then, and I will shew you a little nest in which I enjoy more comfort and quietude of mind than I fear you will experience in the White House.

On another occasion, in 1844, the same scholar, who had become the first American writer to achieve international success and recognition, extended another invitation, this time to a niece:

> I hope you will all make your contemplated visits to New York in the course of the winter; it will serve to break up the monotony of the season, though, for my part, if I could only be in my little cottage, looking out from its snug, warm shelter, upon the broad expanse of the Tappan Sea, all brilliant with snow and ice and sunshine, I think I should be loath to leave it for the city.

The man was Washington Irving, nearly forgotten today, but, in his day, the man most responsible for proving to stuffy Englishmen that the colonies could produce literary talent the equal of that in Europe. The "little Dutch cottage on the Hudson" he had referred to was his home, "Sunnyside," one of the quaintest houses in America.

Before Irving's time, the house had been called "Wolfert's Roost" and "The Snuggery." It went back all the way to the late 1600s when Dutchman Wolfert Ecker built it. A century later, Jacob Van Tassel owned it and saw it ransacked and torched by Revolutionary War marauders.

Irving was born in 1783, not long after the house was destroyed. Handsome in his youth, he achieved fame for his appealing fables of early Dutch life along the Hudson River ("Rip Van Winkle" and "The Legend of Sleepy Hollow") and enjoyed huge popularity for an affecting blend of gentle satire and wistful melancholy. His personal letters throbbed with emotional reflections that at times plumbed self-indulgence to the fullest and approached heartwrenching despondency. But publicly, he exhibited conviviality and basked in others' company. A lifelong bachelor (a condition he blamed on the death of his betrothed at a young age), he enmeshed himself within family and friends and entertained royally. At various times in his life he was a lawyer, newspaper essayist, humorist, historian, biographer, and diplomatic ambassador.

He bought the farmhouse, that had blossomed from the ashes of Van Tassel's ruins, in 1835 and restructured it after his own sense of romance and whimsy. The humble stone cottage grew into the angular eccentricity it now is. Corbie gables arose on the outside, barrel ceilings and arches within. The house borrowed bits of both Gothic and Romanesque styles. The roofs sprouted weathervanes, and wisteria climbed along the facade.

Irving rhapsodized over what he had wrought. "I am living most cozily and delightfully in this dear, bright little home, which I have fitted up to my own humor," he wrote in 1836. "Everything goes on cheerily in my little household, and I would not exchange the cottage for any chateau in Christendom."

He added even more features: a three-storied, spired pagoda adjacent to the main house for his servants and overflow guests; a bathtub with running water (a bit of a novelty then) and a hot water tank in the kitchen; a good-sized pond, his "Little Mediterranean," set amidst the woods; a modified Gothic icehouse for the chunks of solidified water taken from the pond during winter's freeze.

Today, the house is furnished with period antiques and much of Irving's tangible legacy. His study displays the stacks of books exactly as he had assembled them and the desk at which he wrote his final work, his five-volume biography of George Washington (for whom he had been named). His rosewood piano still stands in the Federal parlor, where he often serenaded his nieces on the flute while they provided counterpoint on the upright. Above the study rests his bedroom with his chair and cane and the canopied bed in which he died on November 28, 1859, at 76. All in all, it still fits his own apt summary: "a little, old-fashioned stone mansion, all made up of gabled ends, and as full of angles and corners as an old cocked hat."

Gardens, orchards, and forested trails surround the Little Mediterranean.

Sleepy Hollow Restorations oversees Irving's estate and offers wintry skating and sledding weekends, period cooking, summer picnicking, Christmas candlelight tours, and Halloween weekends in which Irving's "Sleepy Hollow" tale comes to life with filmed and live retellings of the saga of Ichabod Crane and the specter of the Headless Horseman. Costumed guides escort tours of the interior daily (except Tuesdays and major holidays) during customary daytime hours from March through December (and weekends only during January and February). After the half-hour tour, visitors can explore the grounds at their leisure. A visitor center and book store adjoin. An average admission is charged.

Sunnyside is in Westchester County, just above New York City.

It overlooks the Hudson from its eastern shore, a mile south of the Tappan Zee Bridge. To reach it, drive to the northern limits of Irvington on U.S. Highway 9 (Broadway) and follow signs.

Related sites are nearby: the Washington Irving Memorial (Broadway at West Sunnyside Lane), a bust of Irving and a frieze of some of his famous literary creations sculpted by Daniel Chester French, the man who chiseled a seated Abraham Lincoln within Washington, D.C.'s Lincoln Memorial; the site of the old bridge across the Pocantico River that inspired the scene in which the Headless Horseman flings the pumpkin at Ichabod Crane (a couple miles north along Broadway in Sleepy Hollow); and, a little farther north, rambling Sleepy Hollow Cemetery where the great storyteller sleeps the sleep of the ages within a large fenced family plot (the grave is marked, and a map may be obtained from the office during weekday hours).

NORTH CAROLINA

THE WOMAN WITH A THOUSAND CHILDREN

In 1909, Angela Marsh, the seven-year-old daughter of a senator, received a doll named Rosie as a gift.

Three-quarters of a century and 1,000 dolls later, Angela Marsh Peterson gave Rosie to the nation as a gift.

In between, she was a teacher, counselor, travel agent, and recreation director who never lost her fascination for dolls. Hunting for them throughout a lifetime of extensive travel, she married, raised two children, and retired to High Point, North Carolina in the 1970s. She first exhibited her dolls in 1983 at the First Wesleyan Church, then moved them to the Wesleyan Arms Administration Building three years later. The collection expanded and became the Angela Peterson Doll and Miniature Museum, moving to the Professional Building in 1992.

Rosie is an octogenarian now, one of the oldest dolls in the 1,500-artifact exhibit. She has plenty of company: more than 100 Shirley Temples of all sizes and descriptions; Raggedy Anns and Barbies; dolls of papier-mache and paper dolls; closed-mouth bisques; rag dolls and wood dolls; Parian dolls and tin heads; French boudoir dolls; bread dough and goose egg dolls; a doll made of seaweed; flea dolls, fully detailed and with parasols, despite being only slightly larger than Lincoln's nose on the copper penny (a magnifying glass is required to view them); Mussolini and Hitler dolls; and a thundering herd of sevenscore elephants that, while not dolls, highlight the Africa and South America Room.

The dolls congregate according to ethnicity, period, and type. Three dozen dolls, some with period clothing worth more than the models, frolic in the Nursery. The Middle East Room contains full-size adult mannequins specially made for their owner. The Children's Room spotlights a rare Santa Claus holding a bottle of Coca-Cola. Another room gathers dolls from the Orient. "Angela's Village," a city of doll houses, includes a parsonage with tongue depressors as roofing shingles and a Negro Cabin with Pork and Mammy character dolls created by the aunt of "Gone with the Wind" author Margaret Mitchell.

The Nativity Scene reconstructs the birth of Christ as interpreted by 50 wooden and terra cotta European dolls, some dating to the 15th century, and all wearing clothing contemporary to their eras. Flyers, containing Peterson's own text, explain that the dolls don't appear to look Biblical because, centuries ago, the European artists had no knowledge of Biblical clothing styles and robed their dolls in fashions they were familiar with. Thirty-four years of persistent searching were required to collect the 50 dolls. A Crucifixion tableau adjoins the Nativity and includes a button that, when pressed, triggers a jolt of "lightning" in the background. Chairs and a sofa are provided in the religious room.

Many of the dolls still wear clothing once made for them by the collector decades ago; her handwritten notes explain their significance.

A huge model of the house Peterson lived in at 2210 Dudley Avenue, Parkersburg, West Virginia is the ultimate doll house. Complete to the most minute detail (interior clocks, doilies, candles, even drapes made from pieces of the drapery within the actual house), Orville Smith's model relies on an electric pulley to reveal each of the three stories of the house, displaying all the rooms in amazingly lifelike fidelity. Miniature dolls stand in for the actual members, including little Angela, of Senator Harvey Marsh's family. The real structure gave way to a gas station in 1967.

More than 50 countries are represented in the museum. Though Peterson's personal collection provides the exhibit's spine, other collectors have either lent or donated portions: Anne Frazier's

100 European and Oriental dolls; Marietta M. Forlaw's Shirley Temples; and Gary Smith, co-designer of the museum along with Peterson, loaned his elephants on parade.

"I never bought a doll I didn't like and never sold a doll after it was mine," Peterson once stated. It shows...in the 14 miniature scenes she created...and in the main gallery's display cases of rarities like a solid wax Montaniri, and late-1800s English dolls, and brown-eyed blonde bisques.

The museum drew 8,000 visitors during its first year in its present location.

The museum is open daily, except Mondays, during usual daytime hours (only afternoon hours on Sundays), and charges a moderate admission fee. It is at 101 West Green Drive, a one-way street nearly at the crossroads of U.S. Highways 311 (Main Street) and 29-70 and the Business Loop of Interstate Highway 85. You might expect to stay a half-hour to an hour.

It shares the building with the much larger Furniture Discovery Center, a museum to furniture manufacturing. High Point has more than 100 furniture plants, essentially making it the "Furniture Capital of the World," as it bills itself. The center provides a step-by-step look at how wood becomes furniture. A discounted ticket admits visitors to both museums.

High Point can immerse you in the world of furniture with show room tours and the Furniture Library, the world's largest collection of books devoted to...you guessed it. The High Point Museum/Historical Park displays furniture as well as other items. Mendenhall Plantation, a 19th-century Quaker estate, and Castle McCulloch, a same-era English castle, offer free tours. City Lake Park and Oak Hollow Lake provide recreational activities.

High Point is also about 200 miles east of the center of the Great Smoky Mountains.

The stairs along Chimney Rock...
where acrophobia and claustrophobia meet.

WALKING IN THE FOOTSTEPS OF THE LAST OF THE MOHICANS

You can follow the historic footsteps of the Last of the Mohicans, heroic warriors who fought the French and Indian War in upper New York State, by walking along the Cliff Trail, clinging tightly to the sheer mountainside. You'll walk along Nature's Showerbath, Inspiration Point, and Groundhog Slide, where Uncas and Chingachgook of the doomed Mohican nation chased Magua, the Huron Indian who had kidnapped lovely Cora and Alice Munro, daughters of a slaughtered British commander.

You can pretend you're Hawkeye, the intrepid white frontiersman, braver than Daniel Boone or Davy Crockett, who roamed the New York frontier waging war against the savagery of Magua's Hurons, by striding the Skyline Trail, winding around the cliffs of Henderson Augen gneiss, passing the Devil's Head outcropping, and ascending to 2,480 feet at Exclamation Point. Your reward will be a good view of 404-foot-high Hickory Nut Falls from the Peregrine's Rest vantage.

But it's all make-believe. Though there was a real French and Indian War that ravaged a good deal of the New York frontier 20 years before the Revolutionary War, Hawkeye, Uncas, Magua, and the others were all fictional characters from James Fenimore Cooper's most famous novel, "The Last of the Mohicans." Further, the Cliff and Skyline Trails are not even in New York, but in Chimney Rock Park in western North Carolina, the scene of much of the exterior filming of the 1992 hit movie based on Cooper's novel. But the thrills are just as good as if Cooper's figures were real...and the high-altitude trails were in the Adirondacks and not on the fringes of the Great Smokies.

The 1,000-plus-acre park is owned by descendants of Dr. Lucius Morse, a Missouri physician who relocated to North Carolina for its climate, became entranced by Chimney Rock, and bought 64 acres of the mountain in 1902.

A three-mile twisting drive winds around the forested mountain from its entrance at the village of Chimney Rock, gaining nearly 900 feet in elevation by the time it reaches a parking lot. The park's central figure, Chimney Rock itself, a 500-million-year-old granite promontory rising 1,200 feet above Hickory Nut Gorge and the Rocky Broad River and overlooking Lake Lure and surrounding mountains, hovers 315 feet above the parking lot; its verticality vaguely resembles a chimney. It can be reached either of two ways: a fast 26-story ride in an elevator buried at the end of a near-200-foot tunnel that, along with the shaft, was blasted out of the mountain's rock shortly after World War II; or a demanding journey up the endless stairs between Vista Rock and Pulpit Rock and alongside Chimney Rock. Many visitors ride the elevator up and take the stairs down.

The serpentine stairways are a highlight for the unclaustrophobic and steady of foot. The stairs along the Chimney are tight and get narrower at the spiral along the Rock Pile. Needle's Eye presents a near-vertical downward spill: 10 easy steps before a 180-degree turn; then 96 tougher steps before a 30-step spiral; and finally a 36-stair plunge to the bottom. The Grotto is a sheltered rest area roughly halfway between Chimney Rock and the parking lot. The Subway is a shortcut through Pulpit Rock forcing you to hunch over for a few yards through the low-ceilinged overhang. Moonshiner's Cave, holding an actual still in a labyrinth below Vista Rock, contains 58 stairs.

Even the Skyline Trail, high atop the mountain, includes stairs, hundreds of them, some going up and some going down, and some tough stretches across exposed tree root gnarls. Rest stops are plentiful and complimentary guide maps suggest the trail will take 45 minutes (we did it in a half-hour, even pausing for photographs). It ends atop Hickory Nut Falls, a thin strand of water cascading over a much wider cliff and presenting a considerable roar. The Skyline intersects with the Cliff Trail near the falls.

The .7-miles Forest Stroll, rising 200 feet and the easiest of the trails, leads directly to the bottom of the waterfall.

Detailed trail guides augment the walks with information on flora and fauna. Adjacent to Chimney Rock, the Sky Lounge contains a gift shop, snack bar, and outdoor patio requiring no effort to experience and offering a view comparable to that obtained from the trails. Picnic facilities and a nature center are also present.

The park is open daily, weather permitting, during the day and early evening. A surprisingly high per-person admission ($9 in the mid-'90s) is charged; but single-season passes cost less than double that amount. Walking all the trails, squeezing through all the crevices, and stopping for a lunch or picnic will take a half-day.

The village of Chimney Rock at the bottom of the mountain has dozens of souvenir shops, specialty stores, and restaurants.

The park is about 25 miles east of Asheville, gateway to the Smokies, on U.S. Highway 74.

NORTH DAKOTA

THE FORT WHERE SOLDIERS VANISHED INTO THE MIST

On May 17, 1876, more than half a thousand mounted soldiers moved out of a fort on the west banks of the Missouri River in what is now North Dakota. Civilians and Indian guides rode with them, and a pack train - wagons chock full of food, supplies, and the munitions of war - rumbled alongside.

The regimental band played the strains of "Garry Owen," their informal theme song. Wives and family members waved goodby; some dabbed at their eyes.

The morning mist along the riverbank melded with the first rays of the sun to create the illusion that the soldiers were riding into the air, borne aloft on the dense haze that cleaved earth from sky. To the women back at the fort, the soldiers seemed to be ghosts riding off into eternity.

Their commander was a dashing, impetuous Civil War veteran who had barely made it through West Point before becoming a temporary brigadier general shy of his 24th birthday. He enjoyed a reputation as an Indian fighter chiefly for an 1868 slaughter of noncombatants in an assault on an Indian village in Oklahoma. He had survived a court-martial and had eased out of military and political scrapes. Some said he harbored presidential ambitions and wanted one more battlefield laurel. He was 36 years old, with a thick walrus-like mustache that made him look older. Magnetic and quirky, he had married the most beautiful girl in his Michigan home town and ate raw onions the way others ate apples.

And on May 17, 1876, he led half a thousand men through a shroudlike mist on a mission that was to culminate 39 days later on the rolling hills above another river in Montana that men were to paint red with blood...and history was to record as the Battle of the Little Bighorn.

The fort that Lieutenant Colonel George Armstrong Custer left that day was dismantled in the 1890s when the close of the Indian Wars made it expendable. It lives now as the reconstructed Fort Abraham Lincoln State Park, a few miles south of Mandan, North Dakota on State Highway 1806. The whole fort has not been restored. Only the house in which Custer lived with his wife stands on its original location. Brick and concrete piles mark the sites of the officers' quarters.

Forts of the American West did not resemble the heavily stockaded enclosures so routinely depicted in old movies. Fort Lincoln was actually wide open, no outer protection encircling its four dozen major buildings and a like number of smaller shacks and outbuildings. That's usually the first surprise awaiting visitors.

The second generally comes when they enter the authentic reconstruction and see how comfortable and modern it was when either or both of the Custers lived there from November 1873 until shortly after his June 25, 1876 death. A veranda runs along the length of the northern and eastern sides of the wooden frame house, and a slanted bay window off the 32-foot-long parlor lends an unmilitary air. The Custers held dinners, dress receptions, plays, musical recitals, and card games frequently to break the monotony of outpost life. The house included a piano and a harp, a library, and a billiard parlor.

Costumed guides conduct half-hour tours of the house, speaking as though it is still 1876 and the Custers are merely away during your visit. They refer to Custer as "the General," in deference to his Civil War rank, point out his writing desk, and tell anecdotes about him. Period furnishings fill in where authentic furniture no longer survives.

Nothing controversial is mentioned about one of the most

controversial figures ever to wear an American uniform, either a flamboyant, colorful master tactician or a vainglorious jerk, depending on your perspective. Custer is no hero to Native Americans or their sympathizers. He conducted an expedition into the Indians' sacred Black Hills burial ground in 1874 and found gold, triggering a rush of prospectors, settlers, and landgrabbers which, in turn, led to hostilities that spawned Custer's punitive 1876 expedition into Montana and produced one of the most famous battles ever fought. A confrontation between the two cultures would have occurred anyway (Custer had been sent to Fort Lincoln to establish an intimidating presence for the Dakota Territory Indians the government viewed as renegade), but the gold strike hastened the inevitable.

The Custer House is the first of five scheduled for reconstruction; the others include a commissary, barracks, guardhouse, and granary.

Visitors can also see reconstructed blockhouses, breastworks, the post cemetery, a visitor center, and a trading post-gift store.

Of particular interest is the reconstructed partial Mandan Indian village just north of the visitor center, timber and earthen lodges built in the 1930s by the Civilian Conservation Corps on the site of a much larger summer Mandan village. Historical markers describe life among the Mandans who lived there from about 1650 to 1780, when a small pox epidemic and repeated attacks from the Dakota Indians leveled their populace. One memorable marker explains the brutal O-Kee-Pa ritual, pictured graphically in the 1970 movie "A Man Called Horse," in which males hung from ropes passed around the sliced-open muscles of their chests and shoulders.

The 1,000-acre park includes a campground, picnic area, nature trail, and winter activity trails. The walk from the visitor center to the Custer House is about a half-mile, and a horse-drawn wagon with canvas top and rubber tires also covers the distance for a small fee.

The North Dakota Parks and Recreation Department operates the park, placing equal emphasis on both cultures. In 1989, when the house first opened, 40,000 visitors toured. The park crams an ambitious schedule into its summer season, including a number of Native American cultural and craft exhibitions, an annual Frontier Army Days festival with historical recreations, a walking drama with re-enactors posing as the fort's famous inhabitants, a fur traders' rendezvous, a horse race, and living history demonstrations.

The park grounds open daily around 8 a.m. till dusk; a moderate per-vehicle entrance fee is charged. The free museum has similar hours from Memorial Day to Labor Day, then closes by end of afternoon from September through November, and opens only by appointment the rest of the year.

The Custer House hours nearly match the park's from Memorial Day to Labor Day but shorten to afternoons only for September and October; the house is closed the rest of the year. A moderate fee is charged.

The historic sites and museum can be toured in a couple hours. Be prepared for the stiff breezes of the North Dakota plains any time of year.

Nearby Mandan and Bismarck, on opposite sides of the Missouri, provide historic buildings and sites, an art gallery and zoo, shopping malls, seasonal festivals, and dining and gambling cruises aboard the "Far West," a replica of a famous riverboat.

George Armstrong Custer's many idolaters may also want to visit other sites associated with him: New Rumley, Ohio, his birthplace, where a statue and outdoor exhibit highlight the famous native son; Monroe, Michigan, his boyhood home, where a magnificent horseback statue, historical markers, and museum honor his memory; the Washita Battlefield outside Cheyenne, Oklahoma, where Custer's troops surprised and massacred Chief Black Kettle's village in 1868; any of the western forts associated with him, like Kansas' Fort Riley (near Manhattan) and Fort Hays (near Hays); the Little Bighorn Battlefield National Monument in Montana; and the military cemetery at West Point, New York, where a monument marks his purported grave (although the site is controversial, and his bones may actually lie mixed with those of his men in a common heap on the battleground where he breathed his last).

THE MUSEUM IN A MALL FOR A FORGOTTEN MAN

It may be the only museum of its kind - a rectangular line of continuous display cases and a television monitor replaying historic film at regular intervals - all in one wing of a shopping mall in Fargo, North Dakota.

The museum-in-the-mall honors a native son who achieved great fame for himself and his boyhood town... for awhile, before thudding to earth, never again to rise as high.

The native son did something no one else had managed to do and won instant celebrity. Then when he could never again duplicate the feat, he endured jeers from the same people who had cheered him on. Along with Lou Gehrig, whose career and life became victims of the disease that now bears his name, he was the most tragic man who ever wore the honored pinstripes of the New York Yankees.

Roger Maris did something on Sunday, October 1, 1961 that no one else ever did. Not Babe Ruth, not Ted Williams, not Mickey Mantle, not Hank Aaron. He hit a baseball, bearing the fingerprints of Tracy Stallard of the Boston Red Sox, into the stands of Yankee Stadium. It was the 61st time that Roger Maris had hit a home run during a regular season game that year. Only Babe Ruth, in 1927, had ever hit as many as 60 home runs in a regular season before. Roger Maris' 61st home run, coming in the last game of the season, broke Ruth's 34-year-old mark, the most sacrosanct single-person record in all of sports.

Not only did he take dead aim at Babe Ruth's home run record with amazing consistency throughout the year, he shared the Herculean task with another teammate, the much more famous Mickey Mantle who batted directly behind him in the daily batting order. The two competed head-to-head throughout the season, chasing the ghost of Babe Ruth, the most famous and beloved Yankee star, the most magical name in the history of sport.

A single-season record, which pits endurance, good health, skill, and luck in equal doses against a clock that is always running, is generally more difficult than a record amassed over an entire career; everything has to go right without a serious miscue...and, if one occurs, you may never have a chance again. A career record, by contrast, is more easily attained by an exceptional athlete gifted with longevity. Hank Aaron surpassed Ruth's career home run record rather easily - just by hitting home runs over the long haul in an excellent career; but he never put together a single season that approached Ruth's best.

Though Roger Maris had won the American League's Most Valuable Player Award in 1960, he could not equal Ruth's popularity for millions of baseball fans around the country. The people of Fargo and his friends, of course, cheered Roger Maris on as the home runs mounted in early 1961, but most enthusiasts of the game wanted Ruth's mark to stand forever. Were it to be broken, they figured, better it be by Mantle, a Yankee star since 1951...not this Maris who had only come to the team in a December 1959 trade with Kansas City.

Through the season, Maris and Mantle battled each other and the legend of the deceased Babe Ruth. Baseball had never seen such a prolonged two-way race against the clock for the most cherished record in the sport. Though the two teammates roomed and even palled around together, the media sought to heighten the drama and manufactured a rivalry between them. The press incorrectly reported that they didn't get along, didn't much like each other. Mantle and Maris laughed the rumors off, but the public believed them and sided with Mantle, a two-time Most Valuable

Player, a decade-long Yankee, the heir apparent to Ruth, Gehrig, and Joe DiMaggio - the all-time Yankee greats. An easy-going type fond of alcohol, jokes, and parties, Mantle got along with everyone, while Maris, more private and family-oriented, seemed a bit too keyed-up, too tightly wound. When an injury forced Mantle to play hurt and sit out games during the last few weeks of the season, the intense pressure and scrutiny spiraled nearly out of control and shifted entirely to the young man from Fargo.

All alone in his pursuit of an undying legend, with part of the country pulling for him and part rooting against him, Roger Maris persisted. Once far ahead of Ruth's 1927 home run pace, he hit nothing but a drought in the waning moments of the season. Games came and went, but the home runs dried up.

Finally, on October 1, the last day of the season, the last game of the season, Maris faced his last chance. Tied with Babe Ruth at 60 home runs, he could count on at least three and probably four at-bats. He wasted the first one, flying out to left field. But on the next chance, he popped a 2-0 pitch to right, a 365-footer, and the record was his. All alone with 61 home runs.

The specter of Babe Ruth still haunted him. Baseball Commissioner Ford Frick decreed the record books would show two single-season home run marks: Ruth's 60 in a shorter 154-game season (commonly played in baseball's earlier years) and Maris' 61 in a 162-game campaign. The so-called "asterisk" stigma remained with Maris for years to come.

Roger Maris collected his second consecutive Most Valuable Player Award at the end of the 1961 season on the strength of his remarkable feat while under fire - a pressure-cooker performance Ruth never had to undergo in the pre-television era of the 1920s when press coverage was more genteel and less frenetic. But Maris' detractors immediately denigrated his accomplishments: he needed more games than Ruth did; he needed Mantle out of the way; he would never do it again.

On that last one, they were right. Neither he nor anyone else - until the magical 1998 season in which Mark McGuire hit 70 home runs and Sammy Sosa added 66 - ever repeated his 1961 pyrotechnics.

His home run production predictably tailed off - 33 in 1962, 23 in 1963, 26 in 1964. Injured in 1965, he missed most of the games and hit only eight home runs. He never again regained his power stroke. Fans booed him at first, then ignored him as the Yankees, beset with age, went from World Series kings to league cellar dwellers.

Always quiet, colorless, and pedestrian in his interviews, Maris occasionally flared at reporters. But by then, he had become a scapegoat, and the writers cut him no slack, vilifying him, creating the image of a hot-headed, mean-tempered prima donna.

The Yankees unceremoniously dumped him at the end of the 1966 season, trading him to the St. Louis Cardinals, even-up for a little-known player generously referred to as a "journeyman infielder." Maris found out about the trade after the media had announced it to the country.

He played steadily but unspectacularly for the Cardinals, enjoying harmonious relations with his new team, fans, and even the media.

When he retired after the 1968 season, ironically Mickey Mantle's last as well, he left with 275 career home runs, 851 runs batted in, and a .260 batting average - solid figures, but generally not good enough for a real run at enshrinement in the Baseball Hall of Fame. He had just turned 34, young for retirement for a player of his stature. But his injuries had affected his swing and cut his efficiency, and his psyche buckled under the strain of years of criticism. He had had enough of baseball.

He assumed operation of a beer distributorship in Florida, a business set up for him by the owner of the Cardinals, Gus Busch, of Anheuser-Busch fame.

In 1974, he became eligible for the Hall of Fame. Mantle sailed in. Maris didn't even come close to getting enough votes, nor would he ever throughout the next 14 years of his eligibility.

He maintained a low profile in his post-baseball career, seldom making headlines. He scrupulously avoided Yankee Stadium in the Bronx, returning finally in 1978 for opening day ceremonies and, most memorably, in July 1984 for a ceremony in which the Yankees publicly retired his famous "9" jersey number. By then, he had developed cancer of the lymph glands. Both times, he received hearty sustained applause, a rarity for him. "When you die, they always give you good reviews," he said.

The Yankees honored him with a plaque in their revered Memorial Park beyond centerfield:

> ROGER EUGENE MARIS AGAINST ALL ODDS IN 1961 HE BECAME THE ONLY PLAYER TO HIT MORE THAN 60 HOME RUNS IN A SINGLE SEASON IN BELATED RECOGNITION OF ONE OF BASEBALL'S GREATEST ACHIEVEMENTS EVER HIS 61 IN '61 THE YANKEES SALUTE HIM AS A GREAT PLAYER AND AUTHOR OF ONE OF THE MOST REMARKABLE CHAPTERS IN THE HISTORY OF MAJOR LEAGUE BASEBALL ERECTED BY NEW YORK YANKEES JULY 21, 1984.

He returned to Yankee Stadium one more time for opening day ceremonies in 1985. After that, he weakened, became bloated, grew very sick. His doctors drained fluid from his body, gave him transfusions, introduced antibodies from laboratory mice into his system.

On December 14, 1985, he died in a Houston hospital of cancer at 51. Babe Ruth had also died of cancer...at 53. Even in death, Maris had fallen short of equaling the Bambino's numbers. Several national obituaries threw in gratuitous parting shots about his problems with the press.

He was eulogized in Fargo, the town he had not lived in since 1957, on December 19. Mantle served as one of a dozen pallbearers. Another Yankee teammate, Bobby Richardson, in his eulogy in St. Mary's Cathedral, acknowledged that Maris might not win election to the Baseball Hall of Fame. But, he added, "Roger is in God's Hall of Fame. In life, the honors are soon forgotten. God's Hall of Fame is for eternity."

His father, brother, wife, children, and grandchildren survived him.

Though many cities could claim Maris as a native son or resident, Fargo is the only one to commemorate him. Its Roger Maris Museum, tucked into a wing of the West Acres Shopping Center, at Interstate Highway 29 and 13th Avenue South, presents his life to the shopping public and the curious via scores of memorabilia: photographs; mannequins wearing his Number 9 uniform; his bats, caps, and gloves; trophies, plaques, and awards he won at various levels of athletic competition; literal crowns given him signifying his home run crown; some of the actual home run balls he belted during his quest of the record in 1961, including the 56th, 57th, 58th, and 60th (number 59 was never acquired, and number 61 reposes in the Hall of Fame); photographs showing his final at-bat at Yankee Stadium, long after his retirement, on July 22, 1984; and a filmed record of his final 12 home runs of the historic 1961 campaign.

You don't walk into the museum, you walk alongside it and peer through the glass cases at more than 150 objects. Measuring 72 feet in length by 10 feet in height, it opened on June 23, 1984, when its honoree was still alive, under the sponsorship of the Fargo American Legion Post Number 2 (Maris had played American Legion ball in Fargo in 1950 and '51). The museum is available as long as the mall remains open, and it maintains the customary mall hours. It can be viewed in five minutes or a couple hours.

Fargo also remembers him with memorial plaques at Lindenwood Park on Roger Maris Drive and a garden named in his honor at the American Legion's Jack Williams Baseball Park.

In addition to the mall, Fargo has gambling casinos, golf courses and swimming pools, winter sports, summer concerts and craft shows at Trollwood Park, and Bonanzaville, U.S.A., a recreated pioneer village. Annual festivals include the Red River Valley Winter Festival in February, the Scandinavian Hjemkomst Festival in June, and the Merry Prairie Christmas in December. Forty miles northwest of Fargo is the 2,063-foot KTHI-TV Tower, the tallest structure anywhere in North America.

The most poignant perception of Maris' legacy is in Holy Cross Cemetery, north of West Acres Shopping Center and not far from Hector International Airport on the outskirts of Fargo (go north on I-29, exit at 19th Avenue North, drive east until you cross University Drive, turn north and proceed to 32nd Avenue, turn west (or left), and drive to the third cemetery - Holy Cross; the Maris grave is in block 15, a half-dozen graves in from an access road by an open field).

A flat stone, bearing his full name and an inscribed cross separating his birth and death dates, marks the site. Above the grave, a tombstone in the shape of a ball diamond carries his surname squarely in the middle. Underneath the name, an etched figure, in Maris' familiar home run stance, connects with an imaginary baseball. The stone also holds brief extracts from the plaque in Yankee Stadium: "61 '61" and "AGAINST ALL ODDS."

Flowers occasionally surround the base. Otherwise, nothing provides the slightest clue that a famous person lies underneath. You are unlikely to ever encounter anyone at the grave, for Fargo is not a popular tourist destination, and Roger Maris is still the "Forgotten Yankee."

Yankee legend Lou Gehrig, in the midst of the illness that shortened his playing career and eventually took his life, called himself "the luckiest man on the face of the earth." In a way, Roger Maris may have been the unluckiest man on the face of the earth, although he never publicly said that.

And yet, when alone in the cemetery with the legacy of the man the public would not let surpass Babe Ruth, the roar of a jet taking off from nearby Hector International Airport almost seems a deafening roar of belated applause...and the plane's trajectory, visible above the grave, almost becomes a titanic home run unleashed into the stratosphere in tribute to the ghost of a man seeking his final peace.

Perhaps the liberation of death has given Roger Maris the justice denied him in life.

OHIO

RIDING OUT WEST...AND WRITING OUT WEST

He had a stone-cold visage, a gaunt stare, with eyes that ranged from hauntingly sad to penetrating and determined. He gave in to dark moods, became hopelessly depressed, and was one of the greatest writers of the early 20th century. Franz Kafka?

He attacked life with robust zeal, loved the outdoors, rode horses, and could hardly contain himself when he wasn't fishing, hunting, or playing baseball. He mastered a literary style that became his alone. Ernest Hemingway?

He went to Hollywood and became even more famous when his greatest works made the transition to film. During his heyday, he made more money from his films than any other writer in Hollywood. F. Scott Fitzgerald?

He became associated with one part of the country and wrote of it so convincingly that his name alone foretold readers what to expect. His name defined a whole genre of fiction. William Faulkner?

During his life, his prolific works far outsold the writings of Kafka, Hemingway, Fitzgerald, and Faulkner. Indeed, he became far more famous than any of them and owned more loyal readers than any other writer before World War II.

His name was Zane Grey.

Descended from a great-grandfather who carved a rustic dirt path through the Ohio wilderness in the vanguard of settlers pushing westward, young Pearl Zane Gray, born in 1872, grew up too tough to stick with so effeminate a first name. He also changed the spelling of his surname to complete the transformation.

As a kid in Ohio, he converted a cave into a secret meeting

place where he and his cohorts read passages from popular books of the day. In school, he became a practical joker and a bit of a brawler. He studied dentistry to please his father and played baseball on the semi-professional level. "I hated the lecture rooms," he complained. "My thoughts wandered afar...to dreams of what might come true."

He set up his dental practice in Manhattan, but an article he submitted to an outdoors journal spurred him to write a book on the life of his great-grandfather's sister, a minor Revolutionary War heroine. When no one published it, he borrowed money and did it himself. Hooked on writing, with little to go on save his wife's devotion, he quit dentistry, honed his craft, and, with his wife's money and writing tips, endured a string of rejections.

"The Heritage of the Desert," published in 1910, became his first major success and established the western formula he would mine the rest of his life. He followed it later with "Riders of the Purple Sage" and never looked back.

He fished both major oceans, hunted bear in Arizona, and sought adventure and inspiration in ruggedly beautiful places. He wrote simply of the great West he had fallen for, churning out more than 3,000 words a day at peak proficiency (1,000 is usually considered a good output) and at least one or two formulaic westerns every year. He seldom rewrote anything in his Lackawaxen, Pennsylvania home. Eventually, his name became so bankable that Hollywood cranked out one to five filmed adaptations of his works every year. He left the East for California in 1918, eventually settling in Altadena. But he roamed the world as often as he stayed home. In 1923, he constructed a hunting cabin in Arizona.

He renounced Arizona the following decade when the state refused to exempt him from adhering to a new limited bear-hunting season. Yet about the same time he left Arizona in pique, never to return, he gave up hunting. And in the last decade of his life, the man, who as a youngster had wanted nothing more than to "kill bars and bufflers," championed the right of wild animals to live in the wilderness into which nature had delivered them.

A stroke felled him in 1937, but he recuperated and wrote again. Finally, in 1939, he died at 67 of a heart attack.

He never received the critical acclaim of his more erudite literary contemporaries. But, more than anyone else, he created the genre of American fiction we now call the "western" and became the most popular best-selling author of his generation.

His life is commemorated in Ohio's flat heartland, where he was born and grew up. The National Road/Zane Grey Museum houses extensive holdings: first edition copies of his books; posters of films adapted from his works; original manuscripts, including his "Riders of the Purple Sage" masterpiece, his longhand prose virtually correction-free; photographs donated by his family; key possessions and items of clothing; a notebook he kept in 1906 of "Striking Phrases & Sentences," his first entry being the foreboding "The nothingness of human life." A 30-minute film dissects his life, and a life-size mannequin of him sits in a Morris chair, writing prose with a pencil and legal-size tablet on a lapboard, in a room meant to duplicate his California study.

It is only a portion of the museum operated by the Ohio Historical Society. The main thrust traces the evolution of the National Road, the nation's first highway as imagined by George Washington and Thomas Jefferson - 600 miles of land cleared for a toll road between Cumberland, Maryland and Vandalia, Illinois. The road required decades of hard work in the 19th century and officially became U.S. Highway 40 in 1926. In between, it provided a direct, safe route for the goods, produce, and livestock of the western regions to reach eastern markets, connected the Chesapeake Bay with the Ohio and Mississippi Rivers, and became the first large-scale road constructed by the United States of America.

Zane Grey's great-grandfather, Colonel Ebenezer Zane, blazed Zane's Trace through a portion of Ohio in exchange for the government's permission for him to locate his Revolutionary War land grants near the crossings of key streams. His trace became a forerunner of the National Road.

The museum utilizes a unique design: three of its four interior walls visually present the drama of the National Road; nearly two dozen subsections of a 136-foot continuing diorama span the history of the roadway, chronologically and geographically. The miniature figures and settings, as lifelike as photographs, portray the road in gritty realism: its laborious construction from a wilderness; its heavy usage by cattle drovers, conestoga wagons, and migrating westerners; the birth of towns and cities along its edges; its displacement by the railroad in mid-19th century; and its eventual re-emergence with the advent of automobiles. Key scenes prevent stark vignettes: animal congestion along the road by the waystations that arose to accommodate the sudden influx of people; procedures used to cross the Ohio where it interrupted the continuance of roadway; paving the road with macadam in the early years of the 20th century. The diorama was constructed by the Historical Society in 1973, when the site opened.

Along the 136 feet of diorama, the museum posts nine conveyances of the types that actually traveled the great road: a Concord coach sleigh of 1847, an uneven-wheeled bicycle of the late 1800s, and early 20th-century automobiles, among others.

One corner of the complex poses realistic mannequins in reconstructed versions of the wheelwright and blacksmith shops and lodging taverns that came up along the first "Main Street of America." The central room houses a vast collection of Zanesville art pottery and decorative tile, the single-most important regional industry.

The National Road/Zane Grey Museum is open daily from May through September during normal daytime hours (and daily, except Mondays and Tuesdays, during March, April, October, and November) and charges a moderate fee. You can lightly touch on everything, including seeing the film, in an hour or two. It is just south of the road it honors, present U.S. 40, in Norwich, 12 miles east of Zanesville.

A trip to Zanesville can round out the day. An early state capital and the country's former pottery center, it contains Zane Grey's birthplace, pottery factories, an art center, riverboat cruises on the

Muskingum River, and the so-called "Y"-Bridge, the only three-pronged bridge in the country, designed to carry the old National Road, and now U.S. 40, over the intersection of the Muskingum and Licking Rivers.

TOMB WITH A VIEW

It is the tallest Doric column in the world, the fourth-highest manmade monument in the country, the nation's only 350-foot historic shaft surrounded by water, and an international memorial and military cemetery.

And it is nearly unheard of outside Ohio.

It is Perry's Victory and International Peace Memorial, the focal point of Ohio's South Bass Island in Lake Erie, five miles south of Canadian waters.

It celebrates the significant American triumph in the War of 1812 that occurred on September 10, 1813, about 10 miles northwest of the island, when Master Commandant Oliver Hazard Perry defeated a British flotilla and won control of Lake Erie, a key point on the continent. Perry responded with a line that became immortal: "We have met the enemy and they are ours...."

At 352 feet, the memorial cowers only to the St. Louis Gateway Arch (630 feet), the San Jacinto Monument near Houston (570 feet), and the Washington Monument in the nation's capital (555 feet). A square observation tower at the 317-foot level crowns the pink granite column. An 11-ton bronze urn, 23 feet high and 18 feet wide, with lion heads and lights to guide ships at night, rises above the viewing platform. Charts, textboards, and recorded words describe the battle on the deck which surveys the lake and nearby islands with breathtaking clarity, catching hair-raising gusts of wind at the same time.

Back at ground level, a visitor center contains a museum and book store. The bodies of three American officers and a like number of British officers killed in the engagement lie beneath the floor within the memorial's rotunda, making it international in scope. The National Park Service oversees the memorial, free except for a modest elevator fee.

The monument overlooks the small village of Put-in-Bay, an amalgam of shops, lodges, and restaurants. On most weekends, tourists can easily outstrip the village's population of about 100 or so.

The monument is open from late April through the end of October during daytime hours (which expand into the evening during the summer).

Virtually no one goes to South Bass Island for the memorial alone, however. Though small (3.75 miles long and 1.5 miles wide), the island is a fine one-day or weekend destination, an all-encompassing stop where you can get away from mainland traffic and still feel civilization within your grasp. The island's highlights include: sand beaches; fish hatcheries; a daytime touring train that allows patrons to get on and off at will; a number of historic mansions; a mock Viking longhouse with a museum; the mouldering body of John Brown (not the abolitionist, but his namesake son) in Crown Hill Cemetery; parks, one of which includes the remains of the Victory Hotel's grand natatorium which once held the distinction of being America's first coed public swimming pool; a winery tour; two caves; a state biological science research center, lab, and science library; scenic lookouts and hiking trails; an old Coast Guard lighthouse; and a marina.

A town hall, school, library, post office, churches, and basic services keep the community going year-round.

South Bass Island is the southernmost in a chain of islands stretching north and south within the American part of the lake, and no bridge connects it with the mainland. But you have choices: snowmobile across when the lake freezes in winter; take your own boat and dock it at the marina; charter the small private planes that fly between Port Clinton on the mainland and Put-in-Bay Airport; or, as most people do, take either of two ferries departing regularly from different points - Port Clinton (a 10-mile ride connecting with the village of Put-in-Bay) and Catawba Island (a three-mile ride going to Lime Kiln Dock at the island's southern tip). Cars, vans, bicycles, adults, and children are all taken across for varying one-way rates (average for ferry service). An island shuttle bus also connects the two docks and the village. Sea gulls follow the track of the boats, swooping down and around. And when fog enshrouds the lake, nearby islands loom sepulchrally in the distance.

The ferries operate from mid-April to mid-November and occasionally do not cross cars both ways in a single day (warning is given ahead of time). The airplanes fly throughout the year.

THE WONDERFUL WIZARD OF WOOD

The world's greatest sculptor in stone may have been Michelangelo Buonarroti, but the world's greatest carver in wood was probably someone you never heard of.

A man who, as a boy, amassed a second-grade education and carried snakes in his pocket to frighten little girls.

A short man with a booming baritone and an intractable mane of hair that shot out in all directions in waves of stubborn individualism.

A man who received a vision one day in 1913 and then spent 400 hours making 31,000 precise cuts with a knife in a block of black walnut (13 inches long, three-quarters of an inch wide, and five-eighths of an inch thick) to create a tree that opened up into 511 interconnecting plier-type branches, an astounding feat that eschewed rulers, drawn lines, and mathematical principles and became a "Ripley's Believe It or Not" exhibit.

A man who dedicated four decades to carving authentically detailed wooden models of steam engines, using a scale of a half-inch to the foot. A man who carved ebony, ivory, walnut, applewood, and pearl in fashioning as many as 15,000 individual parts for each model and using little-known arguto wood (an oily raw material) for bearings and moving parts to ensure the wheels actually rotated without having to be oiled. A man who carved two to four versions of every model because he donated some of his originals to museums.

A man who had to teach himself how to read and write.

A man who at 14 went to work in a steel mill and remained

there for a quarter-century to help support a wife and a family that grew to include five children. A man who spent the remaining hours of the day fixing things around the house, spending time with his family, and carving.

A man whose lunches often consisted of whole wheat bread, rolled oats, and raw carrots in a day when cholesterol had yet to be heard of.

A prankster and practical joker who often surreptitiously nailed fellow workers' shoes to benches, secretly substituted wedge-shaped wooden blocks for slices of pie in friends' lunch pails, and who cozened coworkers into thinking he could bite through a steel nail by using one he had filed nearly in two beforehand.

A man who rejected a $75,000 offer from industrialist Henry Ford for 15 of his miniature models as well as an offer of a yearly stipend if he would carve exclusively for the auto magnate.

A mechanical genius who couldn't master the art of driving a car and motored his Model-T sedan onto curbs and sidewalks and into creeks.

A man who, in 1933, spent 1,600 hours carving a single train model, the Great Northern, with 7,752 accurate parts, including those which would never be seen hidden within the works.

A man who could produce a functioning pair of pliers with 10 precise cuts in a single block of wood (three and a half inches long and one-half-inch square) in no more than 20 seconds with no shavings or sawdust, a trick he learned from a hobo and perfected by doing tens of thousands of times.

A man who died on June 8, 1973, at 87, in the little town of Dover, Ohio, where he had resided all his life. A man whose talent won him the title "World's Master Carver."

Ernest "Mooney" Warther has been dead for a generation now. But his legacy thrives at 331 Karl Avenue where he lived, worked, and exhibited his work. The museum is not called Warther's Wonderland anymore and it can no longer squeeze all its display items into one room. His wife's collection of buttons (her lifelong passion) - some 73,000 (with 50,000 more in reserve), all different, some shaped as animals and vehicles, and arranged in symmetrical quilt patterns along the walls and ceilings - now fills his old museum.

A newer, larger museum that joins his old workshop (still holding his simple tools and a part of his 25,000 arrowheads) with the modern shop where the family continues to produce the handmade cutlery Mooney Warther turned to after quitting the steel mill currently displays his artifacts: a letter from President Franklin D. Roosevelt thanking him for sending a cane in 1933 (the cane now reposes in the Little White House in Warm Springs, Georgia); a walnut walking cane with a grip containing a parachute, a bust of Charles A. Lindbergh, and a model of the plane that the aviator flew across the Atlantic Ocean in 1927; a walnut and ivory model, with movable parts, of the mill where he had worked, carved from memory three decades later (the mill foreman pounds his fist in anger as one worker dozes and another eats a repast of rhubarb pie and cheese); the elaborate wooden tree exhibited by Ripley's; a jewelry box of ivory and mother of pearl resembling the Parthenon.

And, of course, also exhibited are the five dozen units that compose his history of the steam engine/railroad: Hero's engine of 250 B.C. in Alexandria, Egypt; a whirling aeoliphile of 1st-century A.D. Greece; Sir Isaac Newton's proposed locomotive of 1680; the "Best Friend," the first locomotive built in America (1830); the DeWitt Clinton, which traveled at 15 mph in 1831; the Union Pacific Railroad's Mallet of 1941, at 604 tons, the biggest steam engine ever built; the eight-foot-long Empire State Express, made from a single 81-pound elephant tusk and 11,000 parts and mounted on a stone arch bridge carved from ebony; and, his greatest curiosity, the Nashville, one of four locomotives that hauled the funeral train of Abraham Lincoln (whom he idolized) from Washington, D.C. to Illinois (the eight-foot model includes a black ebony engine, coal tender, and three passenger coaches, the last bearing the carved body of the assassinated president in its coffin, finished in one year's time on the 100th anniversary of Lincoln's death).

The guided 75-minute tour includes a quarter-hour slide show on Warther's life. Tour guides explain how, at 80, he made a pair of his trademark wooden pliers with 10 knife cuts for Johnny Carson on "The Tonight Show" in 9.4 seconds, how he never sold any of his carvings but rather gave them away, and how notables such as Frank Lloyd Wright, Perry Como, and the Rockefeller family acquired some of his work.

After the tour, visitors can see the exhibit rooms at their leisure, visit the gift shop where Warther cutlery can be purchased, walk the grounds and flower gardens where the family used to play, and picnic near the parking lot with its antique steam locomotive, caboose, handcar, and mock train station.

A concession stand is on the premises. The entire site can be done in two or three hours, even including a pilgrimage to Dover Burial Park to see the unmarked grave of Ernest Warther. Visitation is a brisk 100,000 a year.

The Warther Museum is open daily, except major holidays, during customary daytime hours. An average fee is charged for the tour; the gardens and grounds are free. The site is just east of Interstate Highway 77 in the western part of Dover, about 75 miles south of Cleveland. Signs direct you from the off-ramp to nearby 331 Karl Avenue.

Dover is in the middle of Tuscarawas County which brims with little-known treasures: Fort Laurens State Memorial on the site of a Revolutionary War fort; Zoar Village State Memorial, a German Separatist restoration; Gnadenhutten State Monument, the reconstructed site of one of America's most vicious butcheries; Schoenbrunn Village State Memorial, a Moravian reconstruction; "Trumpet in the Land," an historical outdoor drama; Sugarcreek, a Swiss village; Newcomerstown and its Temperance Tavern Museum and exhibits on native sons Woody Hayes (longtime Ohio State football coach) and Cy Young (baseball's winningest pitcher in whose honor the Cy Young Award was named). Football's Hall of Fame lies just 20 miles north of Dover in Canton.

OKLAHOMA

THE GREATEST INDIAN WHO MAY NEVER HAVE LIVED

He may have been the greatest Indian who ever lived. He is also the most unknowable.

Things start getting fuzzy with his birth. He was born in 1760...or about 1770...or maybe 1776...in Taskigi, in what later became Tennessee, to a Cherokee mother and a white father whose name was Nathaniel Gist...or perhaps George Guess...or maybe George Guest.

He supposedly became a blacksmith, silversmith, and artist, though nothing remains of his handiwork. He lived in Georgia...or Alabama...or maybe both.

Though illiterate, he realized the Cherokees could have a written language similar to that of the white race and, from 1809 to 1821, set about achieving it. He attempted to come up with a unique symbol for each word in the spoken Cherokee language but rejected the idea when the sheer enormity of words defeated his efforts. At length, he hit upon a formula that worked: he fashioned a written character for every sound or syllable within the spoken Cherokee language. He identified 85 different sounds, constructed a like number of characters, and called his invention an alphabet (although it was more properly a syllabary, using spoken sounds and not individual letters as its basis). He taught the syllabary to his daughter Ahyoka, one of numerous children he had with several wives. Usage spread, enabling the Cherokees to become a literate people - the only Native Americans with their own written language.

He went to Arkansas in 1818...or 1823... and, in 1828, acted as one of several delegates in the Treaty of Washington, which took the Cherokees' Arkansas land from them in exchange for parcels in Oklahoma. He moved to the site near modern Sallisaw, Oklahoma and built a homestead currently preserved by the Oklahoma Historical Society.

In the early 1840s, perhaps 1842, he journeyed to Mexico where oral history insisted a faction of his nation had gone prior to the Revolutionary War. His purpose was either to convince his lost tribesmen to return to America and rejoin their brethren in Oklahoma or to teach them his syllabary, possibly both. He found them but grew ill and died, reputedly on the trek home in 1843, perhaps August, to be buried near San Fernando, Mexico, in a small cave tucked within a hillside...or maybe somewhere else. His grave has never been found.

Then, more than 100 years later, Traveller Bird published a book entitled "Tell Them They Lie The Sequoyah Myth" that skewed the whole scenario. It alleged that the Cherokees had had a secret syllabary for hundreds of years prior to its discovery by the white race. The book further said that westward-expanding whites had assuaged their guilt over evicting the Indians from their just lands by dismissing them as uncivilized savages, incapable of deep thought and uneducable, perhaps a step higher than buffalo on the evolutionary ladder (and, thus, fit to be removed at will). But the white discovery of an indigenous Cherokee syllabary had suddenly threatened the moral justification for depriving the Indians of their land. So the white race had then methodically set about exterminating every Cherokee who knew of the secret syllabary. Then, as a dodge against discovery of what they had done, the white charlatans had concocted a fake person - the famous "Sequoyah" - whose white education, they claimed, had been responsible for inspiring him to invent the syllabary. They then groomed a number of malleable Cherokees who could be bribed into going along with the story - thus, the many discrepancies in the age and background of "Sequoyah." So alleged the book.

Many historians dismissed the controversial story, demanding proof. Others acknowledged the sketchiness of the original Sequoyah biography and said the truth might lie somewhere between the two explanations.

Regardless, some "Sequoyah" built a single-room log dwelling in Oklahoma in 1829. Years after this Sequoyah's death, George Blair, another Cherokee, purchased the cabin from the owner's widow and added another room. The structure had survived more than a century when the Oklahoma Historical Society acquired it in 1936. The Works Progress Administration removed the added room, returning the cabin to its original appearance, and protected its fragility by enclosing it within a larger stone building, sealing it off from nature's whims. The cabin became a National Historic Landmark in 1966.

Today, visitors can enter the house within a house, filled with period items and furniture, including a spinning wheel of 1820s vintage that was sold along with the house to Blair in 1855 and that carries the Blair family's oral cachet of having been made by Sequoyah.

Displays on Cherokee history, culture, and language, including a plow supposedly made by Sequoyah, line the interior walls surrounding the historic cabin.

The 10-acre grounds include a visitor center built in part from logs supposedly hewn by Sequoyah, a picnic area, and a spring that Sequoyah may have excavated and contained within a well. A statue of Sequoyah, quill in hand, awkwardly looking skyward, commands the lawn leading down to the well and picnic area.

The visitor center includes exhibits. Staffmembers give guests computer printouts of their names spelled out, both in Cherokee script and phonetically, and tell them of the wealth of presidents (George Washington, Franklin D. Roosevelt, George Bush, etc.) related to the Guess-Guest-Gist family.

Among the estimated 36,000-40,000 annual visitors are numerous Native Americans; more Indians live in Oklahoma than in any other state, and descendants of Sequoyah still live in the area.

The Sequoyah Home is open weekdays (except Mondays and state holidays) during normal daytime hours, with afternoon hours on weekends. Admission is free. The home is several miles northeast of Sallisaw in Sequoyah County in eastern Oklahoma, just a few miles east of Akins on State Highway 101. Signs indicate the route. A half-hour to an hour should be sufficient.

If you want to steep yourself in Native American culture, visit nearby Tahlequah, the capital of the Cherokee Nation, second-most populous (after the Navajo). Among its attractions are: the Cherokee Heritage Center, a recreated 16th-century village; the Cherokee National Museum; the Trail of Tears outdoor dramatization of the forced expulsion of the Cherokees from their eastern lands; Adams Corner, a reconstructed 19th-century Cherokee community; the historic Cherokee Capitol Building, former Cherokee Supreme Court Building, and former Cherokee National Prison; the Cherokee Square gift shop and visitor center; Lake Tenkiller and its recreational activities; and perhaps a chance to meet Wilma P. Mankiller, the first woman elected principal chief.

THE UNBUILT HOME OF THE MOST BELOVED AMERICAN

The most popular American of his time had taken his wife to a Los Angeles rodeo, then bid her goodby. He flew to Seattle where he met a famous aviator who had gone around the world in eight days, then a smashing record. The two Oklahomans - one, an experienced flyer, the other, an air enthusiast who had logged hundreds of hours riding shotgun - were to fly to Alaska because the aviator was pioneering a new passenger route across the top of the globe to Russian Siberia. The famous American considered flying with him to Moscow and then meeting his wife somewhere in Europe (plans would be formulated later) to tour awhile and then return together to the states.

The two Oklahoma friends flew in a plane that was a bit too heavy in the nose to Juneau, Alaska and then on to Dawson, in Canada's Yukon province. The famous American pounded away with two fingers on his portable typewriter, working on future newspaper columns, stopping to chat with friends and well-wishers, and posing for photographs (everyone wanted to be photographed with him). Then on to Aklavik in Canada's Northwest Territories. And then back to Alaska - Fairbanks, Anchorage, and Fairbanks again.

At some point, the famous American finished his typing. The last word his fingers struck out on the keys was "death."

The aviator and his famous companion took off again for Point Barrow, the northernmost part of the great Alaskan wilderness.

They landed about 15 miles south to seek directions from Clare Okpeaha, an Eskimo seal camp owner. The famous American undoubtedly said something, but his words went unrecorded. The aircraft pulled back up in the air a short ways on the final leg to Point Barrow.

Suddenly, the engine failed and died completely. Gravity yanked the front-heavy plane downward, and it crashed headlong into a shallow, two-foot lagoon, then landed backward, its underside facing up. The aviator's watch stopped at 8:18 p.m., the moment of impact. The famous American's watch still ticked at 3:30 a.m., when the rescue team reached his body in the tangled carnage of the red monoplane, a hybrid Lockheed Orion and Explorer Special.

The news stunned the world. Memorials sprang up everywhere. CBS and NBC radio pulled the plug on their programming for a half-hour of silence in memoriam.

The date of the crash was August 15, 1935.

The aviator was Wiley Post.

The famous American was Will Rogers.

Imagine an actor as popular as Clint Eastwood...a witty comedian as famous as David Letterman...a sage social commentator as respected as Walter Cronkite. Throw in a dash of the populist appeal of Ross Perot, minus the stridency, and a bit of the athletic showmanship of Michael Jordan. Then combine them all into one person and kill him off at the height of his fame. You'll have an idea how America greeted the sad news of the death of Will Rogers.

He was born with part-Cherokee blood in the pre-statehood Oklahoma Territory and died in the pre-statehood Alaskan glacial wilderness. Though predominantly white, he identified with his Native American descent and oft remarked his "Ancestors didn't come over on the Mayflower, but they met 'em at the boat." He achieved his success not on reservations but in the white world.

Growing up on a ranch, he became a cowboy-cattle driver in the waning days of the Wild West. He acquired riding and roping skills and made his lariat do things most trick artists could only dream of. He took his act on the road in Wild West shows and honed it in vaudeville performances. He became a star in Ziegfeld's Follies and on Broadway. Then he became an actor. When he died, box office receipts had made him America's greatest draw.

But other arenas provided even greater renown for the man with the southern drawl and unruly shock of hair plunging down his forehead in an era when no civilized man allowed his hair to behave thusly. He combined a soft-spoken delivery, affable charm, and perceptive wit.

Hundreds of newspapers ran his syndicated weekly column on politics, the state of the world, and human foibles. He spoke on the radio and in public appearances. He hobnobbed with politicians, statesmen, and royalty as an unofficial yet universally acclaimed public envoy. People doted on his words of advice and politicians sought his humor-laced barbs. He succeeded where politicians failed; he won over an entire nation with trenchant observations cast off with a self-deprecating nod:

> - Our foreign dealings are an Open Book, generally a Check Book.
> - ...with Congress, every time they make a joke, it's a law. ...And every time they make a law it's a joke.
> - So here we are in a country with more wheat and more corn and more money in the bank, more cotton, more everything in the world - there's not a product that you can name that we haven't got more of than any other country ever had on the face of the earth - and yet we've got people starving. We'll hold the distinction of being the only nation in the history of the world that ever went to the poor house in an automobile.

His plain-speaking identification with the common man and natural awkwardness won him the admiration of the downtrodden, oppressed, unemployed, and dispirited. He parlayed his homespun appeal into a multifaceted career that earned him $500 a broadcast minute and a reputation as "America's Ambassador to the World."

He would never make it today, of course. His halting manner of speaking, the hand invariably going to his head to scratch the scalp, the slouching posture, the jaws mechanically working a wad of gum as he spoke would type him as a cornpone rube. Even as a young man, he looked avuncular. But he was both a quintessential product and prototype of his times - and both essences are captured at the Will Rogers Memorial in Claremont, Oklahoma, near the site of his birth and the place where he intended to retire.

Several memorials honor him: the Will Rogers State Historical Park at Pacific Palisades, California - the house in which he lived during his fame; a pair of monuments at or near his Alaskan death site; a statue in the Capitol's Statuary Hall in Washington, D.C.; the Will Rogers Shrine of the Sun in Colorado Springs, Colorado.

But the memorial at Claremore, dedicated in 1938 on land owned by the most popular American of his time and donated to the state by his widow, houses the largest collection of Rogers memorabilia and the most affecting tribute to Oklahoma's favorite native son. A dozen or so rooms and corridors, packed with relics of his life, draw an estimated quarter-million to a half-million annual visitors. More than a dozen realistic dioramas depict facets of his life, from childhood to the fatal crash. Hundreds of photographs, movie stills, and theatrical posters and lobby cards crowd the walls. His prized saddle collection reposes in a room nearly a museum in itself.

The family room displays exhibits on his wife, parents, and children. A television set endlessly plays his films, and easy chairs are scattered throughout.

Another room, devoted to his film career and lined with artifacts, boasts another television showing his films and comfortable sofas and chairs in which to watch them.

An adjacent room contains more dioramas and photos, as well as items from his home; yet another television shows old footage of his consummate dexterity with a lariat.

Other rooms display a recreation of his den (with a radio broadcasting his speeches) and a collection of bronzes of his famous likeness.

A large room concentrates on his entertainment career. One of the 13 dioramas created by Joseph Jacinto (Jo) Mora shows his first radio broadcast on KDKA in Pittsburgh in 1922. Above the diorama, a TV screen continually runs his most famous radio broadcast. A quarter-life sculpture by Tex Wheeler and Clyde Forsythe, "Will Rogers Astride Soapsuds" (his favorite horse), holds court in the center, dwarfed by Torres Rojas' immense "The Spirit of Will Rogers" mural covering the rear wall.

Mementos line corridors and fill display cases everywhere: his costume and script from "A Connecticut Yankee in King Arthur's Court," one of his most famous films; columns he typed on his portable typewriter, handwritten vaudeville notes, telegrams; envelopes addressed to him with only his picture cut out and pasted on or in cryptograph or bearing one of his famous catch phrases - a tribute to his fame; scrapbooks and letters from the famous and anonymous.

A near-200-seat theater shows documentary films on his life, a library provides research on him, and a book store sells souvenirs. Jo Davidson's larger-than-life statue of Rogers, hands characteristically thrust into pants pockets, slouching slightly in a fully-buttoned suitcoat (a duplicate of the one that stands in Washington), fills the center of the foyer, overlooking the outside vault where he, his wife, and two children are buried atop the hill on which he had wished to build a retirement home where he could sit and rock and watch his native state. Another statue, Electra Waggoner's "Riding into the Sunset," shows Rogers astride his horse and stands vigil just east of the grave.

The memorial's most somber room lies off the foyer. Its walls hold 33 newspapers, whose bold type and huge letters proclaim Rogers' death, as well as telegrams of condolences to his widow from America's famous. Jo Mora's sober, sparse "Lonely Death" diorama shows the broken wreckage of the plane on the northern

Alaskan tundra, as Clare Okpeaha, the Eskimo, calls out in vain, trying to contact anyone still alive.

The darkened room, poignantly highlighted by the stark diorama, contains the final haunting relics: his last column, three pages long, bearing his distinctive style replete with misspellings and faulty grammar that editors later corrected; his last will; his final clothing (gray suitcoat and hat, brown tie, shoes); a running light cover from the airplane; his death certificate listing the cause as "multiple fractures, crushing injuries;" his pocket items (watches, a pocketknife, glasses, three-cent stamps, a magnifying glass, and a Coin-Trik Block Puzzle).

The Will Rogers Memorial immerses visitors into the world of its subject. Even a cursory visit will gobble up an hour; taking in everything, including some of the films, will take half a day. Admission is free, but a moderate donation is suggested. Signs point the way to the memorial at 1720 W. Will Rogers Boulevard in Claremore, off State Highway 66, just northeast of Tulsa. The site is open daily, except Thanksgiving and Christmas, during customary daytime hours.

Affiliated with the memorial is the Will Rogers Birthplace Home outside Oologah, about 12 miles distant. Only the first floor is available for touring, and it includes the bedroom where he was born with the crib that held him. To reach it from Claremore, take State Highway 88 north. Just prior to reaching Oologah, an historical marker to Rogers stands at the intersection of 88 and local road NS411. Turn right onto 411 and drive for two miles, then turn right on local road EW38 which takes you to the site. Unlike the memorial, the house can be quickly toured. The house is also free and has the same hours.

OREGON

WHERE AMERICA'S RICHEST MAN GOT RICH

It was the final destination for Lewis and Clark on their epic continent-crossing journey of 1804-06.

It overlooks the point where one of America's mightiest rivers meets the world's mightiest ocean.

It made a fortune for America's first great millionaire.

It became part of the "Graveyard of the Pacific," a triangular patch of treacherous water that claimed hundreds of lives and ships with its turbulent fury.

It is Astoria, the biggest little city in the northwestern corner of Oregon.

Meriwether Lewis and William Clark reached the site of modern Astoria, then a wilderness, in November 1805. They had traveled from St. Louis up the Missouri River, then gone deep into the northwestern wilds through the Clearwater and Snake Rivers, and finally pushed west along the Columbia River to the Pacific Ocean, completing their mission of mapping a connecting route from mid-continent to the coast. By December, they had hastily constructed Fort Clatsop, their winter shelter, a half-dozen miles southwest. In March of the following year, having survived winter's harshness, the explorers left for home.

A few years later, resourceful fur businessman John Jacob Astor, who was to become America's richest man and sire a line of namesake millionaires that continued into the 20th century (including one who perished aboard the Titanic), moved in. By April 1811, his trapping crew had begun constructing Fort Astoria to protect his fur empire operations. It became America's first permanent fortification west of the Mississippi River. The fort's buildings fell into disuse in later years, after Astor's company had milked the rivers of pelt-bearing animals. Eventually, the buildings came down, replaced by a larger community known simply as Astoria.

Over the decades, an inordinately high number of ships foundered, sailed onto spits or snags, or mysteriously disappeared near the prosperous community by the ocean's edge that lured traders and trappers, pioneers and seafaring adventurers. Casualties mounted: 26 people on the William and Ann, a British barkentine, in 1829; the entire crew of the U.S.S. Shark, a naval survey schooner, in 1846; 42 on the steamship General Warren in 1852; 25 on the schooner Sunshine in 1875; 33 on the Rosecrans, a tanker, in 1913; 34 on the steamship Iowa in 1936. The area gained a ghoulish reputation as a boneyard for boats.

Today, Astoria is an historic, scenic town of about 10,000 people. Fort Clatsop, just off U.S. Highway 101, is a reconstructed national memorial staffed by living history re-enactors. It is open daily during daytime hours and charges a modest fee. The site of Fort Astoria contains an historical marker and a reconstructed blockhouse on the corner of Exchange and 15th Streets. It is always available and free. The Columbia River Maritime Museum at 1792 Marine Drive, open daily during the day for an average admission, recounts the history of the region and the dynamic river that claimed so many victims at its junction with the ocean. Astoria also has two other museums (the Heritage Center and Uppertown Firefighters Museums) and an historic home (the Captain Flavel House).

Two structures provide the best view of both the majestic Columbia at its widest expanse and the distant Pacific.

The 123-foot Astoria Column, built in 1926 to celebrate Astoria's famous past, rises above the crest of Coxcomb Hill, perching 635 feet above the river. Nearly 170 stairs twist upward inside the cylindrical shaft, leading to a square observation platform that overlooks the Clatsop Spit, the Pacific Ocean, the Astoria-Megler Bridge (one of America's grandest and longest), the Columbia at its thickest, the high cliffs of neighboring Washington, and the 3,283-foot Saddle Mountain and the nearby Oregon peaks. The column is open daily till dusk and is free.

The 4.5-mile-long Astoria-Megler Bridge, connecting Astoria with Megler, Washington, ascends steeply on both ends before meeting at an apex high above the river and beneath twin canopies of steel A-frame girders. Opened in 1966 as an alternative to a long ferry crossing of the often agitated river, the bridge holds a spot in the "Guinness Book of World Records" as the continent's longest continuous-truss bridge. A modest one-way fee is charged (worth it alone for the thrill of rising high above the Columbia).

Astoria has restaurants, lodging, and a shopping district at Pier 11. If you want to see the exact spot where river gives way to ocean, venture into Fort Stevens State Park, 10 miles northwest. You can clam along the shoreline, visit a military reservation whose gun emplacements once guarded the entrance against foreign invasion, and peer through the water, when shallow, at the hulk of the Peter Iredale, until 1906 a functioning British barkentine. And Highway 101 undulates past a glut of beaches and recreation areas as it hugs the craggy Oregon coastline to the south.

Astoria draws more visitors during warmer months, but the views are good year-round.

PENNSYLVANIA

A snowy serenade: one of the many attractions at Koziar's.

A KOZIAR CHRISTMAS

If you dread the Christmas season, read no further.
 If you revel in it, however, there's a place in Pennsylvania you should know about.
 Before the lights come on, Koziar's Christmas Village is deceptively sedate. But with the power throttle forward, the village's megawattage startles motorists with the sheer brilliance of more than half a million lights, nearly nuclear in luminosity.
 Upon closer inspection, the yellowish-orange glow assumes successions of orderly shapes. Lights outline buildings, pergolas, and passageways. They form decorations, too: circles, trees, stars, bells, horse-drawn wagons, candles, ornaments. Lights make up a giant American flag atop the silo next to the barn, highlight a ferris wheel, and spell out seasonal phrases like "Merry Christmas."
 Koziar's Christmas Village is gaudy beyond all hope of reclamation. It is also absolutely great.
 The average-priced admission gains you entrance to the grounds for as long as you want. Everything else costs extra: food and drinks, souvenirs, Christmas merchandise, the obligatory picture of the kids with Claus.
 But it's the lights that make Koziar's unlike anything else you've ever seen: Santa's Gift and Refreshment Barn with dozens of different seasonal designs outlined in a dazzling three-level panoply of color; exhibit houses you either enter or peer into; the lake with its rippling reflections of riverbank colors; a dock with a tree-like pyramid of lights leading to a bright star; the Christmas House, most elegant of the buildings, where snowmen serenade with viola and piccolo as lights dance throughout; a wonderland walkway of car-

toon characters, where fabled figures of folklore pop up at every turn to greet you amidst trellised lights overhead.

The illuminated paths wend around a blinding maze of colored lights, stopping here to present tigers celebrating Christmas in the jungle, pausing there to observe deer frozen in midstep in a snowy setting, detouring everywhere for "Christmas beneath the Sea" or "Merry Christmas from the Land of Oz" or a reverential look at the story of Jesus.

Appropriately titled lanes ("Christmas Avenue," "Santa Claus Lane") transport visitors to an old-fashioned bakery shop, a toymaker's shop, Raggedy Ann's Ice Cream Parlor, an olden church, a presentation on how different countries celebrate Christmas, a one-room schoolhouse. Another area tells the "'Twas the Night Before Christmas" tale. Santa is everywhere, whether surveying his North Pole operations or welcoming children to his lap in the post office.

Christmas music, sometimes traditional, sometimes jazzed up for disco effects, sometimes played with a country twang, sometimes crooned by chipmunks, emanates throughout to help get you in the mood (in case the lights don't do the trick). When you round one bend and enter another thematic area, you catch a measure or two of carols in conflict.

On cold days, Santa's Gift and Refreshment Barn, the Bavarian-flavored Das Ist Wunderbar eatery, and other indoor stops offering an assortment of moderately priced hot and cold snack foods are welcome heated ports in which to rest and warm up. But don't expect to escape the Christmas sights and sounds in them (like we said, if you don't like Christmas, don't come to Koziar's).

Christmas Village began modestly, even accidentally. Starting in 1948, William M. Koziar constructed annual Christmas displays at his farmhouse for his family - wife Grace and four children. He expanded them each year, gradually encompassing the barn, lake, and paths. Eventually, people started calling it the "Christmas House" and asked if they could see it closer. At length, the financial possibilities became evident, and it opened as an attraction. It now bills itself as "The Greatest Christmas Display in the U.S.A." (which it probably is). Display World magazine gave it a first prize for the "Best Outdoor Christmas Display in the World" (which it, also, probably is).

Koziar's Christmas Village is a seasonal attraction. At this writing, its hours are: 7:30-9:30 p.m. on October weekends; 5:30-9:30 p.m. on Fridays, Saturdays, and Sundays from November 1 to Thanksgiving; and thereafter until January 1, 6-9 p.m. weekdays and 5-9:30 p.m. weekends.

You can do Koziar's in an hour or two, including the mini-zoo that sometimes features live animals. Bring the camera. And the kids; they'll love it. And remember, each succeeding week into the season will be colder than the one before it, as Jack Frost settles in for his wintry stay; dress appropriately. The best time to visit is probably October or early November; the weather will be warmer, the crowds thinner, and the anticipation of Christmas all the greater.

Christmas Village is just west of Bernville (northwest of Reading) in Berks County. When in Bernville, follow signs for Koziar's and be prepared for that first view of a half-million lights as you reach the crest of the last hill along the country road.

Skiers can see Koziar's in conjunction with a ski jaunt; Mt. Heidelberg Ski Area adjoins it. And Reading is famous for its outlet malls.

THE BIRTH OF THE BRETZEL

Sometime around 610, a European monk combined religion and dough in an inspired moment of heavenly hunger. He took a lump of dough, rolled it into a slender spindle, crossed both ends, twisted them once to make a knot, and folded them inward against the knot to make three loops. The whole process signified his spiritual beliefs: the open ends of the doughy spindle represented outstretched arms to God; the crossing of the ends symbolized folded hands in prayer; the twisted knot at the center meant the holy rite of marriage; and the final folding down of the twisted ends that formed the inner loops symbolized the Christian concept of three distinct persons in one God - Father, Son, and Holy Ghost. He then baked the uniquely shaped dough, removed it from the oven, called upon God's blessings, and consumed it.

The tasty staple became known as the "bretzel." In time, it came across the ocean to America. And in 1810, bretzels began to be baked in a Pennsylvania community that had been around since 1743 when Moravian immigrants had arrived and named the town after a Bohemian village that had given birth to the Moravian church some 300 years earlier.

The town became known as Lititz (with the accent on the first syllable). An educational facility, later to become Linden Hall (212 East Main Street), the first girls' boarding school in America, arose three years hence. And during the Revolutionary War, the town set up a military hospital for George Washington's army after the Battle of the Brandywine. Now known as Brothers House, it sits at Cedar and Main Streets, and offers guided tours.

Then in 1861, Julius Sturgis began mass-producing the thousand-year-old product, since Americanized to "pretzel," in a 1784 stone and timber building that he transformed into America's first commercial lard pretzel bakery. The Sturgis Pretzel House, at 219 East Main Street (or State Highway 772), is on the National Register of Historic Places. A plaque sponsored by the National Pretzel Bakers Institute proclaims the site "THE FIRST PRETZEL BAKERY IN THE NEW WORLD."

A modest fee gains you admission to the bakery and a complimentary pretzel. The brief tour includes a demonstration of how to make pretzels: you are given a lump of dough to fashion into a pretzel; it then briefly soaks in a kettle of baking soda which provides both its rubbery firmness and brown sheen; it then gets a salt bath and is consigned to an oven more than 200 years old for baking at 550 degrees for seven to 10 minutes; it eventually emerges as a soft-dough snack, which you can buy, along with several of its siblings, at three for a dollar (guides frequently throw in an extra one at no charge).

The tour continues in the rear of the bakery where hard pretzels are made, 245 each minute, five tons a day. Machine-made, they pass through conveyors into 500-degree ovens and then into cooling receptacles where they harden at a mere 300-degree slow bake over 90 minutes.

The front rooms of the historic house-bakery offer a wide variety of Pennsylvania Dutch craft items and pretzels in all weights and tastes (oat bran, cheese, whole wheat, saltless, chocolate-dipped, etc.) and often at outlet store prices (eight-pound bags for $3.98).

The bakery is open daily, except Sundays and major holidays, during daytime hours. July and August are the busiest months, and 100,000 visitors arrive annually; we had a tour all to ourselves.

But there's more to Lititz than pretzels. In 1871, General John Augustus Sutter, a native of Baden, Germany, came there to spend his final years. He had founded Sacramento, California's capital, in 1839, when it was still a Mexican province. He acquired cattle, horses, and extensive holdings. What should have proved his fortune proved his ruin instead. When gold was found on his land in 1848, hundreds of thousands of scavengers flooded his property, determined to rake a portion of the yellow rock for themselves. The gold rush of 1849 epitomized American enterprise and greed and ruined Sutter. He helped at first, dispersing food and materials from his store. But the squatters panned his gold, purloined his horses, and slaughtered his cattle.

The worst was still to come. When the U.S. gained California, it failed to recognize Sutter's claim to the land Mexico had given him. Just a few short years after the gold rush, Sutter was broke. His home later burned down. In 1871, he moved east to seek redress of his grievances, to no avail. He died in Washington, D.C. at 77, embroiled in legal wrangling and embittered. He is buried in the Moravian cemetery near the entrance gate (just south of the intersection of East Main Street, Church Avenue, and the Moravian Congregation Church). An historical marker at the intersection of Lemon and South Broad Streets tells his sad tale. A flat stone marks his grave; few visitors come.

Then in 1930, the Wilbur Chocolate Company, founded in Philadelphia in the 19th century, moved to Lititz to set up its manufacturing operations as the Wilbur-Suchard Chocolate Company. Currently at 46 North Broad Street, it averages over 68 million pounds of chocolate a year. The complex includes a chocolate museum, factory outlet, and manufacturing center. Safety and insurance restrictions preclude a manufacturing tour, but visitors can peek into small rooms where selected chocolate pieces are being made.

Its Candy Americana Museum continually runs a five-minute short ("Wilbur Chocolate: 'The Perfect Blend'") that explains the chocolate process: 170-pound bags of harvested cocoa beans enter America; beans are cleaned and stored in silos, then journey to aspirators and winnowers where shells are broken to get at their nibs; nibs get roasted, then ground into chocolate liquor (which contains no alcohol) which then meets pure cocoa butter and sweetener in a marriage brokered in heaven; refiners crush the blend into a fine consistency for 24 hours; the batch is then tempered (cooled and reheated) for texture. The result is chocolate, truly the food of the gods.

The museum exhibits chocolate boxes, tins, barrels, and containers of all sizes, with names that make up a who's who of candy manufacturers, and any and all artifacts connected with chocolate: a cocoa bean roaster; a two-stage grinder; 170 international hot chocolate pots (Limoges, Haviland, Bavaria, Royal Munich, etc. - relics of the early 18th century when European aristocracy preferred hot chocolate to coffee), each valued at $50-1,000, depending on the amount of gold leaf and intricate design; a machete used to clear a cocoa tree area; a cocoa bean pod, shells, and nibs.

The outlet store offers hundreds of varieties of candy at some pretty good prices (candy-dipped apricots at $7.50 a pound, for example, in the mid-'90s). Free samples and the ever-enticing smell of chocolate are hard to resist. Candy Americana Museum is open daily, except Sundays and major holidays, during usual daytime hours; it is free.

Lititz also contains craft and specialty stores, restaurants, festivals and flea markets, and the Lititz Springs Park, just south of Wilbur's. The village is in Lancaster County, the heart of Pennsylvania's famous Dutch country.

A LITTLE MAN, A LITTLE TOWN, A LARGE LEGACY

Laurence Gieringer nurtured a fascination with life in miniature since his days as a small child. He tinkered with making small models of everything he saw. Using a scale ratio of three-eighths of an inch to one foot, he dedicated his life to creating miniature buildings, taking drawing lessons as a boy and later visiting New York City's American Museum of Natural History and the Metropolitan Museum of Fine Arts to observe their miniature exhibits and finally financing his hobby with carpentry and painting work.

His wife Dora and children Paul and Alberta eventually joined him in his hobby, the spouse creating trees and shrubs, the children doing little people and detail work. His hobby became a career in the 1930s when people who saw his handiwork urged him to turn professional and the Reading Eagle published a feature on the small village he had created solely for his family. The Rainbow Fire Company offered its building as a display hall, with admission fees donated to charity. In 1938, the village had grown to 1,500 square feet. Newspapers and magazines called it the greatest miniature village in the world. It relocated a number of times, finally settling down in its present 8,000-square-foot location.

A devout Catholic who had bestowed subtle religious touches to the village, Laurence Gieringer, a native of nearby Reading, was working on a Jewish synagogue when death claimed him on January 13, 1963. His family chose not to finish the synagogue and have refused to modernize the village in the intervening years to ensure it always reflects its originator's conception.

Even today, Roadside America is an American original and, in the words of its current owners (descendants of the founder), the first of its kind, America's original miniature village.

It is meticulously wrought to the smallest detail. Buildings assembled, brick by brick...macadam roads and dirt paths looking real...trains, trucks, cars, buses, horse and buggy tandems authentically made...cows, horses, and donkeys nodding their heads...fallen trees clogging streams with actual running water looking so real you expect to see branches bending in the breeze...water running into pools and streams, cascading over falls from promontories, looping in arches across fountains.

The noise level is high. Water gurgles everywhere. Hymns issue from church steeples. Trains clack around tracks. Trolleys scurry throughout streets. Press a button, and the circus comes to town, blaring calliope music.

Activity abounds. Lights flash on rescue, service, and police vehicles parked at curbside. Elephants in the zoo stand on their hind legs.

The train station in the village of Fairfield welcomes visitors. More than a dozen buses, sporting the names of actual transit companies of the past and present, choke the thoroughfares, discharging and picking up passengers. A load of coal slides down a chute into a basement bin while someone shakes a bedspread from an upstairs window. A boy flies a kite. Press another button, and you activate kids in a park: children glide back and forth on swings and teeter-totter up and down. Dogs circle a hydrant. The Victoria Theater still packs them in to see Mickey Rooney and Spencer Tracy in "Boys Town," playing regularly since 1938. Kaufmann's displays four floors of furniture through its windows. A hobo walks the tracks, as Barnum & Bailey gives another rehearsal before hitting the road.

You leave Fairfield and walk through Luray Caverns. Press more buttons and run oil wells and a windmill. Tour a farm, a rail yard, a country club. Worship at the Shrine Church, modeled after an actual church at the bottom of the Tyrolean Alps' Dolomite Mountains near modern Bolzano, Italy. Watch the rabbit hide in its hole, as the hunter raises his rifle. A roofer pounds a rafter. Large goldfish, looking like whales next to the miniature canoes and dock, navigate a pond.

Sleepy Hollow is next. More buttons activate a trolley, street organ, hot-air balloon, water wheel, and coal mine elevator. A cutaway view of the underground anthracite mine, a canal boat, a covered bridge, and a section of the San Francisco-Oakland Bay Bridge all await.

A brochure provides step-by-step descriptions, but unlisted surprises lie hidden everywhere: a mountaintop winter village with skaters and skiers (and visible from the highest of the three tiers of walkways that surround the perimeter of Roadside America); a pair of pueblo mountainside scenes set into both sides of one of the corners; a fight to the death between Indians and settlers/soldiers and a tableau of Virginia's Endless Caverns tucked into both sides of another corner; a hidden prehistoric scene depicting a primeval dinosaur swamp.

Nearly every bit of wall background is painted to resemble actual landscape and conceal doors and storage compartments.

At least once an hour, the five-minute "Night Pageant" envelops the village. Overhead lights dim to the strains of "Now the Day Is Over." All activities cease, individual house lights come on, and the city twinkles in the darkness. Pealing bells replace the hymn, seguing into a spirited rendition of the "Star-Spangled Banner." A current of air plays against a wall flag, rippling it. When the national anthem concludes, Kate Smith's booming voice intones "God Bless America," as the walls light up with images of the Statue of Liberty and Christ watching over mankind. A mirror mounted on the rear wall catches the reflection of the city lights and doubles the size of the village. Visitors actually think they're skyward peering down upon a huge metropolis. Then the house lights rise, and visitors continue touring at their own pace.

Roadside America consists, in part, of thousands of board feet of wood, two tons of sheet iron, over 20 tons of stone, nearly 10 tons of plaster, four tons of sand, three barrels of tar, over 200 bushels of moss, dozens of gallons of paint, and more than 200 yards of canvas. Hundreds of feet of piping carry 6,000 gallons of water per hour through the village's lakes, rivers, and waterfalls; five electric pumps circulate it. Four thousand figures, human and animal, congregate around 300 buildings. Some 200 railroad and trolley cars operate on nearly a half-mile of track. Miles of precise electrical wiring and hundreds of light bulbs supply the electricity. Surgical lamps double as stars in the heavens. Transformers, speaker systems, amplifiers, four-channel tape playback units, motors, 10,000 miniature trees...only death stopped the expansion.

"Be prepared to see more than you expect," boasts a blurb on the building's facade. It is not an overstatement. Though an ideal stop for children, the artistic intricacies of Roadside America make it even more appealing to adults. You can tour it in a half-hour, but you'll miss most of the hidden details. A minimum of an hour is recommended.

Roadside America is at Exit 8 of U.S. Interstate Highway 78 at Shartlesville, Pennsylvania. A large gift shop adjoins, and the Pennsylvania Dutch Gift Haus, operated by Alberta Bernecker, the surviving daughter, and her family, serves food and more souvenirs next door. Open daily, except Christmas, during normal daytime hours, the attraction charges a moderate fee and receives more visitors during rainy days than pleasant ones, according to the owners.

-SHAY

THE ISLAND OF NO RETURN...ALMOST

In olden days, before white men came in abundance, Indians glided past the island in canoes. They moored their canoes and set foot on it, hunted for game in its wooded interior, fished off its banks, camped in its clearings. Muskrats scampered about its marshes, squirrels climbed its trees, ducks swam its waters, and snakes slithered around wherever they had a mind to.

The island was in the Susquehanna River, much farther away from its Cooperstown, New York mouth than from its bowels in Havre de Grace, Maryland, where it spills into the Chesapeake Bay.

The Indians have long since gone from this part of the New World, but the animals still inhabit its fringes and watery channels. Black rat snakes still find their way to the edges of the mainland on either side of the island. Birds artfully soar around the island's highest promontories

The highest point on the island is not a tree or a craggy cliff, but a manmade device...a cooling tower, to be precise. The island is no ordinary island, but rather a nuclear niche in a placid waterway, a road open to snakes and birds and muskrats but closed to the public, a place only authorized personnel may enter. A bridge crosses from the mainland to the island, but security guards prevent unwanted visitors from using it.

The island is just southeast of Harrisburg, the capital of Pennsylvania. It is famous because something that never should have happened there happened there.

It is Three Mile Island, the scene of America's closest-yet brush with nuclear catastrophe.

Three Mile Island has two sets of reactor containment complexes (TMI-1 and TMI-2) and their attendant buildings. A reactor core contains over eight million half-inch-long uranium pellets, each holding uranium atoms capable of being split to create heat-generating fission. Hot water (600 degrees and under high pressure to prevent boiling) circulates through the reactor, sending heat from the core to tubes within steam generators, as feedwater enters the generators and boils into steam as it reaches the hot tubes. The steam leaves the generators for the turbine-generator assembly where it rotates a shaft, creating electricity...all for the benefit of mankind. Water from nearby cooling towers extracts the heat from the spent steam and converts it into warm water vapor. The spent steam condenses again into water which, purified and heated, returns to the steam generators.

When it works, it works well. When it doesn't, you might be meeting your maker sooner than you expected.

TMI-2 debuted as a commercial energy producer in December 1978. Just three months later, on March 28, 1979, as it was proceeding at full capacity, a feedwater pump ceased operations. The plant shut down, and a relief valve opened on cue to alleviate pressure and temperature buildup, allowing water and steam to exit the reactor for a tank in the bottom of the reactor building. With the return of normal pressure and temperature, the valve should have closed tight.

It didn't. And America's worst brush with nuclear disaster began.

The valve remained open for more than two hours, freely permitting radioactive coolant water that covered the fuel core to wind up on the basement floors of the reactor and its auxiliary buildings. The accidental release of coolant water shot the reactor temperature up and induced some uranium fuel to melt.

When workers noticed the problem, shut the valve, and added coolant water into the reactor, some overheated fuel rods broke. And close to a million gallons of contaminated water swirled around the basement of the reactor and affiliated buildings.

The catastrophe marked the end of TMI-2's brief run as an energy producer. It also presented the nation with an unparalleled cleanup operation fraught with nuclear hazards.

The Three Mile Island Visitors Center and Energy Education Center, on the eastern shore of the river, recounts the near-nightmare detail by detail. Information kiosks, textboards, artifacts, interactive televisions and telephones, and a 13-minute film, "The TMI-2 Chronicle," explain both how the crisis occurred and how the 11-year cleanup process solved the problem. General Public Utilities Corporation (GPU), which owns the island and operates it through its subsidiary GPU Nuclear Corporation, its customers, the U.S. Department of Energy, U.S. Nuclear Energy, Japanese Nuclear Energy, and the states of New Jersey and Pennsylvania shared in the $1 billion expense required to extract more than 150 tons of damaged fuel and core debris and relocate them to the U.S. Department of Energy's Idaho National Engineering Laboratory. Some 10,000 people contributed to the massive mop-up without casualties.

The GPU's visitor center emphasizes education over entertainment and provides a plethora of information on nuclear energy. Because of its nature, it is highly technical and presented in studious manner. This is not Disneyland with special effects, but rather a sober look at nuclear technology. A communications rack holds complimentary booklets, statement papers, and newsletters explaining the accident and other company particulars.

Though much of the technology is far above the average person's comprehension (ours included), the exhibit also contains general interest material: a cross-section view of stuffed animals found either on the island or in its surrounding waters; a map of the country with lit pegs everywhere a nuclear facility functions (you may be surprised at their number and how close they are to where you live); tools used in the meticulous cleanup; "Rover," a test model of one of nine remote vehicles used to go where no humans were allowed; vice grippers designed to extract small debris items; a mannequin dressed in nuclear debris reclamation attire (cotton coveralls, several sets of thick rubber gloves, cloth boots covering shoes, tape to prevent the passage of air through any seams; full-face respirator).

An outdoor observation platform opposite the infamous TMI-2 Reactor Building provides free swivel telescopes trained at the imposing four-foot-thick steel-reinforced concrete outer walls of the containment reactors and their concave cooling towers looking even more threateningly monolithic.

Today, 99 percent of the damaged reactor core has been removed and, with it, 300,000 pounds of core debris. Small amounts of contaminated material, impossible to get at and unable to get out, remains trapped within. GPU has no intention of reactivating the notorious unit. A paper entitled "Unit 2 in Profile" and published in October 1991 explains: "TMI-2 is expected to remain in monitored storage until sometime in the next century when it will be decommissioned along with TMI-1."

TMI-1, meanwhile, churns out 860 million watts of electricity for more than half a million homes, garnering accolades for its performance (the most efficient nuclear power plant among the world's 357 units in 1989, according to Nucleonics Week) and setting records (the longest continuous run - 479 days - by a light water reactor in the world in 1990-91).

The visitor center is .6-miles south of the monitored bridge to the island, about three miles south of Middletown along State Highway 441. Hours are limited to afternoons on Thursdays, Fridays, and Saturdays (Sundays, too, between Memorial Day and Labor Day). The site is free. Tours of the actual facility have become a casualty of "downsizing" which "has pretty much cut them out," according to informed personnel (call 717-948-8829 to see if there is any chance of a tour). Surprisingly, a small gift counter sells souvenir TMI items. Crowds are sparse, and the center usually attracts visitors for a half-hour or so; absorbing all the technical information will cost you the whole afternoon.

For those who want a taste of something more palatable, Hershey, with its amusement park and chocolate candy tour, lies fewer than 20 miles northeast.

Even in its emasculated condition, TMI-2 still sends a chill up the spine - a behemoth no longer belching a steady stream of steam upward, yet stolidly squatting as a reminder of what we can only hope, with fingers crossed, will forever be known as our worst nuclear accident.

RHODE ISLAND

AMERICA'S MOST FAMOUS $1 PAINTING

It may be the most recognizable painting in the world, even more familiar than the "Mona Lisa" or "The Last Supper." And chances are you hold it in your hand every day, not even realizing it.

It is known as the Boston Athenaeum portrait of George Washington. You see an engraved version of it whenever you hold an American dollar bill face up.

The man who painted the original is considered one of America's greatest portraitists. He lived in New York, Philadelphia, Washington, D.C., and Europe. He is most closely identified with Boston where he lived the final two decades of his life.

Yet he was born in Rhode Island atop America's first operating snuff mill, established in 1751, a house where tobacco was pulverized into snuff, then a popular product, nearly a staple for socially conscious New England men.

"At the head of Petaquamscott Pond, in the Narragansett country, in Rhode Island, shut in by trees and far away from the din and stir of the world, there stands an old-fashioned, gambrel-roofed and low-portaled house, by the side of a tiny stream," wrote George C. Mason in 1879. "This old house, so seldom visited and so little thought of, has a history, for it was the birthplace and early home of Gilbert Stuart, the artist."

As a boy, Gilbert Stuart drew pictures with chalk and charcoal on the sides of the family barn. Showing promising talent, young Gilbert received a commission to paint portraits of two prominent local Rhode Islanders at age 13. It soon became obvious he would not be succeeding his father in shredding tobacco for a living. In

1775, while still a teen-ager, he sailed for England to hone his craft with master artists of the day. He returned to America in 1792, nearing 40 and with a reputation as a formidable portraitist, yearning to limn the likeness of President George Washington, an American he esteemed.

He painted Washington a number of times and the likenesses of about a thousand others, including presidents, politicians, statesmen, war heroes, society matrons, and prominent private citizens. Of his famous Washington portraits, including the one that served as the model for the engraving on the dollar, Stuart remarked, "When I painted him, he had just had a set of false teeth inserted, which accounts for the constrained expression so noticeable about the mouth and lower part of the face. ... I wanted him as he looked at the time."

He eventually settled in Boston and died there of gout in 1828 at 72, rather penurious. Despite his artistic success, he had yielded to high living, convivial generosity with friends, financial disdain, and a marked disinterest in ensuring that he received proper recompense for many of his works. He was buried in the Boston Common Cemetery.

His portraits, famed for their facial precision and knack of capturing their subjects' inner character ("I copy the works of God, and leave the clothes to tailors and mantua-makers," he once responded to a suggestion he spend as much effort on other parts of the portraits), rank among the greatest American works and now hang in renowned art galleries on both sides of the Atlantic.

His artistic talent and temperament (at times, exacting, even imperious) often gave others the impression he came from the continent. When asked what part of England he hailed from, he once responded, "I was born in Narragansett. ... Six miles from Pottawoone, and 10 miles from Poppasquash, and about four miles from Conanicut, and not far from the spot where the famous battle with the warlike Pequots was fought." And when his questioner mistook his explanation for some exotic place in the East Indies, he added, "East Indies, my dear sir! It is in the State of Rhode Island, between Massachusetts and Connecticut River."

The Gilbert Stuart Birthplace & Museum still stands in extensively restored form, containing period furnishings not original to the site and reproductions of some of its most famous resident's works. A family room occupies the first floor, with the birthing and keeping rooms and the master bedroom filling the upstairs. The basement holds the kitchen and an actual 18th-century snuff mill, newer than Stuart's father's original, transplanted from England and emplaced where America's first snuff mill once stood. An exact copy of the large wooden water wheel that harnessed the nearby mill stream is also present.

Near the house along Mattatuxet Brook is a "fish ladder," so called because of the springtime run of spawning herring, jamming the waters as they swim in heat from the ocean to the river to the pond near the home.

The Gilbert Stuart Memorial, Inc. operates the Registered National Historic Landmark at 815 Gilbert Stuart Road in Saunderstown daily (except Fridays), from late morning through the afternoon, April through early November. Visitation averages over 4,000 annually. A modest fee is charged, and the site can be toured in an hour or less.

The house is between U.S. Highway 1 and State Highway 1A about seven miles due west of Newport across Narragansett Bay. A popular seaport and beach resort, Newport has millionaires' mansions, an aristocratic pedigree, storied history, and fine restaurants and shops.

SOUTH CAROLINA

AMERICA'S FIRST GREAT CIVIL WAR BATTLE

It was the largest massing of Americans against fellow Americans in armed combat since the beginning of the country. At stake was a hill nearly straddling the border between the Carolinas, a 60-foot-high plateau about a third of a mile in length, an extension of the Blue Ridge, just south of the North Carolina line.

Major Patrick Ferguson held the high ground against a massed horde led by a cadre of officers whose names have now been forgotten: William Campbell, Benjamin Cleveland, William Hill, Edward Lacey, Charles McDowell, John Sevier, Isaac Shelby, James Williams, and Joseph Winston. The hill proved less than impregnable, and the attacking army stormed the top in less than an afternoon's fighting. The army on the hill hoisted white flags of surrender, but the attackers ignored them and shot and hacked apart the defenseless men. Joseph Sevier, one of the attacking soldiers, echoed the sentiments of many when he yelled, "The damned rascals have killed my father, and I'll keep loading and shooting till I kill every son of a bitch of them!"

Major Ferguson, commanding the entrenched soldiers atop the hill, never lived to see the most savage part of the fighting. He was shot from his horse. The attackers recovered his body, stripped it naked, and urinated on it. They hated him more than anyone else in that part of America because he had trained his men and led them on brutal missions killing fellow Americans, torching their homes, and raping the countryside. It was their way of returning the favor.

The violence continued even after the battle had ended. A

week later, nine captives were strung up as war criminals after hasty kangaroo court trial. One particularly boorish conquering officer looked at the corpses dangling from the trees and uttered, "Would to God every tree in the wilderness bore such fruit as this!" Captives who couldn't keep up with their forced march to prison were stabbed and beaten to death where they fell.

Such was the Battle of Kings Mountain in South Carolina, on a per-capita basis much more vicious than Gettysburg or Antietam or Shiloh.

It may be surprising to realize this horrendous civil war encounter didn't take place during the Civil War. We're not talking North and South or Grant and Lee here. We're referring to America's first great civil war, the Revolutionary War.

First, for the unitiated, some facts: the Revolution was not as neatly defined as we have come to believe; it was not us against them, George Washington against the British, bluecoats against redcoats.

The reality was far less coherent. Roughly one third of the American colonists supported independence from England, one third opposed it, and one third either didn't know who to favor or tried to remain neutral. Soldiers on both sides wore uniforms of blue, red, green, brown, and pastel colors in between. Soldiers were not the only ones to bear arms; the unusually barbaric war, that spread into private homes as well as designated battlefields, pitted soldier against soldier, militiaman against militiaman, homesteader against Indian, and all possible combinations of the above. Women fought to defend their children from the scalping knife. The conflict infiltrated every corner of the continent where people lived. The British actively encouraged the Indians to raid frontier American settlements, and the Indians, thinking it the only way to halt unwanted white trespassing on their ancestral lands, responded enthusiastically. The frontier shot up in flames, as Indians battled pioneers, each unwelcome act of hostility begetting one in return. America exploded into a headlong skein of vendetta warfare that killed innocent men, women, and children of all ages.

Back in the eastern cities, unoffending civilians were tarred and feathered, rubbed with animal manure, whipped, slashed, and killed for their political leanings alone.

The Civil War, for the most part, featured men in blue fighting men in gray. The Revolution, in which participants often didn't even wear uniforms, turned into a cauldron of venom, spilling over into backyards and into kitchens.

In the midst of this turmoil that christened the country in crimson came the battle that became the first major clash between brothers in the nation's history. Of the 2,000 men who fought at Kings Mountain, only one (Major Patrick Ferguson, commanding the pro-British faction) was not an actual American.

The war in the Carolinas had become especially brutal by October 7, 1780, when pro-independence militiamen from the Carolinas, Tennessee, and Virginia trapped Ferguson's army on Kings Mountain. There was no love between those two conflicting groups of Americans. The attacking force was out for blood, intending to settle a score dating back to the previous May in South Carolina when pro-British Americans had surrounded a group of pro-independence Americans attempting to surrender, skewering and stabbing them at will, killing 100, mangling 150 more. The attackers also wanted to atone for the loss of a dozen of their compatriots who had been hanged in Georgia and others who had been turned over to the Indians for certain torture and death.

Such was the ferocity of the "gentlemanly" Revolutionary War.

Today, the National Park Service runs the battlefield, among the most faithfully preserved sites in America. A paved footpath, marked with a couple dozen markers and monuments, snakes its way around the knoll, where attackers advanced, and through the heart of the defensive line at the crest. The markers include audio narratives and graphically tell the vicious story:

> - These resolute frontiersmen had fought wilderness and Indians to protect homes west of the mountains. Ferguson's threats to "...lay their country waste

with fire and sword" brought them to Kings Mountain bristling for a fight.
- Shout Like Hell and Fight Like Demons!
- They fought stubbornly at Kings Mountain, and the brief engagement took a heavy toll in killed and wounded. The surviving Loyalists surrendered their arms to the Patriot victors, crying for quarter or mercy, but bitter feelings ran strong and pleas went unheeded.

Rest benches are regularly placed along the slightly more than mile-long trail which, true to the terrain of the site, ascends and descends by turns. Unlike most battlefields which have been manicured and monumented to death, this one still looks almost exactly as it did more than 200 years ago. The hill is there, the trees encroach everywhere, with nothing visible save the wilderness that enveloped both attacker and defender that bloody day when the frontier shrieked aloud in the report of the rifle and the wail of the wounded. Five monuments break the pattern of the trees; the two most affecting are those marking the place where Ferguson took his fatal hits and his grave, a traditional Scottish cairn.

A visitor center at the base of the trail houses a film and diorama, displays, and a gift shop. The battlefield is the centerpiece of Kings Mountain National Military Park, one of the nation's largest at nearly 4,000 acres, which also contains hiking trails. Kings Mountain State Park, a separate entity, adjoins and offers hiking and riding trails, camping, and swimming at Lake Crawford. As is customary in hiking little-used mountain trails, be alert for poison ivy and reptiles. The site is open daily, excepting major holidays, during usual daytime hours and is free at this writing. The visitor center and the walking tour will take an hour or two and will give you a better perspective on the civil war that we somewhat mistakenly call the Revolutionary War. Don't expect Gettysburgian throngs of people.

Kings Mountain National Military Park is nearly on the North

Carolina border, just southwest of Gastonia. Follow signs on U.S. Interstate Highway 85.

Of related interest is Cowpens National Battlefield, another Revolutionary War battle won by the Patriots, about 30 miles west on the interstate and State Highway 11. Both can be toured in less than a day.

SOUTH DAKOTA

REESE'S PEEWEES

In 1937, Sheldon F. Reese, a grain entrepreneur from South Dakota, embarked on a trip around the world. While traveling, he indulged in a rather strange activity, particularly for a man in those days. He began checking out and buying dolls from the countries he traveled to. His sister had asked him to do it for her as a favor. But something he had not foreseen happened. He began buying some dolls for himself. He traveled often in ensuing years.

Some 45 years and 4,000 dolls later, his treasures ended up on permanent display in a European-type castle equipped with a drawbridge, flags, turrets, battlements, crenelations, and stained glass windows. The dolls are dispersed through 400 different settings over a thousand square feet of the Enchanted World Doll Museum, a collection that pales most other doll museums and is among the world's best.

Doll aficionados are hard pressed to find any types or eras unrepresented in the stunning collection: 19th-century Bru bisques and French Bebe Mothereaus; Gebruder Heubach character dolls; ball-jointed French Jumeaus of the 1800s; wax dolls, including a Cinderella and Prince Charming in their court finery; Kestner Company German dolls with realistic blown glass eyes; a nursery of bent-limb dolls, a style introduced by Kammer & Reinhardt of Germany in the early 20th century; a 1910 Gibson Girl and a 1915 Mein Liebling; a brood of Kewpies with chubby faces, sideways smiles, and four tufts of hair; a Florodora by Armand Marseilles, a workhorse dollmaker of 100 years ago; three-faced babies with rotating heads.

The dolls are made of virtually every material - bisque, china, wood, paper, steel, aluminum, brass, leather, rubber, vinyl, plastic, clay, wax, stone, shells, and nearly three dozen other materials, including such exotic substances as salt, dried fruits, and cornhusks.

The settings employ both painted and three-dimensional backgrounds in their quest for variety. Large-jointed dolls frolic on a haystack in front of a red barn in "Fun on the Farm." A 44-inch Handwerck-Halbig girl pets a dog as a Depression-era Shirley Temple holds the reins of a horse. French females converge around a chess table, drinking tea and chatting about memories that span more than a century. A doctor and nurse check in on the Dionne quintuplets. King Henry VIII presides over all six of his ill-fated wives in "In the Royal Courtyard." Paul Bunyan, sculpted of wood, stands with his axe and cross-saw amidst a forest. Bisque beauties picnic in a meadow that surveys bluish-white mountains in "Springtime in the Rockies." A Japanese Jesus rises from the dead, and a Japanese Holy Family greets visitors at a stable at the base of Mount Fuji - unique, original, one-of-a-kind Oriental dolls. "Sunday Services" are conducted in a church for dolls in front of a gilded altar as nuns belt out joyful music from the choir loft. Jack (of Beanstalk fame) peers upward at giant boots descending through a cloud layer on the ceiling of the museum. Teddy bears enjoy a picnic in the great outdoors.

The museum also displays doll houses, buggies, dishes, glassware, and other accessories in corridors that weave throughout the interior.

A gift shop sells more affordable dolls along with the customary line of souvenirs. A moderate fee is charged; visitation usually takes about an hour. The museum is open daily during normal daytime hours from April through November and into the evening during summer months.

A non-profit charitable and educational foundation, the Enchanted World Doll Museum is at 615 North Main Street in Mitchell, South Dakota, directly across from the Corn Palace, a famous tourist stop and convention center. Mitchell also contains several museums, an art center, and a prehistoric Indian village.

THE SACRED SOIL OF THE SIOUX

It is perhaps the most sacred Native American site on the North American continent. The Sioux called it "mako sica;" whites referred to it as the Badlands. Half of a national park lies within its boundaries. It comprises one of the premier collections of Native American art in the country, the burial grounds of the two greatest Indian war chiefs of the plains, and the scene of the most infamous massacre of Indians in American history.

And it is generally unknown, lost amongst its big-ticket tourist neighbors: Mount Rushmore, Rapid City, the incessantly advertised Wall Drug, and the slot machine madness of Deadwood.

It is the Pine Ridge Indian Reservation, nearly 1.5-million acres near the southwestern corner of South Dakota. Its tribal capital at Pine Ridge on U.S. Highway 18 is just north of the Nebraska line. The Oglala Sioux, the centerpiece of the seven-tribe Teton Lakota Nation, populate the reservation and govern themselves with an elected president and council.

The reservation's cultural highlight is the internationally acclaimed Heritage Center at the Red Cloud Indian School which showcases historic 19th-century Sioux beadwork artistry alongside current bead and porcupine quill art. The center also displays a permanent collection of contemporary Native American paintings, sculptures, and graphics, including works donated annually by the Red Cloud Indian Art Show, the largest national competition of its type in the country. Open to the public since 1969, the competition runs from the second Sunday in June to the same point in August, drawing international art critics, collectors, and pre-eminent buyers. The center also contains a gift shop selling more affordable Indian artwork and souvenir items to visitors who might not have the resources to purchase the finest Indian art treasures offered during the show.

The Heritage Center stands on consecrated ground. During the 19th century, nearly unconquerable Red Cloud, war chief of the Oglala Sioux, asked his white subduers to build a school for the Indian children. In 1888, Jesuits built the Holy Rosary Mission and have ever since operated it with Franciscan nuns. The former school now houses the Heritage Center, and the current complex includes a collegial setting with administration buildings, classrooms, housing, a quarter-mile track, and a Gothic church with original artwork by Sioux artist Felix Walking.

A decidedly Catholic cemetery reposes atop a slight hill overlooking the mission and Highway 18 on the northern outskirts of Pine Ridge. Like virtually all Native American graveyards, it honors its dead with profusions of flowers, wreaths, and colored banners or strips of cloth woven or tied together atop individual graves...and personalized items attesting to private feelings of affection, like the metallic colored egg that reposes in the middle of little Mary M. Two Two's final resting place. Wooden crosses rise alongside sturdier ones of metal or stone, while granite crosses crown more contemporary tombstones. A life-size statue of the crucified Christ towers above everything.

The peaceful plot serves as a rather incongruous repository for the bones of Red Cloud himself, one of the most doggedly fearsome and skilled tacticians who ever fought the United States Army. Named for a flaming meteorite that had illuminated the skies, he reputedly counted some fourscore coups - human kills - and led plains Indians in the so-called "Red Cloud War" of 1866-68. Either he or his chiefs attacked Fort Phil Kearny in Wyoming a purported 50 times within a few years and wiped out an entire Army detachment under Captain William J. Fetterman. After treaties stopped the violence, the middle-aged Red Cloud tried to secure favorable rights for his tribesmen. He accepted life on the Pine

Ridge Reservation in the 1870s and died there on December 10, 1909, well into his 80s.

One of the cemetery's more elaborate tombstones marks his grave, a combination of granite and cement with a couple crosses, a raised bust of the chief in full feather bonnet, and a scrap of scripture from 2 Corinthians: "Brethren, be of one mind, have peace and the God of peace and of love shall be with you."

The Red Cloud Indian School distributes a card containing an invocation, attributed to Red Cloud, in response to one offered by white commissioners in 1870 "that these heathens be claimed for the inheritance of our Lord and Savior." Red Cloud responded by touching the earth, raising his arms skyward, and saying aloud:

> Oh great Spirit, I pray you to look upon us. We are your children and you placed us first in this land. We pray you to look down upon us, so that nothing but truth shall be spoken in this council. We do not ask for anything but what is right and just. ... You are the protector of those who use the bow and arrow, as well as those people who wear hats.

A two-sided historical marker, horribly defaced, summarizes Red Cloud's life just east of the cemetery alongside the highway.

Another famous Oglala Sioux war leader lies buried on the reservation. Crazy Horse led a far shorter life - bayonetted in the back before he was 40. Almost a mystical figure, he never signed a peace treaty ("You cannot sell the ground you walk on," he said), never permitted his picture to be taken (he believed it would capture his spiritual essence), and never indulged in unnecessary bloodletting or massacres. He fought in most battles waged on the plains in the 1860s and '70s, often challenging his opponents by riding full-tilt through a hail of bullets to slay his enemy at close range and then riding back unharmed, a stunt that earned him his name.

His greatest triumph occurred in 1876 when he helped defeat George Custer's Seventh Cavalry on the hills above Montana's Little Bighorn River. He prophetically predicted a bullet would never end his life. His death by the blade on September 5, 1877, at Fort Robinson, southwest of the reservation, resulted from miscommunication and treachery.

His parents reclaimed his body and returned it to the Badlands, where only a handful of Indians participated in its unmarked burial. Today, no one knows its exact location. Most studious speculation pinpoints the vicinity of Manderson, about 12 miles north of Pine Ridge, as the likeliest spot. His bones may forever remain as unconfined in death as his spirit was in life. An extensive two-sided historical marker south of the little hamlet of Wounded Knee on State Highway 44 discusses his life.

The reservation also holds the mass graves of the scores of victims of Wounded Knee, America's most publicized massacre. "Ghost Dancing," which was a cultural response to a last-gasp attempt at wresting ownership of their own destinies once again, had pervaded the plains Indian reservations in the late 19th century. The Army stepped in to present a strong presence everywhere, including the Pine Ridge Reservation. On December 29, 1890, when soldiers searched Indian lodges for weapons, a medicine man urged warriors to resist. Tempers flared, and an initial act of violence led to a massive volley of sustained fire from the same Seventh Cavalry that Crazy Horse had defeated years earlier. When the smoke cleared, an estimated 150-300 Indian men, women, and children, including many unoffending, unarmed victims, lay dead on the wintry ground. Photographs of the bodies, frozen in deathly grimaces, limbs protruding stiffly in the snow, transfixed the nation and came to symbolize the final brutality inflicted by the military on the people of the plains.

A two-sided historical marker along the roadside in Wounded Knee, near the heart of the tragedy, tells the story. A hill rises to the west, the site from which the Army's Hotchkiss guns destroyed the Indian village. The crest of the hill now holds a mass grave, a trench dug for the victims by the soldiers. A tombstone, surrounded by the distinctive colored strips of bright cloth and pouches of tobacco and spiritual artifacts unique to Indian cemeteries, bears witness to the "MANY INNOCENT WOMEN AND CHILDREN WHO KNEW NO WRONG" who "DIED HERE."

A trip through the reservation for the above sites and a stop at the Badlands visitor center and any of the trading posts along the roads will take a half-day. Everything, except what you purchase, is free. A sojourn within the reservation will help you absorb the sensitivity, culture, artistry, and tragedy of a people whose ancestors were informed by newcomers that there was simply no room for them in the country of their birth.

TENNESSEE

How Tennessee recalls Davy...just beyond Lawrenceburg.

TENNESSEE'S TRIBUTES TO A LEGEND

Ever since his life ended in blood and smoke at dawn on a Sunday in March 1836, his life and legacy have been sanctified by hero worshippers and trivialized by iconoclasts until few non-scholars know anything about him.

Yet he was, a bit in life, a lot in legend, one of the most famous Americans of the 19th century.

He didn't much look like any of the actors who played him in movies. He wasn't "Born on a mountain top in Tennessee," as Tom Blackburn's lyrics to a 1950s hit song averred. He didn't serve as the conscience of Congress during a checkered career in the House of Representatives. And he may or may not have died as heroically as he did in the motion picture images from "Davy Crockett King of the Wild Frontier" and "The Alamo."

Yet there really was a Davy Crockett, although he preferred to be called "David" and so signed his name. He volunteered to fight Indians in the Creek War of 1813-14 in Alabama and Florida. A simple man with common interests, he participated in bear hunts and eked out a modest living for himself and his family as a Tennessee hunter and mill operator. He successfully entered politics on the local level and went on to serve three terms in Congress where he became famous for helping champion the rights of Indians and frontier homesteading squatters and also for taking lengthy absences from legislative sessions to go on self-promotional trips to major American cities. He gained a reputation as a colorful storyteller and humorist. The last of three electoral defeats and an abiding dislike for the politics of President Andrew Jackson, a retired general he had served under during the Creek War, embittered him, and he left his family to pursue a political career in Texas, then champing at the bit over independence from Mexican sovereignty. He rode into San Antonio two weeks before a Mexican army invaded and wound up defending the Alamo, a mission-turned-fort-turned-deathtrap. He distinguished himself during its siege and died a debated death - either while enmeshed in combat or by execution after surrendering.

To quest the real David Crockett, it is necessary to either read recent revisionist books or journey to Tennessee, his home state. The Volunteer State claims him from east to west, paralleling his gradual westward migration.

The first stop is the Davy Crockett Birthplace Historic Site in Davy Crockett Birthplace State Park. Though born in the shadow of the Appalachian Mountains, Crockett grew up in a valley near Limestone, close to the easternmost tip of the state. The 65-acre park surrounds the August 17, 1786 birthplace site near the Nolichucky River's junction with Limestone Creek and features a reconstructed cabin, visitor center and museum, picnic pavilions and tables, a campground and swimming pool, a short hiking trail, and a flower garden surrounding a monument and enclosed by a wall comprising stones from each of the United States. Another stone marker, reputedly the original cabin's door stone, now emplaced between the rebuilt structure and the Nolichucky, marks the approximate site of the first cabin little Davy called home.

The visitor center doesn't contain any Crockett artifacts but nicely atones with a vivid display that presents him to generations who know nothing of him. A television monitor shows an eight-minute film, produced by Kyle Stirling for the state department of conservation in 1990, that juxtaposes images of the real Crockett with visages of the reel Crockett. A case holds items from the Davy Crockett merchandising boom of 1955 spawned by Walt Disney's immensely popular television series. Color stills, posters, and lobby cards from the numerous Crockett films complete the Fess Parker-John Wayne screen persona that so many contemporaries confuse with the real man.

Another wall holds seven paintings of Crockett taken from life, defining nuances of facial detail and showing the frontiersman resplendent in collars, vests, and suitcoats, altogether a rather handsome man with an angular face, long pronounced nose, sideburns well below the ears and extending onto the cheeks, and flowing hair - sometimes parted on the side, sometimes down the middle.

Other walls peek into his life (and afterlife) roles: homesteader, hunter, smalltime businessman, politician, symbol, and legend. Along the way, new realities start to replace hoary myths. "Davy Crockett" was a sharpshooter, prodigious Indian fighter, the most unique politician to ever stride the halls of Congress, a fierce hunter who wrestled bears and cougars, and the mightiest hero of the Alamo. But "David Crockett" was more a skillful hunter than an unerring marksman, a so-so soldier who fought in a couple engagements and then paid someone to finish off his term of enlistment when he tired of military regimen, an average politician who lost as often as he won, a simple man fond of telling homespun stories and gifted with an engaging style, and a man who sought political and economic redemption in a new land rent by revolution and about to martyr him in a battle that forever elevated him into a national hero of mythic proportions.

The museum displays period clothing, implements, accouterments, and weapons that Crockett would have been familiar with. A gift rack sells books and souvenirs.

The Crockett birthsite is just south of U.S. Highway 321/11E, about halfway between Johnson City and Greeneville. An historic marker to "DAVID CROCKETT" along the highway signals your approach. After that, merely follow signs; Davy Crockett Road takes you to the site. The campground remains open year-round; the free visitor center conducts daily daytime hours. Every year on the Friday, Saturday, and Sunday closest to August 17, the site celebrates his birth with music, food, and exhibits.

The next Crockett cabin is in Morristown, about 40 miles west, and just south of the major intersection of U.S. Highway 11E (East Andrew Johnson Highway) and North Haun Drive East.

It occupies the junction formed by Morningside Drive and Ridgelawn Avenue. An historical marker identifies the site as the place where David's father kept a home and crossroads tavern after the family left the Nolichucky. David lived here during a good share of his adolescence until his marriage a few days shy of his 20th birthday. A reconstruction, now called the Crockett Tavern Museum, utilizes wood from neighboring homes of early American periods and stands close to the site of the original cabin. The site has nothing belonging to Crockett (most of those artifacts are preserved in the Alamo, the Tennessee State Museum in Nashville, and the Smithsonian in Washington, D.C.); but, unlike the reconstruction in Limestone, this facsimile allows visitors to enter and tour its three floors. Authentic period frontier furnishings abound, and a basement museum collects numerous antique items and reserves space for a small gift area.

The tavern museum's hours have fluctuated in recent years, but it is generally open during normal daytime hours from around mid-spring to mid-fall; a moderate admission is charged.

The third reconstructed Crockett cabin occupies 218 South Military Street, just south of the town square in Lawrenceburg on U.S. Highway 64 (the David Crockett Highway) in south-central Tennessee. An historical marker lists the site as Crockett's residence from 1817-22 when he entered local politics as a town commissioner, justice of the peace, militia colonel, and state legislator. The one-room cabin supports period antiques and a few Crockett-related items. Wall plaques testify to Crockett's life and career, and a table holds a number of binders brimming with newspaper clippings and photocopies on a wealth of Crockett topics.

Tennessee's only statue of David Crockett, an heroic life-size bronze, modeled after John G. Chapman's painting of the hunter with long rifle, powder horn, and leather brimmed hat, dominates the nearby town square.

David Crockett State Park, a 1,100-acre recreation center, lies a half-mile west on the Crockett Highway, on the site of the honoree's distillery and grist and gunpowder mill operations. The park includes a lake, two campgrounds, hiking and bike trails, swimming pool, entertainment amphitheater, picnic areas, restaurant, and interpretive center with a half-dozen rooms focusing on Crockett's many facets. It possesses a few Crockett relics: a froe blade and brush hook that he may have owned; a couple letters he wrote to his publisher in 1835; and references to him in newspapers of the day.

The exhibits also provide little-known pioneering facts: an average-sized bear (300 pounds and 6.5-feet tall) yielded 180 pounds of meat; bear grease was used to lubricate hair and waterproof moccasins; Crockett operated the only distillery in the county for awhile, grinding out 13.5 bushels of grain a day. The room on Crockett the Hunter includes a recipe for roast raccoon and sweet potatoes that serves four and begins by instructing would-be chefs to "skin and clean one large coon." Another room poses the question "What Did Crockett Look Like?" and answers with seven portraits from life. The visitor center occasionally shows commercial Crockett films and is open daily during usual daytime hours from Memorial Day to Labor Day.

The park is open year-round, the reconstructed cabin likewise when visitors appear (the caretaker lives next door). Both are free. Like Limestone and Morristown, Lawrenceburg also celebrates Crockett's birth annually with its Crockett Days.

The fourth reconstructed Crockett cabin stands just outside Rutherford in northwestern Tennessee on U.S. Highway 45W. It contains several split logs from the original which was dismantled in the 1930s for eventual preservation. Crockett moved to the Rutherford Fork of the Obion River in 1823 and lived there, off and on, while a congressman in Washington, D.C., eventually leaving in late 1835 for his unwitting date with death in Texas. While living in western Tennessee, he hunted, conducted business, and served in the state legislature.

A few miles west of its original site, the cabin houses the usual assemblage of period relics. Crockett's mother, who died scant months before her son did, lies buried in an adjacent grave. The cabin site comes alive every year for its version of Davy Crockett Days. And even neighboring Crockett County, where Crockett never lived, hosts its own annual Crockett festival at its county seat - the city of Alamo. The cabin is open daily from May to October and charges a modest admission.

Seldom has any one man inspired such a dose of festivals and celebrations at any one time throughout an entire state.

Tennessee has even more memorials to one of its favorite sons. A bust in profile, executed by Belle Kinney Scholz, adorns the grounds surrounding the county courthouse in Trenton, 12 miles south of Rutherford.

Fifteen historical markers perpetuating snippets of Crockett-related lore dot the Tennessee landscape from east to west and north to south.

Crockett graves speckle the state's cemeteries, from his mother's in Rutherford to his eldest son's in Paris to the northeast.

And though Crockett is not buried anywhere (his corpse was burned by the Mexican Army after his March 6, 1836 death), the most affecting Crockett grave is that of his first wife who died in her 20s shortly after the birth of their third child. Though a tombstone marks the site, it is impossible to locate without precise directions.

An historical marker to "POLLY FINLAY CROCKETT" on U.S. Highway 64 in Franklin County, between Maxwell and Beans Creek, provides your first clue:

> David Crockett, his first wife and their
> children settled on a homestead a few miles
> east about 1813. She died in 1815, following
> her husband's return from the Creek War. She
> is buried in an old cemetery overlooking
> Bean's Creek, about five miles southeast.

Just south of the marker and a short distance to the east is an unmarked rural road. Take it exactly two miles to an intersection with a stop sign. Turn left onto another similar road and follow it two more miles. Then turn left onto what appears to be a private drive and go past a house and silos on your left. After .2-miles, you'll encounter a cul-de-sac that may or may not be impeded by fallen tree limbs. Dismount at this point and proceed on foot to your right on a somewhat worn footpath through a thicket. The grave awaits you in utter solitude. No one else will ever be there.

If David Crockett ever truly loved any woman, it was probably the woman whose remains lie beneath you (he wed his second wife more to provide a mothering influence for his children than because he was deeply smitten). His "autobiography" (written by a congressman-friend) calls Polly "a tender and loving wife." He buried her in a forest, placed rocks above the sod, and bade her farewell. The site, now as then, is hopelessly forlorn.

Visiting all the Crockett sites in Tennessee means touring the state. Each reconstructed cabin and museum/visitor center will take a minimum of a half-hour to an hour. Other visitors should be slight...unless you time your trip for one of the Crockett observances; if so, expect good down-home food and music.

THE SEA THAT NEVER SEES THE LIGHT OF DAY

According to the local story now accepted as fact, a young boy stumbled upon what he thought was a small pool in his underground explorations in eastern Tennessee. As water swirled around his ankles, he stopped in his tracks and cast a stone into the darkness ahead. He heard the noise of the rock striking deep water and sinking. He stepped back carefully, knowing the pool was far deeper than he had imagined.

He had discovered what the Guinness Book of World Records has since called the "world's largest underground lake" - 4.5 acres of water 300 feet below ground, a portion of the Craighead Cavern network.

During the Civil War, Confederate soldiers entered the caverns to mine saltpeter for use in making gunpowder. Other area settlers occasionally used the coolness of the caverns as a refrigerator for food. And in the 20th century, local entrepreneurs held parties in what they called their "Cavern Tavern."

The Lost Sea, as it is now known, holds a Registered Natural Landmark designation from the Department of the Interior for its body of water and great plenitude of anthodites, rather scarce crystalline oddities often called cave flowers.

More than an underground lake, the Lost Sea offers the usual cavern environment of various formations rising from the floor or hanging from the ceiling in 58 degrees of consistent year-round temperature.

A futuristic-looking bright yellow tube transports visitors down a sloping paved path into the underground world. Without the aid of stairs or an elevator, the path continues its descent past a flowing formation called the Cascades, an alcove with an authentic moonshine still, a rock called the Bear's Paw (which, alone of all the formations, you may touch), the Veil of Tears, Soda Straw Stalactites, Hanging Rock Chamber, the Keel Room, a small waterfall with thin streams trickling through open air, and the squat entrance to the sea itself, blasted from the heavy rock overhead to afford a modern entrance.

The site is old. An historical marker outside documents the discovery of the skeleton and footprints of an eight-foot Pleistocene jaguar.

But it is the great sea that provides the wonderment. Floodlights interspersed at regular intervals along the perimeter of the lake illuminate the underground expanse, casting reflections on the green water and delineating the craggy loops and whorls of the arched rocky ceiling, giving it the appearance of a natural dome. No-frill pontoon boats float alongside a dock that extends over the lake from the shore. The boats' partial glass bottoms provide a view of the water they skim through. Trout populate the lake, freely swimming under the boats, breaking the surface of the water as they leap upward to snare morsels of food tossed by tour guides. Occasionally boats pass each other as they navigate the rippling waters in search of cozy corners where the ceiling curves downward to meet the lake. The experience is cool, dark, and a bit eerie.

The complete tour lasts a little less than an hour, with the boat ride accounting for about a third of it.

The way out is all uphill. The slopes are generally moderate, but people with walking or respiratory problems might find the ascent a bit taxing. As with all caves, the Lost Sea is not for people with claustrophobia.

Above ground, the privately owned complex features craft stores, a trading post, a general store, a nature trail and picnic area, and a restaurant in the appropriately named Lost City.

The site is open daily, except Christmas, until dusk; a slightly above-average fee is charged. Crowds are respectable but not overwhelming. It is just on the outskirts of Sweetwater, off State Highway 68, three miles east of U.S. Interstate Highway 75, roughly halfway along the 110 miles separating the major cities of Chattanooga and Knoxville. The Tennessee entrance to the Great Smoky Mountains lies about 70 road miles west.

TEXAS

THE ALAMO YOU REMEMBER

In 1836, 200 Texans and transplanted Americans enacted one of the world's most famous fights to the death against 2,400 Mexican soldiers.

Everyone remembers the Alamo. But when they visit what little is left of the fort in the middle of San Antonio today and find it overtaken by center-city sprawl and heavy traffic and tourism, they appear bewildered because it doesn't resemble what their minds remember.

What they remember is actually the image of coonskin-capped John Wayne firing at the enemy from within a spacious fort in the middle of vast open lands in a 1960 movie called "The Alamo," a movie filmed on location 125 miles west of San Antonio on the outskirts of Brackettville, an elaborate movie set built specifically for the film.

In an ironic sense, the fake Alamo is actually more realistic than the real one. Very little of the original survives, and what remains has been severely overhauled and changed for necessary preservation. The result leaves the masses of visitors who tour the popular site perplexed. Even David Crockett, James Bowie, William Travis, and the other mere mortals who became legends on March 6, 1836 would never recognize the bastion they defended were they to somehow reappear.

But transplant them in Alamo Village, where John Wayne "died" in defense of Hollywood history, and they would feel right at home.

Alamo Village came about because of Wayne's $12-million

epic (then a record amount of money for a film). Reviled upon initial release for its lumbering pace, preachy script, and inverted historical characterizations, the film garnered respect for its action sequences and realistic sets. Many serious film critics today still consider the sets the movie's best asset. They resulted from a deal consummated by Wayne, the film's producer and director, and James T. "Happy" Shahan (pronounced SHAY-han), the owner of the 35-square mile Shahan HV Ranch. Shahan's crew built a fairly accurate set from 1957-59, then turned it over to Wayne for his film. Shahan's Alamo Chapel, the famous Alamo facade that everyone recognizes, exactly matches the original's dimensions. The construction crew built the remainder of the oblong compound at a three-quarter scale and added a neighboring village 300 yards away to serve as a realistic mockup of 19th-century San Antonio.

"The Alamo" was far from the only movie filmed at the site. Though Shahan has allowed film crews to adapt existing structures to their specific needs, the Alamo set has remained fairly stable during the production of more than 75 theatrical motion pictures, television programs and series, documentaries, travelogues, and commercials. Among the most famous projects filmed on the site are "Two Rode Together," "Bandolero," and the landmark TV western miniseries "Lonesome Dove."

The HV Ranch became a location for movies even before the construction of Alamo Village. While serving as Brackettville's mayor in the 1950s, Shahan wooed filmmakers to his virginal western land to inject money into the local economy. He succeeded; film crews shot "Arrowhead" there in 1950, "The Last Command" in 1955, and "Five Bold Women" in 1958.

When filming does not occur, the entire village serves as a western theme park with a couple dozen Wild West buildings. The Wagon Room houses the owner's collection of wagons, buckboards, stagecoaches, carriages, buggies, surreys, and hearses. The Tack Room and Stockyard, Stagecoach Barn, and Old West Prop Room contain exactly what they imply they do. Most of the collectibles in the various buildings also double as movie props, when film crews come to town. Symbiosis, Texas-style.

Other buildings contain museums: one for Johnny Rodriguez, a country and western singer whom Shahan discovered in 1969; another for John Wayne and scores of photographs, posters, and props from his epic film.

Souvenirs are available at the Trading Post, General Store, and Indian Store. Food and drink can be had in the Cantina, the village's center of activity. You can also get married in the Olde San Fernando Church, a rather faithful replica of the real one in San Antonio.

Special activities occur throughout the day during the summer season (Memorial Day to Labor Day): stagecoach and horse rides; the "Western Melodrama," a street shootout with juvenile humor; and free entertainment from the Cantina stage. Prior to his 1996 death, Happy Shahan himself occasionally took the stage to tell anecdotes and trade secrets about the filming of "The Alamo" and "Lonesome Dove." The genial host also treated special visitors (who did not necessarily have to be celebrities) to his backstage office where walls staggered under the weight of framed pictures and cast cards, gifts from the famous he had known over the years. Labor Day brings the summer season to a close with horse races and name singers.

Permanent studios and other buildings, when filming occurs, may be temporarily closed to the public.

The village part of Alamo Village is where most tourists spend their time. But the Alamo portion is a favorite for students of history and Alamo buffs who can stroll the interior of the Chapel, resembling the ruinous state it was in during the battle, and walk along the barracks, within the animal pens, and up the earthen cannon embankments and pretend they are back in 1836.

Alamo Village is open daily during normal daytime hours, except the week preceding Christmas. An average admission is charged. Several hundred people may visit during a summer weekend, fewer during a weekday. During the off-season, you may nearly have the run of the place to yourself.

Brackettville is west of San Antonio on U.S. Highway 90. From there, take local road 674 north about seven miles and look for signs for Alamo Village.

The Amistad National Recreation Area and the cities of Langtry and Del Rio (famed for their connection with Judge Roy Bean, the legendary "Law West of the Pecos") are within easy travel distance.

And while at Alamo Village, especially in the parking area next to the Alamo itself, expect to see some members of Shahan's registered Texas longhorn herd. Many of them are the children of the supporting animal actors used in Wayne's film. They like to lick paint from cars. Otherwise, they're harmless.

A DOUBLE DOSE OF DALLAS DELINQUENTS

They lived fast, died young, and left an indelible, if unwarranted, mark on the pages of early 20th-century history.

He was bad from the start. At nine, he had already been deemed "an incorrigible truant, thief, and runaway." When a teen, he turned to grocery store and gas station stickups with his older brother Buck. He survived a high-speed chase and shootout with police in 1928.

In early 1930, just barely out of his teens, he met the person he was forever to be linked with, a tattooed teen-ager whose married name was Thornton, a fellow Texan lacking in perceptiveness and common sense. Though he was a nasty, unsavory sort with few compensating features, she fell for him. And when he went to jail for burglary later that year, she smuggled a gun in to him, helping him escape.

He was recaptured and returned to prison. Despite killing a fellow prisoner, he won parole in 1932 and promptly stole a car with his girlfriend. Police closed in, captured her, and put her in jail.

In the meantime, he went on a killing spree in Texas and Oklahoma. She joined him upon her release. He continued his depraved pastime, kidnapping law enforcement officials, hitting a National Guard armory, robbing small banks and grocery stores, senselessly killing more victims, and evading police entrapments, often with his paramour.

Brother Buck joined the tandem along with his wife and an unfortunate simpleton named William Daniel Jones. The quintet expanded operations, hitting federal armories, grocery stores, restaurants, loan offices, banks, and gas stations in Texas, Oklahoma, Kansas, Missouri, Iowa, Minnesota, and Indiana, stealing cars, killing police officers and marshals, and winning gun battles. A sanguine scuffle with the law in Iowa in July 1933 took Buck's life and wounded the others.

Unchastened, the lovers continued their criminal ways alone, constantly traveling one step ahead of the law, escaping another hot pursuit in Texas that wounded them anew in November, springing friends from prison, and, as always, robbing and killing.

Both were socially maladjusted. In the summer of 1933, she stopped a cop in Oklahoma City, Oklahoma, asking directions, then blasted his head off with a shotgun.

Suffering from addled brains, they stole as much for the amoral thrill of it than from necessity, often robbing everyday people and frequently indulging a demoniac kick to kill policemen.

Plain and rather unattractive, they were small; he appeared weaselish, she matronly. Though her hair has always been described as blonde, her photographs show dark tresses and lawmen who knew her said her hair was red. Neither of them resembled the handsome actors who later played them in contrived cinematic bits of fancy. Future bank robber extraordinaire John Dillinger called them "punks" in 1933 and said they gave "bankrobbing a bad name."

Though some romantic chemistry existed between them, he was a homosexual who paired off with several of his male gang members. She was healthily heterosexual and often proved it with his male gang members.

The press publicized their two-bit escapades, labeling him "The Rattlesnake" and her "Suicide Sal," once even publishing a long poem she wrote about their exploits, a whimsical epic that ended with the limerick:

>Some day they will go down together,
>And they will bury them side by side.

To a few it means grief,
To the law it's relief,
But it's death to Bonnie and Clyde.

The end came at 9:20 in the morning, May 23, 1934, on a country road (now State Highway 154) near Gibsland, Louisiana. Texas highway patrolman Frank Hamer had stalked the duo for months. His men leveled a barrage of bullets at a gray Ford sedan. Nearly 200 rounds later, Clyde Barrow was slumped behind the car's steering wheel, shoeless, 25 bullets in his body, and Bonnie Parker Thornton's head was between her knees, a portion of a sandwich in her mouth and 23 bullets riddling her. Both corpses' hands held guns.

They were not buried side by side, as Parker had fatalistically predicted, but nonetheless lie close to each other, about seven miles in a straight line, in Dallas. Barrow is interred in Western Heights Cemetery at 1617 Fort Worth Avenue (U.S. Business Route 80), just northeast of the Cockrell Hill section of Dallas and east of U.S. Interstate Highway 30 as it leaves Grand Prairie. Parker is due north in Crown Hill Memorial Park at 9718 Webbs Chapel Road, just north of Dallas' Love Field Municipal Airport.

Parker's grave is more accessible. A flat stone with a small inlaid plaque marks the spot behind a high squared-off row of evergreens very close to the office building. A small white cross rises from the earth at the marker's head. Artificial flowers are sometimes nearby. Her epitaph contains a bit of poetry not composed by her:

BONNIE PARKER
OCT. 1 1910 - MAY 23, 1934
AS THE FLOWERS ARE ALL MADE SWEETER BY
THE SUNSHINE AND THE DEW, SO THIS OLD
WORLD IS MADE BRIGHTER BY THE LIVES
OF FOLKS LIKE YOU.

Poetic license, even in death.

Barrow's grave holds the southwestern corner of Western Heights Cemetery north of the thoroughfare. A much smaller plot, Western Heights dates to the 1850s and is fenced in. Visitors cannot gain access unless they inquire for the keykeeper at neighboring houses on the side street east of the cemetery (he will gladly oblige and open the cemetery gate for a brief visit). An historical marker along Fort Worth Avenue attributes maintenance of the cemetery to the Trinity Oaks Church of Christ and lists as the graveyard's residents Texas pioneers, soldiers of the Civil War and both World Wars, "AND CLYDE AND BUCK BARROW." The stone the brothers share is likewise flat along the ground and contains a terse phrase ever popular among tombstone inscriptions:

> BARROW
> CLYDE C.   MARVIN I.
> MAR. 24, 1909   MAR. 14, 1905
> MAY 23, 1934   JULY 29, 1933
> Gone but not forgotten

In the early 1990s, twin flowering bushes flanked, shaded, and partially obscured the stone. A long rectangular warehouse sprawls to its rear.

You'll likely encounter no one else at the graves while you're there. Both can be seen in about an hour's time - the tangible legacy of two of America's most overrated, overglamorized cult heroes who parlayed adventurous daring, myopic intelligence, graphic insensitivity, and a suicidal drive into early death and a legacy of blood, bullets, and brainless brutality.

If you finish both graves early in the day, you've got the city of Dallas at your disposal.

A TEXAS-SIZED TRENCH IN THE PANHANDLE PLAINS

It plummets 800 feet down from its 3,500-foot-high rim into rock strata a quarter of a billion years old. Dinosaurs and mammoths once thundered along its terrain. Indians roamed its canyon, searching for strong wood for their bows and arrows. Gullies and ravines course everywhere. Red-rocked mountains pierce the sky from its trenches.

It is "Palo Duro," adapted from a Spanish phrase for a tough cedar bush native to the canyon. Its craggy spires and riverine valleys resulted from the procreative interplay of wind and water over a million or so years.

In a way, it is part of the Rocky Mountains, its rim being a portion of the Caprock Escarpment of high plains, called Llano Estacado, flanking the eastern base of the Rockies from Wyoming to the Lone Star State.

Long after the dinosaurs thudded their way across the flat subtropical marshes within the huge crevices that now compose the canyon, other species moved in. The buffalo that once grazed there have died out, but deer, coyotes, foxes, raccoons, prairie dogs, rabbits, beavers, skunks, lizards, rattlesnakes, roadrunners, turkeys, quail, eagles, and hundreds of other species still call it home, moving among the mesquite and cedar trees, yucca and sagebrush, southwestern flowers, and palo duro trees.

The exploratory conquistadores of Francisco Vasquez de Coronado may have been the first white visitors during their 1541 sojourn in pursuit of the elusive Seven Cities of Cibola. Proselytizing missionaries, pioneers and settlers, and prospectors in search of gold followed. "Comancheros" came, too - Mexican and Indian bandits who robbed Gold Rush wagons, stole horses, livestock, and provisions, and took hostages to trade with other brigands in Palo Duro's hidden nooks.

On September 28, 1874, Colonel Ranald S. Mackenzie's 4th Cavalry invaded Palo Duro to roost out bands of marauding Comanches and Kiowas. A largely bloodless battle succeeded in inducing the renegades back to their reservations.

Shortly after the battle, cattle baron Charles Goodnight moved in, started a huge ranch that encompassed 60,000 cattle, and welcomed famed Quahadi Comanche Chief Quanah Parker as a guest.

Today, after a brief flirtation with the National Park Service in the 1930s, the site is Palo Duro Canyon State Park, a fantastically carved hole in the ground two dozen miles southeast of unredeemingly flat Amarillo prairie in Texas' panhandle. At 16,403 acres, it is the largest contiguous state's largest park. The state-owned portion is just a small part of the far greater canyon extending 120 miles across the panhandle under private ownership.

It has a single entrance and exit, a paved road that loops down, around, and out of the canyon bottom. The Coronado Lodge, an interpretive center atop the northern rim, explains its history and geology.

Farther into the canyon, the Goodnight Trading Post sells souvenirs, food, and camping equipment. Nearby stables rent horses. Across the road, the 1,650-seat Pioneer Outdoor Amphitheatre hosts summer drama. Natural acoustics, fashioned from the harmonic interaction between the curved theater and the canyon wall, allow the slightest sound to carry resoundingly. The musical "Texas", an annual extravaganza, rings the celestial rafters under the stars against a backdrop of a 600-foot-high cliff stretching to the canyon rim.

The narrow-gauge Sad Monkey Railroad takes visitors on a brief excursion through Timber Creek, offering close-up views of

Permian and Triassic Era formations like the Spanish Skirts and Triassic Peak (whose highest point amazingly resembles the mournful simian visage that gave the train its name). A fast-food outlet at the depot provides window service.

The eight-mile-long paved road continues along the floor of the canyon, following the flexures of the Prairie Dog Town Fork of the Red River, crossing six washes, adhering close to five campsites and a number of trailer areas and picnic and scenic overlook sites, and slithering between the Rock Gardens of Fortress Cliff, Capitol Peak, and Mesquite Mesa. A popular hiking and riding trail begins at a parking lot near Wash Number 2 and winds west and south past Sunday Canyon, Devil's Tombstone, and Castle and Lighthouse Peaks.

Permits are required for overnight camping and are obtainable from park rangers. Campsites come equipped with the usual amenities. Campers frequently delight in sitting around their nighttime fires, the utter canyon quiet broken only by the wail of the coyotes atop the high-above crags.

A state park that has the distinctive feel of a national park, Palo Duro also doubles as an amusement center: live drama, a mock railroad, historical markers, promontories and gullies, side streams to hike, and mountainous hills and caves that cannot all be experienced in a single day.

Palo Duro Canyon State Park is south of Amarillo and east of U.S. Interstate Highway 27. Pick up State Highway 217 east of the city of Canyon and take it a dozen miles east to the park entrance. The park is open throughout the year until 10 p.m. A moderate per-vehicle fee is charged. A ride on the Sad Monkey Railroad and a ticket to "Texas" cost extra. The railroad runs daily during the summer and on weekends during the other seasons. Theater performances start at sunset most evenings during June, July, and August; for information or reservations, call 806-655-2181 or write to "Texas," Box 268, Canyon, TX 79015. The summer season is the busiest.

Much of what time and humanity have unearthed from the

canyon, whether dinosaur skeletons, prehistoric fossils, or Spanish armaments, is displayed in the Panhandle-Plains Historical Museum at 2401 4th Avenue, just east of the intersection of State 217 and U.S. Highway 87, in nearby Canyon. The museum also features a pioneer village and considerable exhibits on the history of the Texas plains. It is open daily, except major holidays, during daytime hours and is free.

Taken together, the park and the museum constitute one of the best buys for your money in all of Texas.

UTAH

The rays of the sun blessing the mountains of the Mormons.

THE MOUNTAINS OF THE MORMONS...AND THE ROADS TO THEM

Somewhere in those blurry days between the Mesozoic and Cenozoic Eras, a rough 65 million years ago, the earth retched a few times, buckling a giant slab of its crust and creating a 100-mile-long fold, as though a baker had rolled a bumpy layer of dough back upon itself and neglected to smooth out the lumps. The initial upheaval and subsequent wind and water erosion created a striking mix of canyons and mountains - domes and crags of Navajo sandstone, cliffs and walls of Kayenta and Wingate sandstone.

Migrating pioneers came smack up against a portion of this so-called "Waterpocket Fold," a smaller 20-mile-long ridgeline of 1,000-foot-tall white domed rocks, looking a little like the architectural facade of the nation's capitol in Washington, D.C. The impressive but impassable barrier looked to them like coral, and they called the impediment "Capitol Reef." Though Indians had lived within the nooks of the fold for centuries, it was the westering Mormons, entering the Utah wilds in search of hospitable water-fed valleys, who first recognized it for modern man.

They tilled its more arable regions in the late 1800s and remained till the middle of the 20th century. Rumor had it they stayed because the landscape was at once desolate and beautiful and because, as the last part of the contiguous United States to be explored and mapped, it offered the persecuted sect immunity in which to practice its polygamous lifestyle.

The Mormons prospered, operating their Old Fruita Schoolhouse from 1900-41, instructing their offspring as the ancient Indians had done with their petroglyphs, chiseled into rock walls, a millennium earlier.

Today, the Mormons are gone, and the federal government has moved in. It is now called Capitol Reef National Park, one of the most ruggedly beautiful and least visited spots on the face of the earth.

Much of the quarter-million-acre park in south-central Utah is off limits to visitors in conventional vehicles because of its remoteness. But what remains is choice.

State Highway 24 pierces the park in its northern quarter, passing the scenic Twin Rocks, Chimney Rock, Castle, and Capitol Dome.

At the visitor center, a 25-mile round trip scenic drive intersects with the highway and parallels the western side of the giant north-south fold, showcasing the heart of the park with its majestic Egyptian Temple, a monolith with sheer fluted columns atop a sloping base.

Two twisting gullies, Grand Wash and Capitol Gorge, feed off the drive and enter unpaved sections cutting through the canyon bottom beneath high curving rock walls. One of the few east-west breaks in the otherwise impenetrable Waterpocket Fold, Capitol Gorge contains a wall where early pioneers inscribed their names and dates of passage. Modern visitors are strongly discouraged from adding theirs to the so-called Pioneer Register that today serves as a time capsule. It can be reached via a one-mile trail at the end of the northern segment of the unpaved road.

Both gorges offer hiking trails. The Cassidy Arch, named for western outlaw Butch Cassidy and his Wild Bunch, who reputedly used the wash as a hideout, is along Grand Wash. The washes are enticing, but enter them cautiously and never during a rainstorm or before an impending one. Solid waves of water, taller than a man and leavened with rocks and twigs, crash through the gorges almost without notice when heavy rains create flash floods.

More than a dozen hiking trails, varying in round trip length from a quarter-mile to nine, dot the landscape from above Highway 24 south to Capitol Gorge. Visitors with high-axled vehicles can tour the unpaved drive amongst the 700-foot monoliths of Cathedral Valley, the northernmost part of the park, featuring some of its most spectacular scenery. The Burr Trail Road and Notom-Bullfrog Road, entering the fold far south of Capitol Gorge, peek into the Strike Valley from the Muley Twist Canyon rim and peer at the 11,000-foot Henry Mountains ringing the park along the east.

The park is open daily, except Christmas; the visitor center has normal daytime hours. The per-vehicle entrance fee is moderate and good for a week. Snow occasionally cloaks the escarpments and crevices in winter, but most of the road-served areas are passable. Camping is allowed, and food and more durable lodging is offered beyond park premises.

You can also eat the fruit of the Mormons' toil. Visitors can freely sample small amounts of apples, cherries, peaches, apricots, and such from trees in the Fruita orchards, an early-20th century community along the banks of the Fremont River still tended by rangers. Various picking seasons during the year allow larger quantities to be obtained for a fee.

No matter how you reach the park, you'll experience a stunning prelude that may help you understand why the Mormons decided to stay in the midst of such rugged barrenness. If you approach from Salt Lake City on the north, you'll enter by way of Highway 24, passing Fishlake National Forest and curving around a quartet of mountains upwards of 11,000 feet.

Entering from the northeast and the Moab area, you'll course along the Fremont River and slip between the Caineville Mesas, with their steel gray, white, and tawny strata, on Highway 24. You'll also drive alongside 6,358-foot Factory Butte, one of the world's premier rock formations, its gigantic setbacks, symmetrical ridges, and grooved sides giving it the appearance of a mythological temple.

If you're coming from Monument Valley and the southeast,

State Highway 95 previews White Canyon and Natural Bridges National Monument, three sweeping arches, and Lake Powell and the Glen Canyon National Recreation Area (a place for which the word "awesome" was invented), before flanking the eastern face of the Henry Mountains and joining Highway 24.

Those entering from Zion and Bryce Canyon National Parks and points southwest will follow State Highway 12 as it skirts Kodachrome Basin State Park and 9,000-foot Canaan Peak and winds up, over, and around the fabulously colored Escalante Canyons, deeply furrowed gorges with undulating cliffs, shrub-studded plateaus, sinuous washes, lush gardens atop steep ledges, and several waterfalls and natural bridges. One skyline summit, in particular, thrusts you on a narrow shoulderless road with plummeting canyons on either side. The Escalante and Anasazi Indian Village State Parks are nearby. After leaving the canyons, Highway 12 slices through the Dixie National Forest, glimpsing peekaboo views of the Waterpocket Fold's western wall before hooking up with Highway 24 near the park entrance.

Capitol Reef and especially the drives to it are ideal for people who have visited Salt Lake City or Bryce or Zion and think they've seen Utah.

VERMONT

A DOUBLE DIP OF CHIPS AND QUIPS

In 1963, when John F. Kennedy was still president of the United States and Vietnam was a year away from burning its imprint into the American psyche, two New York youngsters prone to wanton waistlines met in a seventh-grade gym class in Merrick, Long Island.

Fifteen years later, they had become soulmates and business partners. Their venture started out small: a five-dollar correspondence course to teach the rudiments of their craft; and $8,000 of their life savings. On May 5, 1978, they opened their business at the corner of College and St. Paul Streets in Burlington, Vermont...and, in short order, became an institution.

You'd think a product indulgently loaded with fat and calories might not make it in an age of health awareness, cholesterol counts, and fiber. But Ben Cohen and Jerry Greenfield mined gold when they decided to make an extra-rich premium ice cream, load it with nuggets of fruit, nuts, and candy, and package it as a dense, solid treat heavy on flavor and sweetness and hang the calories. Ben & Jerry's packaged pints, introduced in 1980, often pack more than 1,000 calories each (an outrageous amount in an era of tofu and diet soda) and a whole day's supply of fat. Even their frozen yogurts frequently carry more calories and fat than other manufacturers' ice creams.

But the people who eat the stuff don't seem to mind. Ben & Jerry's has spread to all 50 states and several countries. Three manufacturing plants operate in Vermont.

Masters of unconventional publicity, Cohen and Greenfield

created the world's largest sundae at St. Albans, Vermont on April 15, 1983 - 27,102 pounds and tens of millions of calories. In 1986, they dished out free scoops of what they called "That's Life Apple Pie & Economic Crunch" ice cream on Wall Street after the October 19 stock market crash. In 1988, they appeared at the White House to receive a U.S. Small Business Persons of the Year award from President Ronald Reagan (they dressed for the presentation but later said they never again wore ties). In 1991, daily tours of their Waterbury manufacturing plant and headquarters swelled to more than 200,000 visitors, making it Vermont's most popular tourist draw.

The tours continue today, every 15-30 minutes, each lasting about a half-hour and starting when a guide, reflecting the owners' tongue-in-cheek approach, rings a cowbell in the plant's lobby-gift shop. Visitors view a humor-laced 10-minute film explaining the Ben & Jerry's story.

Then they monitor the production lines where, each day, blenders mix 17-19,000 gallons of milk with cream and stabilizers for seven minutes. The mixes then set in a tank room for eight hours before liquid flavoring is added. Next the batches chill out in 22-degree freezers, and chunky ingredients, if appropriate, are plopped in. Air is introduced to prevent the mixtures from becoming solid blocks of ice (Ben & Jerry's is far more dense than other manufacturers' ice creams because far less air - 17-20 percent, rather than the customary 40-50 percent - is injected). Fruits and swirls are dropped in, and the ice cream is packaged into 200,000 pints and banished to the deep freezer for two hours of frigidity at minus-70 degrees.

Visitors sample paper cupfuls of that day's production flavor, the obvious highlight of the tour, and then enter the quality assurance room where employees quarter 96 packaged pints a day for visual inspection. A narrow Hall of Fame corridor contains memorabilia and pictures, jocularly presented, of the company's short history.

Tours end where they began - in the spacious gift shop where both unique and tacky items are available. An attached "Scoop Shop" serves the whole Ben & Jerry's rich, artery-clogging line of flavors, some three dozen in all (including the amusingly named Cherry Garcia, Chunky Monkey, Wavy Gravy, etc.), at reasonable prices.

Outside, visitors can round out the tour by indulging in bingo, food, face painting, swings, and so forth at an amusement area with picnic tables.

An estimated quarter-million people annually line up for the tours.

Billed as "Vermont's finest ice cream," Ben & Jerry's donates much of its product to nationwide community fundraisers, contributes 7.5 percent of its profits to its own foundation which funds non-profit social improvement activities, and offers its employees profit-sharing opportunities in what it calls "caring capitalism." Each employee also gets three complimentary pints of ice cream a day.

Tours cost a very modest amount and occur daily during daytime hours (expanded to 8 p.m. during July and August). Ice cream is not produced on Sundays, holidays, and special company celebration days nor after mid-afternoon on Wednesdays and Saturdays.

Ben & Jerry's Factory Tour and headquarters is along State Highway 100, just north of Waterbury, in the heart of northern Vermont's ski country.

THE LIBRARY OF POOR LONELY VERSES

Helen Wilhelmina Wernecke once fell in love with a businessman, a Union College man. Things happened, and she got pregnant. People considered her beneath his social level; she was only a worker for the General Electric Company. He refused to marry her, so she aborted the fetus in a day when abortions were illegal.

On December 29, 1934, she wrote a poem:

> Small, square cards like little white hearses
> Carry the corpses of my verses.
> Verses written at home, in cars
> At break of dawn or beneath the stars.
> Verses written at instant thought
> Verses that time has dearly bought.
> Verses that laugh because they are glad
> Verses that cry because they are sad.
> Small square cards like little white hearses
> Carry gently and carefully my poor lonely verses.

She wound up marrying another man and had a family with him. The marriage eventually ended in divorce. A second marriage came and went, too.

When a neighbor killed himself in the early 1950s, she remembered him in verse:

> His heart was sick and his soul was sore
> And he could not wait to die—

> He took his life that he might be
> God's neighbor in the sky.

The woman who had once written, "I'd die without my inside - my wonderful self of dreams," died on June 19, 1960, in Middlebury, Vermont, at 49.

Her legacy exists in only two places: the memories of her family; and the Brautigan Library in Burlington, Vermont - "America's only library of unpublished writing" - which carries the world's only public copy of "The unpublished poems of Helen Wilhelmina Wernecke," as compiled by her daughter, Ann Nevin, a professor at the University of Vermont.

About 300 volumes of typed manuscripts occupied shelf space in the narrow rectangle, formerly a book store, that became the Brautigan Library at 91 College Street, nearly hidden behind a garden and the adjoining Vermont Institute of Massage Therapy. Then in January 1996, the Brautigan moved farther up the street to the Fletcher Free Library's top floor.

The individual manuscripts, bound within hard covers for easier storage and durability, run the gamut of topics in both fiction and nonfiction. Some of the writing is good, some is sophomoric. The library's guidelines don't discriminate qualitatively:

> We don't judge the works we receive.
> Each book is treated with equal
> importance and given an equal opportunity
> to be read by the public. ... It is up
> to the writer to determine if his or her
> work is worthy....

Consequently, some oddball items slip in on the shelves:

- Carol D. Holoboff's "My Mom," a treatise on how to prepare a child for "the rituals of death and funerals;"

- Albert E. Helzner's "The Long Range Effect of a Birth," "The Long Range Effect of Abortion and other Essays About Life in the Universe," "Some Challenging Essays for You to Think About," "More Challenging Essays for You to Think About," "365 Bits of Wisdom to Enrich Your Daily Life," etc.;
- A. Alexander Stella's "War Dodger," the story of Larry Ice as he experiences "enlightenment" while in the throes of "drugs, disenchantment and despair;"
- Stephen B. McNeal's "Shoot Bullets Through Me," the fiction of two hitchhikers "thrown together by the road;"
- Martha Truable Sexton's "A Simpler Time and Place," the story of her life and 55-year marriage;
- Etherly Murray's "Autobiography about a Nobody" ("...when was the last time you read the biography of an interesting nobody?");
- Stephen Andrew Bort's "Three Essays Advocating the Abolishing of Money" ("The injustice...is that our fundamental human needs must be earned through labor and purchased with income.");
- Donald McNowski's "The McNowski Papers Letters from a Small Mind or A Man with a Idea;"
- Stuart Chaulk's "Chapterbook" ("By examining an archeology of myself, I come up with a printed nothingness.");
- Carla A. Schwartz's "I'd Be Your Roadkill, Baby," a collection of poems;
- Delilah Della Rose's "How to Murder Your Husband and Not Get Caught. By Someone Who Did It."

The manuscripts come in the mail, often with incomplete addresses ("Library of the Unknowns," "Library For People With Tales To Tell"). Nominal fees (roughly $50-100, depending on manuscript size) are charged to cover binding and related costs.

The submissions are bound, assigned identification numbers, and placed on shelves according to general topics: family, natural world, spirituality, love, humor, future, adventure, street life, war and peace, social/political/cultural, meaning of life, poetry, all the rest.

Some manuscripts contain skillful narratives. Others are self-indulgent hodgepodges too blandly conceived to ever offer much appeal. Some bear the imprint, deservedly or not, of hundreds of publishers' rejection slips; others were written only as personal reminiscences never intended for publication. Some should have been published; others should never have been written.

Founder Todd Lockwood flatteringly says the collection contains some "very naked stuff." Going through the volumes, all identically bound in generic covers, is like perusing someone's diary and ferreting out the most intimate thoughts. Only with a difference. The authors of these volumes very much want someone to read their memories to help validate their existences, justify their lives, perhaps even grasp slight sprigs of immortality.

The library is doubly one of a kind: America's only library of unpublished writing and also the only public repository for each bound manuscript anywhere in the world. And therein lies its sense of fragility. Imagine the consequences of an act of nature; if something were to happen to the library, the individual life mementos perish as well. The "poor lonely verses" grow even lonelier.

The bound volumes generally do not leave library premises. Once, a sizable number of them, shelves and all, flew to Seattle for display in an arts fair. But the idea is to come to the library and curl up in the chairs with a good manuscript for an afternoon of alternative reading, imbibing of the unpublished musings of some of the talented and talentless...and some of America's most sentient scribes who either had the ill luck to be one step out of synchronization with the publishing world or were merely unconcerned with publishing at all.

The name "Brautigan" derives from a very real writer, Richard Brautigan, who described a library of unpublished manuscripts in one of his books ("The Abortion," 1970). A counterculture figure with cult appeal, he killed himself in 1984. The library honors him by using, as symbolic bookends, mayonnaise jars (because mayonnaise figures prominently in one of his books) and also by soliciting letters and notes from anyone on any topic on the occasion of his birthday every January 30 (these submissions are bound into book form as well).

But the Brautigan Library's value is not in commemorating a very published writer who indirectly lent his name to it. The library is Todd Lockwood's realization of Richard Brautigan's inspiration. The library is, according to Lockwood, "a place for ideas, a place where stories can be told, a wisdom exchange. We're the other Library of Congress."

The library's treasures are the otherwise anonymous lives which inhabit its pedestrian shelves, populating them with experiences, ideas, and feelings as human, honest, and real as those in any hardbound book in a conventional library or book store.

The Brautigan Library is a tribute not to Richard Brautigan, who had his day in the sun. Nor even to Todd Lockwood, its guiding force. It is a tribute, a memorial, a living tombstone to Martha Truable Sexton, Etherly Murray, A. Alexander Stella...and Helen Wilhelmina Wernecke whose "poor lonely verses" can now transcend mortality's bonds and breathe anew, perhaps even to endure into another century and touch the soul of some unforeseen stranger yet to be born.

The Burlington area also includes the Ethan Allen Homestead Historic Site as well as that Revolutionary War hero's ostentatious grave, several museums and product manufacturing tours, lake cruises, malls and shopping districts, restaurants and lodging, and access to recreational activities on Lake Champlain.

VIRGINIA

A TRIP TO TOBACCO ROAD

In 1492, Christopher Columbus did not discover the New World but he did stumble across its inhabitants smoking, sniffing, and chewing tobacco.

In 1585-87, English colonizers brought tobacco seeds from North Carolina to Sir Walter Raleigh who grew them and introduced pipe smoking to genteel English society.

In 1613, tobacco was used as currency; a wedding cost 200 pounds of raw tobacco, payable to the minister.

In 1619, Americans had planted tobacco so exclusively that they had to be told to occasionally vary their fields with corn.

In 1624, England monopolized the sale of American tobacco and began charging customs duties, in a way, sowing the "seeds" for the future rebellion of the United States.

In 1776, during the darkest days of the Revolutionary War, Commander-in-Chief George Washington stressed the importance of getting tobacco to the poor soldiers in the field: "I say, if you can't send money, send tobacco."

Washington and Thomas Jefferson grew it in the 18th century. Two centuries later, Generals John "Black Jack" Pershing and Douglas MacArthur implored the government for cigarettes for America's fighting men. Franklin D. Roosevelt placed it on the list of essential foodstuffs during his presidency.

Like it or not, tobacco - the crop that, when cured, becomes cigarettes - has contributed about as much to the success of America as any other single factor.

The Philip Morris Manufacturing Center in Richmond, a not

impartial observer, vigorously documents the history of tobacco from the days around the time of Christ to the present in the lobby of its sprawling plant. A chronological dateboard, with text, display case exhibits, artifacts, photographs, and a recording of New York bellhop Johnny Roventini's famous primordial bellow ("Call for Philip Morris"), nearly surrounds the inner lobby of the visitor center, chronicling tobacco's importance through the ages with fact, nostalgia, and wit. A 17-minute Philip Morris Training Center film ("Tobacco Seed to Pack"), shown several times an hour, maintains that a two-million-job, $60-billion economy results from the one acre given to tobacco of every 400 acres consigned to other crops in America.

Visitors board guided trams that undertake half-hour tours through the heart of the manufacturing complex. The production areas are noisy (headphones are worn by guests, earplugs by employees), remarkably clean, and rich with the sweet aroma of cured tobacco. Uniformed employees, wearing badges distinctively like Marlboro red and white cigarette packs, tend conveyors that march up to 10,000 cigarettes a minute through belts and chutes and into the rectangular pocket-size boxes millions of Americans depend on to get them through their everyday lives.

The whole process unfolds before your eyes. Each day, a million pounds of cured Bright Leaf, Burley, and Oriental tobacco, cut and blended and freshly shipped, comes up via suction pumps from holding reservoirs beneath the floor. The tobacco pneumatically rushes through tubes at 20 mph and emerges as "cut filler" wrapped and sealed by 270-degree heat within the white paper so familiar to cigarette smokers.

At the same time, another part of the modular apparatus converts "tow," a spongy, gauze-like substance, into cigarette filters. Plug wrap encircles the filters, and they head to the tipping section at a blinding 55 mph where they are joined to the "cut filler" and gold-colored tipping paper that millions of American lips puff on every day.

Conveyors carry the finished cigarettes to the acronymic "OS-

CAR" ("overhead spiral conveyor and reservoir") which hurries them to a packer that drops them down into chutes for assembly. Each family of 20 is then wrapped within foil and a preprinted label that forms the pack. A stamp-like colored seal is applied to the top, and the whole package receives an outer skin of transparent polypropylene and a tear tape and finally a jolt of heat to seal everything together.

Voila. Thousands of packs of cigarettes completely made in less time than it takes to smoke a single butt.

The statistics are overwhelming, even when watching the lightning speed at which cigarettes are made: Bay 1 (one of several bays in the 1,600,000-square-foot facility built from 1970-73 on 200 acres for $225 million) converts tobacco, paper, and tow into 10,000 finished cigarettes per minute and fills 500-550 packs each minute in an area large enough to hold more than three football fields; at the Richmond plant alone, 1.3 billion cigarettes are processed daily from one million pounds of tobacco, enough for five smokes a day for every living American of any age and enough cigarettes to stretch from the manufacturing center to San Francisco's Golden Gate Bridge; about $7 million in cigarette taxes are generated each day, more than $75 a second.

Philip Morris is not just blowing smoke with those numbers.

The actual Philip Morris, a London tobacco shopkeeper, capitalized on an incident in the 19th-century Crimean War in which British soldiers noticed their Russian enemies' fondness for cigarettes. When the soldiers returned to England, they said they'd like domestic smokes of their own. In the 1850s, enterprising merchant Morris coined a motto ("quality - for people of quality") and set about cornering the market.

In 1919, Philip Morris and Company Ltd., Inc., controlled by American stockholders, incorporated within Virginia. The company flourished, eventually growing to include such disparate holdings as Kraft General Foods International, Mission Viejo Realty Group, Inc., and Miller Brewing Company. It is now the world's largest consumer packaged goods firm and controls Entenmann's,

Jacobs Suchard, Jell-O, Log Cabin, Maxwell House, Nabisco, Oscar Mayer, Post, Sanka, and others. Fortune magazine annually ranks it among the world's top performers in profits, assets, and total sales.

The tour concludes in the gift shop, overlooking the production floor, where smoking adults are given a complimentary pack of any of the cigarette brands manufactured by Philip Morris and where various products, related and unrelated to cigarettes, are sold. The gift shop also shows videos on cigarette production, both in actual time and slow-motion. And a two-wall display uses frozen-frame cutaways to delineate the step-by-step assembly process.

The center, which is one of several Philip Morris area plants, offers free weekday tours during daytime hours (except during the week of July Fourth, the days between Christmas and New Year's, and holidays on which the plant is closed). No photographs are allowed inside. Some 45-50,000 visitors tour annually. Tour guides scrupulously avoid promoting cigarettes and controversy.

To reach the center, take the Bells Road (Exit 69) ramp from U.S. Interstate Highway 95 in southern Richmond and turn north on Commerce Road to the plant entrance. Signs point the way, and a giant rectangular block, resembling a cigarette and bearing the names of the company's various brands, stands by the plant on the west side of the interstate.

The Philip Morris Manufacturing Center tour is an exceptionally fascinating and educational look at one of the world's most popular commodities and its production.

Those who have strong feelings against the consumption of tobacco, however, may wish to tour elsewhere in Richmond.

THE GREATEST MAN YOU NEVER HEARD OF

The man many consider the most brilliant American reposes atop a gentle hill not far from Charlottesville, Virginia. A scholar, author, architect, scientist, philosopher, and eminent man of letters, he wrote words that ring with the full resonance of emotion, truth, and power. He was a man who ardently believed in the worth of mankind and who strove all his life to enlighten fellow men with the loftiest of principles.

Thomas Jefferson?

Try Walter Russell...the greatest man you never heard of.

Walter Russell was born, quite humbly, on May 19, 1871, in Massachusetts. His formal education ended at age nine when his impoverished parents pulled him out of school and put him to work in a dry goods shop. He took art classes, financing them with another job, and parlayed three months of music lessons into a juvenile career as a church organist and music teacher. He also composed. Famed Polish pianist Ignace Paderewski, who had once overheard him playing, stumbled across him years later and badgered him into playing a particular waltz he had written.

An art editor for Collier's Weekly and a wartime correspondent and artist for Collier's and Century, he painted "The Might of the Ages," a visual metaphor illustrating what he called "the power of thought in the making of civilization." The canvas featured two dozen recognizable historical figures (Julius Caesar, Cleopatra, Joan of Arc, Christopher Columbus, William Shakespeare, Napoleon Bonaparte, George Washington, etc.), all in period attire, commingling in New York City to watch the modern colossi which man had wrought - mighty ships ruling the East River under the towering Brooklyn Bridge. America's National Academy ridiculed it and called it puerile. Undaunted, Russell exhibited it, by invitation, at the Turin International Art Exposition in 1900. It toured Europe triumphantly and won awards. When the National Academy, hat in hand, approached him in embarrassment, asking to display it, he firmly told the Academy what to do with its hat.

He painted sensitive studies of children, including the progeny of Theodore Roosevelt, sketching them from memory after having spent hours observing them. The Ladies' Home Journal chose him to scour the country, painting America's dozen most attractive children.

Around World War I, he switched to adult portraiture.

And then he underwent his full renaissance. He wrote books and articles and lectured. He designed buildings (New York City's Hotel des Artistes on West 67th Street, the original Hotel Pierre on Park Avenue, Alwyn Court at Seventh Avenue and 58th Street, and Gothic Studio on 79th Street) and popularized the duplex studio apartment.

He communicated with the great of his day including presidents from Theodore Roosevelt to Franklin D. Roosevelt and scientists Thomas Edison and Albert Einstein.

He became a skillful equestrian and owned black Arabian stallions. He won figure-skating medals, even at 69 beating rivals half his age.

He switched from painting to sculpture, with no formal training. He sculpted scores of busts of famous people. One of his FDR busts greets visitors at the former president's New York home.

He created a larger-than-life statue of inventor Charles Goodyear for an Ohio memorial.

FDR's optimistic words on mankind's Four Freedoms (freedom of speech and religion and from want and fear) inspired a massive idealized statue of the freedoms as metaphorically personified by four angelic figures, right-angled to each other, facing outward, their upward-pointed wings united, one to another, behind them.

He embarked on the greatest sculpting challenge of his life, his finished masterpiece, a 28-figure setting of author Mark Twain and the principal characters of his novels. Perfectly symmetrical, the figures balance each other geometrically on either side of the seated author in dead center.

IBM founder Thomas Watson invited him to address corporate employees, salesmen, and executives on the concept of fair ethics in business that for decades served as IBM's benchmark.

He saw fortunes come and go. He offered $5,000 for a particular black Arabian and then, when the owner balked, plunked down $50,000 for the entire stable of horses, house, and 40 acres. He lost $300,000 in the panic of 1907. He viewed financial setbacks as only "valuable stepping stones to success."

His most signal accomplishments came in science. With no rudimentary training, he communicated with great empirical minds like Einstein and comprehended what their formulas meant even before they did. He discovered the concept of the isotopes of hydrogen and formally introduced it to a scientific panel; years later, his assertions were proved correct. He revised the Periodic Table of the Elements in 1926, foreshadowing the actual discovery of neptunium and plutonium with his proffered uridium and urium. The American Academy of Sciences conferred a Doctor of Science degree on him in 1941.

When asked how an uneducated man could comprehend such unfathomable realities, he responded that, in May 1921, God had called him to a "high mountain of inspiration and intense ecstacy." While there, his consciousness was freed from his body and thrust "wholly in the Mind universe of Light, which is God." He explained that all knowledge resides in that "Mind universe of Light" and can be tapped if one becomes "One with that Source." He claimed the revelation allowed him to understand "what Jesus meant when He spoke of 'the Light of the world.'"

He spent the rest of his life discussing how to find God, the source of light and fount of knowledge, and live in union with that all-purposeful knowledge and channel one's abilities to that awareness to be a part of the totality of life.

He ran afoul of the government after World War II when his book "Atomic Suicide?" warned of the dangerous implications of a nuclear world. He identified ozone depletion long before other scientists announced it to the world. Deeply committed to nuclear energy, the government attempted to stifle his message.

He died - a term he would strongly disagree with - on the 92nd anniversary of his birth, May 19, 1963.

A keenly intensive man with a striking physical appearance (piercing eyes, bald head, Vandyke beard, a visage professorial in repose but unremittingly stern when flashing self-assured determination), Walter Russell was one of the most intellectually daunting, spiritually haunting of human beings.

His art, sculpture, medals, photographs, books, correspondence, philosophy, and soul still permeate the house where he took his final breath - Swannanoa, atop the Blue Ridge Mountains in west-central Virginia. It is a museum now, the largest repository of his mortal essence. His statuary occupies pedestals and mantels everywhere. A model of the multi-character Twain memorial sits against an interior wall. A model of the "Four Freedoms" fills the center of one room (the original is in Florida). "The Might of the Ages" hangs nearby. His sketches of children decorate one room, sharing space with display cases of photographs of him and the buildings he designed. Some of the letters he received from the famous are displayed.

Visitors see a much more cheerful place than the dilapidated shell that greeted Russell when he became its owner in 1948. The Italian Renaissance mansion features marble highlights in its design and construction, Georgia on the exterior, Italian Carrara and Sienna on the inside. A grand marble staircase leads to a 10-foot stained glass window, crafted by Louis Tiffany and considered his masterpiece - an ascetic figure, Christlike in its piety, against a backdrop patterned after New York's Hudson River. A domed ceiling rises above.

A moderate fee is charged for admission to the three-story edifice with its twin frontal towers and a guided tour that may stretch from a half-hour to an hour, depending on available personnel and visitation.

The house also serves as the headquarters of the University of Science and Philosophy, a disciplined educational institution founded by Russell to promote the study of man for his intellectual, cultural, and ethical development and continued survival in an increasingly threatening world. The school entices those attuned to the Russell message with home study courses, annual seminars, and workshop weekends. A gift shop sells books and writings by Russell and his accomplished wife Loa, an author, philosopher, and artist who both drew inspiration from her husband and inspired him and who urged him to buy the rundown mansion and turn it into a "Shrine of Beauty."

Three terraces of manicured lawns and paved walkways lie to the rear of the house. A pool, holding individual likenesses of each of the Four Freedoms, and an arbor flank either end.

An ascendant "Christ of the Blue Ridge," a figure of Jesus, eyes and face heavenward, hands reverentially clasped in prayer - the inspiration of Lao, the product of both Russells - surmounts a double-tiered plinth and commands the focal point of the highest terrace. The 30-foot statue is a model of a 600-foot work that Walter Russell intended others to build after his death. It marks the approximate site of the graves of both Russells (she died on May 5, 1988). He desired no conventional tombstone, no traditional memorial words. Seasonal flowers and shrubbery surround the terraces; rest benches are everywhere.

Few people know of Swannanoa ("Land of Beauty" in its West Indian translation; "The Mother of Heaven" or "The Absolute" in East Indian). Some 7,000 visit each year, many simply because it is within two dozen miles of Jefferson's home in Charlottesville. Some admit to finding God or the secrets of life and death at Swannanoa. Others mine its inner tranquility and harmony or its architectural grandeur.

A few miles east of Waynesboro, Swannanoa is open daily during normal daytime hours. Leave U.S. Interstate Highway 64 at the marker for Highways 76/250 and turn right onto East 250. From there, follow signs for Swannanoa on the mountain above a Holiday Inn. And be prepared to meet the most intriguing man you never heard of.

WASHINGTON

WASHINGTON'S FAVORITE FAIRY FOOD

Before the birth of Christ, Egyptians mixed grapes and nuts with rosewater and the nectar of bees to produce a sweet treat favored for its reputed wholesomeness. Through the centuries, the Greeks called their version "lokoumi," and Turks referred to theirs as "rahat lacoum." The Armenians used the term "locoum" (which translates into "to give rest to the throat"). Several hundred years ago, traders brought it to mainland Europeans who called it "Turkish delight" and willingly consumed it.

During World War I, two Armenians named Mark Balaban and Armen Tertsagian brought it to America and updated it. They mixed apples and walnuts in a jelled base, then dusted the pliable candy with powdered sugar and called the pieces "aplets." They marketed their product in Washington as "The Confection of the Fairies" but eventually dropped the phrase when marketing experts figured the connection with the mythological imagery of ambrosia and nectar might be a bit obscure for consumers. The candy simply became "Aplets."

Another brand was added later: a blend of apricots and walnuts called "Cotlets."

Today, the business is run by a grandson of one of the founders. It is formally called "Liberty Orchards," but everyone throughout the state knows it as "Aplets & Cotlets." The product line has greatly expanded to include numerous variations: strawberry-walnut; pineapple-macadamia nut; raspberry-pecan; orange-walnut; blueberry-pecan; peach-walnut; banana-macadamia; passionfruit-macadamia; cherry-walnut; papaya-macadamia; guava-macadamia;

rose-pistachio; cinnamon-walnut; etc. Because high-fat chocolate is not an ingredient, the candy weighs in with fewer calories.

"Aplets & Cotlets" are made in only one place in the world: 117 Mission Street in Cashmere. Free samples are there for the tasting. And complimentary quarter-hour tours head out through the production and assembly lines every 15 minutes, overseeing all the key operations: cooking the blend of fruit juices and purees, sugar, pectin, cornstarch, and flavorings in large copper kettles; adding nuts when the jelled batch has reached the proper consistency; pouring the mix into trays for leveling with rollers and 24-hour cooling in refrigerated racks; slicing the molded masses of congealed confection into uniform rectangular pieces; dusting with cornstarch, enrobing with powdered sugar; packaging and wrapping. Though some machinery is used, most phases of the process are accomplished by hand.

The tour and browsing and buying time in the gift shop (where many varieties of the products you just saw being made are for sale) can easily fit into an hour. Tours are offered daily during normal daytime hours from May to December; during the other months, tours occur most weekdays. The plant is located on U.S. Highway 2/97 in Cashmere, about 85 miles east of Seattle, as the crow flies.

Cashmere also offers the Chelan County Historical Museum with its reconstructed pioneer village, a shopping district on Cottage Avenue, and occasional street festivals.

It is only a dozen miles southeast of Leavenworth, one of America's most authentic reconstructed Bavarian villages. In the 1960s, the burghers of Leavenworth decided to turn a 1920s railroad and lumber town that had gone sour into a delightful blend of German music, food, architecture, and atmosphere cozying up to the Wenatchee Mountains, the foothills of the Cascade Mountain Range. The names ring true - Das Feinkostgeschaft, Herzenslust, Das Meisterstuck - and the window flowerboxes, old-fashioned street lights, shuttered windows, performing arts gazebo, and steeples and cupolas almost fool you into thinking you've left America. The Bavarian Ice Festival (second weekend in January), Maifest (second weekend in May), Autumn Leaf Festival (last weekend in September to the first weekend in October), and Christmas Lighting Festival (first two weekends in December) are among the dozen special events throughout the year.

Cashmere and Leavenworth are on the southern end of the Cascade Loop, a breathtaking drive that swings along the Wenatchee and Columbia Rivers, several lakes and dams, and Puget Sound, with major stops at Tumwater Canyon, Lake Chelan National Recreation Area, North Cascades National Park, and Deception Pass Bridge, altogether some of the greatest scenery on the continent.

And, yes, you can find individual packs of Aplets & Cotlets nearly everywhere.

A cross and a teddy bear...remembering little Dallas Desautel on the lonely knoll of Nespelem.

THE LONELY KNOLL OF NESPELEM

It is a lonely, haunting place, a knoll that surveys a few humble homes nestled in the flats among the hills surrounding Nespelem, an unknown village in northwestern America. The homes are functional, nothing more, nothing less. Some have fencing for horses and cattle. Cars are scattered throughout.

The lonely knoll stands as a silent sentinel, seldom bearing the tramp of human footsteps in its solitude, only catching the wind as it rustles by. Its only entrance is a dirt path leading to a gate of upright posts and horizontal crossboards. A fence encloses the perimeter, shutting it off from the outside world.

Time and memory seem to have forgotten the lonely knoll. Grass, weeds, and wildflowers rise high in places, sometimes almost choking the flags, sculpted figures, and statues of Christ that struggle to be seen above the tangle. The handwritten notes and letters, never answered, lie on the ground, weathered by rain and sun.

The lonely knoll is the home of little Dallas Desautel. His pinwheel juts up from the ground, rotating when a breeze catches its petals. His toy vehicles, miniature cars, trucks, and such, are parked on the loose gravel that is his playground, near his little plastic dinosaurs. His stuffed teddy bear sits on its haunches, slumping a little to the side, its coat a bit ratty from exposure to the elements. Its right paw touches a folded piece of paper, a personal handwritten note of affection for little Dallas.

Dallas will never again see the dinosaurs or the toys or the pinwheel. He'll never read the letter addressed to him. He'll never again hold the teddy bear, his little buddy.

The lonely knoll is now the home of Dallas Desautel (1983-87). He shares it for all eternity with hundreds of others...and his faithful teddy bear. A wooden cross, its crosspieces nailed together, a few sprigs of attached plastic flowers lending color to its gray drabness, stands at the head of the low mound that covers little Dallas. Vases of flowers and plants protect the cross on either side. A small metal marker, supplied by a funeral home, rises from the foot of the mound; it lists Dallas' name and years of life. The teddy bear and the note of affection and remembrance tell the rest of the story.

The little knoll in Nespelem, within Washington's Colville Indian Reservation, is one of the most heartbreaking spots on the face of the earth.

A contemporary granite marker recalls little Harry Joe Owhi: "GOD BLESS OUR BABY BOY." His July 1959 birth and July 1961 death are also inscribed, and a reclining deer, bordered by twin flower blossoms, completes the frieze. A flower vase stands by the stone.

Elsewhere, wooden crosses lie in a line atop gentle mounds of earth. Encircling rocks outline many of the individual mounds; and personal objects - molded or sculpted birds, Indian figures, religious statues, etc. - salute the honored dead for all eternity. Native American cemeteries are colorful, highly personal, and evocative; Nespelem's is one of the most poignant.

One grave, in particular, stands out. A towering tree a few paces to its side often casts shadows upon it. A monument resembling an obelisk, taller than a person, contains a bas relief bust of a famous Indian. A variety of objects - animal skulls with racks, garlands, evergreen bows, colored paper streamers, wreaths, flowerpots, piled stones, and glass jars with feathers, coins, and candles - surrounds the base. It honors Heinmot Touyalakekt ("Thunder Traveling to Loftier Mountain Heights"), the most famous of the Nez Perce, a tribe that had for decades prided itself on never having engaged in hostilities with white Americans.

The isolation of the ancestral homes of the Nez Perce in the area where modern Idaho, Oregon, and Washington converge helped minimize outside contact. But that changed when white pioneers found gold on their land in the years before the Civil War. White government agents inflicted fraudulent treaties on the Nez Perce in order to seize more land.

In 1871, Heinmot's father counseled him with his dying breath:

> When I am gone, think of your country. You are the chief of these people. ... Always remember that your father never sold his country. ... This country holds your father's body. Never sell the bones of your father and your mother.

Heinmot used eloquence and logic in bargaining with the whites, but they ultimately had their way. When the Nez Perce complied with an order to move to a reservation, hostilities erupted and a full-scale war began. Heinmot remained an influential figure off the battlefield as his tribe, along with other bands of Nez Perce, arduously traversed more than a thousand miles of Idaho, Wyoming, and Montana, crossing the Bitterroot and Rocky Mountains, fighting battles and skirmishing with the pursuing U.S. Army, desperately trying to make the Canadian border.

In October 1877, 35 miles short of Canada and freedom, the Nez Perce faced a besieging army near the Bear Paw Mountains. The army attacked. Snow fell and blanketed the bodies of the dead. Hungry, tired, sick, wounded, broken in spirit, the Nez Perce looked to Heinmot.

He came forward to speak words that became the most famous ever uttered by a Native American to his white conquerors:

> ...I am tired of fighting. Our chiefs are killed. ... The old men are all dead. ... He who led the young men is dead. It is cold and we have no blankets. The little

> children are freezing to death. My people, some of them, have run away to the hills, and have no blankets, no food; no one knows where they are - perhaps freezing to death. I want to have time to look for my children and see how many I can find. Maybe I shall find them among the dead. ... I am tired; my heart is sick and sad. From where the sun now stands, I will fight no more forever.

The man America calls Chief Joseph spent nearly the last 30 years of his life on reservations, exiled from the homeland his father had urged him never to leave. White America rejected all his pleas for the remnants of his small band to resettle their ancestral home. He died in 1904 on the Colville Indian Reservation, his heart and soul shattered by a white world unable to accommodate his presence on the land of his birth.

An historical marker to Chief Joseph stands in Nespelem, down the hill from the cemetery.

The scenic reservation, halfway between Seattle and Spokane, is just north of Grand Coulee Dam, the world's largest concrete structure, with its visitor center, overlook, and summer nighttime laser light show. The cemetery is off State Highway 155 on the northern outskirts of Nespelem.

Native American cemeteries, even if overgrown with weeds and tall grass, are emotional reminders of undying love, commemoration, and the natural beauty of the human spirit renewing itself through the generations.

On the surface, the little knoll in Nespelem is unremittingly lonely. But, deep within its soul, throbbing with sentiment and resonant of voice, resides the legacy of Chief Joseph...and the enduring love of a teddy bear for its little boy.

THE WOMAN WHO WED TO GO WEST

Young, auburn-haired Narcissa Prentiss, charming, lively, intelligent, gifted with a lovely singing voice, and said to be beautiful, grew up in western New York in the early 19th century and became a schoolteacher. But when she applied for missionary work among the western Indians, the Protestant American Board of Foreign Missions rejected her. Her problem? She was a single woman.

She agreed to marry Marcus Whitman, a physician and preacher, if he agreed to take her west. On February 18, 1836, they married in a moving ceremony. As emotions overcame her friends and they cried, Narcissa sang the last lines of the hymn "Yes, My Native Land! I Love Thee:" "Let me hasten far in heathen lands to dwell."

The following morning, the newlyweds set out for the wilds of the Oregon wilderness. It proved a taxing honeymoon - 3,000 miles of rugged terrain over six months. They journeyed along a roughhewn path known only to Indians and fur traders, a route soon to become famous as the Oregon Trail. She and one of her fellow missionary travel companions became the first white women to journey across the continent, the first white women the Pacific Northwest Indians ever saw.

The Whitmans established Waiilatpu ("place of the people of the rye grass"), a mission among 400 Cayuse Indians. They taught them to read and farm, attempted to convert them to Christianity, and provided medical help for their ailments.

On Narcissa's 29th birthday, her only child, Alice Clarissa, was born - the first child born to citizens of the United States in the vast northwestern lands. Narcissa's journey across the continent and the birth of her child convinced thousands of Americans back east that the Pacific lands could be settled, prompting a great westward migration. The mission expanded to become a welcome oasis for the migrants, a place where food, supplies, medical attention, and rest could be obtained.

But tragedy dogged the Whitmans.

On June 23, 1839, two-year-old Alice Clarissa drowned. Griefstricken, the Whitmans took in a dozen children - white orphans, boarders, and half-bloods who claimed Indian mothers and mountain men fathers. Narcissa seemed happy. "Here we are," she wrote, "one family alone, a way mark, as it were, or center post, about which multitudes will or must gather this winter. And these we must feed and warm, to the extent of our powers."

But despite the extended family and the hundreds of travelers to care for, Narcissa often grew melancholy. The Cayuse resisted the introduction of Christianity and feared the heavy influx of white settlers would threaten their lands.

In 1847, a measles epidemic transmitted from that year's wagon train infected the Cayuse who had no immunity to the white disease. Despite Marcus' efforts to save them, half the Cayuse died. A half-blood named Joe Lewis, bent on stirring up trouble, told the superstitious Cayuse the Whitmans had purposely poisoned the air to kill them. His lies worked.

On November 29, 1847, the Cayuse attacked the mission, killing 13 people - men, women, and children - and capturing some four dozen others. The mutilated bodies of Narcissa and Marcus were hastily buried in a shallow grave, only to be shortly dug up and gnawed on by scavenging wolves.

Word of the unprovoked slaughter prompted Congress to act. The following year, a bill created the Oregon Territory, the nation's first formal territorial government west of the Rocky Mountains.

Today, the Whitman Mission National Historic Site exists on the spot where the Whitmans lived and died, a tribute to the earnest attempts of two transplanted easterners to bring religion, civilization, and comfort across a continent.

A 27-foot monument crowns the hill Narcissa often stood atop to catch a glimpse of Marcus returning from one of his several trips away from the mission. It provides a panoramic view of the entire valley where the mission once functioned. An easy self-guiding walking trail with wayside markers takes visitors along the excavated foundations of the mission house and assorted buildings, the site of a tombstone to little Alice Clarissa who drowned in the nearby Walla Walla River, and the scene of the mass grave where the remains of the victims were interred.

A visitor center displays exhibits and sells souvenirs, and a picnic area is nearby. Demonstrations of pioneer activities are provided during the summer.

Whitman Mission National Historic Site lies along U.S. Highway 12, about six miles west of Walla Walla, Washington. A modest admission is charged, and the site is open daily, excepting major holidays, during customary daytime hours. The site can be toured within an hour or two.

Hells Canyon National Recreation Area is a few hours southeast along the Snake River in Oregon.

WASHINGTON, D.C.

BLOOD, SEX, AND LINCOLN'S SKULL

On August 4, 1862, Carleton Burgan, a private in Company B of Purnell's Maryland Legion, entered General Hospital in Frederick, Maryland, his mouth oozing sores, his tongue dry, his body dripping with sweat. Prior to checking in, he had taken massive amounts of calomel, a powerful purgative of mercurial chloride, which physicians had said would cure his pneumonia. But the overdose had caused gangrene; and, by the 21st, it had chewed away his upper mouth, palate, and right cheek and approached his right eye. By the 27th, it had created a gaping hole in the right center of his face.

On October 1, surgeons removed his right superior maxilla (upper jawbone) to stanch any residual gangrenous action. Gurdon Buck, a surgeon from New York, and Thomas Gunning, a New York dentist, worked on restoring his face. A half-dozen intricate surgical procedures rendered Burgan the first facially restored patient and paved the way for future reconstructive surgery.

Hideous before and after photographs of Burgan, plaster casts of his face, and his actual maxilla are displayed at the National Museum of Health and Medicine of the Armed Forces Institute of Pathology run by the Department of the Army in the nation's capital. Part-tent freak show, part-X-rated sex exhibit, part-scientific archives, the museum is shocking, titillating, bizarre, scholarly, and fascinating.

Carleton Burgan's cheek is not the only curiosity on display. In unheralded fashion, the museum showcases: the bullet that killed Abraham Lincoln, shattered shards of his skull, and locks of his hair removed from near the bullet's entrance; part of the spinal cord and vertebrae from his assassin, John Wilkes Booth; a young female brain shrunken by syphilis; and an embarrassingly large collection of prophylactics from 1920 to 1988 (Sheiks, Ramses, Chariots, and Rubber Ducky condoms).

The condom display boldly discusses the history of sexual protection since 1564 when fish bladders and animal skins served as "penis caps." A prophylaxis kit, made by the Comfort Manufacturing Company in 1942 for members of the U.S. Army and carrying specific personal instructions on its proper usage, now rests on a shelf for anyone to read. Scores of posters of early 20th-century vintage illustrate the anti-venereal disease message physicians tried to get across ("Surgeon Sage Says - Only a poor boob pays his money, loses his watch, gets the syph, and brags that he's had a good time").

Venereal disease occupies a large portion of the museum, and wax models of earlier eras, used by physicians as visual aids, are startlingly real: a face bearing the scars of tertiary syphilis, circa 1870; disconnected penises partially eaten away by gonorrhea and primary syphilis, circa 1893 and 1917; and a syphilitic tongue from 1910. Photographs of actual victims, faces horribly mutilated by open syphilitic lesions, adorn the wall in graphic abundance.

Two cutaway models of the male and female sexual organs, life-size and correct in every way, down to the smallest vein and curliest hair, often surprise visitors.

And the amount of real body parts on display overwhelms all but the most jaded. Actual male and female pelvises are shown to illustrate the narrowness of the former and the breadth of the latter, part of the exhibit explaining why childbirth is often difficult for humans and not for animals, who possess broader pelvic expanses.

A line of skeletons, ranging from four months in the fetal stage to five years in actual life, stands rigidly at attention.

A smoker's cancerous lung, overtaken by dark black tar and carbon buildups and white areas where cancer was growing at the time of death, sits in a preservative-laced container. Adjoining glass boxes show a 76-year-old iron miner's lung shot through with black hematite and a coal miner's lung darkened from years of inhaling coal dust. A nearby cutaway depicts syphilitic aortitis, an "aneurysm rupturing into the esophagus."

In another area, a scarred portion of the interior wall of a heart chamber denotes damage done by cardiac arrest.

Other exhibits show cancer robustly strangling the lining of someone's large intestine...colon polyps...kidneys, both whole and in cross-section slivers...liver slices (looking like what you might eat from a plate, minus the onions)...syphilitic cirrhosis livers, fatty livers, and plastinated sections with metastatic carcinomas. These are not clay or plastic models, but parts of once-alive human beings.

More than Abraham Lincoln's naked bones are exposed. Fragments of femurs, fibulas, and phalanges rest in display cases echoing a somber story of mortal lives ruined by the armaments of the Civil War. In some instances, bullets that tore limbs apart rest embedded in the bones lining the trophy cases. The right knee of an unnamed soldier, its patella gone, carries the "spherical ball" that blew it away.

Among miscellaneous jaws, elbows, and lower arms is a partially shattered skull. Text tells the tale:

> Cranium of a black soldier recovered in 1876 from Morris Island, SC near the battery of Fort Wagner. The shell fragment shown entered behind the left ear and exited through the right temporal region. Ft. Wagner, under siege by union troops from July 10 to Sept. 6, 1863, was the site of a battle on July 18, 1863 involving the 54th Massachusetts Volunteers, a black regiment.

The details may sound familiar; they were the basis for "Glory," a hit movie of recent years.

Many of the exhibits go beyond grisly into ghoulish. In the "Health and the Human Body" section, markedly cooler to accommodate the plethora of human parts stored everywhere, you can stretch your finger through a small hole in a plastic container and touch the inside of someone's stomach (it feels rubbery and cold). You can gape at a giant stomach-shaped hairball, removed from the stomach of a 12-year-old girl who ingested her hair for six years. You can peer into the chalk-like white stomach of some forgotten person who died of "Phenol Poisoning," a probable suicide.

The most arresting - and disturbing - section is "Human Growth, Reproduction & Development." Fetuses on parade, from early term to ninth-month, and looking white and plastic in their solution-filled glass cases, are explained thusly:

> To the best of our knowledge, their survival was prevented by natural causes or accidents. The sutures seen in some cases result from autopsies that were performed.

It does not quite prepare you for what you see: a potential human Cyclops, with a single eye implanted in the forehead, a victim of Cyclopia; a bloated dwarf, victim of Achondroplasia; a half-human, half-tadpole creature illustrating "Sirenomdia (fusion of lower limbs)...thought to be produced by alterations in early development of the blood vessels. Resultant defects include a single lower extremity with backward facing knees and feet, resembling the flipper of a mermaid;" "Conjoined Twins," tragic genetic accidents joined either at the head (two eyes, one nose, one mouth, three ears) or at the chest (looking like little dolls, with adorable reddish-blonde hair, except for the gutwrenching joining of their chests); and an example of Anencephaly (congenital absence of the brain and spinal cord) - a troll-like figure, horrifying to look at, with bulging eyes, curled ears, and a darting tongue.

The accompanying text offers a modicum of comfort:

> Most embryos and fetuses with gross genetic abnormalities are aborted spontaneously during the first trimester since those abnormalities are not compatible with life. Other fetuses with abnormalities may survive the pregnancy but be stillborn. Occasionally, survival is possible after birth.

You keep telling yourself it's only a museum, as you move from one shocking scene to another. You are essentially touring a macabre cemetery, looking at the body parts of dead people. When you view the skeleton of an achondroplastic dwarf, reflecting a congenital disorder that caused bones to cease growing in an early stage, and read the explanation, you understand the difference between a dwarf (abnormal trunk-to-limb ratio) and a midget (normal trunk-to-limb ratio but abnormally short height), yet you still recoil at the sight of the skeletal structure of an elderly woman who once lived. What if she had been your mother? Your daughter?

Likewise, viewing the presumed skull of an Ohio hotel worker whom British novelist Charles Dickens met and wrote of in his "Notes on American Travel" and who died of syphilis in 1868 strikes a discordant chord. She may have been a prostitute, as Dickens implied, but seeing the cold skull that once encased her every thought - since reduced, in the exhibit's text, to a "specimen" showing "characteristic lesions of tertiary syphilis: destruction of areas of bones and the presence of nodules and cavitations of the cranial vault" - strips her in death of any scrap of dignity she may have clung to in life.

Not everything is morbid. Interactive video displays throughout the "Health and the Human Body" room provide personalized and general information on skin, the heart, the lungs, the stomach, the kidneys, and the liver. An exercise bicycle gauges your pulse. Another video by the Lincoln display allows visitors to see how Lincoln's wound would be monitored by computer technology today.

An entire wing traces the "Evolution of the Microscope" with hundreds of models. Other sections explore the "History of Medicine," "Medical Instruments," and "AIDS." Hundreds of syringes, lancets, medicine chests and kits, cutaway models of hospital railroad cars, ships, and wagons, trephining instruments, saws, dental tools, eyeglasses, hooks, spatulas, and ophthalmoscopes vie with the cadaver parts for your attention. Bloodletting, the once-revered medical procedure that killed George Washington, is explained; five live leeches crawl around in a bowl. Information pulses around every corner. Up-to-date brochures on AIDS, Alzheimer's, and other current maladies are free for the taking.

A descendant of the original Army Medical Museum started in 1862 to further advances in both medicine and surgery, the museum rotates its exhibits. That may explain why a pickled testicle of gargantuan proportions formerly on display might be unavailable during your visit. Highly regarded in health circles, the museum helped develop a vaccine for typhoid fever, made films warning of venereal contagion, and furthered the study of worldwide disease. The museum became a National Historic Landmark in 1965 and adopted its current name in 1989.

A trip to the National Museum of Health and Medicine is intriguing and delivers information with a resounding wallop. It is also deeply disturbing. Adults might wish to counsel small or impressionable children if they bring them along.

The museum is free and open daily, except Christmas, during normal daytime hours. An estimated 80-100 people visit each day.

The museum suggests a stay of at least one or two hours. It is located in Building 54 of the Walter Reed Army Medical Center between Georgia Avenue and 16th Street in the Northwest quadrant of Washington, D.C. It is scheduled to move to the downtown section in close proximity to the other federal buildings sometime around the turn of the century.

Researchers may avail themselves of the museum's document and specimen archives.

A final footnote: a visit to the museum may diminish your appetite for either food or sex immediately afterward.

WEST VIRGINIA

GOD'S GOLD

It is a diamond in the rough. A grandiose, gaudy structural gemstone in a state not noted for them. A literal palace of gold amidst twisting roads and potholes, rural hills and the all-pervasive smell of coal.

Seasonal flower gardens, four ornate gazebos, and a hundred small fountains surround one of the most serenely beautiful spots in America - a temple of gold with globe-topped balustrades, filigreed walls, and scalloped arches and domes, a sumptuous palace for a man who never lived there, a tribute to the earthly memory of A. C. Bhaktivedanta Swami Prabhupada, the Indian-born Abhay Charan De who became a spiritual master of Krishna consciousness, one of America's least-understood religions.

Recorded eastern music swells the air. Members of the Krishna community and nearby West Virginians tend the flower gardens whose roses have won awards for their beauty.

The interior of the Palace of Gold is opulent beyond words. Photographs cannot do it justice.

The galleries around the inner rooms radiate gold: baseboards, cornices, chandeliers, doors, window casings, ceiling mirror frames, urns. Sunlight plays through the vibrant colors of two dozen stained glass windows. Marble luxuriates in dark green shades on the inner walls and in diamond patterns on the floors. Austrian and Czech crystals decorate a succession of chandeliers.

Intricate royal peacock windows flank the front and rear ends of the palace. Each holds a peacock crafted in gold and surrounded by hundreds of stained glass pieces. The peacock is special to Krishna "devotees" (pronounced "da-VO-tees") because the Lord Krishna adorned his hair with that bird's feathers. Imported teakwood predominates throughout.

The interior rooms become an ornate museum to Prabhupada (pronounced Prah-bup-AH-dah). The study exhibits a wax figure ("murti") of a bespectacled Prabhupada studiously translating Vedic scriptures from Sanskrit and Bengali into English on a marble table. A teakwood altar to the deities Krishna and Radha holds a pair of antique Chinese vases donated by Alfred Ford, grandson of automobile industrialist Henry Ford. Wainscoting beautifies the walls and floors. The heads of lions, revered for their embodiment of spiritual strength, symbolize Krishna's message to mankind and quietly roar out from wall panels and the chair upon which the murti sits.

The bedroom seems lifted directly from "1,001 Arabian Nights." A gold brocaded spread covers a single bed underneath a handsome painting of Krishna as a child. A teakwood wardrobe with bas relief carvings of Krishna in childhood activities and a teak-filigreed chair decorate either side of a door of gold and glass. Hourglass urns repose on the floor, and a two-tiered chandelier centers a ceiling of hundreds of hand-painted flowers. Italian Botticino marble and amber Persian onyx compose the walls.

An adjoining bathroom features a 300-pound sink of gray-orange marble with rose quartz, 22-karat gold faucets.

The inner sanctum is the opulent Temple Hall, with colored lights and incense, surrounded on all sides by a majesty only hinted at in the previous rooms. The entrance doors combine flowers, lotus stalks, and elephants - all important symbols in India - in teak beneath a scalloped arch highlighted by thousandth-inch-thick gold leaf (the total 22-karat gold measures 8,000 square feet and weighs five pounds, according to devotee guides). The vaulted ceiling, containing idealized murals and anchored by an antique French chandelier with immense Marie Antoinette pendants, towers above symmetrical marble pillars surmounted by gold capitals and cornices. Oil paintings adorn the walls.

A sculpted teakwood entrance, itself a miniature palace, frames a deeply recessed altar within the Temple Hall. A murti of Prabhupada sits regally on a black and white onyx, bejeweled, golden throne under a massive gold-encrusted canopy; jewels and gold ornament his crown, scepter, and ceremonial robes, as befits an honored representative of God (the human Prabhupada actually wore customary pajama-like trousers and robes of much humbler fabric).

The central dome weighs 30 tons and encircles a 4,200-piece crystal ceiling.

Devotee members of the community, formally called New Vrindaban and founded in 1968 on a rural farm by Kirtanananda Swami Bhaktipada, constructed the palace and elaborate grounds with over 250 tons of imported marble, teakwood, and precious raw materials in homage to Prabhupada who sanctioned Bhaktipada, a chief disciple, to start the community in America. Many of the workers who toiled throughout the 1970s on the monumental project still reside within the community.

Dying in 1977, Prabhupada did not live to see the completion of the palace. Plans still call for more additions: the near half-mile-long Gardens of Transcendental Knowledge, replete with fountains, waterways, cascading waterfalls, a golden-glass conservatory for tropical plants mentioned in scripture, and an interfaith garden where statues of God and/or His prophets as interpreted by all the world's major religions (Jesus, Buddha, Muhammad, etc.) will stand; and a Radha Krishna Temple, "the world's largest solid granite temple carved in the classic Vedic style."

The palace basement holds a gift shop with both imported and locally made items, Nathaji's Palace Restaurant where Krishna meatless strictures meld eastern foods with western culinary habits, and an art gallery and lounge with scriptural quotes covering Baha'i, Buddhism, Christianity, Confucianism, Hinduism, Islam, Jainism, Judaism, Sikhism, Zoroastrianism, and Native American beliefs.

The heart (perhaps "soul" would be a more apt metaphor) of New Vrindaban is a few hundred yards northwest and down a road from the eminence the palace occupies. A large manmade pond, gazebos, and a pair of immense sculpted dancing deities point the way. A larger-than-life elephant kneels at the entrance of the parking lot. Just beyond are the community's living quarters and monastery, office, natural health food store, fruit juice and frozen dessert stand, guest lodge and cabins, conference center, and traditional Krishna church. The Temple of Understanding, as ornately spectacular in design as the Palace of Gold, displays a likeness of the Christian Jesus kneeling and conducts early morning, noon, afternoon, and evening services for devotees and visitors. Early morning means just that - 5 a.m. Breakfast follows at 7:30, to provide an idea of New Vrindaban's priorities. Between services, devotees frequently chant delicately flowing singsong melodies for the glorification of Krishna.

New Vrindaban conducts four annual interfaith conferences for the exchange of other holy traditions.

For those, whose only contact with the sometimes-bald, white-robed "Hare Krishnas" has been in airports and who view them as cultish, weird, and threatening, a few words of explanation might be helpful. A Temple of Understanding sign explains the "Deities of the Lord:"

> Although there's only One Eternal and Supreme God, He appears in different forms at different places according to the different time and circumstances. In other words, He expands Himself to assume different personalities to accomplish His purposes.
> Just like an actor, the Lord plays various roles for His enjoyment. Each of these personalities has different aspects and qualities, and performs various activities (called pastimes). Each devotee of the Lord is attracted to one or another of these

transcendental personalities. Even though God is One, He provides a variety of ways to capture the heart of His devotee.

Just as one devotee may be attracted to Lord Jesus Christ, others are attracted to Lord Krishna, Lord Rama, Lord Jagannatha or any other bona-fide form of the Lord. In this way, the devotee always thinks of God with love and devotion.

Devotee guides explain further:

We chant the name of God when we say, "Hare Krishna, Hare Krishna, Krishna Krishna, Hare Hare, Hare Rama, Hare Rama, Rama Rama, Hare Hare," because it is the only way to perfection. The Lord has many names. People chant the name of Jesus or Yahweh or Allah. Christ is Krishna in other languages. Jesus is our guru, which is the highest tribute you could pay anyone.

Prabhupada came to America and accepted other faiths. He was more concerned with people developing a love for God than with developing an alien system. He said, "I'm not trying to teach you something new. I'm just trying to tell you what you've forgotten." He was always respectful of other religions.

Devotees define Krishna consciousness as love of God and point to Prabhupada's emergence in America as a divine mission from his spiritual master (Srila Bhaktisiddhanta Saraswati) to spread the eastern Krishna consciousness to the western world. Prabhupada didn't invent the Hare Krishna movement; he only brought it to America.

One painting along the gallery in the Palace of Gold foreshadows the cynicism and intrigue with which westerners frequently greet the Krishna faith. The "Changing Bodies Exhibit" graphically shows the essence of a human soul passing through a succession of bodies, fetus to child to adolescent to adult to elder to skeleton, and then resuming the same cycle in another series of bodies. It metaphorically pictures reincarnation, the transmigration of a unique soul from one host to another. The initial shock of the inevitability of death vanishes with the realization that the soul eternally goes on. Devotees comment:

> The soul is indestructible. Though we cannot scientifically discover the soul or consciousness and see it through a microscope, it is mentioned in every religious tradition in the world. Just because something cannot be perceived through empiricism does not mean it does not exist. Does love exist?

An average fee is charged for a devotee-guided tour of the Palace of Gold; it lasts 30-45 minutes. Touring the outside grounds is free. No proselytizing pressure is applied.

The New Vrindaban community may also be toured free at your own leisure. Devotees may approach you, but in a friendly, nonconfrontational manner smacking only of hospitality.

When entering the Palace of Gold and the Temple of Understanding, you must place shoe covers over your footwear; they are provided at the entrances.

The grounds are open year-round till dark. The summer season is the busiest; at other times, you may have an entire tour to yourself.

The Palace of Gold is just a few miles south of Limestone in Marshall County in the northern spoke of West Virginia thrusting up between Ohio and Pennsylvania. From U.S. Highway 250, take "Limestone Hill-Palace Road-44" east for 3.7 miles; you'll notice signs along the bumpy way. But nothing will prepare you for the fragrant incense, eastern music, symmetrical beauty, and ethereal serenity of the sight at the end of the road. And you don't have to be a Krishna to experience that.

WISCONSIN

LIONS AND TIGERS AND BARABOOS

The "Greatest Show on Earth" got that way because of human freaks and oddities that Phineas Taylor Barnum, the father of the circus, and others of his ilk exhibited, anomalies of nature like: Carlos Leal ("Senor Diablo"), the human fire eater; the Siamese Twins Chang and Eng, joined at the breast, who wed different wives in a quadruple-ring ceremony and together sired 22 children; Jo-Jo ("The Dogface Boy") who had an unusual amount of hair on his cheeks and forehead; and Anna Swan who massed 426 pounds on a 7'11" frame.

The "Greatest Show on Earth" got that way because of the enterprising children of German-born August Rungeling and Salome Juliar - brothers Al, Alf, Charles, Henry, John, and Otto, who changed their surname to Ringling and started the most famous dynasty ever associated with lions, tigers, and dancing bears.

The "Greatest Show on Earth" got that way because of Irvin Feld, the showman who created the Ringling Bros. Barnum & Bailey Clown College and introduced famed big cat trainer Gunther Gebel-Williams.

The "Greatest Show on Earth" got that way because of clowns like Otto Griebling, Lou Jacobs, and Emmett Kelly.

There's a place in America that honors freaks and impresarios and clowns. It is Circus World Museum, where visitors roam the stables, cookhouse, dressing tents, and private quarters of a circus backyard.

At Circus World Museum, an 85-foot trailer used by the Ringling Bros. Barnum & Bailey Circus provides information on everything about the behind-the-scenes operations of press agents and banner tackers and bill posters.

Circus World Museum exhibits the last center pole ever used by the Ringling Bros. Barnum & Bailey Circus - 62 feet of Oregon fir, one of four supports for the celestial canvas that covered three performing rings and 10,000 audience seats in 1956.

The W. W. Deppe Wagon Pavilion at Circus World Museum holds a segment of the world's largest collection (more than 150) of ornate, gaudy, brilliantly colored circus parade wagons, many of them once owned by Wilbur W. Deppe, a former circus entrepreneur: the 5.5-ton Pawnee Bill Bandwagon, built in 1903 for the Pawnee Bill Wild West Show, with American flag pennons, gold-painted friezes, and silver-filigreed flourishes; the Swan Bandwagon of 1905, a white chariot with golden swans, cherubs, and sea creatures emerging from rolling blue waves, formerly owned by Walt Disney Productions and featured in the movies "Jumbo" and "Toby Tyler," among others; the Two Hemispheres Bandwagon, the largest circus wagon ever constructed; and a Bostock & Wombwell Bandchariot that dates back to the Civil War era and is the oldest extant wagon.

That same pavilion also houses: the world's largest collection of American circus carvings; an immense concentration of posters and canvases advertising seemingly every circus that ever existed; exhibits on circus paraphernalia; an actual circus train showing the proper loading order of cars (stock cars for animals, coaches for personnel, flatcars for wagons, and advertising cars for advance publicity people); scores of historic circus photographs; the shoes and wristwatch worn by tightrope walker Karl Wallenda when he plunged to his death; and a wall of information on freaks, whose exploitation in side shows predated circuses (they were first exhibited in England in the 16th century; the first-known American show involved a female dwarf in 1771).

Circus World Museum's Irvin Feld Exhibit Hall & Visitor Center explains how President Woodrow Wilson inspired a catchphrase by throwing his hat into the ring of the Ringling Bros.

Circus in 1916 to signify his desire to run in that year's presidential race.

The Ring Barn Building displays the last red and blue Ringling Bros. flag ever flown above the Big Top (July 15, 1956, in Pittsburgh, Pennsylvania), just before circuses began turning to arenas, coliseums, and auditoriums. It also honors clowns in a hall of fame setting and provides a huge miniature cutaway version of a traditional outdoor Big Top circus and an electronic question and answer board that quizzes visitors on circus knowledge.

The Elephant Barn holds a Wild West exhibit featuring Buffalo Bill's restored ticket wagon and relates facts about the film actors who first started in circuses (William "Hopalong Cassidy" Boyd, Hoot Gibson, Kirby "Sky King" Grant, and Buck Jones).

Circus World Museum conducts train-loading and clown demonstrations. A walk along Water Street, outside the grounds, showcases historical markers identifying landmark buildings associated with the Ringling name: the Wild Animal Barn with its intact sunken hippopotamus tank; the Elephant Barn where rings, formerly used to tether a herd of elephants, still hang; the hotel where three floors of rooms housed many circus employees.

The Circus World Museum is in Baraboo, Wisconsin, where on May 19, 1884, the Ringling Brothers, the quintessential circus family, pitched their first circus tent. They remained there till 1918 just before their merger with Barnum & Bailey, another giant circus conglomerate.

Circus World Museum started in Baraboo in 1956 with a stock car, a coach, and eight baggage wagons. It now owns the greatest collection of circus artifacts and information in the world. The State Historical Society of Wisconsin owns the National Historic Landmark. It's where to go if you want to find costumes worn by circus midgets Michu and Juliana for their twice-daily staged weddings in 1976-77 and Gunther Gebel-Williams' sequin-laden black, silver, and gold boots, pants, and vest worn during his November 18, 1990 career swan song performance in Pittsburgh and Emmett Kelly's costume worn by actor Henry Fonda when portraying him in "Clown."

Circus World Museum includes a petting zoo, the Robert L. Parkinson Library and Research Center (the world's largest circus history respository), concession stands, an animal menagerie (where elephants are kept when not performing), "doodoo-doodledoodle-doodoo-doodoo" music concerts throughout the day, a film on Gebel-Williams in the Feld Exhibit Hall theater, gift shops, and picnic facilities. It straddles the narrow Baraboo River near one of its more prominent bends along Water Street, just east of the intersection with Broadway. Signs point the way throughout Baraboo.

The city in south-central Wisconsin, northwest of Madison, formerly served as the home base for the great American circus before Bridgeport, Connecticut, Sarasota, Florida, and currently Venice, Florida.

The entrance fee - around $10 during the mid-90s - buys a day's admission, good for all demonstrations and programs, a circus parade through the dusty streets of the complex, and as many of the one-hour actual circus performances under a real Big Top as you care to take in. We gave Circus World Museum nearly eight hours and had to spend the last couple hours just taking a slow walk past exhibit corridors, letting our eyes merely bounce from one staggering information board to another. The museum complex constantly expands its holdings.

Hours fluctuate. The visitor center and select exhibit buildings on the north side of the river remain open all year during normal daytime hours. Both sides of the Baraboo, including the south (where the Big Top and demonstration shows occur), open during prime tourist season (early May to mid-September); during most of July and August, the daily hours extend to 10 p.m.

Wisconsin Dells, the state's most famous natural phenomenon and a major tourist destination, is just 15 miles north.

A SECLUDED SLICE OF SCANDINAVIA

It's a land of elves and trolls, twisting rills and manicured meadows, where the trills of Scandinavians long gone still softly echo in the hollows among the hills.

But it was just 40 acres of virgin wilderness along a ridge in southern Wisconsin when Osten Olson Haugen of Tinn Telemarken, Norway bought it in 1856, intent on carving out for himself and his family a slice of the old country. He selected the tract because its hill-snuggling valleys reminded him of his roots. He felled trees and used the lumber to construct his Norse simulation: a stue (or dwelling house), where he would live; a stabbur (storage house) for grain, bread, and meat; a cow barn and horse shed. A spring provided drinking water. The land supported farming and grazing.

The Haugens doubled the size of their valley farm over the next six and a half decades. Some of the children married and moved; the parents stayed and died. In 1920, the remaining family left, and the buildings were empty.

In 1927, Isak J. Dahle, a businessman of Norwegian descent, purchased the valley and its buildings. Fashioning it into a summer residence for his family, he christened it "Nissedahle - The Valley of the Elves." He spent the last decade of his life transforming the estate into a faithful reproduction of a Norwegian community. He drained the soggy bottomland, carved shallow pools from the fields, turned stables and storage barns into cottages, repaired buildings, and constructed new ones (a springhouse and a new cottage with a sod roof).

He also imported the famous "Norway Building" in 1935. The "stavkirke," a model of a 12th-century Norse Christian church, had arrived in the United States from Trondheim, Norway in 1893 for exhibit in the World's Columbian Exposition in Chicago. Sculpted pine wood dominates the vaulted ceiling, the faces of Norwegian monarchs hanging from exposed beams, and a series of acutely angled peaks with dragons lurching from gables. Shingles shaped like dragon scales cover the roof.

Visitors began showing up at his "Little Norway" restoration. Dahle's sister, Mrs. Asher Hobson, who obtained the grounds upon his death in 1937, showed the buildings for free at first. But the increase in visitation necessitated tour guides and groundskeepers which eventually meant fees.

Little Norway still draws crowds, an estimated 30-38,000 annually during its six-month season (May-October). Guided tours last 45-60 minutes and depart from the gift shop where ethnic music always plays and employees wear authentic Norse attire. The path twists downward into the valley past carved gnomes, elves, fairies, and trolls and by all the dozen buildings of log construction with peaks, cupolas and distinct blue window, door, and trim paint. The buildings contain antiques, old implements, and furniture typical of Norse pioneering life. Many relics of the Haugen family still fill tables, shelves, and walls. Rosemaling, Norwegian folk art, adds luster to trunks, tablecloths, and pottery. Harvest cradles with wheels and runners, six-legged rockers, and "sleep-tight" beds make up part of America's largest private collection of Norwegian artifacts.

The main cabin, formerly the Haugens' livestock barn, houses a kitchen and dining room where cattle once trod. The long tables contain secret compartments concealing feather ticks and convert into instant beds. The walls nearly collapse under the weight of wooden spoons and ale bowls with carved dragon heads. The upstairs loft includes squat, squarish canopied bunk beds (called "himmelseng"), in which occupants slept nearly sitting up, their backs propped against thick pillows).

The stue, where the Haugens lived, holds portraits and period furniture in two compressed rooms, one downstairs, one upstairs, connected by a steeply angled six-step ladder that Mrs. Haugen climbed every day, toting a child and a lantern. Upstairs, two single beds meet at right angles to one another, joined by an oversize square pillow, upon which the heads of both occupants touch, the only allowable intimacy the L-shaped placement allows. In front of the pillow, where the beds join, a "grievance" bench faces outward, inviting antagonistic spouses to sit together and make up before heading off to bed in their separate horizontal directions.

The stavkirke holds a wealth of artworks and antiques: an original 1873 musical manuscript of the young Edvard Grieg, Norway's celebrated composer; jewelry, glassware, and silver; hand-carved wooden chests; a wedding sleigh; and men's and women's bootjacks, the ladies' with a hinged modesty board to prevent milady's ankle from being seen while her boot was removed.

The stalde once housed a team of horses; farm implements now decorate it. The laden, formerly a granary, is now a cottage. The stabbur once used to keep foodstuffs fresh for the long haul; accordingly, it rests on four raised pegs to protect it from animal intrusion, and 18 inches of open space separate the top stair from the front door to deny rodents access.

The administration building sports a sod roof. In Norway, such roofs often topped houses built into hillsides; grazing goats kept the grass low (Little Norway's sod is cut by maintenance workers).

Picnicking is allowed, and a gift shop sells a wide variety of Scandinavian items, including fine-crafted jewelry, coverlets, and figures. Admission is about average for the length of the tour.

Little Norway is just northeast of Blue Mounds in Dane County. In the Blue Mounds area, follow County Road ID east until it intersects with County Road JG; then pursue JG a short distance to the access road for Little Norway. The site is well-marked.

Just to the east, Mount Horeb, the self-styled "troll capital of the world," prides itself on craft, specialty, and antique shops, museums, and carved trolls who peer at you from every corner of its downtown area. Little Norway is also close to the House on the Rock, near Spring Green, Wisconsin's premier attraction, one of the most awesome collections of virtually everything collectible.

WYOMING

HOW TO GO TO HELL IN WYOMING

It bleeds brown and white in its various striations. The white sometimes appears gray, even blue, depending on the time of day and position of the sun. The brown alternates tan with amber. Brush and grass grow on the bottom. Pinnacles sprout from unseen depths. Deep creases furrow the walls. Caves pit the sides like disfiguring pockmarks. Bony gullies undulate along the valleys. Multi-colored stone pyramids rise and fall. Shrubs poke out from the unlikeliest outcroppings.

It appears desolate, impenetrable, foreboding.

At length, your eyes may seem to deceive you. You may notice what appears to be a small patch of color moving at the very bottom of the abyss. Eventually, you'll notice the microscopic blotches of color may wave at you, as you stand at cliff's edge, and show themselves to be fellow human beings prowling through this Devil's Den, this Satan's Snare. The intrepid adventurers often turn out to be children who are relatives or friends of the people who manage the lodge and restaurant atop the heights.

Welcome to Hell...Wyoming-style.

Plunked nearly in the dead center of the state, Hell's Half Acre is a natural curiosity directly south of U.S. Highways 20 and 26, about halfway between Waltman and Powder River, two rural route intersections some half a hundred miles west of Casper.

Hell's Half Acre is actually 320 acres of starkly jagged terrain bearing an artist's palette of earthtones, compressing the color, grandeur, and topographical variety of the Grand Canyon and Bryce Canyon into a limited area. Hell's Half Acre is privately owned.

There are no interpretive markers, no specially constructed observation points, no switchback trails cut by modern man, no rules or regulations. It is simply a hands-on visual wonder, created by nature over millennia in the usual erosive way.

A portion of it can be seen from the highway; it is that close to the road. From the parking lot at the top, a short walk of a few dozen yards leads to any of several natural vantage points overlooking the steep drop. If you decide to descend, remember there are no maintained trails anywhere. You'll have to slide down an end where the descent is least-steep. Good sneakers or hiking boots are a must. You can't really get too lost down at the bottom if you keep track of the sun and the section of rim you descended; common sense dictates a return to the surface before nightfall, however.

The first men to inhabit the rugged valley probably had reddish complexions. A concentration of buffalo bones and flint arrowheads indicates that Native Americans probably induced herds of buffalo into the canyon for butchering. The lone historical marker at the top mentions that Captain B. L. E. Bonneville and white visitors ventured to the site in 1833.

The site brochure refers to it as "the only natural geological phenomenon of its kind in the United States" and "320 acres of beauty in the middle of the open plains." It also maintains that the Indians knew the area as "Burning Mountain" because of "vapors which could be seen rising." The vapors are gone, but deer and smaller wildlife are there in abundance; expect to see them at night. And if you're present during an electrical storm, as we were, expect a particularly eerie experience as lightning flashes across the chasm and thunder reverberates through the benighted recesses.

A motel, campground, restaurant, gas station, and gift shop are just off the highway. Crowds are not a concern; you may well be alone. The site is free.

Hell's Half Acre is near Casper, which has historical, wildlife, and art museums, a fish hatchery, and the midsummer Central Wyoming Fair and Rodeo. And the popular Yellowstone and Grand Teton National Parks are to the west.

And there are far worse things to do in Wyoming than going to Hell.

BIBLIOGRAPHY

Much of the source material for this book came from the sites themselves: brochures, complimentary tourist newspapers and publications, postcards, newspaper clippings, and other material usually considered "throwaway" items to be picked up by visitors while touring and casually discarded shortly thereafter. Full bibliographic credits are rarely included in such items. Whenever possible, full documentation is provided in the following sources.

Books and Booklets

_____. Cathedral of the Pines Wedding Book. 1994.
_____. Desert of Maine.
_____. DeWint House National Shrine.
_____. Franklin D. Roosevelt's Little White House and Museum. Atlanta: Georgia Department of Natural Resources.
_____. Memorial Stones and Gifts.
_____. Pictorial History of The Cabin Home in Garden of Eden.
_____. Prabhupada's Palace of Gold. Bhakti Books, 1986.
_____. Roadside America. Shartlesville, PA: Roadside America.
_____. Self Guided Hike/Bike Tour South Bass Island. Columbus, OH: The Ohio State University, 1985.
_____. Sermons in Stone The Life and Work of Brother Joseph. Cullman, AL: The Ave Maria Grotto.
_____. Sleepy Hollow Restorations Interior and Exterior Views of the Historic Sites. Sleepy Hollow Restorations, Inc., 1983.
_____. The Baha'i Faith. Wilmette, IL: Baha'i Publishing Trust.
_____. The Complete Guide to America's National Parks. Washington, D.C.: National Park Foundation, 1992.

_____. The Crockett Tavern-Museum.

_____. The Memorial Bell Tower.

_____. The Music House. Berrien Center, MI: Penrod/Hiawatha Company, 1988.

_____. The Shawnee Is Camping. U.S. Department of Agriculture, 1981.

_____. The Story of Aplets & Cotlets.

_____. The TMI-2 Story. GPU Nuclear Communications, 1991.

_____. The Wayfarers Chapel.

Allen, Maury. Roger Maris A Man for All Seasons. New York: Donald I. Fine, Inc., 1986.

Asbell, Bernard. When F.D.R. Died. New York: Holt, Rinehart and Winston, 1961.

Baigell, Matthew. A History of American Painting. New York: Praeger Publishers, 1971.

Baker, Carlos. Ernest Hemingway A Life Story. New York: Charles Scribner's Sons, 1969.

Bedinger, M. S. Valley of the Vapors Hot Springs National Park. Philadelphia: Eastern National Park & Monument Association, 1991.

Bellavance-Johnson, Marsha, and Lee Bellavance. Ernest Hemingway in Idaho. Ketchum, ID: The Computer Lab, 1989.

Bendure, Glenda, and Ned Friary. Hawaii A Travel Survival Kit. Berkeley, CA: Lonely Planet Publications, 1990.

Betts, Glynne Robinson. Writers in Residence American Authors at Home. New York: The Viking Press, 1981.

Biser, Sam, ed. A Vital Message from Lao Russell. Waynesboro, VA: University of Science and Philosophy, 1986.

Bishop, Jim. FDR's Last Year April 1944-April 1945. New York: Pocket Books, 1975.

Boatner III, Mark M. Landmarks of the American Revolution. Harrisburg, PA: Stackpole Books, 1973.

Boslough, John. America's National Parks. Lincolnwood, IL: Gallery Books, 1990.

Brock, Robert M. *The Apache Trail Guidebook.* Apache Junction, AZ: Orion Publishing Company, 1987.
Brown, D. Alexander. *The Lewis and Clark Expedition.* Harrisburg, PA: American History Illustrated, 1982.
Bryant, Lorinda Munson. *Pictures and Their Painters.* New York: John Lane Company, 1907.
Butler, Rev. John V. *Churchyards of Trinity Parish in the City of New York.* Corporation of Trinity Church, 1969.
Caldwell, Mark. *The Last Crusade.* New York: Atheneum, 1988.
_____. *Saranac Lake: Pioneer Health Resort.* Historic Saranac Lake, 1993.
Caploe, Andrew B. *A Guide to New York City Museums.* Cultural Assistance Center, Inc., 1981.
Clark, Ella E., and Margot Edmonds. *Sacagawea of the Lewis and Clark Expedition.* Berkeley, CA: University of California Press, 1979.
Clark, Glenn. *The Man Who Tapped the Secrets of the Universe.* Waynesboro, VA: The University of Science and Philosophy, 1989.
Collins, Dr. Reba N. *The Will Rogers Memorial.* Claremore, OK: The Will Rogers Memorial, 1979.
Colten, James. *The Apache Trail.* Apache Junction, AZ: Superstition Mountain Research Center, 1980.
Cornwell, Ilene J., and Deborah K. Henderson, and Cary R. Henderson. *Travel Guide to the Natchez Trace Parkway between Natchez, Mississippi, and Nashville, Tennessee.* Nashville: Southern Resources Unlimited, 1984.
Croft Mine Joint Powers Board. *Guide to the Croft Mine Historical Park.* Crosby-Ironton, MN.
Cromie, Robert, and Joseph Pinkston. *Dillinger A Short and Violent Life.* Evanston, IL: Chicago Historical Bookworks, 1990.
Culbertson, Judi, and Tom Randall. *Permanent Californians.* Chelsea, VT: Chelsea Green Publishing Company, 1989.
Curry, Tom, and Wood Cowan. *Famous Figures of the Old West.* Derby, CT: Monarch Books, Inc., 1965.

Dalton, David. James Dean: The Mutant King. San Francisco: Straight Arrow Books, 1974.

Davidson, James Dale. An Eccentric Guide to the United States. New York: G. P. Putnam's Sons, 1980.

Delgado, James P. America's National Parks. New York: Portland House, 1990.

Dunee, JoAnne. Portage Glacier and Turnagain Arm. Anchorage, AK: Ultima Thule Publishing Company, 1988.

Editors of Sunset Books and Sunset Magazine. National Parks of the West. Menlo Park, CA: Lane Publishing Co., 1983.

Editors of The Colorado Express, The. The Colorado Express Pocket Guide to Colorado. Denver: The Colorado Express, 1981.

Eubank, Nancy. The Lindberghs Three Generations. St. Paul: Minnesota Historical Society, 1975.

Eyster, Irving R., and Darlene Brown. Indian Key. Long Key, FL: 1976.

Feil, Elisabeth. Chimney Rock Park Forest Stroll. Chimney Rock Park, 1990.

_____. Chimney Rock Park Skyline-Cliff Trail Loop. 1989.

Foreman, Gary L. Crockett The Gentleman from the Cane. Dallas: Taylor Publishing Co.

Franks, Ray. Palo Duro Canyon State Park. Franks-Zulauf Publishing Company, 1966.

Frome, Michael. National Park Guide. Chicago: Rand McNally & Company, 1985.

Fulcher, Bob. Crockett's Woods A Self Guided Tour of the Davy Crockett Bluff Trail. Tennessee Department of Environment and Conservation, 1993.

Gallos, Philip L. Cure Cottages of Saranac Lake. Saranac Lake, NY: Historic Saranac Lake, 1985.

Hancock, Harold B. A History of Kent County Delaware. Dover, DE: Dover Litho Printing Company, 1975-76.

Hansen, Harry, ed. Colorado A Guide to the Highest State. New York: Hastings House, Publishers, 1970.

Haughey, Homer L., and Connie Kale Johnson. Jack London Homes

Album. Stockton, CA: Heritage Publishing, 1987.
Hayes, John P. Mooney The Life of the World's Master Carver. Midvale, OH: Dove Publishing Company, 1977.
Herndon, Venable. James Dean A Short Life. New York: Doubleday and Company, 1974.
Holland, James W. Andrew Jackson and the Creek War: Victory at the Horseshoe. University, AL: University of Alabama Press, 1968.
Hopley, Samuel P. "He Built an Altar." 1967.
Josephy, Jr., Alvin M. Chief Joseph's People and Their War. The Yellowstone Association, 1964.
Kane, Joseph Nathan. Facts About the Presidents. New York: Permabooks, 1960.
King, Joseph A. Winter of Entrapment. Toronto: P. D. Meany Publishers, 1992.
Kochmann, Rachel M. Presidents A Pictorial Guide to the Presidents (sic) Birthplaces, Homes, and Burial Sites. Osage, MN: Osage Publications, 1987.
Kouwenhoven, John A., ed. The New York Guidebook. New York: Dell Publishing Co., Inc., 1964.
Kubek, Tony, and Terry Pluto. Sixty-One The Team/The Record/The Man. New York: Macmillan Publishing Company, 1987.
Lane, Hana Umlauf, ed. The World Almanac & Book of Facts 1981. New York: Newspaper Enterprise Association, Inc., 1980.
Lossing, Benson J. Pictorial Field-Book of the Revolution. 2 vols. New York: Harper & Brothers, Publishers, 1860.
Mack, Jim. Haleakala The Story Behind the Scenery. KC Publications, Inc., 1989.
Magee, Judy. Cavern of Crime. Smithland, KY: The Livingston Ledger, 1973.
Martinez, Raymond J. Mysterious Marie Laveau Voodoo Queen. New Orleans: Hope Publications, 1956.
Mason, George C. The Life and Works of Gilbert Stuart. New York: Burt Franklin Reprints, 1972.
Mathews, Wendell, ed. Will Rogers: The Man and His Humor.

Racine, WI: Glenheath Publishers, 1991.

McGrane, Martin Edward. The James Farm. Madison, SD: Caleb Perkins Press, 1987.

Mead, Howard. Little Norway. Blue Mounds, WI: Little Norway, Incorporated.

Messick, Hank. King's Mountain The Epic of the Blue Ridge "Mountain Men" in the American Revolution. Boston: Little, Brown and Company, 1976.

Milton, Joyce. Loss of Eden A Biography of Charles and Anne Morrow Lindbergh. New York: HarperCollins Publishers, 1993.

Moore, Marie. Shrine of the Pines. Paul Bunyan Press, 1982.

Murphy, Dan. Lewis and Clark Voyage of Discovery. Las Vegas: KC Publications, Inc., 1988.

Nash, Jay Robert. Bloodletters and Badmen. New York: M. Evans and Company, Inc., 1973.

National Lexicographic Board, eds. Illustrated World Encyclopedia. 21 vols. New York: Illustrated World Encyclopedia, Inc., 1967.

Olson, Virgil J. and Helen. Capitol Reef The Story Behind the Scenery. KC Publications, Inc., 1990.

Phelps, Dawson A. The Natchez Trace Indian Trail to Parkway.

Phelps, Richard H. A History of Newgate of Connecticut. Salem, NH: AYER Company, Publishers, Inc., 1984.

Pitch, Anthony S. Washington, D.C. Sightseers' Guide. Potomac, MD: Mino Publications, Inc., 1992.

Reese, Eunice. Enchanted World Doll Museum. 1988.

Robotti, Frances Diane. Key to New York: Empire City. New York: Fountainhead Publishers, 1964.

Russell, Walter. The Secret of Working Knowingly with God. Waynesboro, VA: The University of Science and Philosophy, 1993.

Russell, Walter and Lao. A Vision Fulfilled! Waynesboro, VA: University of Science and Philosophy, 1989.

Sangster, Tom and Dess L. Alabama's Covered Bridges. Bay Minette,

AL: Coffeetable Publications, 1989.
Scar, Ethel C. The Great American. Winterset, IA: The John Wayne Birthplace.
Schneider, Norris F. The National Road Main Street of America. Columbus, OH: The Ohio Historical Society, 1987.
_____. Zane Grey. Zanesville, OH: published by author, 1967.
Settle, Jr., William A. Jesse James Was His Name. Lincoln, NE: University of Nebraska Press, 1977.
Shumard, George. Billy the Kid. Mesilla, NM: Mesilla Southwestern Old Times, 1972.
Sifakis, Carl. The Encyclopedia of American Crime. New York: SMITHMARK Publishers, Inc., 1992.
Smith, Helen Henry. Vikingsholm. Sunnyvale, CA: K/P Graphics, 1973.
Snyder, Gerald S. In the Footsteps of Lewis and Clark. National Geographic, 1970.
Stocker, Joseph. Travel Arizona. Phoenix: Arizona Highways Book, 1984.
Synnestvedt, Sig, ed. The Essential Swedenborg. New York: The Swedenborg Foundation, Inc., 1984.
Taylor, Robert. Saranac. Boston: Houghton Mifflin Company, 1986.
Thompson, Ernest T. The Fabulous David Crockett. Rutherford, TN: David Crockett Memorial Association, 1956.
Thompson, Erwin N. Whitman Mission National Historic Site. Washington, D.C.: National Park Service, 1964.
Towner, Jim. The Unofficial Guide to Fort Abraham Lincoln State Park. 1988.
Trachtman, Paul. The Gunfighters. (The Old West series). New York: Time-Life Books, 1976.
Trudeau, M.D., Edward Livingston. An Autobiography. Garden City, NY: Doubleday, Doran & Company, Inc., 1934.
Tshudy, Barbara Ann. The Pretzel Story.
Van Name, Fred. William Gillette...as Sherlock Holmes. 1981.
Wagenknecht, Edward. Edgar Allan Poe The Man Behind the Leg-

end. New York: Oxford University Press, 1963.
Waller, Robert James. The Bridges of Madison County. New York: Warner Books, 1992.
Weisfeld, Victoria. The Trudeau Institute A Century of Science 1884-1984. Trudeau Institute, Inc.
Wocl, Edward. Gillette Castle State Park. 1978.
Zajicek, Chris O. Wildlife Drive Guide J. N. "Ding" Darling National Wildlife Refuge.
Zamonski, Stanley. Buffalo Bill The Man and the Museum. Frederick, CO: Renaissance House, 1987.

Magazine and Newspaper Articles

_____. "Festival set this weekend." Free Press (Islamorada, FL), March 29, 1989, p. 8.
_____. "Indian Key Festival Commemorates History." Island Navigator (Pine Key, FL), April 1989, p. 1.
_____. "Islamorada Prepares for Indian Key Fest." The Reporter (Tavernier, FL), March 30, 1989, pp. 1 and 21.
_____. "Mysterious visitor leaves tribute to Poe." Press & Sun-Bulletin (Binghamton, NY), January 20, 1995.
_____. "No peace on the 'Garden Island'." Press & Sun-Bulletin (Binghamton, NY), September 14, 1992.
_____. "North from the Battery, Seeking Washingtoniana." The New York Times (New York), February 13, 1987, pp. C1 and C33.
_____. "Photographer snaps image of Poe's mysterious visitor." Press & Sun-Bulletin (Binghamton, NY), June 26, 1990, p. 2A.
Armbrister, Trevor. "Fire in the Sunshine Silver Mine." Reader's Digest, June 1973, pp. 21-30.
Ballard, Delores. "Come to Tupelo, Miss., for music, shopping...and Elvis." Press & Sun-Bulletin (Binghamton, NY), March 6, 1994, p. 9C.
Bell, Bob Boze. "Billy the Kid." Arizona Highways, August 1991,

pp. 4-11.

Blakely, Mike. "Alamo Village The stuff westerns are made of." Texas Highways, May 1985, pp. 36-43.

Brown, Joseph E. "The Apache Trail." Arizona Highways, January 1989, pp. 4-13.

Campbell, Mary. "'Bridges' spans gap between two lives." Press & Sun-Bulletin (Binghamton, NY), August 1, 1993, p. 13C.

Crenson, Matt. "Rabies, not drink, blamed in Poe's death." Press & Sun-Bulletin (Binghamton, NY), September 12, 1996, p. 1C.

Denato, Pat. "Waller fans will be pleased with 'Waltz'." Press & Sun-Bulletin (Binghamton, NY), October 13, 1993, p. 3D.

Denike, Lisa. "Mystery covers body in Poe's grave." The Baltimore Evening Sun; reprinted in The Press & Sun-Bulletin (Binghamton, NY), January 21, 1984.

Duckworth, Ed. "Where Be Ye Buried 'Bonney' Billy?" De Baca County News (Fort Sumner, NM), May 30, 1985, pp. 2-4.

Feron, James. "A Winter's Day at Sleepy Hollow." The New York Times (New York), February 17, 1984, p. C29.

_____. "The Tarrytowns: Reliving History on the Hudson." The New York Times (New York), August 16, 1985, pp. C1 and C25.

Gardner, William H., and Jack Metcalfe. "The Lawman Who Triggered a Legend." Sunday News (New York), April 7, 1968, pp. 10C-C11.

Heffernon, Rick. "Tonto Natural Bridge." Arizona Highways, August 1991, pp. 28-35.

Keating, Bern. "Pathway Through History Today Along the Natchez Trace." National Geographic, November 1968, pp. 640-67.

Kraft, Scott. "Truth lies buried with Jesse James." The Evening Press (Binghamton, NY), October 3, 1979.

Kriss, Claudine. "Great lake, great islands." USA Weekend, June 22-24, 1990, p. 18.

Levathes, Louise E. "Kamehameha Hawaii's Warrior King." National Geographic, November 1983, pp. 558-99.

Page, Jake. "Was Billy the Kid a superhero - or a superscoundrel?" Smithsonian, February 1991, pp. 137-48.

Rogers, Joe. "Jump in the car and retrace historic Natchez Trace trail." Press & Sun-Bulletin (Binghamton, NY), November 22, 1992, p. 12D.

Shay, Jack. "Broome Carousels: A Ride Of A Lifetime." Broome Pennysaver Plus (Johnson City, NY), May 25, 1993, pp. 1 and 6.

_____. "Broome Carousels: The Cost of Re-birth." Broome Pennysaver Plus (Johnson City, NY), June 8, 1993, pp. 1 and 6.

_____. "Carousels Through The Years." Broome Pennysaver Plus (Johnson City, NY), June 1, 1993, pp. 1 and 6.

Shepard, Richard F. "Landmark New York Dwellings Still Speak of Bucolic Times." The New York Times (New York), May 29, 1987, pp. C1 and C4.

Thomasson, Robert E. "Connecticut Castle Shows Actor's Flair and Mystery." The New York Times (New York), June 25, 1982.

Tighe, Michael. "'Diamond in world of coal' showcases amateur authors." Press & Sun-Bulletin (Binghamton, NY), September 15, 1991.

Tourangeau, Dixie. "New Adams Visitor Center Opened." Courier, Fall 1993, p. 19.

Villiers, Alan. "The Man Who Mapped the Pacific." National Geographic, September 1971, pp. 297-349.

Tourist Magazines and Newspapers

Adventure Guide to Oklahoma's Green Country. Green Country Marketing Association, Inc. (Tulsa, OK), 1992.

Alabama/Louisiana/Mississippi TourBook. American Automobile Association (Heathrow, FL), 1994.

Alaska 1991 Official State Guide & Vacation Planner. Alaska Tourism Marketing Council (Juneau, AK).

Alaska Travel News. Alaska Travel News (Anchorage, AK), July/August 1991.
Amish Country News. Lancaster, PA, June 1993.
Arizona/New Mexico TourBook. American Automobile Association (Heathrow, FL), 1994.
Arkansas/Kansas/Missouri/Oklahoma TourBook. American Automobile Association (Heathrow, FL), 1994.
A tourist's guide to Hays and Northwest Kansas. The Hays Daily News, June 7, 1992.
California/Nevada TourBook. American Automobile Association (Heathrow, FL), 1994.
Car Trekker Colorado Car Trekker Travel Guide. Colorado Travel Tapes (Littleton, CO), 1992.
Circus World Museum 1991 Official Souvenir Program. Circus World Museum (Baraboo, WI).
Circus World Museum 1993 Souvenir Program. Circus World Museum (Baraboo, WI).
Colorado/Utah TourBook. American Automobile Association (Heathrow, FL), 1994.
Connecticut/Massachusetts/Rhode Island TourBook. American Automobile Association (Heathrow, FL), 1994.
Discover Carson Country. Nevada Appeal (Carson City, NV).
Discover Us. Star-Herald (Scottsbluff, NE), Summer 1992.
Explore Alaska 1991 Visitors Guide. Anchorage Daily News.
Fairmount Home of Distinguished People. Fairmount, IN, 1988.
Florida TourBook. American Automobile Association (Heathrow, FL), 1994.
Fort Abraham Lincoln State Park Gazette. Fort Abraham Lincoln State Park (Mandan, ND), Summer 1990.
Georgia/North Carolina/South Carolina TourBook. American Automobile Association (Heathrow, FL), 1994.
Gone West! The Jefferson National Expansion Historical Association (St. Louis), Winter 1985.
Hertz Drive Guide Hawaii. Honolulu Publishing Company, Ltd. (Honolulu), November 1991-February 1992.

Idaho/Montana/Wyoming TourBook. American Automobile Association (Heathrow, FL), 1994.

Illinois/Indiana/Ohio TourBook. American Automobile Association (Heathrow, FL), 1994.

James Dean The Life and Legend 1931-1955. Chronicle Tribune (Marion, IN), September 26, 1992.

Kentucky/Tennessee TourBook. American Automobile Association (Heathrow, FL), 1994.

Maine/New Hampshire/Vermont TourBook. American Automobile Association (Heathrow, FL), 1994.

Maui Beach Press. Hawaii Press Newspapers, Inc., November 4-10, 1991.

Maui Fun. Marine Planning International (Lahaina, HA).

Meet the Town Saranac Lake New York 1990-91. Galas Unlimited (Saranac Lake, NY), 1990.

Michigan/Wisconsin TourBook. American Automobile Association (Heathrow, FL), 1994.

Mid-Atlantic TourBook. American Automobile Association (Heathrow, FL), 1994.

Minnesota Explorer. Minnesota Office of Tourism (St. Paul), Spring/Summer 1993.

Nebraska Visitors Guide. Nebraska Travel and Tourism (Lincoln, NE).

New Jersey/Pennsylvania TourBook. American Automobile Association (Heathrow, FL), 1994.

New York TourBook. American Automobile Association (Heathrow, FL), 1994.

1991-92 Long Beach Peninsula Visitor's Guide. Chinook Observer (Long Beach, WA).

1993 Brainerd Lakes Area Guest Guide. Range Printing (Brainerd, MN).

'91 Seward Visitors Guide. Seward Visitors Guide (Seward, AK), 1991.

North Central TourBook. American Automobile Association (Heathrow, FL), 1994.

North Tahoe/Truckee Week. North Tahoe Week Publishing Co. (Tahoe Vista, CA), June 8, 1994.

101 Fun Things to Do at Lake Tahoe. Tahoe Tourist Promotions (Kings Beach, CA), Summer 1994.

Oregon/Washington TourBook. American Automobile Association (Heathrow, FL), 1994.

Our Daily Bread. The Swedenborgian Church (Ft. Myers Beach, FL), June 1994.

Sanibel Captiva Islands Chamber of Commerce. SEE (Sarasota, FL), 1989.

Sonnenschein auf Leavenworth. Leavenworth, WA, 1991.

Southern Iowa 9 Tourism. Southern Iowa 9 Tourism (Winterset, IA), 1993.

Southwest Wisconsin's Uplands 1993 Free Visitors Guide. The Uplands Inc. (Mt. Horeb, WI).

Spotlight Big Island. Spotlight Hawaii Publishing (Honolulu), November 1991.

Spotlight Kauai. Spotlight Hawaii Publishing (Honolulu), November-December 1991.

Sun Valley Guide. Express Publishing Inc. (Ketchum, ID), Summer 1994.

Tennessee Travel Guide. The Guide Company, Inc. (Nashville), 1986.

Texas TourBook. American Automobile Association (Heathrow, FL), 1994.

The Baha'is. Baha'i International Community, 1992.

The Cascade Loop Traveler's Guide. Cascade Loop Association (Wenatchee, WA), 1991.

The Fairmount Reporter. Fairmount, IN, Winter 1992.

The Great Circus Parade 1987 Souvenir Program. Event Promotions, Inc.

The Tennessee Conservationist. Tennessee Department of Conservation (Nashville), July/August 1986.

This Week Big Island. Hagadone Hawaii, Inc. (Honolulu), November 4-10, 1991.

This Week Kauai. Hagadone Hawaii, Inc. (Honolulu), October 28-November 3, 1991.
This Week Maui. Hagadone Hawaii, Inc. (Honolulu), November 4-10, 1991.
Tourism Times. Sweetwater, TN, Spring 1993.
Tourism Treasures of Southern Illinois. Southern Illinoisan, June 26, 1988.
Utah! 1986 Travel Guide. Utah Hotel Motel Association, Inc.
Utah's National Parks. American Park Network (San Francisco), 1992.
Vacationland. Crosby-Ironton Courier (Crosby, MN), July-August 1993.
Wheaton Village Times. 1992.
Will Rogers Memorial nears 55th birthday. Written by Joe Carter.

Broadsides, Brochures, Fliers, Leaflets, Postcards, Etc.

Alamo Village Movie Location.
Alligator Facts.
America's Stonehenge. America's Stonehenge Inc., 1992.
A National Park Full of Top Family Attractions. Tourist Attraction Committee (Hot Springs National Park, AR).
Angela Peterson Doll and Miniature Museum.
An Illustrated Self-Guide of the Ave Maria Grotto. The Ave Maria Grotto (Cullman, AL). Written by Rev. Aloysius Plaisance, OSB, Ph.D.
Antiques Crosby, Minnesota. Published by the dealers listed.
Aplets & Cotlets Fall 1993 Gift Guide.
A Self-Guiding Walk Through the Gardens and Sanctuary of Wayfarers Chapel.
A Tour of Historic Saranac Lake. Historic Saranac Lake (Saranac Lake, NY), 1988. Written by Mary B. Hotaling.
Baha'i; House of Worship Peace Tapestry.
Baraboo Area. Ad-Lit Distributing Co., Inc. (Wisconsin Dells, WI).

Baraboo Wisconsin. Baraboo Area Chamber of Commerce (Baraboo, WI).

Bear Facts.

Buffalo Bill Memorial Museum. Curt Teich & Co., Inc. (Chicago), 1957.

California's Old Faithful in Napa Valley Calistoga. Written by Sybil McCabe.

Capitol Reef. U.S. Department of the Interior, 1992.

Capitol Reef Trails.

Carson City Mint's Press No. 1. Nevada State Museum (Carson City, NV). Written by Douglas McDonald.

Cathedral of the Pines.

Cave-In-Rock. Hardin County Chamber of Commerce (Cave-in-Rock, IL).

Cave-In-Rock State Park. State of Illinois Department of Conservation, 1987.

Charles A. Lindbergh House. Minnesota Historical Society.

Charles A. Lindbergh State Park Summer Trails. Minnesota Department of Natural Resources, 1993.

Cherokee Heritage Center.

Chimney Rock Park. 1992.

Chimney Rock Park Trail Map. Chimney Rock Company, 1992.

Circus World Museum.

Circus World Museum 1993 Summer Schedule of Events.

Colonel Harland Sanders Museum. Kentucky Fried Chicken (Louisville, KY).

Covered Bridge Map.

Croft Mine Historical Park.

Cullman Alabama. Cullman County Chamber of Commerce Convention and Tourism Bureau (Cullman, AL).

David Crockett State Park. Tennessee Department of Environment & Conservation, 1992.

Davy Crockett Birthplace State Park. Tennessee Department of Conservation, 1990.

Descriptions of the Buildings of the Miniature Kingdom.

Desert of Maine.
Donner Memorial State Park. California Department of Parks & Recreation (Sacramento, CA), 1991.
Early American Cashmere.
Enchanted World Doll Museum.
Exit Glacier A Window into Time. Alaska Natural History Association, 1988.
Experience Madison County, Iowa! Madison County Tourism Council.
Experience Northwest Kansas. RDF & Associates, Inc. (Hays, KS).
Explore our Kit Carson Trail Carson City. Convention and Visitors' Bureau (Carson City, NV).
Fairmount Historical Museum, Inc. Users Guide.
Federal Hall National Memorial, New York City. National Park Service, 1975. Written by Bruce Bliven, Jr.
Fordyce Bathhouse Visitor Center. Department of the Interior.
Fort Abraham Lincoln Foundation. Bismarck, ND.
42nd Street River to River. 42nd Street E.T.C., Inc., 1984. Written by Gerald R. Wolfe.
Franklin County, Massachusetts Mohawk Trail. Franklin County Chamber of Commerce (Greenfield, MA).
Fraunces Tavern Museum. Fraunces Tavern Museum, 1989.
Ft. Abraham Lincoln State Park. North Dakota Parks and Recreation.
Garden of Eden.
General Patton Memorial Museum.
Geologic Wonders of Western Nebraska and South Dakota. South Dakota Department of Tourism, et al.
Gilbert Stuart Birthplace & Museum.
Gillette Castle State Park. State of Connecticut Department of Environmental Protection (Hartford, CT).
Green Mount Cemetery. Baltimore, 1976.
Guide to Hiking & Horse Trails Kings Mountain State Park Kings Mountain National Military Park.
Guide to Historical Sites of New York City. Metropolitan Historic

Structures Association, 1980.
Haleakala Hiking and Camping Guide. Hawaii Natural History Association, 1991.
Haleakala Ka Lu'u o ka 'O'o. Hawaii Natural History Association, 1990.
Haleakala National Park. National Park Service, 1991.
Hell's Half Acre.
Hell's Half Acre. Sanborn Souvenir Co., Inc. (Denver).
Heritage Trail. The Friends of the Heritage Trail (New York).
High Point Visitor's Map.
Historic Lititz Pennsylvania 1993 Shopping Directory. G&J Ideas (Myerstown, PA), 1993.
History of Sunshine. 1988. Written by Robert L. Anderson.
Horseshoe Bend. National Park Service, 1981.
Hot Springs. U.S. Department of the Interior, 1993.
Hot Springs Mountain Tower. Hot Springs Advertising & Promotion Commission (Hot Springs National Park, AR).
Hot Springs National Park Guide to a Dream Vacation.
Indian Key State Historic Site. Florida Department of Natural Resources (Tallahassee, FL).
Jack London State Historic Park. California Department of Parks & Recreation (Sacramento, CA), 1994.
James Byron Dean. 1986. Written by Ann Warr.
James Dean Fan Club Information.
Jesse James Historic Sites.
Jesse James Wax Museum.
Kenai Fjords National Park. Seward, AK.
Kenai Fjords National Park Alaska. Department of the Interior, 1987.
Kings Mountain National Military Park, South Carolina. 1988.
Kipahulu. Hawaii Natural History Association, 1989.
Koziar's Christmas Village.
Koziar's Christmas Village. Koziar's Christmas Village (Bernville, PA).
Landmark Along the North Platte A Guide to the Summit Trail

System. Oregon Trail Museum Association.

Largest Prehistoric INDIAN BURIAL PIT in the Middle West.

Lewis and Clark Trail. U.S. Department of the Interior, 1991.

Little Norway.

Lookout Mountain Colorado. Curt Teich & Co., Inc. (Chicago), 1963.

Lost Sea.

(Madison County Bridges postcards). Joe Graham & Co (Winterset, IA).

Madison County Covered Bridge Festival. Winterset, IA.

Map and Guide to Lower Manhattan From Shoreline to Skyline. The Port Authority of New York and New Jersey, 1988.

Miniature Kingdom.

Minnesota State Parks. Minnesota Department of Natural Resources.

Missouri Botanical Garden Visitors' Guide.

Museum of American Glass at Wheaton Village Millville, New Jersey. New Jersey State Council on the Arts.

Museums of New York City. Metropolitan Transportation Authority, 1988.

Natchez Trace Parkway. 1989.

National Museum of Health and Medicine. Department of the Army (Washington, D.C.).

National Park Service Areas in Western Nebraska. Department of the Interior.

National Road/Zane Grey Museum. Ohio Historical Society.

Nevada State Museum.

New Echota on Your Own. Georgia Department of Natural Resources.

1993 Historic Sites Travel Guide. Minnesota Historical Society (St. Paul).

1993 Map & Directory Tuscarawas County Visitors Guide. Tuscarawas County Convention and Visitors Bureau (New Philadelphia, OH).

Old NEW-GATE Prison and Copper Mine.

Outdoor Illinois Magazine's Guide Map to Historic Hardin County in the beautiful Ohio River. Hardin County Chapter, Shawnee Hills Assn (Rosiclare, IL).
Pennsylvania's Roadside America. Roadside America, Inc., 1985.
Perry's Victory and International Peace Memorial. National Park Service, 1986.
Philip Morris Manufacturing Center. Philip Morris U.S.A. (Richmond), 1991.
Pioneer Health Resort A Tour of Historic Saranac Lake. 1991.
Portage Valley Chugach National Forest. United States Department of Agriculture, 1988.
Prabhupada's Palace of Gold.
Roger Maris Museum.
Romance of Beautiful Swannanoa. 1989.
Sail the Lost Sea. Colourpicture (Boston).
Schedule of Services 1994.
Schmidt's Coca-Cola Museum.
Scotts Bluff. U.S. Department of the Interior, 1991.
Self-Guided Walking Tour Constitution NYC Bicentennial. The New York City Commission on the Bicentennial of the Constitution (New York). Written by John Hammond.
Shawnee National Forest. U.S. Department of Agriculture (Harrisburg, IL), 1971.
Shrine of the Pines.
Sleepy Hollow Restorations Calendar of Events 1986.
Southern Illinois. Southern Illinois Tourism Council (Marion, IL), 1986.
Southern Illinois 1988 Guide to Fairs Festivals and Special Events. Southern Illinois Regional Tourism Council (Marion, IL), 1988.
Southern Illinois Scenic Southeast. Illinois Office of Tourism, 1980.
Southern Illinois Shawnee National Forest. Southern Illinois Tourism Council (Marion, IL), 1987.
Southern Illinois Shawnee National Forest Guide. Southern Illinois Regional Tourism Council, 1988.

Souvenir Folder of the Ave Maria Grotto. The Ave Maria Grotto (Cullman, AL).
Sturgis Pretzel House.
Sunnyside. Sleepy Hollow Restorations (Tarrytown, NY), 1983.
Tappan: A Walk through History. Tappantown Society (Tappan, NY).
The Baha'i Faith. Baha'i Publishing Trust (Wilmette, IL), 1991.
The Birthplace of John Wayne.
The Brautigan Library. The Brautigan Library (Burlington, VT).
The Brautigan Library. Burlington, VT. Written by Todd Lockwood.
The Bridge of Flowers Shelburne Falls Massachusetts. 1984.
The Crockett Tavern Museum.
The Duck Stamp Story. Department of the Interior.
The Heritage Center at Red Cloud Indian School.
The James Dean Gallery.
The John Dickinson Plantation. Delaware State Museums.
The John Dillinger Historical Wax Museum.
The Mohawk Trail Visitor's Guide. The Mohawk Trail Association (Charlemont, MA).
The Monadnock Region Map & Guide. Monadnock Travel Council (Keene, NH), 1992.
The Music House.
The Nature Trail at the Charles A. Lindbergh House. Minnesota Historical Society (Little Falls, MN). Written by Muriel Poehler, Agnes Girtz, and Virginia Berguson.
The Oklahoma Historical Society's Sequoyah's Home Site. Oklahoma Historical Society, 1993.
The Original Roadside America Inc.
The Slaves and Free Blacks of John Dickinson. The Afro-American Historical Society of Delaware (Wilmington, DE).
The Story of Swedenborg and the Swedenborgian Church. Communications Support Unit of the Swedenborgian Church (Boston), 1992. Written by Vicki Dixon.
The Story of the Miniature Kingdom.
The Trudeau Sanatorium. 1949.
Tonto Natural Bridge.

Tonto Natural Bridge. Norman Mead Russell Mead (Tempe, AZ).
Tonto Natural Bridge. Smith-Southwestern, Inc. (Tempe, AZ).
Tonto Natural Bridge State Park.
Visit Fairmount Indiana. Fairmount Historical Museum (Fairmount, IN).
Visit Little Falls on the Mississippi. Little Falls Area Chamber of Commerce (Little Falls, MN).
VISIT Sleepy Hollow Country. Sleepy Hollow Restorations (Tarrytown, NY).
VISIT the Baha'i House of Worship.
Visit the Museum. The Babe Ruth Museum (Baltimore).
Wallace District Mining Museum. Wallace, ID.
Warther Museum.
"Welcome" to Fairmount Indiana Home of James Dean.
Welcome to the Baha'i House of Worship. Baha'i House of Worship, 1990.
We Remember Dean International. Written by Sylvia Bongiovanni.
Western Nebraska Scottsbluff Gering. Scottsbluff/Gering United Chamber of Commerce (Scottsbluff, NE).
Wheaton Village. New Jersey State Council on the Arts.
Whitman Mission National Historic Site. U.S. Department of the Interior, 1993.
Wilbur Chocolate Company Candy Americana Museum and Wilbur Chocolate's Factory Candy Outlet.
Will Rogers Memorial and Birthplace.
World Famous Baths. Hot Springs Advertising & Promotion Commission (Hot Springs National Park, AR).
Your Guide to Mitchell's Feature Attractions. Mitchell Convention Visitors Bureau (Mitchell, SD).
Your Self-Guided Tour to the Buffalo Bill Memorial Museum.

Newsletters

Fort Mims Arrow. Vol. 5, No. 2, 1992. Bay Minette, AL.
The 23. Vol. 3, No. 1, December 1992. The Brautigan Library (Burlington, VT).

The 23. Vol. 4, No. 1, Winter 1994. The Brautigan Library (Burlington, VT).
The 23. Vol. 4, No. 2, Spring 1994. The Brautigan Library (Burlington, VT).

Compilations, Papers, and Reports

"Questions and Answers Regarding TMI." Backgrounder, July 1992. GPU Nuclear Communications.
"Sunshine Mine Fire." (Binder of news clippings exhibited in Wallace District Mining Museum, Wallace, ID).
"Unit 2 in Profile." Backgrounder, October 1991. GPU Nuclear Communications.

Atlases and Maps

Full Color Topographic Map of Hawai'i. Honolulu: University of Hawaii Press, 1988. Executed by James A. Bier.
Full Color Topographic Map of Maui. Honolulu: University of Hawaii Press. Executed by James A. Bier.
Geographia's 5 Borough Atlas New York City. Jersey City, NJ: Geographia Map Co., Inc., 1982.
Haleakala National Park. Evergreen, CO: Trails Illustrated, 1991.
Hot Springs National Park, Arkansas Map. Springfield, MO: Riley Marketing, Inc., 1990.
Ketchum Sun Valley Hailey Area Map. Hailey, ID: Starr Map Company, 1994.
Louisville. American Automobile Association, 1985.
Map of the Chugach National Forest Alaska. U.S. Department of Agriculture, 1989.
New York State Atlas & Gazetteer. Freeport, ME: DeLorme Mapping Company, 1987.
Palo Duro Canyon State Park. 1992.
Rand McNally Road Atlas. Chicago: Rand McNally & Company Offices, 1989.
Tonto National Forest. United States Department of Agriculture, 1986.